Therapeutic Recreation Programming:
Theory and Practice

Therapeutic Recreation Programming:
Theory and Practice

by

Charles Sylvester, Judith E. Voelkl, and Gary D. Ellis

Venture Publishing, Inc
State College, Pennsylvania

Production Manager: Richard Yocum
Manuscript Editing: Valerie Paukovits, Richard Yocum, Michele Barbin, and Julie
    Klein.
Cover: Sandra Sikorski Design 2000

Library of Congress Catalogue Card Number 2001089377
ISBN 1-892132-20-6

Table of Contents

Preface

*We have forgotten that know-how is a dubious endowment unless
it is accompanied by other "knows"—by "know what," "know
why," and—most important of all at the present moment—"know
whether."*

—Joseph W. Krutch (1959)

In this age of unbelievably powerful technology, where enough know-how
exists to destroy ourselves, our world requires knowledge not subsumed under
"tools and techniques" for humanity to progress in terms of freedom, justice,
and well-being. With attention to Krutch's sage advice, we have tried to
enhance the knowledge or "knows" of therapeutic recreation by writing this
text. World peace may not be at stake, but we believe other worthwhile values
are relevant, such as health, community, self-determination, and the quality of
life. Therefore, we wish to discuss briefly how we approached this important
goal.

Know-how refers to the technical knowledge used by therapeutic recreation
practitioners in their daily work. Judging by texts, journals, workshops, and
conferences, there has been a steady increase over the years of information on
the how-to of therapeutic recreation. This is a welcomed development, because
technical knowledge is indisputably important. Imagine carpenters who do not
know how to use their tools, math teachers who cannot add and subtract, or
physicians who cannot read x-rays and set broken bones. The negative consequences of technical ignorance and incompetence are obvious, resulting in
shoddy construction, poorly educated children, and inept medical treatment.
Accordingly, we pay due attention in this text to the technical side of therapeutic recreation programming, such as goal-writing, documentation, and discharge planning.

As essential as technical knowledge is, however, we contend that it is
inadequate and potentially harmful unless it is wrapped in a web of comprehensive knowledge. Indeed, therapeutic recreation has been too absorbed in know-
how at the neglect of other areas of knowledge. Technical knowledge receives
enormous attention because it consumes so much of practitioners' time as they

do assessments, lead groups, chart client progress, and develop discharge plans, not to mention management tasks that must be done. Technical knowledge also results in the overt display of skill, which is a key characteristic of professionalism. Technical knowledge and skills are pointless, however, unless we understand the ends, conditions, and implications of their use. For example, technology makes it possible for children to attend summer camp far from home. It has also made it possible for children to commit murderous carnage in schools. Technology connects people worldwide via the Internet; yet it also produces social disconnection by decreasing the amount of face-to-face interaction people experience. In therapeutic recreation, technical knowledge has been used to foster freedom and to deny it (see Sylvester, 1987).

Other domains of knowledge are required for therapeutic recreation specialists to perform ethically and effectively. This body of knowledge is intellectual in nature, involving a thinking process that gives form, content, and direction to the techniques of practice. Flexner (1915), in his classic study of professions, was emphatic that professions were fundamentally intellectual, claiming that "the real character of the activity is the thinking process; a free, resourceful, and unhampered intelligence applied to problems and seeking to understand and master them—that is in the first instance characteristic of a profession" (p. 902). Thus, while we have included programming know-how required of therapeutic recreation specialists, we have sought to embed it with the other "knows" that constitute a comprehensive understanding of therapeutic recreation programming.

Know-what relates to the purposes of therapeutic recreation. All fields have moral viewpoints oriented to a particular value or set of values. It is well-known that the field of therapeutic recreation has experienced decades of debate regarding its values and purposes. Knowing what should be done is imperative because it delves into the purposes to which know-how is then applied, providing a moral blueprint that guides the use of technical knowledge. In Chapter 1 we discuss the foundations of therapeutic recreation, and examine its ideals, values, and principles.

Know-why is synonymous with *theory,* meaning here a process of rational explication. Theory provides understanding of all sorts of phenomena, from the origin of the universe to why people do not fall off the face of the earth to why choice and control lead to increased self-esteem and improved mental health. Explaining why therapeutic recreation is good, effective, or beneficial goes hand in hand with understanding the purposes of therapeutic recreation. Similarly, understanding the purposes of therapeutic recreation helps to suggest the moral, historical, and scientific phenomena therapeutic recreation needs to explain. Science, history, and philosophy are not independent departments;

they are complementary areas of inquiry and knowledge. Although there have been signs of improvement, including better research, more rigorous philosophical analysis, and critical study of practice models, therapeutic recreation has substantial room to enhance its theoretical knowledge. The body of knowledge in therapeutic recreation is still top-heavy with techniques, yet featherlight with theory. Accordingly, the core of this text consists of chapters that emphasize the theoretical aspects of therapeutic recreation programming, including models of practice, counseling, assessment, learning, and evaluation.

Know-whether pertains to moral judgment, perhaps the most important knowledge a professional can possess. Therapeutic recreation practitioners regularly face moral situations and dilemmas. Wishing for readers to reflect upon the ethics of therapeutic recreation programming, we have included a chapter on professional ethics.

We decided to add one more "know" to Krutch's list—*know-who*. "Who" refers to the people therapeutic recreation serves, those individuals we refer to as "clients" or "patients." In the abstract, the "client" is a faceless creature whose existence is often interpreted from the perspective of the dominant culture. Therapeutic recreation programming has been guilty of being "culturally encapsulated" in the dominant culture. In reality, therapeutic recreation serves individuals of all races, ethnicities, genders, religions, ages, geographic locations, socioeconomic levels, and sexual orientations. While all clients desire to lead lives that are healthy, productive, and fulfilling, their needs and interests are significantly shaped by their cultural backgrounds. Therapeutic recreation specialists must be aware of and sensitive and responsive to cultural differences among the people they serve. As such, we have attempted to avoid the "one size fits all" approach to therapeutic recreation programming. We have included a chapter on multicultural considerations of therapeutic recreation programming. Further, we have tried to be attentive to multicultural factors as they relate to such topics as assessment and interventions.

One of the hallmarks of this text is our effort to situate the technical knowledge of therapeutic recreation programming in a more comprehensive body of ethical, social, scientific, and philosophical knowledge. Therapeutic recreation professionals must be more than narrow specialists skilled in the tasks of administering assessments, writing goals, documenting behavior, and processing activity experiences. They must understand what ends or purposes are worthy of their technical know-how. Furthermore, they must understand the theoretical bases of their work so the "best practices" of therapeutic recreation are founded on valid knowledge. Moreover, professionals must understand the ethical dimensions and implications of their work. Finally, they must understand who they serve, not simply in terms of their diagnoses, but in relation to their cultural contexts. We want this text to enable students to exercise the most important and difficult of all competencies—intelligent action ethically applied to the needs and problems of a culturally diverse society. We hope, in other words, to bring theory (thinking) and practice (doing) together, where they belong.

We offer a few final comments for readers' consideration. This text deals with the topic of therapeutic recreation programming. It does not attempt to cover all subjects that fall under the broad umbrella of therapeutic recreation practice. We have restricted ourselves to the traditional components of therapeutic recreation programming: assessment, planning, implementation, and evaluation.

Furthermore, texts are inherently limited for at least two reasons. First, they tend to become dated fairly quickly. Second, because of space limitations, most texts must favor breadth over depth. In order to minimize these limitations, we have included lists of recommended readings for the core topics comprising this text. The authors, all educators, strongly believe that a text should be supplemented with readings from books and journals that address the vital ingredients of therapeutic recreation programming more thoroughly. We encourage instructors to use these readings and others they have found to supplement this text. Moreover, we urge readers to remain informed by keeping abreast of the current literature as it pertains to the topics and issues of therapeutic recreation programming.

Lastly, we wish to thank everyone who has assisted with this project. Miriam Lahey and Cathy O'Keefe read chapters and provided invaluable suggestions. Naomi Yoshioka created graphics and checked the accuracy of the references. Ken Mobily and Sandy Negley read the entire book, and their recommendations led to substantial improvement. Venture Publishing editors Michele Barbin, Valerie Paukovits, and Richard Yocum were more patient and supportive than we could have expected. We would also like to thank the students who read preliminary drafts and offered their candid remarks, especially Debbie Cleveland and Susan Jung. All of you have made this book even better. Finally, we are indebted to the love and support of our families, friends, and pets. No matter what life deals us, you make everything worthwhile.

We did not ask a luminary from the field of therapeutic recreation to contribute a preface testifying to the "cutting-edge brilliance" of this text. Whatever this book is or is not, we want readers to make up their own minds. As readers move through the rest of the text, therefore, we encourage them *not* to treat what they read as the final word on therapeutic recreation programming, because it is not. Of course, we hope what we have written meets your critical approval and above all meets the challenges of practice. Where it does not, however, it is your responsibility to imagine how to improve it and then to put your ideas to the test. We wish you the best of luck with your hard work and worthy mission.

Charles Sylvester
Bellingham, Washington

Judith Voelkl
Iowa City, Iowa

Gary Ellis
Salt Lake City, Utah

References

Flexner, A. (1915). Is social work a profession? *School and Society, 26,* 901–911.

Krutch, J. W. (1959). *Human nature and the human condition.* New York, NY: Random House.

Sylvester, C. (1987). Therapeutic recreation and the end of leisure. In C. Sylvester, J. Hemingway, R. Howe-Murphy, K. Mobily, and P. Shank (Eds.), *Philosophy of therapeutic recreation: Ideas and issues, Vol. 1* (pp. 76–89). Alexandria, VA: National Recreation and Park Association.

Section
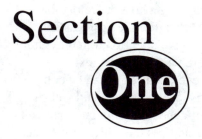

Conceptual Foundations

Behind all organized efforts to better the human condition is a frame of reference that provides concepts and values to guide the actions of those who seek change. Try as one might, it is impossible to move in any direction without ideas and values. Therefore, nothing is better than the practical realization of good ideas that serve a worthy purpose. Sometimes, however, the ideas and values that move people to action are obscure, ill-conceived, incoherent, or simply wrong. Accordingly, the ideas and values we operate by must be made clear, coherent, complete, and justifiable for two chief reasons. First, they serve as a compass, showing the way for individuals who subscribe to them. Second, they allow individuals to examine their legitimacy as proposals for improving life. Section One of this text concerns itself with the core ideas and values of therapeutic recreation programming.

Chapter 1 discusses the importance of a conceptual foundation for professions and the development of a legitimate foundation for therapeutic recreation. Therapeutic recreation programming is a set of skills, techniques, methods, and processes, including assessment, planning, and evaluation. Virtually anything can be assessed, planned, and evaluated, however, which raises questions about the purposes that programming intends to achieve. Chapter 1 seeks to establish the purposes of therapeutic programming by assessing the needs of society. We conclude that an orientation to leisure is the most justifiable and legitimate argument for the existence of therapeutic recreation and the operations of programming.

Chapter 2 is an innovation. The current body of knowledge in therapeutic recreation programming implies "one size fits all." In other words, the assumption is that therapeutic recreation programming should be standardized, making it equally applicable to all people who share a diagnosis. Even where differences are acknowledged, they are usually interpreted from a Western cultural perspective. Yet society is far more culturally diverse than has been acknowledged in therapeutic recreation programming. Age, ethnicity, gender, class, religion, geography, and sexual orientation are among a host of factors that collectively constitute a multicultural society. Although more progress is needed than can be accomplished in this text, we give attention to multicultural considerations in Chapter 2 and throughout the remainder of the text.

Therapeutic recreation practice is rarely, if ever, neutral. It can be conducted in ways that respect people's dignity, privacy, autonomy, and well-being. It can also harm people, violate their confidences, manipulate them, and do them injustice. Accordingly, in Chapter 3 we address the ethics of therapeutic recreation practice by introducing the subject of ethics, exploring several prominent ethical principles, and discussing the resolution of moral dilemmas.

We finish Section One by critically examining models of therapeutic recreation practice. Models describe and explain the components of therapeutic recreation programming. The form that therapeutic recreation practice takes will significantly depend on the model or models to which practitioners subscribe. Therefore, we examine the strengths and weaknesses of the major models in therapeutic recreation.

In summary, Section One provides a broad foundation and vision of therapeutic recreation programming. It stresses the importance of working out a moral and conceptual foundation of therapeutic recreation. At the same time, it makes clear our commitment to a foundation oriented to leisure theory. Section One further emphasizes the importance of a multicultural approach to therapeutic recreation programming. Justice demands that therapeutic recreation not only serve everyone, but also that its services reflect the multicultural diversity of the people it serves. Besides justice, therapeutic recreation programming must be ethical in all other respects. Moreover, therapeutic recreation practitioners must be capable of recognizing and resolving moral dilemmas. Finally, Section One reviews the major models that give practical direction to therapeutic recreation programming.

Chapter

1

Creating a Conceptual Foundation for Therapeutic Recreation: Examination and Legitimation

There is nothing more important than a sound conceptual foundation for any social endeavor. A conceptual foundation consists of a system of ideas that explains something at its most basic level. For example, the foundation of Christianity is the word of God. Everything that Christians think and do is founded on that fundamental source. Sometimes multiple foundations exist for a particular practice. Government, for instance, is based on different conceptual foundations. Monarchy is founded on the belief in a hierarchy of rulers and ruled, descending from God to kings down the line to the common people. Democracy, on the other hand, is grounded on the fundamental principle of universal political equality under law. A foundation, then, is the ultimate source of explanation and justification upon which theory and practice are based. It is not final in the eternal sense of never changing. Most foundations transform over time as conditions change, making alternatives possible and necessitating alterations. Nonetheless, a systematic set of basic beliefs and values should be clearly evident at a given time.

Prior to discussing professional foundations in therapeutic recreation, we want to comment briefly on the relation between philosophy and foundations. By *philosophy,* we mean thinking about the ideas that form the theory and practice of therapeutic recreation, including its basic beliefs and values. Paraphrasing philosopher Hannah Arendt, philosophy is "thinking about what we are doing." As such, we need to think carefully about how we "do therapeutic recreation," because there is no divine or absolute blueprint. Furthermore, we want therapeutic recreation to consist of the best ideas possible for the purpose of effective practices and worthwhile results. The activity of philosophy seeks to understand what makes something logically and morally sound. It searches for and critiques reasons for regarding some ideas and actions as good and others as bad. For example, is it a "good idea" to stress choice in therapeutic recreation, even when persons in our care may make bad choices? Shank and Kinney (1987) questioned the nature of and limits to leisure choices in clinical settings, while Sylvester (1992) defended the freedom of leisure. On another front, how can leisure or recreation be "ordered" as a "prescription" when by definition they are free and autonomous acts? Do recreation and leisure even matter when people are ill? Is health an absolute value or are other values equally or more paramount? This is philosophy at work. It is a constructive process because it leads to richer and deeper understanding about matters that significantly affect the lives of the people therapeutic recreation serves. We can never stop thinking about the consequences of the actions we have in mind for clients. After all, we too may be "clients" one day, subject to the forces of therapeutic recreation. If we care about how we may be treated, then we should certainly care about how we treat others. Therefore, philosophy is indispensable to the development of a foundation that is built on good ideas for the good of people.

Unfortunately, in our judgment too many persons have little patience for philosophy, considering it abstract, impractical, and irrelevant. Ignoring philosophy is costly, even though those who avoid it may not recognize their own ignorance (see Sylvester, 1989a). By acknowledging the importance of philosophy in therapeutic recreation practice, and by becoming more proficient at all levels, we can develop a firm and functional foundation that is sufficiently flexible for changing times. Indeed, there cannot be a foundation without philosophy. The question is whether our ability to do philosophy will be up to the task of building a strong profession.

The foundation of a profession consists of the principles and values a field stands for and stands on. What a field stands *for* refers to its purpose, mission, or "calling." For example, education stands for knowledge and learning. What a field stands *on* refers to the fundamental beliefs and values that explain and justify the field's existence in relation to its purpose, which gives guidance to theory and practice. A foundation states to the world, "This is *who* we are and *why* we are here." A foundation, therefore, is the single most important structural dimension of a profession, providing a rational basis for its existence as a legitimate social institution. Without it a field literally has nothing to support its existence.

The paramount importance of a conceptual foundation has not escaped the attention of therapeutic recreation. Reynolds and O'Morrow (1985) asserted that "No single issue could be more important or require more urgent attention from the profession of therapeutic recreation than the development of a well-defined occupational philosophy" (p. 35). In a study conducted by Witman and Shank (1987), therapeutic recreation leaders considered the development of a central mission to be first among 14 characteristics of professionalization. Out of the many urgent tasks, issues, and challenges facing the profession of therapeutic recreation, Kraus and Shank (1992) declared, "If we were to select a single most important priority, it would probably be the need to develop a sounder philosophical base for the field" (p. 16).

Although respected sources have spoken to the importance of a well-developed professional foundation, the outcome has not been as impressive as the testimony. The creation of a rationally coherent and morally compelling professional foundation for therapeutic recreation has been marked by mixed results. Although there have been enough fruitful efforts to have sustained therapeutic recreation during its brief history, it still lacks the maturity characteristic of such professions as law, medicine, and education. One obvious explanation is that being far younger than these fields, therapeutic recreation simply has not had the opportunity to develop a sound foundation. This is partially true, but there are other reasons why therapeutic recreation has not yet developed a firmer foundation. Several of them are worth reviewing, for if a solid foundation is ever to be achieved, it will require the critically intelligent efforts of students when they become professionals.

Peterson (1989) contended that a major barrier to professionalization was therapeutic recreation's "inability or unwillingness . . . to take a stand on philosophical content" (p. 22). We doubt that unwillingness is the problem; professionals have never been shy to *take* a stand. Peterson may be correct, however, in questioning the field's ability to *develop* a stand. Compared to other fields, only a small fraction of the discussion taking place in therapeutic recreation qualifies as philosophical discourse. Since willingness does not seem to be a serious impediment, the problem results largely from the scarcity of professionals who have the skill, background, and the inclination to conduct serious conceptual analyses.

The most likely candidates for the job are educators. Yet Compton (1989) exclaimed that there are "few individuals [in education] who are in a position to conduct such inquiry" (p. 487). Most educators are not prepared to perform the inquiry necessary for examining and building foundations. A number of factors contribute to this deplorable situation. The main culprit, however, is professional education. The vast majority of educators do not have sufficient preparation in history, philosophy, and social and political theory to conduct social analyses. Consequently, philosophy and critical theory are insufficiently understood and rarely practiced. Furthermore, as Hemingway (1987) explained, "philosophical discussions of therapeutic recreation are too often isolated from relevant sources in the main currents of philosophical inquiry or from philosophically informed discussions of social issues affecting the field" (p. 1).

Professional education in therapeutic recreation has generally placed little emphasis on critical inquiry. Based on the scarcity of adequate philosophy in the literature, students must get a much richer diet of philosophy, as well as social and political theory. To do so, they must be exposed to a wider variety of literature and must practice critical inquiry themselves. Clearly, this will require leadership from educators.

The tendency to borrow foundations from other fields is another reason for an inadequately developed foundation. Lahey (1987a) asserted that therapeutic recreation has expediently adopted the logic and language of medicine at the expense of creating its own foundation. To be sure, therapeutic recreation should study assiduously the foundations of other disciplines and professional fields, such as nursing, medicine, education, and social work. Where elements from other fields and disciplines are relevant, they should be integrated into therapeutic recreation's foundation, as well as fully explained and justified. Other fields can contribute materials, but therapeutic recreation must build its own foundation.

A final factor is the presence of two professional organizations representing therapeutic recreation: the American Therapeutic Recreation Association (ATRA) and the National Therapeutic Recreation Society (NTRS) (see James, 1998). This discussion cannot account for the existence of or the advantages and disadvantages of two professional organizations. In terms of clarity, coherence, consistency, consensus-building, and maximizing resources, one organization would probably be best; but that does not look likely. As long as two organizations do exist, the development of a foundation will require constant cooperation between them. An example of productive collaboration is the joint ATRA-NTRS (1993) statement, *Therapeutic Recreation: Responding to the Challenges of Health Care Reform*. Furthermore, in 1998 ATRA and NTRS formed the Alliance for Therapeutic Recreation (NTRS, 1999, p. 5) and signed a resolution that pledged communication, cooperation, and collaboration for the benefit of consumers and the profession (James, 1998, pp. 34–35).

Of course, every profession has differences. Indeed, differences are desirable, because the alternative is lock-step dogma, which produces no dissent, but also no growth. With a shared foundation, therapeutic recreation has the potential to become a community of professionals who can not only tolerate, but also appreciate their differences while remaining united around a common set of beliefs and values. Such an effort would be remarkably difficult. It would require patience, persistence, leadership, integrity, communication, and, above all, wisdom. Perhaps therapeutic recreation has not matured enough to take on such a challenge. Hopefully, it will be ready in the future.

Regrettably, organizational politics, motivated by the desire for power and control, remain a barrier to the cooperation required to construct a single foundation. Far too much professional rhetoric, some under the disingenuous cloak of "research," is driven by the self-serving interests of organizational cliques. As long as power, prestige, and profit, rather than the public interest, shape therapeutic recreation's discourse and inquiry, a *legitimate* foundation is impossible. For the good of the public and in a spirit of professional coopera-tion, both professional organizations can facilitate rather than frustrate profes-sional foundations.

For these and other reasons therapeutic recreation has not developed an adequate foundation, impeding professionalization and the ability to serve the public (see Sylvester, 1998). Besides dealing with these problems, therapeutic recreation must adopt two basic approaches as it proceeds to build a founda-tion. First, it must do what Compton (1989) suggested by returning regularly to the fundamental question *"Why does therapeutic recreation exist?"* The function of a foundation is to explain in basic terms what justifies the existence of a field. Why is it needed? What purpose does it serve? A probing exploration of that simple question will effectively launch the construction of a foundation and keep it on course. Second, examining and justifying the existence of therapeutic recreation will require a liberal education to complement the technical preparation typical of professional education. Current problems in therapeutic recreation are not primarily rooted in the lack of competence, as some have implied (see Russoneillo, 1992; West, 1993). As important as technical competence is, it can be ineffective and even harmful unless it is guided by a legitimate set of foundational beliefs and values forged from a broad base of knowledge. E. L. Boyer (1987), former president of the Carnegie Foundation for the Advancement of Teaching, recommended "enriched majors" that allow students to place their specialized fields in social perspective. Grounded in liberal or general education, enriched majors would respond to three essential questions: "What is the history and tradition of the field to be examined? What are the social and economic implications to be understood? What are the ethical and moral issues to be confronted?" (p. 110). The authors of this text will follow Boyer's advice by maintaining a broad perspective of therapeutic recreation and by situating its technical side in the moral, social, economic, and political contexts in which it operates.

Examining and Justifying Professional Foundations

Given its vital importance, how is the foundation of a profession created? The first step toward answering this question is by way of another question: "What is a profession?"

A profession is a skilled service performed for pay. According to this broad definition, virtually any skilled occupation qualifies for a profession, including farming, plumbing, gardening, and hairstyling. The term has also been more narrowly applied to fields that require extensive education to master a body of applied knowledge to serve a legitimate social need. Moreover, certain fields have been distinguished by their principal orientation to public service rather than financial profit. (Some professions, such as law and medicine, have been criticized for permitting the profit motive to interfere with their primary commitment to public service.) What fields qualify for the distinction of a "profession" in the more restrictive sense has generated considerable debate (e.g., Cogan, 1953; Etzioni, 1969; Goode, 1960; Greenwood, 1966; Hughes, 1963; Vollmer & Mills, 1966). Greenwood (1966) asserted that the crucial distinction between a professional occupation and a nonprofessional occupation rests in the former's "fund of knowledge that has been organized into an internally consistent system, called a *body of theory* . . . a feature virtually absent in the training of the nonprofessional" (p. 11). Authorities in therapeutic recreation have agreed that a theoretical body of knowledge is "the basis upon which the occupation claims its professionhood" (Meyer, 1980, p. 46; also see Reynolds & O'Morrow, 1985; Sylvester, 1989).

A body of knowledge is *one* of the main elements of a profession. Prior to the development of a body of knowledge, however, *service-oriented* fields originate to meet a public need. Knowledge is then sought and created to serve that purpose. Kuhn (1970) contended that public service fields, such as law and medicine, *do not* achieve legitimation on the basis of a scientific body of knowledge. Rather they achieve it on the basis of an "external social need" (p. 19). Therefore, while scientific knowledge is required for performing public service and gaining professional status, a legitimate social need is the original seed from which a service-oriented field, such as therapeutic recreation, sprouts its foundational roots.

Therefore, a profession is formed by two core qualities. The first is an altruistic *calling* to serve an area of public need. The second is knowing what is *called for,* which consists of a comprehensive body of knowledge, including theoretical, historical, moral, and technical knowledge. A calling or mission is thus joined by a body of knowledge, together serving the end of public service. Establishing a profession, therefore, requires locating and justifying what a society needs, as well as continually developing a body of knowledge for the purposes of serving that social need ethically and effectively. The apparently simple question, then, is "What does a society need?"

Beyond the more obvious survival needs of food, water, and protection from harm, basic needs are notoriously difficult to determine. Many theorists agree that basic needs have a large conventional component (Griffin, 1986; Miller, 1976; Benn & Peters, 1959). In other words, many needs are not entirely determined by natural circumstances, but instead are dependent on social expectations and cultural norms. Telephones were once a luxury; now they are virtually a necessity. Formal education was not a universal need in early America, and many people had little if any formal education. Today, a person is likely doomed to a substandard life without at least a high school education. Formal education has thus *developed* into a basic need. In the past, what people needed for a state of health was relief from illness and discomfort. People believe they need far more for "optimal" health today, including positive social, physical, emotional, and spiritual states. As society changes, so does the understanding of "basic needs." As such, basic needs cannot be taken for granted, but instead must be given a "fresh interpretation in each social setting" (Griffin, 1986, p. 45).

Therefore, basic needs are not limited to what is required to sustain biological life. Basic needs also comprise society's conception of a *particular kind of life*. Falling below this standard is viewed as a threat to the humanity and well-being of individuals in that society. Needs must be assessed on the basis of what a society considers "the right ends of human life" (Thomasa, 1984, p. 44). Society may deem it desirable to prolong life indefinitely with medical technology, even if it means being hooked to expensive machinery. On the other hand, safe and pleasant communities that offer a variety of enriching activities are also desirable. But life-prolonging services, as opposed to life-enriching services, may be considered more "necessary." Consequently, people who have lived in poverty all their lives may receive state-of-the-art medical care, only to return to squalor after they have been rescued by medical technology. These results are not written solely by the laws of nature, but rather by the way we choose to live as a society.

Much of what we "need," then, depends on the kinds of lives we desire to lead. Determining our needs and the quality of life requires examining our lives and deciding what is in our best interests for the social, economic, physical, moral, and psychological well-being of everyone. When the right goals of living have been discerned, the types of professions that are required and the forms they should take will become evident. Before discussing social needs that justify the existence of therapeutic recreation, however, the meaning of some key words must be examined.

Making Meaning: The Challenge of Defining Terms

In addition to compassion, integrity, and diligence, reasoning is one of the most important attributes of a professional. Reasoning requires the ability to use language. As Socrates wisely recommended, we must define the words we use if we hope to achieve understanding about how we should live our lives. But explaining what we mean when we utter, sign, or write words is not at all simple, as anyone who has tried to define something can attest. Concrete objects, such as rocks and trees, are more readily defined because they can be described according to objective properties, such as weight, size, and shape. Abstractions, like "health," "leisure," and "well-being," however, do not have an objective existence of their own. (When was the last time you saw "leisure" out for a walk or "wellness" losing its leaves?) Rather, abstract ideas or concepts are used to express aspects of our lives that do not have a concrete, independent existence of their own. For example, getting up mid-morning on a weekend, choosing what to wear and eat, thinking about who to vote for on election day, reflecting on which church to attend, deciding whether to hit the books or a few baseballs are experiences related to the idea of "freedom," but none of them is an objective "thing" called freedom. Because ideas cannot be connected to any particular object in nature, they require great intellectual care to explain. Furthermore, because our experiences are affected by social, cultural, economic, political, intellectual, and psychological factors, ideas are complex and dynamic. Moreover, we inherit ideas from different times and places. Therefore, historical knowledge, and the lack of it, affects understanding and communication. Finally, no universal language exists to settle the correct use of words. Meaning must be achieved through communication, which has barriers of its own, such as confusion and distortion.

As difficult as definition is, however, we must make an effort to "make meaning." Just as other professionals, such as judges, nurses, or teachers, are expected to understand and explain the basic concepts upon which their fields are founded, we must also be capable of explaining therapeutic recreation and why it exists. We must be able to communicate clearly and logically the meaning and relevance of such terms as "health," "wellness," "leisure," "inclusion," "autonomy," "normalization," "well-being," and "quality of life." We must not only be able to speak to one another, but also to administrators, coworkers, insurance payers, board members, and, most importantly, to our clients and the general public.

Doing justice to complex concepts that have extensive histories is impossible in the space of a few pages. Rather than just give a series of definitions, however, we plan both to define the foundational vocabulary that guides therapeutic recreation practice and discuss some of the issues and problems surrounding it. This will require historical insight. When words are placed into historical perspective, attitudes and practices can be seen that have impacted the lives of human beings, for better or worse. For example, during most of history, the terms "freedom" and "democracy" were mainly reserved for property owning males. Since then their meanings have been broadened. Understanding the background of words can enlighten us so our ideas lead to actions that are in the best interests of our clients. The following discussion is intended as a launching pad into ideas that, with continuous study and reflection, can make a difference in the care of persons who are ill or injured. We will begin with the ideas of *leisure* and *recreation,* after which we will explore *health, well-being,* and therapeutic *recreation.*

Kelly's (1982) conceptual model of leisure incorporates the three most common definitions of leisure into a single construct. First, leisure is interpreted as *time* when one is free from the necessity of having to do something. Clearly, this element can be problematic when trying to discern what is and is not necessary or obligated. Everyone, however, feels constrained to perform certain tasks to survive as an individual, a society, and a species. For example, most people must work at a job to make a livelihood. One may or may not enjoy work, but a job is usually viewed as being obligatory rather than discretionary. During "free-time," however, constraints are minimized, allowing the greatest degree of freedom for people to do as they wish.

Leisure suggests not only freedom *from* necessity, but freedom *for* something, which implies an action or activity. Leisure-time is the opportunity to turn from an activity one feels one must do to an activity one wants to do. The second dimension of leisure, then, is *activity.* More precisely, it is *freely-chosen* activity. As such, a leisure activity is not determined by its content, but rather by the quality of free choice. As Kelly (1982) explained, "It is the quality of the experience of doing the activity, not the activity itself, that makes it leisure" (p. 21). For this reason working in the garden may be labor to some people and leisure to others.

There is a related element to freely-chosen activity that merits a few words. What motivates an individual to choose a particular activity? Theoretically, leisure is *mainly* motivated by intrinsic reasons. By *intrinsic motivation,* we mean that the activity is chosen because of the meaningful qualities it holds for the individual. An action can also be chosen for *extrinsic* reasons, meaning the benefits it produces, such as knowledge, social relationships, and cardiovascular fitness. Nonetheless, the principal motivation for a leisure activity is derived from the meaning the activity holds for the individual. For example, both baseball and basketball offer beneficial outcomes. Yet one of the authors of this text is indifferent to basketball. He would prefer to live, and die, with bat, ball, and glove on some dusty ballfield. The difference lies in the meaning the action of baseball holds *for him,* even though both activities provide external benefits, such as teamwork and hand-eye coordination. Regardless of extrinsic outcomes, then, free-choice and intrinsic meaning are critical qualities of leisure.

Both choice and intrinsic meaning involve a type of consciousness or attitude toward an action. Therefore, the third element of leisure is *experience*. The perception of free choice and the attitude of doing something for intrinsic reasons are internal aspects of leisure. As Kelly (1982) pointed out, perceptions do not occur in a psychological vacuum; they are responses toward an action. Our perceptions inform us of the quality of the action, whether the action is regarded by the individual as forced or free, futile or fulfilling. On the one hand, a person who is a slave, drugged and chained in a box may say he feels he is experiencing leisure. But we would be wrong to ignore his objective condition, despite his perceptions. On the other hand, a person may have all the free-time in the world, yet not "feel" free because of a compulsive attitude. The "objective" side of leisure—an action that occurs in space and time—and the "subjective" side of leisure—an attitude of intrinsically motivated free choice—are two inextricably related dimensions of leisure.

The term *recreation* is often used as a synonym for leisure activity, a convention we will follow in this text. Recreation generally refers to pleasurable or enjoyable free-time activity chosen for its personal or social benefits. In other words, people seek a particular activity in their leisure—dancing, for instance—because they enjoy doing the activity *and* because they desire certain benefits, such as exercise or companionship.

A distinction between recreation and leisure is sometimes made on the basis of activity that is chosen primarily for its own sake (leisure) and activity that is chosen primarily for its external benefits (recreation). This distinction has produced the issue of "means and ends," which has received much attention in the literature (see Sylvester, 1985, 1996; Mobily, Weissinger & Hunnicutt, 1987; Kraus & Shank, 1992). The debate has revolved around whether recreation is an end, done for its own sake because of the inherent qualities of the activity, or a means, done for the sake of benefits the activity yields.

We agree with Kraus and Shank (1992), who contended that recreation can be both a means and an end. A misconception exists, however, that recreation or leisure activity can be used as a means *by another agent,* such as medical personnel, to produce predictable results. Whether recreation or leisure activity is motivated by intrinsic or extrinsic reasons, the action must be chosen by and remain under the control of the individual for it to qualify as recreation or leisure. The action cannot be prescribed or principally controlled by someone else, even though it may produce salutary outcomes. Most theorists agree that the definitive element of leisure and recreation is freedom. Regarding freedom, Adler (1970) stated:

> In every conception of freedom . . . the free act is that which
> proceeds from the self, in contrast to such behavior on a man's
> part which is somehow the product of another. It is his own act
> and the result it achieves is a property of himself . . . . A man
> lacks freedom to whatever extent he is passively affected, or
> subject to an alien power, the power of another rather than his
> own. (p. 75)

The same principle holds true for leisure and recreation. Unless an action is predominantly characterized by freedom and autonomy, it is not leisure or recreation. Even when recreation or leisure activity is used as a means by the individual, it contains the inherent elements of freedom and autonomy. In situations where an activity is prescribed to treat a condition, it should be called "activity therapy." The term "recreational therapy," however, is a contradiction, for a freely-chosen activity cannot be prescribed. Since language has implications for action, the problem is not simply a question of logic or semantics. The language of "recreational therapy" can lead to abuses of client freedom, autonomy, and self-determination because of the tacit permission it grants for intervening and assuming control in the autonomous domain of clients. There are, of course, appropriate times for professional control. We contend, however, that freedom, autonomy, and self-determination are important values that should be treated seriously. Freedom, autonomy, and self-determination have been normatively legitimated and empirically verified as being essential to well-being (Sylvester, 1995). Recreation and leisure, in turn, have been suggested as vital sources for these goals in the lives of persons with disabilities. Professionals should do everything possible to preserve and protect these values for persons with disabilities, particularly in institutional settings, where they are too often diminished or altogether dismissed.

No issue exists as long as choice reasonably belongs to the individual. The issue begins the moment recreation or leisure activity is coopted as an instrument of control, irrespective of good intentions or potentially salutary results.

Before attempting a definition of therapeutic recreation, a couple of other terms must be examined. *Health* and *well-being* invariably appear in discussions on the purposes of therapeutic recreation. Therefore, we should also make sense of them, since they represent two of the main destinations of therapeutic recreation practice.

Traditionally, *health* has meant the "absence of organic and mental disease," along with relative freedom from chronic pain and discomfort (Dubos, 1980, p. 461). More recent definitions of health have emphasized the *whole* person and a state of *optimal* functioning, rather than just the absence of disease and discomfort. The "holistic" view of health has led to greater recognition of the integrity of body and mind, the role of the person's environment in contributing to disease and health, and the importance of promoting healthful living.

Expanded definitions of health have been criticized, however, for being too broad (see Callahan, 1973; Dubos, 1980; Kass, 1975; Redlich, 1976; Zola, 1977). For example, the World Health Organization (WHO) defined health as a "state of complete physical, mental, and social well-being and not merely the absence of disease or infirmity" (Callahan, 1977, p. 26). By inflating the meaning of health from mental and psychological functioning to social and spiritual well-being, the idea of health has begun to infiltrate every element of life. Temkin (1973) observed that "the prevailing tendency at the present moment seems . . . to take so broad a view of health as to make it all but indistinguishable from happiness" (p. 407).

We see both sides of the issue. A broad definition of health has advantages, including the importance of healthy living and the influence of various environments and activities, such as home, work, and play, on one's state of health. Recognizing the interrelationships among work, play, education, religion, and health is one thing. Defining work, play, education, and religion as *aspects* of health is another thing entirely. We would conclude that a person who is illiterate is more likely than not to be poorly informed. But we would be mistaken to call that person "unhealthy." Similarly, a person who lacks a sense of spirituality may experience life as meaningless, but we would be hard-pressed to label the person as "sick." Furthermore, a person may be fit and free of organic dysfunction, yet lack in other areas of life, such as compassion and leadership. Therefore, while accounting for the affects of nonmedical areas on physical and mental health, these dimensions (e.g., religion, work, play, family, art, and sport) have their own distinctive nature and are important in their own right regardless of their impact on health. If a person were suffering from an incurable disease and had only six weeks to live, our efforts to provide care would not be concerned with restoring health, but rather with other important human values, such as love, faith, and companionship. A definition of health should be broad enough to include the *effective functioning* of the whole person. Yet the whole person and his or her range of needs and desires cannot be subsumed under the idea of health. For that purpose, the idea of "well-being" is proposed.

Discussions among philosophers and social scientists regarding the meaning and measurement of well-being are complex. As Haslett (1994) observed, "many different sorts of things—self-realization, autonomy, health, and so on—have been put forth as what constitutes human well-being . . ." (p. 24). The best this discussion can provide is a general description of well-being, while avoiding its debates and subtleties. Paying attention to the idea of well-being is crucial, however, because, along with health, it is often mentioned as one of the main goals of therapeutic recreation (see ATRA, 1988; NTRS, 1994). Yet descriptions of well-being and its relation to therapeutic recreation beg for content and clarity (see Sylvester, 1989b).

First, well-being includes the basic needs required by human beings for survival, such as food, water, and shelter. Rescher (1972) called the basic requisites of well-being (i.e., health, income, housing, education, and employment) "welfare." He and other theorists agree, however, that a "basic needs" definition of well-being is incomplete (see Finnis, 1980; Griffin, 1986). A human life is deemed deprived or incomplete unless it has the vital qualities that are socially recognized as constituting what it means to be a "human being." Here is where the arguments begin. What are the minimum requirements of well-being, below which a person's humanity is violated? Exactly what are the *legitimate* needs, desires, and interests of human beings? Theorists have agreed that not everything people desire is needed for well-being. In fact, some things people desire, such as addictive drugs, can be detrimental to well-being.

Moral inquiry can inform us about the constituents of well-being, enabling us to reach general, if not complete, agreement. Griffin (1986, pp. 66–67) listed five prudential values that are requisite for a life of well-being:

- Accomplishment,
- Components of human existence (autonomy, basic capabilities, and liberty),
- Understanding,
- Enjoyment, and
- Deep personal relations.

Finnis (1980) also derived a list of elements that comprise well-being:

- Life,
- Knowledge,
- Play,
- Aesthetic experience,
- Sociability (friendship),
- Religion, and
- Practical reasonableness (using one's intelligence to choose and shape one's life and character).

Rescher (1972) listed "consensus happiness requisites" that a just society should provide for the purpose of well-being. Among them, he includes such things as health, equality, prosperity and economic well-being, and leisure.

Finnis (1980) and Griffin (1986) also alluded to leisure as a condition of well-being. Although Finnis's account does not specifically mention leisure, it can be postulated as an essential condition for realizing six of the seven basic goods that constitute well-being, especially play, which flourishes in leisure. Griffin contended that "we need a certain amount (not just of resources, but also of liberty and leisure and education) to be able to make something valuable of our lives" (p. 43). Therefore, while well-being includes health and other basic needs, it also involves a group of values that collectively contribute to a life of worth and dignity. The idea of well-being will be revisited later in the discussion, where it will be especially pertinent in determining what constitutes the "total care" of persons who are ill or disabled.

We finally arrive at the task of defining therapeutic recreation. There is no shortage of definitions. Reviewing several should help set the stage for examining the foundations of therapeutic recreation. Virtually every definition of therapeutic recreation includes the notion of involvement in activity that is oriented to treatment, education, or recreation as a means for improving the health and well-being of persons with disabilities. An early definition of therapeutic recreation developed at the Ninth Southern Regional Institute on Therapeutic Recreation (1969) is suggestive:

> [Therapeutic recreation] is a process which utilizes recreation services for purposive intervention in some physical, emotional, and/or social behavior to bring about a desired change in that behavior and to promote the growth and development of the individual. Therapeutic recreation provides opportunities for participation on one's own volition in activities that bring pleasure or other positive personal rewards. (n.p.)

The dual focus of "purposive interventions . . . to promote the growth and development of the individual" and "opportunities for participation on one's own volition in activities that bring pleasure or other positive rewards" is evident in this definition. Similar principles are apparent in more recent definitions. For example, Kraus and Shank (1992) contended that therapeutic recreation service involves programs and activities purposefully designed to alter dysfunctional conditions and maladaptive behaviors and to contribute to personal enrichment. Carter, Van Andel, and Robb (1995) stated that therapeutic recreation "refers to the specialized application of recreation and experiential activities or interventions that assist in maintaining or improving the health status, functional capacities, and ultimately the quality of life of persons with special needs" (p. 10). Again, practice is aimed at improving the functioning *and* the well-being (quality of life) of persons with disabilities.

The official definitions of ATRA and NTRS are also remarkably alike in terms of their services and goals. According to ATRA (1988):

> Therapeutic recreation is the provision of treatment services and the provision of recreation services to persons with illnesses or disabling conditions. The primary purpose of treatment services, which is often referred to as recreation therapy, is to restore, remediate or rehabilitate in order to improve functioning and independence as well as reduce or eliminate the effects of illness or disability. The primary purpose of recreation services is to provide recreation resources and opportunities in order to improve health and well-being

Compare it to the NTRS (1994) definition, which states:

> Practiced in clinical, residential, and community settings, the profession of therapeutic recreation uses treatment, education, and recreation services to help people with illnesses, disabilities, and other conditions to develop and use their leisure in ways that enhance their health, independence, and well-being.

For the purposes of this text, *therapeutic recreation is defined as a service that uses the modalities of activity therapy, education, and recreation to promote the health and well-being of persons who require specialized care because of illness, disability, or social condition. Furthermore, recognizing the potential of leisure for contributing to the quality of life of all people, therapeutic recreation facilitates leisure opportunities as an integral component of comprehensive care.*

While these purposes (i.e., health, well-being and quality of life), modalities (i.e., treatment, education, and recreation), and commitments (creation of leisure opportunities) are theoretically compatible, they have resulted in a stubborn conflict that has plagued therapeutic recreation for decades. We will address that issue in the next section. First, however, we wish to comment briefly on the relation between recreation and therapeutic recreation.

If the concept of recreation implies beneficial outcomes for individuals, and the word "therapeutic" suggests something that is beneficial, one might argue, as some have, that the term "therapeutic recreation" is a redundancy ("beneficial benefits"). Before we are accused of splitting hairs, however, we wish to make an observation. Writers have attempted to find a way to distinguish between "general recreation" and "therapeutic recreation." In their discussion, Carter, Van Andel, and Robb (1995) stated that:

> Recreation, while closely related to therapeutic recreation, tends to focus on broader, more long-range goals. Although recreation is therapeutic in the sense that it promotes growth and development and may prevent maladaptive behaviors, it does not necessarily assist in diagnosing, treating, restoring, or ameliorating a disease process without some systematic plan and application. (p. 10)

> Therapeutic Recreation . . . cannot be defined by a particular setting or categorical group of individuals. Instead, it must be characterized by the specific process that uses recreation or experimental activities to achieve predetermined health-directed and health-related objectives. (p. 11)

We understand their logic and the reasoning of those who characterize therapeutic recreation as a specialized process. It *is* a specialized service. In *principle,* however, it is really no different than general recreation services. If the purpose of recreation and leisure services is to make life better for human beings no matter where they are found, then all recreation programs *should be* therapeutic or beneficial. This should be true for all people, whether the individual is a middle-aged man recovering from a spinal cord injury in a rehabilitation hospital, a pregnant adolescent, a young mother with AIDS, or a painfully shy and obese nine-year old who is tormented by his peers on the playground. Irrespective of setting, the goal is for people to achieve greater health and well-being according to their needs. As Fred Humphrey (1970) argued, being "therapeutic" is not a professional option or specialization, but rather an ethical responsibility that belongs to all professionals. Therefore, there really is no meaningful distinction in principle and purpose between "general recreation" and "therapeutic recreation." Different settings, of course, will demand different models, methods, techniques, and strategies. Specialization, however, can emphasize dissimilarities rather than common ground. This is unfortunate, because a bond of commonality between general recreation and therapeutic recreation ultimately benefits the people whom both serve. If our job is to make things better for people, and if recreation can contribute to that mission, then we are all therapists *and* we are all recreationists.

Whether conducted in a community or a clinical context, recreation has the potential to benefit the health and well-being of all human beings. The key connection between general recreation and the specialized field of therapeutic recreation lies in the freedom of people to decide for themselves what those benefits will be and how they will be achieved. Some observers recognize two categories of recreation—recreation that is chosen and recreation that is prescribed (see James, 1998). Both technical and popular understanding of recreation, however, have typically recognized its intimate association with freedom. Activities in the forms of art, dance, and games can be prescribed, but people generally understand recreation as relatively autonomous and self-determining. Embodying principles of autonomy and self-determination, recreation empowers people to choose for themselves what those benefits will be. Therein lies its value and uniqueness.

Sorting out and Searching for Foundations

An exhaustive review of the historical foundations of therapeutic recreation is beyond the scope of this text. Readers are encouraged to consult other sources for a comprehensive account of therapeutic recreation's attempts to set professional roots (see Carter, Van Andel & Robb, 1995; James, 1998; Reynolds & O'Morrow, 1985). The following discussion covers basic themes and issues related to the foundations of therapeutic recreation for the purpose of exploring their legitimacy and provides a foundation of therapeutic recreation practice.

From the earliest days, the core issue of therapeutic recreation's identity crisis has been whether the field exists primarily as a medical service or as a recreation service. Proponents of recreation associated with the Hospital Recreation Section (established in 1948) of the American Recreation Society. Supporters of a medical orientation affiliated with the National Association for Recreational Therapy (NART) formed in 1953. In the mid-1960s, however, a new national organization, the National Recreation and Park Association (NRPA) was forming. Some leaders in therapeutic recreation saw this as an opportunity to reconcile differences. In 1966 HRS, NART, and the Recreation Therapy Section of the American Association for Health, Physical Education, and Recreation, merged to form the National Therapeutic Recreation Society (NTRS). For some people the union was a satisfactory solution. For others it represented a marriage of expediency. And for others it must have been an unholy alliance. For the time being, however, the compromise worked for practical purposes.

Despite the creation of a single organization and the introduction of the term *therapeutic recreation* to cover the functions of treatment and recreation, the presence of two distinct professional identities was still evident. According to Miller (1967), there were:

those who see themselves as therapists and those who see
themselves as recreationists. The former concern themselves
with illness and employ recreation as treatment in the rehabilitation process, the latter with leisure time and patients' recreative
needs. (p. 34)

Even with a common organization and terminology, bedrock differences
still existed. Consequently, the debate continued; indeed it escalated. Hoping to
achieve clarity and consensus regarding the field's identity and purpose, the
NTRS Philosophical Issues Task Force polled the NTRS membership regarding
which of four positions it preferred to represent therapeutic recreation. The
positions were largely derived from a study conducted by Lee Meyer (1980) on
the philosophical bases of therapeutic recreation. Position A held that the
purpose of therapeutic recreation was to provide opportunities for persons with
special needs to experience recreation. Position B viewed recreation services as
treatment for enhancing the total functioning of the individual. Position C,
based on a model developed by Gunn and Peterson (1978), interpreted therapeutic recreation as a continuum of services, which included treatment, education, and recreation. Position D included Positions A (recreation) and B
(treatment). Position C was favored by the majority of members who responded to the survey and was accepted in May 1982 as the NTRS Philosophical Position Statement. The continuum model found room for treatment and
recreation, as well as leisure education. Clearly, though, leisure ("leisure
lifestyle") was the overarching mission of therapeutic recreation, with treatment, education, and recreation functioning as contributing services toward that
goal.

The peace was short-lived as dissatisfaction mounted. At least two reasons
account for the discontent. First, many professionals were concerned whether
NTRS could adequately meet the needs of therapeutic recreation professionals,
most of whom worked in healthcare settings. Second, smoldering disenchant-
ment persisted over the principal orientation of therapeutic recreation to
recreation and leisure. Disgruntled professionals asserted that because therapeutic recreation was mainly situated in healthcare settings, its goal should be
identical to other therapies. Like physical therapy and occupational therapy, it
should be a medical specialty designed to help people regain their health.
Although the effort did not materialize until several years after the founding of
the American Therapeutic Recreation Association (ATRA) in 1984, sentiment
was building for change. A contingent in ATRA recommended reforming as
"recreation therapy." Concentrating primarily on treatment, the field of recreation therapy would distance and even divorce itself from recreation and leisure
(see Carter, Van Andel & Robb, 1995, p. 58). Both reasons for creating another

organization are reflected in the comments of Peg Connolly (n.d.), founding President of ATRA. First, she addressed the organizational issue, observing that:

> a need exists for a national, professional association which is *solely* devoted both philosophically and with full financial commitment to the advancement of this important field of service. Since no autonomous, national *professional* organization existed specifically for the advancement of the Therapeutic Recreation profession in healthcare and human service settings as a priority concern, these professionals have joined forces to found ATRA. . . . ATRA can advocate specifically for the needs of Therapeutic Recreation in healthcare and human services as a priority focus rather than a special interest of a diverse organiza-tion (emphases added). (n.p.)

Connolly (n.d.) also attended to the purpose of therapeutic recreation, declaring that:

> ATRA defines the Therapeutic Recreation process in terms of improved human functioning with an emphasis on leisure as a viable concern in human development. *The focus of our services is on the delivery of Therapeutic Recreation as a means to improved independent functioning, not on the provision of adapted or special recreation as an end in itself* (emphasis added).

Despite the renewed emphasis on treatment, leisure remained conspicuous. A promotional brochure published by ATRA (n.d.) stated that "Therapeutic Recreation places a special emphasis on the development of an appropriate leisure lifestyle as an integral part of . . . independent functioning." It continued:

> The underlying philosophy of Therapeutic Recreation is that all human beings have the right to and need for leisure involvement as a necessary aspect of optimal health and, as such, Therapeutic Recreation can be used as an important tool for these individuals in becoming and remaining well. (n.p.)

Deciding not to divorce recreation from its definition of therapeutic recreation, the ATRA Board of Directors adopted the following Definition Statement in 1987:

> Therapeutic Recreation is the provision of Treatment Services
> and the provision of Recreation Services to persons with ill-
> nesses or disabling conditions. The primary purpose of Treat-
> ment Services which is often referred to as Recreation Therapy,
> is to restore, remediate or rehabilitate in order to improve
> functioning and independence as well as reduce or eliminate the
> effects of illness or disability. The primary purpose of Recreation
> Services is to provide recreation resources and opportunities in
> order to improve health and well-being.

Discontent remained, however, over any formal commitment to recreation
and leisure. In comments intended to support a proposed name change of
ATRA to American Recreational Therapy Association (ARTA), West (1993)
advocated a treatment orientation, arguing that:

> It is very important that the name of the Association reflect the
> primary purpose of the organization. Most of ATRA's members
> work in clinical settings. Most of ATRA's resources are devoted
> to the support of the service as a treatment or therapy. ATRA is
> the only national professional association devoted to addressing
> the allied health needs of our field. Today the term "Recreational
> Therapy" is the most politically correct and most commonly
> used term, both within the profession and by those in allied
> health and healthcare, to describe our discipline as a treatment
> modality. (p. 6)

The attempt to change the name of the organization from ATRA to ARTA
was narrowly defeated. This did not deter those who believed that treatment
should be the exclusive focus of the field. Efforts continued within ATRA to
establish a medical foundation for practice. In *Recreational Therapy: An
Integral Aspect of Comprehensive Healthcare* (ATRA, 1993), ATRA's official
definition was wholly ignored. Instead, the document stated that:

> Recreational therapy, also referred to as therapeutic recreation, is
> defined by the United States Department of Labor as a profes-
> sion of specialists who utilize activities as a form of treatment
> for persons who are physically, mentally or emotionally disabled.
> Differing from diversional or recreational services, recreational
> therapy utilizes various activities as a form of "active treatment"
> to promote the independent physical, cognitive, emotional, and
> social functioning of persons disabled as a result of trauma or

disease, by enhancing current skills and facilitating the establishment of new skills for daily living and community functioning.
(n.p.)

Where ATRA will finally come to rest on the issue of its identity remains to
be seen. Because of the sentiment to promote a treatment orientation, efforts
will likely continue not only to alter the name of the organization, but also to
change its definition and goals.

After sorting out the various conceptual orientations, there still appears to
be two foundations. The current ATRA and NTRS definitions share much in
common, including the goals of independence, health, and well-being. Fundamentally, they differ in their orientation to leisure. ATRA's early affirmation of
leisure has weakened as the movement to promote treatment has gained
momentum. Although ATRA's official stance has yet to be determined, recent
events and developments suggest that ATRA is increasingly embracing the
medical orientation implied by "recreational therapy." Russoneillo (1994)
defined this orientation as "the prescription of recreational activities to predict,
prevent and/or treat disease, illness, and pathological conditions as well as to
improve and maintain overall health" (p. 249)

On the other hand, the NTRS (2000) definition of therapeutic recreation
makes an explicit commitment to promoting leisure in the lives of persons who
are ill or injured:

> Therapeutic recreation uses treatment, education, and recreation
> services to help people with illnesses, disabilities, and other
> conditions to develop and use their leisure in ways that enhance
> their health, functional abilities, independence, and quality of
> life.

So, as the saying goes, "The more things change, the more they stay the
same." After nearly 50 years, therapeutic recreation still must decide, as Peterson
(1989) put it, "whether our basic contribution to society is in the domain of
leisure or in the domain of therapy" (p. 22). Resolving the issue must begin
where Peterson suggests—with society. The issue is what does society need in
order for its members to function, grow, and develop as human beings. The
most sound and legitimate foundation for therapeutic recreation, therefore, is
derived from an analysis of the public good. The authors' conviction is that the
most defensible foundation for therapeutic recreation is primarily oriented to
leisure and recreation. An integral role is reserved for treatment where it is
needed for improving functioning so clients can use recreation or leisure
activity in ways that contribute to their health, independence, and well-being

during and after the time they are receiving care. The remainder of this chapter is devoted to making a case for a foundation that includes a commitment to recreation and leisure for persons who are ill or injured.

Making a Case for Leisure

The position of this text is that the most socially legitimate justification for therapeutic recreation is derived from an orientation to leisure for the purposes of health, well-being, and quality of life. Prominent roles are reserved for treatment, education, and recreation as key aspects of therapeutic recreation services. Therapeutic recreation, however, is not a medical specialty. It is a unique human service that complements, but does not duplicate, medical services. The following discussion lays out a rationale for a foundation of therapeutic recreation oriented to leisure. It starts by asking "What would be the status of therapeutic recreation *without* leisure?"

If leisure were removed from therapeutic recreation, what would distinguish it from activity-based therapies, such as occupational therapy, physical therapy, music therapy, and art therapy? In effect, nothing would differentiate it. Consider the following definitions of occupational and recreational therapy in *Glossary for Therapists* (burlingame & Skalko, 1997):

> *Occupational therapy:* A clinical specialty which uses "purposeful activity with individuals who are limited by physical injury or illness, psychosocial dysfunction, developmental or learning disabilities, poverty and cultural differences, or the aging process to maximize independence, prevent disability and maintain health." (p. 188)

> *Recreational therapy:* A clinical specialty which uses leisure activities as the *modality* to restore, remediate or rehabilitate the patient's functional ability and level of independence and/or to reduce or eliminate the effects of illness and disability. (p. 218)

Fundamentally, there is no difference between the definitions. "Purposeful activity" implies that the action is intentional for the purposes of maximizing independence, preventing disability, and maintaining health. The term "leisure activities" in the definition of recreation therapy is used synonymously with "purposeful activity," because in each case the intention is to use activity *prescriptively* to achieve medical goals. As such, the reference to "leisure activities" is misleading, because leisure activities are, by definition, freely chosen, rather than prescribed. The term *leisure* really has no logical place in the preceding definition of "recreational therapy." Conceived solely as treatment ("recreation therapy"), therapeutic recreation is indistinguishable from other activity therapies, such as occupational therapy. It does not meet needs that other activity therapies are not already satisfying or could potentially satisfy by an adjustment in their methods. One might argue that the difference lies in the medium of activity, but therapeutic recreation does not own exclusive rights to the domain of activity. Occupational therapy, for example, also uses activity as its medium.

Another argument holds that therapeutic recreation makes a contribution by preparing clients to function in their communities (ATRA, 1993). Community-based efforts make good sense, but they do not represent the defining characteristic of therapeutic recreation. Other services, such as social work and occupational therapy, should and do work with clients to help them function successfully in the community. Staking claim to the community, therefore, does not by itself justify therapeutic recreation.

If therapeutic recreation is basically assuming the same role as other activity-based services, it faces the problem of duplication. Why should the public support a service that is already being made by other established fields? One retort to that question is that therapeutic recreation is a "bargain" compared to other activity therapies. For example, an ATRA document on health-care reform (ATRA, 1993) contended that:

> Recreational therapy services utilize both individual and small group intervention strategies, therefore, staff/patient ratios are cost-effective. More patient treatment hours per therapist can be generated through the use of such small group interventions. (n.p.)

Cost-effectiveness, however, is not an argument for the existence of a *profession*. Even if therapeutic recreation could demonstrate that its services are delivered more economically than other activity therapies, it would only resolve the problem of duplication, not the question of social need. Furthermore, if the difference between therapeutic recreation and similar fields is mainly cost-efficiency, therapeutic recreation should honestly admit that it is a market competitor rather than an allied field.

We fail to see an adequate social justification for therapeutic recreation without a clear and direct association with leisure. That still leaves unanswered the question "What does an orientation to leisure contribute to a comprehensive approach to care that improves health and well-being?" The following seven fundamental reasons constitute a foundation for therapeutic recreation that is embedded in leisure theory.

1. *Leisure affords opportunity for activity, which has been credited as an effective means for meeting the adaptive needs of human beings.*

Driver, Brown, and Peterson (1991) observed that "the issue is not whether leisure activities produce beneficial consequences. The questions are: What are those consequences? Who benefits? What are the magnitudes of the beneficial consequences?" (p. 7). Although more and better research is needed (Witt, 1988), some of the benefits of play and recreation have been documented. While the body of research findings cannot be listed here for lack of space, we recommend that readers consult two publications. First, *Benefits of Leisure* (Driver, Brown & Peterson, 1991) surveys the research across a broad array of needs, including physiological, psychological, and sociological domains. Second, *Benefits of Therapeutic Recreation: A Consensus View* (Coyle, Kinney, Riley & Shank, 1991) contains extensive literature reviews of the effects of activity in a number of areas, including chemical dependency, developmental disabilities, gerontology, pediatrics, physical medicine, and psychiatry.

Perhaps leisure activity can best be viewed as a stimulus to health rather than a cure for disease. The medical model is inclined to emphasize the pathogenic factors that affect disease. Surely, they should be treated. Mordacci and Sobel (1998) contended, however, that "just as there are factors that destroy health, so there are factors that support, enhance, and produce health" (p. 34). These factors they call *salutogenic* for their beneficial property. Among the myriad salutogens, they identify freedom of choice, humor, love, and intimate relationships. Besides the experience of freedom, leisure provides opportunity for a long list of potential salutogens that promote health, including challenge, laughter, creativity, curiosity, imagination, social relationships, and play for its own sake.

Therefore, the common sense conclusion that benefits come to people who are socially, physically, and intellectually active, as well as emotionally involved, is receiving empirical confirmation. This supports the age-old conviction that activity enhances human growth and development. Exercise does improve cardiovascular fitness. Reading does improve memory. Therefore, leisure activity can contribute to human growth and development and can promote health. Despite the apparent efficacy of activity, however, therapeutic recreation lacks justification if that is the only reason for its existence. In addition to its adaptive benefits, leisure opportunities should be offered for at least six additional reasons.

2. *Leisure contributes to a greater sense of well-being.*

Freedom, autonomy, and self-determination have been identified as defining characteristics of recreation (Brightbill, 1960; Miller and Robinson, 1963) and leisure (de Grazia, 1964; Kelly, 1982; Neulinger, 1981). In turn, recreation and leisure are recognized as vital sources of freedom, autonomy, and self-determination. The relationship between recreation and leisure and freedom, autonomy, and self-determination is morally significant in its own right, because freedom, autonomy, and self-determination are primary norms in American society, valued for their own sake. Furthermore, they have been credited for contributing to psychological well-being (Mannell & Kleiber, 1997). Operationalized as "perceived freedom" (Ellis & Witt, 1986), leisure has been recommended for alleviating "learned helplessness" and enhancing well-being (e.g., Dattilo & Barnett, 1985; Iso-Ahola, 1988; Langer & Rodin, 1976). Leisure has also been recognized for promoting well-being by contributing to positive identity, perceptions of competence, and feelings of enjoyment (Mannell & Kleiber, 1997; Dattilo, Kleiber & Williams, 1998). The psychosocial benefits of leisure are compelling for persons who are ill or impaired as they face challenges regarding freedom, control, competence, identity, and self-determination. Mannell and Kleiber's (1997) contention that leisure is a powerful "autonomy supportive context" (p. 145) can be plausibly extended to other psychological factors that contribute to well-being (e.g., perceived competence, intrinsic motivation, locus of control).

3. *The opportunity of leisure is necessary for meeting the creative-expressive needs of clients.*

Adaptive or functional needs pertain to what is physically, socially, cognitively, and emotionally required for individuals to cope successfully. They are first-order needs because they are necessary for individual functioning and species survival. Earlier the adaptive benefits of activity were acknowledged. But adaptive needs are only part of the picture. Beyond their strictly animal functioning, human beings *make* their own worlds of meaning and value, creating their identity (self-concept) and sense of worth (self-esteem). The other half of the picture is comprised of *creative-expressive needs*. Whether we wish to call these outcomes "existential," "spiritual," or "psychosocial," the important point is that besides the needs to clean, dress, and feed themselves, human beings also need to create and express themselves. Viktor Frankl (1959) claimed that the "search for meaning is a primary force" so powerful that people not only live for their ideals and values, they will die for the sake of them as well (p. 97). Richter and Kaschalk (1996) boldly recommended that therapeutic recreation take on the unique role of helping people whose lives have been disrupted by injury, illness, or impairment to create experiences of personal meaning and worth through the medium of leisure (also see Murray, 1998). The quest for meaning has important implications for healing. In reviewing research on the parallels between psychological and physiological events, Jourard (1964) observed:

> When a man finds hope, meaning, purpose and value in his
> existence, he may be said to be 'inspirited,' and isomorphic brain
> events weld the organism into its optimal, antientropic mode of
> organization. 'Dispiriting' events, perceptions, beliefs, or modes
> of life tend to weaken this optimal mode of organization which at
> once sustains wellness, and mediates the fullest, most effective
> functioning and behavior, and illness is most likely to flourish
> then. It is as if the body, when a man is dispirited, suddenly
> becomes an immensely fertile "garden" in which viruses and
> germs proliferate like jungle vegetation. In inspirited states,
> viruses and germs find a man's body a very uncongenial milieu
> for unbridled growth and multiplication. (p. 53)

Besides creating environments conducive to healing, creative-expressive opportunities provide incentive for living that is both functional and fulfilling. In other words, where people are involved in experiences they care about, they are more likely to take care of themselves *for the sake of* those things that give meaning and purpose to their lives (Sylvester, 1996). When human service fields speak of serving the "whole" person, they make a commitment not only to the individual as a functional entity, but also to the person's life as an expression of meaning and purpose. Both moral and medical reasons, therefore, support the important human need for meaning and value, which the condition of leisure is well-suited to serve.

4. *Leisure is a flexible medium for helping persons with illnesses and disabilities to reintegrate into community life.*

Much has been said and written about the importance of inclusion, mainstreaming, and integration (Hutchison & McGill, 1998; Schelein & Ray, 1988). Out of the many benefits that involvement in community leisure opportunities offer for persons with disabilities, perhaps the most important one is the achievement of an identity. Guess (1981) stated that:

> Participating in a culture is a way of satisfying certain very deep-
> seated human needs. Humans have a vital need for the kind of
> "meaningful" life and the kind of identity which is possible only
> for an agent who stands in relation to culture. (p. 22)

A culture supplies the beliefs, values, and social practices that collectively constitute ways of life that offer people suitable models for achieving personal meaning and worth. A culture provides norms of what is "good," "desirable," "successful," and so forth. To the extent that any person does not have access to culture, he or she remains "invisible," having no means to determine where he or she stands in relation to the world. Bullock and Howe's (1991) reintegration model emphasizes the importance of social participation by way of the concept of "social role valorization." Identity or self-concept comes from interaction with others and participation in social practices and cultural rituals. Ironic as it may sound, an individual identity depends on other people and the available identities found in culture. For persons with disabilities to achieve valued identities, they must have access to the key domains in society and culture where those identities are created and sustained. Community integration is vital because it is in communities where people work, worship, shop, play, interact, and create contexts that provide models for "successful" living. According to Bullock and Howe (1991), "social valorization theory identifies the individual's right and responsibility to assume a valued social role in society and society's obligation to allow the individual to pursue that role without constraint" (p. 9).

Leisure has been increasingly recognized by people as a viable medium for engaging in activities that are seen as worthwhile and meaningful. For example, the Roper Center (1990) reported that for the first time in fifteen years people identified leisure as "more important" in their lives than work. Furthermore, the changing nature and structure of work (e.g., downsizing, automation) suggest that leisure may be playing a greater role in the lives of many people (see Rifkin, 1995). For these reasons, the connection between therapeutic recreation in institutional settings and community recreation and leisure opportunities is vital. All efforts in clinical settings should be aimed at enabling clients to gain access to their communities. In turn, community services should be doing everything possible to facilitate the successful reintegration and inclusion of persons with disabilities into the community. Insofar as community life is essential for meeting human needs, it should be infused into institutional settings as much as feasible. Institutions are notorious breeding grounds for negative identities. Leisure affords opportunities for individuals who are residing in institutional settings to continue to have culturally meaningful and valued experiences. As such, holidays, birthdays, and other important cultural events and rituals are not just "diversions," and should not be referred to as such. They are intrinsically meaningful and significant *immersions* in living that help people form self-concept, self-worth, and significant relationships. From start to finish, the therapeutic recreation process should enable individuals to create identities of choice, form meaningful relationships, and express themselves through social, cultural, and political media. This is best achieved in the community.

5. *The social institution of leisure is an avenue for addressing structural deficiencies that affect the health and well-being of individuals.*

While praising holistic medicine for being sensitive to environmental factors, Freund (1982) also criticized it for being too individualistic and for failing to restructure environments that produce "diseases of civilization" (e.g., cancer, anxiety, depression, and heart disease). He commented:

> Healing is generally accomplished within the narrow confines of a professional setting and tends to be separated from prevention and above all from everyday life. More shelters for the broken humans, better job conditions, more parks, better public transportation, easier access to all of these appear at first to be unrelated to health but are essential to it. These must be important considerations for a holistic/social medicine that is truly "whole," meaning oriented towards changes of economic and social conditions that are unhealthy. (p. 130)

Rusalem (1973) offered similar advice to therapeutic recreation, arguing that because social structures cause illness and injury, disabling environments should be diagnosed and treated. Preventive medicine that addresses environmental deficiencies and dysfunctions that are deleterious to human health and well-being recommends an important role for leisure. The correlation between good health and good habits of living, such as sufficient rest, diet, hygiene, exercise, and the enjoyment of intrinsically motivated activities, is receiving more attention. Similar opportunities should be made for persons who already have disabling conditions in order to prevent deterioration and to promote health and well-being.

Besides the more constructive habits of living cultivated in leisure, structural changes to work—permitting more frequent and flexible opportunities for leisure—are urged. Freund (1982) alluded to shortening the work day so people can become better informed and more responsible for their own health, reducing dependence on healthcare specialists. Expanding the definition of what constitutes "success" by easing the constraints imposed by the work ethic and by recognizing social contributions that occur during leisure will further widen social participation, which is essential to self-concept and self-esteem. Altering social structures in similar ways will make environments more conducive to fitting the needs of human beings. As such, Callahan (1990) called for a "society prepared to make room for those it cannot cure or return to 'productive life'" [work], suggesting a range of services that go "well beyond the narrowly medical" (pp. 148–149). In his critical theory of play, Hearn (1976/77) explained how industrial capitalism distorted and weakened play in order to create a compliant work force malleable to the requirements of factory life and productive labor. The suppression of play has deprived people of opportunities for meeting creative-expressive needs and greatly limited the freedom and control that play affords. Therefore, therapeutic recreation must not restrict itself to narrow, vocational models of rehabilitation, but must address the broader environmental issues that affect the lives of clients, including the environment of leisure. In fact, as rehabilitation embraces quality of life as its goal (Sandstrom, Hoppe & Smutko, 1996), therapeutic recreation would do well to adopt quality of life as its primary mission. Arguably, no other human service field is as well-suited for that role as therapeutic recreation.

6. *Leisure is a significant contributor to quality of life, which is being recognized as the overarching goal of rehabilitation.*
Imagine a world in which individuals with impairments could be rehabilitated to function flawlessly. They could walk, communicate, reason, and relate as well as persons without impairments. Unlike persons without impairments, however, their world is devoid of opportunities to hold jobs, form relationships, participate in their communities, or enjoy the outdoors. In other words, even though they have achieved functional ability, they lack the opportunities that make functioning worthwhile. Such an existence, all too real for some people, would be hell on earth. For this reason, rehabilitation is embracing quality of life as its goal. As Sandstrom, Hoppe, and Smutko (1996) expressed:

> *The goals of rehabilitation are twofold: promote the wholeness and integrity of the person and enable the individual to live a full life with an illness or disability. . . .* In doing so, rehabilitation needs to focus on the care not the cure, not isolated pathologies but the whole person, and on the quality of life of the individual. *. . . Improvement of the quality of life is the central mission of rehabilitation.* (emphases added) (p. 44)

Speaking about therapeutic recreation, Dr. Lynn Gerber (1994/95), a professional in rehabilitation medicine, stated:

> Clearly, quality of life is more than survival and productive capacity. It includes full participation in society. Leisure activities that give a sense of purpose and enjoyment to life must be made possible. Recreation participation must be measured by its ability to provide meaning and dignity to life so that people with disability have reasons to live, not merely exist. (p. 3)

Quality of life refers to the subjective experience that life is good, meaningful, and satisfying. On a phenomenological level—the realm of our subjective experience—most people can attest to perceiving their lives as fulfilling and satisfying as opposed to degrading and despairing. Furthermore, most people can point to particular conditions that are conducive to experiencing their lives as "good," including such things as safe and pleasant surroundings, economic security, social relations, and enjoyable pursuits.

The importance of quality of life has not escaped therapeutic recreation. One of the earliest theorists on the relationship between therapeutic recreation and quality of life, Sylvester (1989b) argued forcefully for placing quality of life at the center of therapeutic recreation's mission. Quality of life is one of the key outcomes of Van Andel's (1998) Therapeutic Recreation Outcome Model. Carter, Van Andel, and Robb (1995) contended that because they produce freedom, satisfaction, and joy, leisure activities are vital "to experiencing a quality of life" (p. 21). Therefore, while extensive study of the relationship among leisure, therapeutic recreation, and quality of life is needed, rehabilitation's embrace of quality of life as a goal invites a central role for leisure and a unique contribution by therapeutic recreation.

7. *All people, including persons receiving healthcare, have the right to leisure for the purposes of health, well-being, and quality of life.*

Lieb (1976) claimed that illness does not turn people into some other kind of creature. Carter, Van Andel, and Robb (1995) made a similar point, asserting that persons with disabilities are still human beings "apart from any impairment, disease, or need they might have" (p. 22). Human beings do not check their humanity at the door when they enter rehabilitation programs. Consequently, they maintain their basic rights. Sylvester (1992) noted that the concept of well-being has served as a principle for determining rights. Arguing that modern life requires leisure for the purpose of well-being, he proposed that "the right to leisure . . . is an indispensable corollary of the right to well-being" (p. 16). Asserting that "disability does not preclude the right to leisure," Sylvester argued that "leisure must be protected and facilitated for people who have limiting conditions, lest they be deprived of their main or only source of well-being" (p. 16). Therefore, leisure is relevant in any setting where people retain their right to live like human beings.

The right to leisure has been affirmed repeatedly in the history of therapeutic recreation (NTRS, 1982, 1990, 1996). Most recently, the NTRS *Philosophical Position Statement* (1996) identified the right to leisure as one of three values that constitutes the field's value structure, proclaiming that "the right to leisure is a condition necessary for human dignity and well-being."

Summary

A conceptual foundation is a critical function for all professions, providing theory and practice with intellectual substance and moral direction. A sound conceptual foundation cannot be developed without philosophy, which is an intellectual process aimed at analyzing and explaining the key concepts and values that ground a field. Although some progress has been made, more philosophical discourse in therapeutic recreation is imperative.

The presence of ATRA and NTRS has also impacted the foundations of therapeutic recreation. Because therapeutic recreation practice, and therapeutic recreation programming in particular, does not operate in a vacuum, students should understand how social and political developments related to professional organizations influence a field's foundation.

Finally, a justification for the profession of therapeutic recreation starts with a legitimate social need or good. The authors of this text contend that an orientation to leisure provides the firmest foundation for the profession. First, leisure activities are gaining empirical support for contributing to growth and development, posing important implications for disease prevention, disability management, and health promotion. Second, leisure contributes to a greater sense of well-being, offering significant psychological benefits associated with freedom, autonomy, and self-determination. Third, in addition to adaptive needs, human beings also have creative-expressive needs. Leisure is often the only, and arguably the best, opportunity to satisfy those needs in rehabilitation. Fourth, without a community to supply meaningful and valued roles and norms, a human being is invisible, a nonperson. Through community-based opportunities, leisure is a flexible medium for helping people to assimilate into cultures in which they can "find" themselves, acquiring an esteemed identity in the process. Fifth, leisure affords a way to deal with structural deficiencies in society, such as noxious and debilitating environments and destructive habits of living, that contribute to illness and disability. Sixth, leisure is a vital resource for quality of life, which is being recognized as a central goal of rehabilitation. Seventh, and finally, all human beings have a right to leisure based on the principle of well-being, which is a goal of therapeutic recreation. Leisure and the related forms of play and recreation are broadly relevant to the needs, values, and interests of human beings with illnesses and disabilities who are receiving medical and rehabilitative care. Any theory of caring for persons who are ill or injured that does not include a prominent role for leisure and therapeutic recreation service is socially limited and morally impoverished.

Recommended Readings

Hemingway, J. L. (1987). Building a philosophical defense of therapeutic recreation: The case of distributive justice. In C. Sylvester, J. Hemingway, R. Howe-Murphy, K. Mobily, and P. Shank (Eds.). *Philosophy of therapeutic recreation: Ideas and issues, Vol. 1*, (pp. 1–16). Alexandria, VA: National Recreation and Park Association.

Richter, K. and Kaschalk, S. (1996). The future of therapeutic recreation: An existential outcome. In C. Sylvester (Ed.), *Philosophy of therapeutic recreation: Ideas and issues, Vol. 2*, (pp. 86–91). Arlington, VA: National Recreation and Park Association.

Shank, J. and Kinney, T. (1987). On the neglect of clinical practice. In C. Sylvester, J. L. Hemingway, R. Howe-Murphy, K. Mobily, and P. Shank (Eds.), *Philosophy of therapeutic recreation: Ideas and issues, Vol. 1*, (pp. 65–75). Alexandria, VA: National Recreation and Park Association.

Sylvester, C. (1992). Therapeutic recreation and the right to leisure. *Therapeutic Recreation Journal, 26*(2), 9–20.

Sylvester, C. (1996). *Philosophy of therapeutic recreation: Ideas and issues (vol. 2)*. Ashburn, VA: National Recreation and Park Association.

Sylvester, C. (1998). Careers, callings, and the professionalization of therapeutic recreation. *Journal of Leisurability, 25*(2), 3–13.

Sylvester, C., Hemingway, J., Howe-Murphy, R., Mobily, K., and Shank, P. (Eds.). (1987). *Philosophy of therapeutic recreation: Ideas and issues, Vol. 1*. Alexandria, VA: National Recreation and Park Association.

Chapter

2

Multicultural Considerations

Therapeutic recreation takes place in a society comprised of various cultures. *Therefore, all therapeutic recreation practice occurs in a multicultural context.* It is reasonable to expect that therapeutic recreation would reflect the cultural diversity of the society it serves. Yet Peregoy and Dieser (1997) contended that therapeutic recreation was based on Western beliefs and values, seriously limiting the field's capacity to serve people whose primary world-view is non-Western. The issue is not that Western cultural values, beliefs, and practices are inherently wrong. Clearly, they have a central and significant role in society. The problem is that therapeutic recreation, which has long advocated the principle of inclusion as it pertains to persons with disabilities, has not sufficiently incorporated cultural inclusion, or multiculturalism, into its theory and practice.

Furthermore, multiculturalism is not just about respecting individuals' cultural beliefs and practices; it is also about oppression. The history of oppression in the United States toward such groups as Native Americans, African Americans, and Asian Americans is shameful (see Zinn, 1980). Although no longer considered a mental illness, until 1973 the American Psychiatric Association listed "homosexuality" among mental and emotional disorders. Homosexuals continue to be an oppressed group. Granted, history cannot be changed and progress has been made. But as a calling to serve society, the profession of therapeutic recreation has the moral responsibility to eliminate discrimination and oppression and to foster opportunities for growth and development according to the individual's cultural frame of reference.

Therapeutic recreation has made formal commitments that support multiculturalism. The codes of ethics of both the American Therapeutic Recreation Association (ATRA; see Appendix A) and the National Therapeutic Recreation Society (NTRS; see Appendix C) take stands on justice and equality. Under Principle 3: Justice, The *ATRA Code of Ethics* (1998) states:

Therapeutic Recreation personnel are responsible for ensuring that individuals are served fairly and that there is equity in the distribution of services. Individuals receive service without regard to race, color, creed, gender, sexual orientation, age, disability/disease, social and financial status.

The *NTRS Code of Ethics* (1990), under Principle VI: The Obligation of the Profession to Society (B. Equality), states:

The profession is committed to equality of opportunity. No person shall be refused service because of race, gender, religion, social status, ethnic background, sexual orientation, or inability to pay.

It goes on to say:

The profession neither conducts nor condones discriminatory practices. *It actively seeks to correct inequities that unjustly discriminate.* (emphasis added)

Both organizations express their obligation to serve people fairly. Although not explicitly stated, it is reasonable to assume that this commitment would include providing services that reflect the cultural backgrounds of clients. The facts indicate, however, that multiculturalism is a seriously underdeveloped area of therapeutic recreation. As such, it is necessary to devote a chapter to it in the foundations section of this text. Multicultural aspects of therapeutic recreation programming will also be addressed throughout the rest of this book. Nonetheless, there is more work to be done in this important area than can be accomplished in this book. Encouraged by signs of progress, such as the contribution of Peregoy and Dieser (1997), let us take this opportunity to call for the comprehensive study and action that multiculturalism warrants. Readers are encouraged to investigate the suggested readings at the end of the chapter.

The Basics of Multiculturalism

According to the U.S. Bureau of the Census' *Population Profile of the United States: 1997* (1998):

By 2000, the non-Hispanic White proportion of the population is expected to decrease to less than 72 percent with just under 13 percent Black; over 11 percent Hispanic origin; 4 percent Asian and Pacific Islander; and less than 1 percent American Indian, Eskimo, and Aleut. By 2050, those proportional shares will shift quite dramatically. Less than 53 percent will be non-Hispanic White; 15 percent Black; over 24 percent Hispanic origin; almost 9 percent Asian and Pacific Islander; and just over 1 percent American Indian, Eskimo, and Aleut. (pp. 8–9)

The ethnic face of America is undergoing dramatic change. In the not too distant future, groups presently referred to as "minorities" will comprise nearly half the population of the United States. The competent therapeutic recreation specialist, therefore, must be able to serve a pluralistic society. Although cultural diversity has always been present in therapeutic recreation, it has only received attention in recent years, leaving much to be learned. As a start, an elementary description of multiculturalism is offered, after which the relation between multiculturalism and therapeutic recreation programming will be briefly explored. We begin with some key terms.

Culture

Cross, Bazron, Dennis, and Isaacs (quoted in Sue, Carter, Casas, Fouad, Ivey, Jensen, LaFromboise, Manese, Ponterotto, & Vazquez-Nutall, 1998, p. 7) define culture as "an integrated pattern of human behavior that includes thoughts, communications, actions, customs, beliefs, values, and institutions of a racial, ethnic, religious, or social group." The distinctive quality of a culture is sharing a way of life distinguished by a common set of beliefs and values. Therefore, the term culture can be applied to almost any group of people who share a way of life (e.g., Western culture; Eastern culture; Hispanic culture; blue-collar culture; deaf culture; youth culture; gay, lesbian, bisexual, and transgendered culture). Furthermore, culture is not static, but instead constantly changes as groups interact with each other. Nonetheless, cultural groups exhibit identifiable features (Axelson, 1993).

Following Pedersen (1994), we define culture broadly to include:

- Demographic variables (e.g., age, gender, sexual orientation, residence, disability),
- Status variables (e.g., economic, educational),
- Affiliations (formal and informal), and
- Ethnographic variables (e.g., nationality, ethnicity, language, religion). (p. 16)

Race

Traditionally, race has been defined by biological traits shared by people, such as hair texture and skin pigmentation. According to Krogman (quoted in Sue et al., 1998, p. 8), race refers to:

> a subgroup of peoples possessing a definite combination of physical characteristics of genetic origin, the combination of which to varying degrees distinguishes the subgroup from other subgroups.

Race also has been classified by the typology of Caucasoid, Mongoloid, and Negroid. The widespread existence of biracial and multiracial individuals, however, makes simple classification on the basis of biology extremely difficult (Sue et al., 1998). Consequently, race may not be a useful referent, except where it is used for purposes of social identity.

Ethnicity

Sue et al. (1998) define ethnicity in terms of group members who:

> share and transmit a unique cultural and social heritage passed on from one generation to the next; these cultural patterns (differences in nationality, customs, language, religion) are more related to national origin rather than physical differences, which may or may not be germane. Ethnicity does not have a biological or genetic foundation and should not be used synonymously with race. (p. 10)

Members of the same ethnic group, sharing a common social and cultural heritage, may nonetheless belong to different cultures. For example, a European American might associate with a blue-collar culture, a homosexual culture, or any number of subcultures.

Diversity

Diversity refers to the constellation of human qualities, including primary characteristics, (e.g., race, age, gender, and ethnicity) and secondary characteristics, (e.g., religion, education, and economic status). Traditionally, the term has been used in the social sciences to express the differences that exist within any particular group. For that reason, a monoculture could exhibit diversity among its members in terms of physical attributes, such as a group of Caucasian males who vary according to height, weight, and so forth. Accordingly, we prefer the term multiculturalism to convey the idea of recognizing and respecting cultural diversity. Nonetheless, multiculturalism and cultural diversity will be used interchangeable in this text.

Multiculturalism

Peregoy and Dieser (1997) explained that "multiculturalism encompasses all aspects of diversity which includes but is not limited to race, culture, ethnicity, language, socioeconomic status, gender and gender orientation, lifestyle, and physical ability" (p. 175). Because we are using a broad definition of culture in this text, multiculturalism, as Peregoy and Dieser (1997) clearly suggested, incorporates a diverse array of characteristics that are central to people's identity and way of life. Multiculturalism is also a way of thinking, offering "a conceptual framework that recognizes the complex diversity of a plural society, although at the same time it suggests bridges of shared concern that bind culturally different persons to one another" (Pedersen, 1994, p. 15). Therefore, multiculturalism is about recognizing and respecting differences among people *and* about common values and goals, such as justice, respect, dignity, and quality of life, that establish a sense of unity among people of different cultures.

We wish to be clear that by advocating a multicultural approach to therapeutic recreation, we are not implying that all cultural beliefs, values, and practices are legitimate. By no means do we support cultures that oppress people by class, gender, religion, or disability. For example, women in Afghanistan suffer severe oppression under the rule of the Taliban regime, whose cultural beliefs have led to women being banished from work and school. The United Nations and the World Health Organization (1997) have appealed to the international community to eliminate the cultural practice of female genital mutilation. Cultural relativism, therefore, does not mean everything is morally acceptable. It requires learning about other cultures and making moral judgments from a perspective broader than one's own cultural norms (World Health Organization, 1997). Despite the emphasis on differences, cultures need to examine themselves collectively by standards of what is good for human beings in general. Obviously, harmonizing different world-views will be difficult, but it is necessary in today's multicultural, global community.

Cultural Encapsulation

Wrenn (1962) has been credited with coining the term "cultural encapsulation," by which he meant "an encapsulation within our world, within our culture and subculture" (p. 445). According to Wrenn, everyone lives in a world-view that is woven over time with the thread of social experience, providing individuals with "cultural cocoons." While everyone has a "cultural cocoon," however, it can create a serious problem when it becomes impervious to other cultural beliefs, attitudes, and practices, enveloping the individual in a rigid enclosure of his or her prejudicial biases. Some of the key features of cultural encapsulation include:

- Defining reality by one set of cultural assumptions and stereotypes, which become more significant than what actually occurs in reality,
- Insensitivity to cultural variation, assuming that one's view is the only real or legitimate one,
- Accepting assumptions without regard to evidence or reason, and
- Failure to evaluate other viewpoints, resulting in taking no responsibility to interpret or accommodate other people's behavior except from one's own narrow viewpoint. (Pederson, 1994)

Ethnocentric Monoculturalism

Ethnocentrism refers to the belief that an ethnocultural group is superior to all others. Monoculturalism involves viewing the world from a single cultural perspective, ignoring all others. Sue et al. (1998) referred to ethnocentric monoculturalism as a combination of cultural encapsulation and cultural racism. They identified five main characteristics:

1. Strong belief in the superiority of one group's cultural heritage, regarding it as the "best way."
2. Corresponding belief in the inferiority of all other groups' cultural heritage.
3. The dominant group uses its power to impose its beliefs and values on less powerful groups.
4. Ethnocentric values and beliefs appear in the programs, policies, practices, structures, and institutions of the society.
5. People assume universality of their world-view, seldom questioning their assumptions about truth and reality. (p. 16)

Perhaps the most blatant example of ethnocentric monoculturalism is the White supremacist movement. Insidious instances of it occur on a regular basis in everyday life, especially where ethnocentric monoculturalism has become institutionalized. Our objective is to avoid cultural encapsulation and to eliminate monocultural ethnocentrism, which requires multicultural competence.

The Multiculturally Competent Professional

Principle 7 of the *ATRA Code of Ethics* (1998) states that "Therapeutic Recreation personnel have the responsibility to continually seek to expand one's knowledge base related to Therapeutic Recreation practice." Under "The Obligation of Professional Virtue," the *NTRS Codes of Ethics* (1990) declares that "Professionals continuously enhance their knowledge and skills through education and by remaining informed of professional and social trends, issues, and developments." Therefore, by becoming multiculturally competent, we are fulfilling our ethical obligations.

Multicultural competence means becoming a professional who is capable of helping people from all cultures to meet their needs and to achieve well-being as they understand it. Multicultural incompetence can contribute to the oppression of people. Multicultural competence, however, makes it possible for the field of therapeutic recreation, as part of the larger recreation movement, to play a role in facilitating recognition, respect, understanding, appreciation, and community in a culturally diverse nation.

Clearly therapeutic recreation professionals must achieve multicultural competence. Based on the work of experts in multicultural education, Peregoy and Dieser (1997) developed an extensive curriculum for therapeutic recreation education and practice, which appears in Table 2.1, p. 42. Their approach is based on attitudes, beliefs, knowledge, and skills regarding one's own culture and the cultures of other individuals. Readers are encouraged to read each component reflectively, using the curriculum as a career long path for becoming multiculturally competent.

In their discussion of frameworks for multicultural training, Peregoy, Schliebner, and Dieser (1997) recommended working toward an integrated model of training in which multicultural knowledge is infused throughout the curriculum. They further suggested that course design be based on three components:

- Awareness: Consciousness-raising regarding one's personal values, sexual biases, beliefs, attitudes and assumptions,

Table 2.1a Helper's Attitude of Own Cultural Values and Biases*

Attitudes and Beliefs

1. Cultural self-awareness and sensitivity to one's own cultural heritage are essential.
    *   Learn to identify cultures that one belongs to.
    *   Understand the cultural heritage of interventions used.
    *   Actively engage in a process of challenging one's attitudes and beliefs that do not support valuing of differences.
    *   Articulate positive aspects of one's own heritage that provide strengths in understanding differences.
    *   Understand the cultural heritage of recreation and leisure activity.

2. An awareness of how one's own cultural background and experiences influence one's attitudes, values and biases about psychological processes.
    *   Identify the history of their culture.
    *   Identify social and cultural influences on their cognitive development.
    *   Articulate the beliefs of their own culture and religious groups as they relate to differing cultures, and the impact of these beliefs in a helping relationship.

3. An ability to recognize the limits of their multicultural competencies.
    *   Recognize when and how their attitudes, beliefs, and values are interfering with providing the best service to a client.
    *   Identify training which contributes to expertise in therapeutic recreation practice.
    *   Provide real examples of cultural situations in which they recognize their limitations and referred the client to more appropriate services.

4. Therapeutic recreation specialists recognize their sources of discomfort with differences that exist between themselves and their clients in terms of race, ethnicity and culture.
    *   Recognize their sources of comfort/discomfort.
    *   Identify differences.
    *   Communicate acceptance of and respect for differences.

Knowledge

1. Acquire specific knowledge about one's own racial and cultural heritage and how it personally and professionally affects their definitions and biases.
    *   Have knowledge regarding their heritage.
    *   Recognize their family's and culture's perspective of acceptable and unacceptable codes of conduct.
    *   Recognize their family's and culture's perspective of recreation and leisure.

2. Possess knowledge and understanding about how oppression, racism, discrimination, and stereotyping affect them personally and in their work.
    *   Identify their identity development.
    *   Provide a reasonable definition of racism, prejudice, discrimination, and stereotype.

Table 2.1a Helper's Attitude of Own Cultural Values and Biases (continued)

3. Possess knowledge about their social impact on others.
   - Define their communication style and describe their verbal and nonverbal behaviors.
   - Describe the behavioral impact of their communication styles on clients that are different than themselves.
   - Provide an example of an incident in which communication broke down with a client from a differing culture.

Skills

1. Seek out educational, consultative, and training experiences to improve understanding and effectiveness in working with culturally different populations.
   - Describe objectives of at least two multicultural related professional development activities.
   - Develop professional relationships with helpers (both inside and outside of therapeutic recreation) from differing cultural backgrounds.
   - Maintain an active referral list. Actively engage in professional and personal growth activities pertaining to working with clients from different cultures.
   - Actively consult with other professionals regarding issues of culture.

2. A constant seeking to understand themselves as racial and cultural beings and are actively seeking a nonracist identity.

Table 2.1b Awareness of Client's Worldview*

Attitudes and Beliefs

1. An awareness of one's negative and positive emotional reaction toward other racial and ethnic groups that may prove detrimental to the therapeutic relationship.
   - Identify their common emotional reactions about people different from themselves.
   - Identify how emotional reactions observed in oneself can influence effectiveness in therapeutic recreation intervention.
   - Describe at least two examples of cultural conflict between self and culturally different clients.

2. An awareness of one's stereotypes and preconceived notions that they may hold toward other racial and ethnic minority groups.
   - Recognize their stereotyped reactions to people that are different from themselves.
   - Consciously attend to examples that contradict stereotypes.
   - Recognize assumptions made concerning different cultures.

Knowledge

1. Possess knowledge and information about particular groups with whom they work. They are aware of the life experiences, cultural heritage, and historical backgrounds of the culturally different clients.

Table 2.1b Awareness of Client's Worldview (continued)

- Identify differences in nonverbal and verbal behavior of different cultural groups.
- Describe at least two models of minority identity development.
- Understand the historical implications of contact with dominant society for various ethnic groups.
- Identify within-group differences of cultures.

2. Possess an understanding of how race, culture, ethnicity, and so forth may affect personal choices, help-seeking behaviors, recreation and leisure behaviors, and disorders.
   - Based upon literature, describe and give examples of how different therapeutic recreation approaches may or may not be appropriate for a specific culture.
   - Describe one system of personality development and how this system relates or does not relate to at least two culturally different populations.

3. Possess knowledge about sociopolitical influences that impinge upon the life of racial and ethnic minorities.
   - Identify implications of concepts such as internalized oppression, institutional racism, privilege, and the historical and current political climate regarding immigration, poverty, and welfare.
   - Explain the relationship between culture and power.
   - Communicate an understanding of the unique position, constraints, and needs of those clients who experience oppression.
   - Identify current issues that affect different cultures in legislation, social climate and so forth.
   - Understanding of how documents and affirmative action legislation affect society's perception (both pros and cons) (sic) of different cultural groups.

Skills

1. Become familiar with research relevant to their discipline that affects racial and ethnic groups.
   - Discuss recent research regarding relevant topics (e.g., mental health, education, recreation/leisure, therapeutic recreation) related to different cultural populations.
   - Complete workshops, conferences, and in-service training regarding multicultural skills and knowledge.
   - Identify professional growth activities.

2. Become actively involved with minority individuals outside the helping setting (e.g., community events, social functions) so that their perspective of minorities is more than just an academic exercise.
   - Identify at least five multicultural experiences in which they have participated within the past three years.
   - Actively plan experiences and activities that will contradict negative sterotypes and preconceived notions they may hold.

* Peregoy and Dieser (1997). Reprinted with the permission of the National Therapeutic Recreation Society.

- Knowledge: Learn about the history and culture of diverse groups, and
- Skill: Develop ability to work with culturally different individuals. (p. 290)

Besides training in undergraduate and graduate programs, continuing education and professional literature should provide regular opportunities for professionals to develop competencies. Whatever means are designed, therapeutic recreation must make a concerted effort to make certain that its professionals are capable of serving all people.

Multiculturalism and Therapeutic Recreation Programming

With few exceptions, the multicultural context of therapeutic recreation programming has been largely unexplored (see Allison & Smith, 1990; Peregoy & Dieser, 1997; Peregoy, Schliebner & Dieser, 1997). Each aspect of the programming process, including assessment, planning, implementation, and evaluation, is replete with multicultural implications. We wish to offer a few examples.

Assessment uses tests, interviews, questionnaires, and other means to gather valid and reliable information about individuals to develop programs that meet their needs for health and well-being. Assessment is expected to be sensitive to individual needs, because decisions based on assessment results may significantly impact a person's life. Yet there is ample evidence that therapeutic recreation assessments on the whole are not culturally sensitive. For example, one of the questions on The Idyll Arbor Reality Orientation Assessment asks: "Professional baseball is played during what season?" (burlingame & Blaschko, 1990, p. 214). The correct response from someone who lives in the United States would most probably be "summer" (even though baseball playoffs extend well into the fall). A Puerto Rican might correctly answer "winter," however, because professional baseball is played during the winter months in Puerto Rico. Unaware of the difference, the individual doing the assessment might incorrectly judge the client as "disoriented" on this item. Activity inventories, which purport to identify leisure interests of individuals, are notoriously biased toward majority activities. Aware of this, some therapeutic recreation specialists are now adapting and developing activity inventories that reflect their clients' backgrounds. Nonetheless, we have not come across an inventory that includes "drag events" among its listing of activities, even though they are a popular leisure activity among some members of the homosexual community. A similar problem related to sexual orientation occurs with pictorial assessments that show only heterosexual relationships.

Therapeutic recreation interventions provide another example that has implications for multiculturalism. Assertiveness training is a popular intervention in therapeutic recreation. Peregoy and Dieser (1997) observed that assertiveness training, while useful for clients who value independence and individuality, can be detrimental to clients from cultures who value congeniality. Another example is the use of sacred rituals, such as American Indian pow-wows, as interventions by individuals who are not members of the cultural group. According to Oles (1992), the misappropriation of Native American ceremonies as "tools" for adventure leadership programs desecrates sacred cultural practices.

Planning is another area of therapeutic recreation programming that suffers from the lack of multicultural awareness. Much of therapeutic recreation is based on the goal of "independent functioning." Over the years, "independent leisure functioning" and "independent leisure lifestyle" have become virtual mantras. Today we are seeing that while independence has an appropriate time and place, it is not the only perspective. We are recognizing that *interdependence* is more highly valued among some cultures. In a culture where interdependence is valued, goals might focus on developing group supports, such as the involvement of extended family. Again, the point is not to "swap" one value or world-view for the other, but to be aware of how goals are mediated by culture and to respond accordingly for the well-being of clients.

Franklin and Rios (1999) provided a helpful inventory for appraising multicultural services using job tasks and knowledge areas developed by the National Council for Therapeutic Recreation Certification. We encourage readers to peruse the list in Table 2.2 and to consider its implications for therapeutic recreation programming as they move through the remainder of the text.

Table 2.2 Cultural Competencies Based on the National Council for Therapeutic Recreation Certification Job Analysis*

Culturally Competent Agency and TR Service Plan

- Program has accurate demographic data about various cultural populations of community served
- Program has the capacity to serve clients from all ethnic and cultural demographics in the community
- Plan takes into consideration diversity of clients
- Board/advisory groups are comprised of people from various cultural populations of the community
- Multicultural events are planned
- Program has identified resource people from various cultural populations of the community
- Program has developed and maintains ongoing direct person-to-person contact with these resource persons
- Program used demographic data to ensure all cultural populations receive equal access and/or equal service as required to meet their needs
- Program has and utilizes a resource library containing up-to-date articles, books, tapes, and other resources related to cultural issues
- Program provides opportunities which help clients understand and appreciate cultural differences
- Program employs ethnic, bilingual, and culturally diverse staff and/or volunteers in positions that have direct contact with clients
- Program has written policies or plans which call for the program to become culturally competent
- Program maintains cultural awareness and support at all levels of the organization

Culturally Competent Assessment for TR Intervention

- Assessments conducted consider cultural differences of populations served
- Plans are in place to determine language proficiency in both native and English language
- Interpreters are available and used to conduct assessments with clients and families
- Assessment results are reviewed, analyzed and interpreted in a culturally competent manner
- Assessment tools are sensitive to cultural differences

Culturally Competent Individualized Intervention Planning

- Individualized plans consider each individual's cultural background (i.e., religion, language, family life, healing beliefs, art expression, recreation)
- Individualized services are delivered with interpreter when indicated
- Individualized goals reflect person's cultural heritage
- Discharge/transition/aftercare plan considers community cultural resources and unique cultural needs

Table 2.2 Cultural Competencies Based on the National Council for Therapeutic Recreation Certification Job Analysis (continued)

Culturally Competent Implementation of TR Services

- Program utilizes resource persons from various cultural populations in the community
- Reasonable accommodation is made to ensure access to services by removing architectural and structural barriers
- Posted information is written in a variety of appropriate languages
- Atmosphere in the program acknowledges and welcomes people from diverse cultural backgrounds through art work, posters, books, and other media
- Opportunities through multicultural events which help clients understand and appreciate cultural differences

Culturally Competent Evaluation of Individualized Intervention Plan

- Clients from all cultural and language backgrounds progress and successfully complete the program in similar ratios
- Program will strive for client satisfaction in culturally diverse ways (e.g., food, personal hygiene, religious activities, holidays, celebrations)

Culturally Competent Documentation

- Documentation strives to be objective and professional and does not reflect personal cultural biases
- Documentation is sensitive to use words describing race and ethnic backgrounds, phrases and negative stereotypes
- Documentation reports use of interpreters and resource persons in delivery of services to address individual needs

* Franklin and Rios (1999).

Summary

Situated in a multicultural society, the profession of therapeutic recreation is expected to provide services that respect, reflect, and respond to the needs of persons from diverse groups. Although there are principled commitments to multiculturalism and some evidence of progress, therapeutic recreation needs to make greater gains in becoming multiculturally relevant. While this book attempts to improve on the multicultural foundations of therapeutic recreation programming, it too remains predominantly Western in its orientation. The authors look forward to making the text more multiculturally informed in future editions as advances are made in research and practice.

Recommended Readings

Pedersen, P. (1994). *A handbook for developing multicultural awareness* (2nd ed.). Alexandria, VA: American Counseling Association.

Peregoy, J. and Dieser, R. (1997). Multicultural awareness in therapeutic recreation: Hamlet living. *Therapeutic Recreation Journal, 31,* 174–188.

Peregoy, J., Schliebner, C., and Dieser, R. (1997). Diversity issues in therapeutic recreation. In D. Compton (Ed.), *Issues in therapeutic recreation: Toward the new millennium* (2nd ed.) (pp. 275–298). Champaign, IL: Sagamore Publishing.

Sue, D. W., Carter, R., Casas, J., Fouad, N., Ivey, A., Jensen, M., LaFromboise, T., Manese, J., Ponterotto, J., and Vazquez-Nutall, E. (1998). *Multicultural counseling competencies.* Thousand Oaks, CA: Sage Publications.

Chapter

3

Professional Ethics

Consider the following scenario: You arrive at work. The morning has already been eventful. Your six-year-old has been going through a period of telling lies. While it has been exasperating, you are encouraged at the moment because you and he had a good talk at breakfast about the importance of telling the truth. Feeling satisfied, you go on to see your first client, a 14-year-old girl with leukemia. As you talk with the nurse about scheduling an upcoming activity, the young girl interrupts. She excitedly exclaims that she will not be able to attend future activities because she is going home in a few days. Caught off guard, you ask her what she means. She explains that her grandmother came to visit her the previous evening. During the visit, her grandmother told her that God was not going to let her die and that she would recover in time for her birthday in two weeks. Her grandmother also promised to take her to Disneyland to celebrate her recovery and birthday. Her mother, a single parent who lives in another state, has openly discussed with her daughter the implications of her condition, trying to harmonize hope with honesty.

What her grandmother told her is clearly not true. She is not going to recover in a matter of weeks. Nor is she going to Disneyland for her birthday. Yet the girl, happier than she has been in months, asks you if you will attend her birthday party and celebrate what her grandmother has told her would be "many more happy birthdays."

What would you do in this case? Would you support the grandmother's lie because it has lifted the girl's spirits, in effect sustaining the falsehood? Would you tell the truth, even though it might upset her hopes for recovery, no matter how remote it may actually be? Perhaps, believing it is none of your business, you would say nothing, leaving it to the family to sort matters out.

Consider another scenario: Among its stated moral principles, the agency you work for subscribes to client autonomy. Recently, you and your colleagues have been instructed by the new administration to require clients to attend all therapeutic recreation activities in order to increase profits by generating more insurance reimbursements. Furthermore, unless you are able to achieve higher levels of attendance, it is likely that your department will lose a full-time position, impairing its ability to provide adequate services.

What should you do in this case? Should you infringe on your clients' autonomy by coercing them into attending programs, understanding that the result will be better services for all clients? Should you respect their autonomy, which would lead to fewer resources for all clients? What if long overdue staff raises, which would help reduce burnout and staff turnover, were at stake?

Imagine one more hypothetical situation. You are leading a leisure education group in an acute psychiatric facility. Several of the women in your group belong to cultures based on male authority, placing women in a subordinate position. In your eyes, the quality of the women's leisure suffers because they are expected to support the leisure interests of their husbands before their own. One woman even works a second job to help pay for her husband's expensive fishing trips. Seeing this as oppression, you encourage the women to examine their beliefs and you implement assertiveness exercises that are intended to help them resist their husbands' control. Are you acting ethically?

These situations are fraught with difficult moral values, bringing us into the realm of ethics. Shank (1996) explained that:

> Whether we realize it or not, *we do* ethics everyday. Over that we have no control as we are constantly faced with situations demanding right action. *How* we do ethics, that is, how we make decisions about the right action to take, is within our control. We should become very familiar with the professional codes of ethics in therapeutic recreation. Additionally, we must become skilled at the process of moral reflection, which requires self-awareness, knowledge, discipline, and practice. (p. 52)

Professional practice is rarely, if ever, neutral. It can be helpful to people in need, conducted with careful regard for what is good and right. It can also be harmful, marred by actions that are bad and wrong. Along with efforts to be optimally effective, therapeutic recreation professionals must also be ethically upstanding.

Ethics involves the study of what is morally good and bad, right and wrong regarding human behavior and human characteristics. The term *morality* usually refers to actual moral behavior, while ethics is used to describe reflection on moral behavior. Following convention, the terms ethics and morality will be used interchangeably in this chapter.

Several other terms require brief definition. *Descriptive ethics* provides an empirical account of the actual moral beliefs and practices of individuals and groups. It attempts to describe what people believe and how they behave.

Normative ethics attempts to state and justify standards of ideal conduct. It is mainly concerned with how people *should* act, rather than how they actually behave. Typically, normative ethics offers general norms to guide and evaluate moral behavior, as well as reasons to justify the prescribed norms (Beauchamp & Childress, 1994). *Conceptual ethics,* also called *metaethics,* is concerned with analyzing the meaning of ethical concepts and methods. For example, conceptual ethics attempts to explain the meaning of such terms as *duty, autonomy, paternalism,* and *informed consent. Applied ethics* is concerned with the morality of specific practices. *Professional ethics* is perhaps the most prominent example of applied ethics, whereby ethical theory is applied to the activities of professions, such as law, teaching, medicine, or therapeutic recreation. A *code of ethics* is a set of statements that articulates the moral obligations and commitments of a group. It serves to guide and evaluate professionals in the moral aspects of their professional activities.

Both the American Therapeutic Recreation Association (ATRA) and the National Therapeutic Recreation Society (NTRS), have codes of ethics (see Appendices A and C). The *ATRA Code of Ethics* (1998) consists of eight principles: justice, autonomy, fidelity, beneficence/nonmaleficence, veracity/ informed consent, competence, confidentiality and privacy, and compliance with laws and regulations. The *NTRS Code of Ethics* (1990) is comprised of five broad areas of professional obligation: professional virtue, professional to the individual, professional to other individuals and to society, professional to the profession, profession to society. Specific principles, such as honesty, competence, respect, privacy, equality, and advocacy, are included under each area. Furthermore, an extensive set of *Interpretive Guidelines* (1994) was developed to assist professionals in interpreting the *NTRS Code of Ethics.* Several of the principles contained in both codes of ethics will be examined later in this chapter.

Although ATRA and NTRS have ethical practices committees, neither one has established policies, procedures, and mechanisms for enforcement. The National Council for Therapeutic Recreation Certification has an ethics review committee to review alleged incidents of unethical behavior as they pertain to certification.

The presence of two codes of ethics for therapeutic recreation might appear to complicate matters. The codes are quite similar with respect to the principles they prescribe. While the *NTRS Code of Ethics* and *Interpretive Guidelines* make for a more extensive and detailed document, the difference is mainly a matter of emphasis growing out of the goals of the respective organizations. Even subtle differences, however, can be significant, leading to conflicts. At first glance, it appears that conflicts could be settled on the basis of which organization an individual belongs. Yet some professionals belong to both organizations, while others belong to neither. Therefore, the question of which code to follow, and the potential for conflict, is a serious matter. It also suggests that a single code of ethics for therapeutic recreation may be preferable.

Before discussing the handling of moral dilemmas, we wish to introduce several of the main ethical principles and issues affecting therapeutic recreation practice. Afterward, we will examine some of these principles in case studies for the purpose of applying ethical reasoning to moral dilemmas.

Well-Being

The concept of well-being forms a broad umbrella covering several other principles, such as autonomy, paternalism, and privacy. In general, well-being pertains to protecting and promoting the welfare of clients, recognizing them as agents capable of social, physical, emotional, spiritual, and intellectual growth. The principle of well-being is typically treated as having two main components: nonmaleficence and beneficence.

Nonmaleficence is signified by the caution to "do no harm," meaning that professionals are required to avoid actions that might injure others. Harm is construed broadly to include social, physical, and psychological injury. As such, professionals avoid actions that might inflict physical and emotional pain as well as those that might tarnish a person's reputation. The duty of nonmaleficence is evident in the *ATRA Code of Ethics* (1998), which states that "Personnel strive to . . . minimize possible harms." The *NTRS Code of Ethics* (1990) declares, "Above all, professionals do no harm." Efforts taken to prevent harm are expressed in the standard of due care, which entails proper training, requisite skill, and due diligence on the part of professionals (Beauchamp & Childress, 1994).

The principle of nonmaleficence assumes unique features in therapeutic recreation. The principle of normalization supports the right of persons who are ill or disabled to take risks as a normal aspect of life. Of course, the right to risk can become problematic in medical settings, where people are being treated for conditions that threaten their health and well-being, increasing the degree of risk and the possibility of harm. Nonetheless, the fact of illness or injury requiring treatment does not by itself preclude the right to take risks. Risk comes in a variety of shapes and sizes, and must be judged on a case by case basis. For example, forming relationships involves risks which can result in emotional pain. Harms must be weighed against benefits, though nonmalficence is usually overriding.

Some therapeutic recreation programs, especially those with an outdoor or adventure component, incorporate risk activities as a part of treatment. Yet risks can result in social, physical, or psychological harm. Discussing experiential education, Hunt (1990) observed that the risk-benefit issue is a morally compelling tension requiring a "delicate balance" (p. 39). Life is full of risks. Furthermore, risk is often the currency of growth. Hunt concludes that "Practitioners . . . are left with a built-in tension in their professional lives. They embrace risky activities and they embrace a commitment to safety" (p. 42). The two goals are not incompatible, but require conscientious moral reflection and empirical analysis of the benefits and dangers of risk. Therefore, the right to risk and the therapeutic use of risk have legitimate roles in therapeutic recreation. A well-developed risk management program that includes continuous moral reflection is indispensable. Although it will not eliminate the potential for harm, it can minimize the possibility while enabling risk to be practiced safely and ethically.

The other dimension of well-being is beneficence. The traditional basis of service-oriented professions, beneficence seeks to confer benefits on individuals in need of education, recreation, and healthcare. Peterson and Gunn's (1984) therapeutic recreation continuum includes a range of benefits offered by therapeutic recreation, categorized by treatment, education, and recreation. The *ATRA Code of Ethics* (1998) states that "Personnel strive to maximize possible benefits . . ." while the *NTRS Code of Ethics* (1990) declares that "[Professionals] do everything reasonable in their power and within the scope of professional practice to benefit [the people they serve]."

The trend toward an outcome-based approach is reflective of the interest in identifying specific benefits of recreation with improvements in individual and social well-being. Therapeutic recreation has been criticized, however, for narrowly defining well-being and quality of life in terms of health status signified by biopsychosocial functioning (Sylvester, 1989). Ignored are the expressive, aesthetic, and spiritual aspects of life that contribute significantly to well-being and to which leisure serves as a vital source. Because of its intimate association with leisure, therapeutic recreation must take a broad stance toward well-being, making certain that it reflects clients' perceptions (see Wilhite, Keller, & Caldwell, 1999).

Autonomy

One of the central components of well-being in Western society is autonomy, which simply means to be self-regulating. Closely associated with freedom and self-determination, autonomy leads to the conclusion that "individuals are free to decide their own destiny" (Shank, 1985, p. 33). Lahey (1987b) contended that autonomy is especially critical for therapeutic recreation, "because freedom and self-determination lie at the heart of leisure experience and are central to the therapeutic benefits it offers" (p. 18). The *ATRA Code of Ethics* (1998) states that "Therapeutic recreation personnel have a duty to preserve and protect the right of each individual to make his/her own choices. Each individual is to be given the opportunity to determine his/her own course of action in accordance with a plan freely chosen." Similarly, the *NTRS Code of Ethics* (1990) asserts that "Professionals respect the ability of people to make, execute, and take responsibility for their own choices. Individuals are given adequate opportunity for self-determination in the least-restrictive environment possible." The cornerstone of autonomy in healthcare is informed consent (Beauchamp & Childress, 1994). Thompson and Ozanne (1982) explained that:

> The principle of informed consent is based on the belief that the client, as a free and autonomous individual, should be a full participant in therapy. In order to accomplish this objective, the client needs to know what the therapist proposes to do and why, what the likely consequences are, and what the alternatives are. Only then will the client be able to make an informed choice. (p. 10)

If informed consent is accepted as a working principle for increasing client autonomy, therapeutic recreation professionals are faced with the possibility that clients may choose to refuse treatment. As long as the role of the professional is to facilitate leisure and recreation, this matter is not a problem, since leisure and recreation by definition involve free choice. Clients should be able to refuse participation in activities labeled "leisure" or "recreation." Furthermore, coercing competent persons into activities against their will violates client autonomy.

Another ethical issue emerges where professionals purport to be conducting treatment. One role of therapeutic recreation is the treatment of functional impairments as a prerequisite to leisure behavior (Peterson & Gunn, 1984). Relative to the area of therapy or treatment, Peterson and Gunn (1984) stated that "within the treatment component, the freedom of choice issue is premature" (pp. 20–21). Approached from the principle of informed consent, however, clients ought to have the right to make decisions that affect their lives, including the right to refuse treatment. Even the simplest treatment procedure may present major consequences for the client's personal beliefs and relationships (Coyne, 1976). Therefore, in light of the popular argument made for self-determination through recreation and leisure, the implications of *Bartling v. Glendale Adventist Medical Center* (1985), a case involving the constitutional right to refuse treatment, should be considered:

If the right of the patient to self-determination as to his own medical treatment is to have any meaning at all, it must be paramount to the interests of the patient's hospital and doctor. The right of a competent adult patient to refuse medical treatment is a constitutionally guaranteed right which must not be abridged. (p. 220)

Decisions regarding acute medical care do not exhaust the concept of autonomy. Autonomous persons are characterized by free choices *and* free actions. Addressing the importance of "everyday autonomy," Collopy (1996) stated:

long-term care ethics have drawn attention to "everyday autonomy," to the many, seemingly small freedoms that allow a frail individual to shape daily life into a coherent sense of identity and self-determination. This daily experience of autonomy can easily be overlooked because it has little bearing on medical treatment and because it simply does not appear on the radar of care providers struggling with efficiency and other *provider* goals. The result is structural insensitivity within long-term care, a generalized failure to see how the personal autonomy of the elderly can thrive or be thwarted in the flow of life's ordinary daily rhythms. Therapeutic recreation could here offer major insights into the expressive freedom of the frail elderly, into the various arenas of daily living that are important to their autonomy, the diverse kinds of care, institutional and community-based, that are needed to support this autonomy. (p. 12)

Although Collopy's attention is aimed at long-term care, his critique can be applied to any setting where individuals receiving care find their lives disrupted and restricted. Therapeutic recreation's emphasis on freedom and self-determination as central elements of leisure and recreation creates a special moral obligation. Beauchamp and Childress (1994) observed that "many autonomous actions could not occur without the material cooperation of others in making options available" (p. 127). Because freedom and autonomy are inherent to leisure, therapeutic recreation should play, as Collopy suggested, a leading role in promoting the everyday autonomy of persons receiving healthcare. Leisure, with its implications for freedom and self-determination, is a fertile field for autonomous decisions and actions. Attempts to characterize leisure as mere "diversion" trivializes the moral significance of leisure as a source of autonomy and self-determination (see Sylvester, 1994/95, pp. 98–99).

A key moral dilemma arises when autonomy meets competence. Complex and controversial, competence pertains to the ability to execute a task (Beauchamp & Childress, 1994), as well as to understand and appreciate the nature and consequences of one's behavior (Annas & Densberger, 1986). Where incompetence can be demonstrated, autonomy may be restricted or overridden for the client's welfare, a practice called *paternalism*. The difficulty rests in clearly determining when someone is sufficiently incompetent to restrict his or her autonomy. Furthermore, while healthcare professionals are inclined to be protective of their clients, they are also mindful that autonomy is among the preeminent values in Western culture. Moreover, autonomy is an indispensable element of leisure and recreation, a principle that therapeutic recreation practitioners are likely to give special respect because of their professional culture.

While it may be a cardinal value, autonomy is not absolute. Instances exist in which people are not competent to make their own decisions or to act independently due to diminished capacity as a result of a temporary or permanent condition. A person going through a period of severe mania is probably not in the best position to make personal decisions, warranting at least some restriction of his autonomy, such as withholding his credit cards. Shank and Kinney (1987) argued that therapeutic recreation risks unethical conduct by indiscriminately adhering to the principle of autonomy, putting the welfare of clients in jeopardy. Unrestricted freedom and autonomy, they point out, can become irresponsible and dangerous, leading to maladaptive outcomes. As a result, they constructed the concept of "pre-leisure" to defend paternalistic practices:

> The concept of 'pre-leisure' behavior is an important one in understanding clinical intervention. The very notion of leisure implies . . . freedom from control. Yet freedom from control requires psychological, social, and affective functioning at a level to ensure that free choice does not result in maladaptive outcomes. (pp. 68–69)

To illustrate this point, they offer the following example:

> Consider the anorexic who, despite weighing only 93 pounds . . . perceives herself as extremely obese and consequently elects to spend her free time jogging and cycling. An unbridled adherence to promoting free choice, and a complete allegiance to personal control believed to be indigenous to the leisure experience can become irresponsible and dangerous. (p. 71)

The idea of pre-leisure has merit. Yet it must be prudently applied to permit autonomy the ethical regard it deserves. Autonomy is a matter of degree (Beauchamp & Childress, 1994). Paternalistic practices based on judgments of incompetence are thus contingent on the particular action or activity. As such, the restriction of some choices and actions on the grounds they are harmful should not preclude other alternatives that preserve a degree of autonomy. The person who is anorexic would have options besides jogging that preserve autonomous leisure while avoiding harmful behaviors. Therefore, the range of leisure choices can be temporarily narrowed without violating the integrity of autonomous leisure. Therapeutic recreation specialists are urged to search for areas of competence in the face of apparent incapacity. Such a principled stance is consistent with an approach to therapeutic recreation practice oriented to ability and autonomy.

Confidentiality

The principle of confidentiality obligates professionals to safeguard clients from unauthorized disclosures of information. The justification of confidentiality is twofold. First, privacy has traditionally been respected as a right enjoyed by Americans. Second, confidentiality is a prerequisite for the trust between client and professional that is necessary for an effective relationship.

The concepts of privacy and privilege can be distinguished for the sake of clarity. The broader of the two, *privacy* refers to the liberty of persons to share personal information at their discretion, thus protecting their private lives from undue scrutiny (Shah, 1970; Siegal, 1979). *Privilege* is a legal term granted by statute protecting the right of clients to withhold testimony during a court proceeding (Corey, Corey & Callanan, 1993). Privileged communication has been usually reserved for relationships between clients and such professionals as psychotherapists, nurses, physicians, accountants, and lawyers. We are unaware of any instance of privilege being extended to therapeutic recreation professionals. It is also important to understand that privilege belongs to the client, not the professional. Therefore, professionals are required to divulge information if a client elects to waive his or her privilege.

Both professional codes of ethics in therapeutic recreation have explicit standards regarding privacy and confidentiality. The *ATRA Code of Ethics* (1998) states:

> Therapeutic recreation personnel are responsible for safeguard-
> ing information about individuals served. Individuals served
> have the right to control information about themselves. When a

situation arises that requires disclosure of confidential information about an individual to protect the individual's welfare or the
interest of others, the therapeutic recreation professional has the
responsibility/obligation to inform the individual served of the
circumstances in which confidentiality was broken.

The *NTRS Code of Ethics* (1990) holds that:

Professionals respect the privacy of individuals. Communications are kept confidential except with the explicit consent of the
individual or where the welfare of the individual or others is
clearly imperiled. Individuals are informed of the nature and the
scope of confidentiality.

It is evident from these statements that confidentiality is not unlimited.
According to Remley (1990), there are three general exceptions to confidentiality in which professionals are expected to reveal information: (1) cases in
which clients pose a danger to themselves or others, (2) cases in which clients
request that their records be released to themselves or a third party, and (3)
cases involving court orders. The limits of confidentiality, therefore, should be
spelled out to clients as a part of informed consent, including conditions under
which information may be shared.

Carefully developed policies and procedures can effectively control the
flow of information. For example, policy should make clear who is authorized
to review progress notes and other documentation. The therapeutic recreation
professional, however, may find special situations that make confidentiality
especially difficult to manage. Frequently characterized by informality and
spontaneity, the activity environment is conducive to the exchange of personal
thoughts and feelings. As such, the professional must be aware that whether in
the office, in the craft room, or around a campfire, clients' personal expressions
must be dealt with in a manner consistent with the principle of confidentiality.

Confidentiality is an intricate issue that requires careful deliberation. Most
professionals would likely agree with the position taken by the Privacy Protection Study Commission (1977) when it observed, "as long as America believes,
as more than a matter of rhetoric, in the worth of the individual citizen, it must
constantly reaffirm and reinforce its protections for the privacy, and ultimately
the autonomy, of the individual" (p. 160). On the other hand, occasions arise
where individual rights must be balanced with the welfare of others. Conflict-
ing claims are thus inevitable. The prudent professional recognizes the inherent
conflicts in the area of confidentiality and seeks resolutions that respect the
rights and welfare of all parties.

Justice

Justice pertains to "fair, equitable, and appropriate treatment in light of what is due or owed to persons" (Beauchamp & Childress, 1994, p. 327). Injustice occurs when people are deprived of some entitlement, such as medical care or legal representation. The idea of justice, therefore, is closely connected with the concept of rights, a relationship that will be discussed shortly. Distributive justice refers to the equitable sharing of social goods, such as income, safety, property, education, and healthcare (see Hemingway, 1987). Lahey (1991), for example, claimed that commercialization and medicalization in therapeutic recreation have resulted in groups such as the homeless and chronically ill elderly not receiving the services they need.

Both codes of ethics in therapeutic recreation embrace the principle of justice. The *ATRA Code of Ethics* (1998) states:

> Therapeutic recreation personnel are responsible for ensuring that individuals are served fairly and that there is equity in the distribution of services. Individuals receive service without regard to race, color, creed, sex, age, disability/disease, social and financial status.

The *NTRS Code of Ethics* (1990) addresses justice in two places. First, under the *obligation of professional virtue,* it reads "Professionals are fair. They do not place individuals at unwarranted advantage or disadvantage. They distribute resources and services according to principles of equity." Second, under the *obligation of the profession to society,* it states:

> The profession is committed to equality of opportunity. No person shall be refused service because of race, gender, social status, ethnic background, sexual orientation, or inability to pay. The profession neither conducts nor condones discriminatory practices. It actively seeks to correct inequities that unjustly discriminate.

Bioethical discussions of justice focus on such issues as the right to health-care, the right to die, resource allocation, and the controversial issues of rationing and patient selection (Beauchamp & Childress, 1994). As a participant in managed healthcare, therapeutic recreation finds itself immersed in the issue of justice. For example, Sylvester (1994/95) and Lahey (1996) criticized the recommendation of the ATRA Reimbursement Committee (1994) to "prioritize the patients we know we can obtain an outcome with and market ourselves as a cost-effective, reimbursable service" (p. 3). What they considered unjust was the possibility of neglecting people who need care because they are not the best candidates for reimbursement. Granted, there will always be tension between a profession's ethical commitments and the hard realities of economics. Yet the tension should be negotiated, as Lahey (1996) suggested, "in terms of [the profession's] basic philosophical and moral commitments" (p. 23), which fall on the side of social justice.

The principle of justice is closely related to the concept of rights. Rights are entitlements considered vital for living a life suitable for a human being. Negative rights signify entitlements of noninterference, such as the rights to speak and worship freely. Positive rights express provisions that should be made for people, such as safety, education, and healthcare. Rights, therefore, represent morally paramount principles that are to be taken seriously by any profession that subscribes to justice. Indeed, the Preamble of the *NTRS Code of Ethics* (1990) declares, "Leisure, recreation, and play are inherent aspects of the human experience, and are essential to health and well-being. All people, therefore, have an inalienable right to leisure and the opportunities it affords for play and recreation." The revised *NTRS Philosophical Position Statement* (1996) and the *National Recreation and Park Association Position Statement on Inclusion* (1997) also endorse the right to leisure.

Space does not permit a detailed analysis of the legitimacy of the right to leisure (see Sylvester, 1992). Nonetheless, we agree with Sylvester's (1992) conclusion:

> leisure allows people to reflect on and to realize many of the personal values that constitute their well-being. As such, modern life requires some measure of leisure for the purpose of achieving well-being. The right to leisure, then, is an indispensable corollary of the right to well-being. (pp. 15–16)

With respect to therapeutic recreation, he goes on to argue:

> Since people who are ill or disabled are human beings, they qualify as *moral agents*. This means they need and are entitled to live a life fit for a human being and to take a hand in determining the kind of life they wish to lead. . . . Thus, leisure must be protected and facilitated for people who have limiting conditions, lest they be deprived of an important source of well-being. Although ability increases the potential range of leisure opportu-

nities, disability does not preclude the right to leisure; it only
modifies its expression while intensifying its importance. (p. 16)

The right to leisure, therefore, is a prominent ethical concern for therapeutic recreation, spanning a range of conditions, such as:

- Equitable distribution of resources and services to persons with disabling
  conditions, such as the homeless mentally ill,
- Oppression based on race, class, ethnicity, gender, sexual orientation, or
  other characteristic,
- Using leisure as a reward or a punishment, and
- Removing clients from recreation programs against their wishes to attend
  other services.

These are just a small sample of instances involving the principle of justice to
which therapeutic recreation must devote serious attention. Although the field
has made appreciable strides in ethics in recent years, issues of social justice
have not received adequate attention (Sylvester & Patrick, 1991).

The preceding principles are representative of important human values.
Understanding their nature is essential for achieving ethical knowledge.
Because values are complex, dynamic, and have a tendency to conflict, ethical
decision making is also demanded. As such, we now turn to ethical reasoning.

Ethical Reasoning

Dealing with moral situations is invariably difficult and often painful. Clear
choices are all too rare, and dilemmas abound. Therefore, the ability *to think*
logically and rigorously about ethics, with attention to detail, nuance, and
complexity, is paramount, as is the capacity *to care* deeply about the welfare of
human beings. The following section provides an elementary basis for ethical
reasoning, drawing liberally on the highly regarded work of Beauchamp and
Childress (1994).

Ethical reasoning aims to solve moral problems by making value judgments. Some people consider ethical reasoning a waste of time because value
judgments are subjective. They argue that moral judgments are simply personal
opinions that cannot be judged objectively. What if we were to say, however,
that persons with severe disabilities should not receive therapeutic recreation
services because funds could be better spent on persons who have more potential for growth and development? Or that people with congenital disabilities
should be euthanized at birth because they will not be as productive and will

cost more to support than "normal" people? Most people would cry out, "But that is wrong!" As soon as it is admitted that some moral situation is better or worse, right or wrong, we acknowledge the validity of value judgments as more than just subjective feelings or personal taste. Value judgments are emotional, social, and intellectual activities in which reasons are offered as means of support. Therefore, while everyone has the *right* to his or her views, not all views are equal. Moral judgments must be evaluated as good or bad on the basis of the reasons used to support them; hence the importance of moral reasoning.

Moral reasoning entails identification of relevant theory, principles, and rules, as well as pertinent facts and circumstances. In this discussion, a theory means a well-developed system of principles that is effective for explaining moral experiences and problems. For example, utilitarianism is a prominent ethical theory that explains moral action on the basis of pleasure and utility. It contends that human happiness consists of maximizing pleasure and minimizing pain. Actions that prove useful for increasing the happiness of the majority of people are considered ethical. Morality, therefore, is explained and justified on the basis of the utility of decisions for promoting the greatest happiness of the greatest number of people.

No ethical theory, however, is perfect. Other theories, such as Kantian and feminist ethics, have strengths as well as limitations. Readers are strongly encouraged to consult Shank (1996) on the subject of ethical theories and their implications for therapeutic recreation (also see Hunt, 1990).

Most moral reasoning in daily professional practice takes place at the level of rules and principles. Rules and principles are guides to moral action; principles are broader in scope, rules are more specific. For example, honesty is a moral principle. Either of the following statements, "professionals should tell the truth" or "professionals should represent their credentials accurately," is a rule, each giving more precise content to the principle of honesty. Autonomy is a principle. The rule "Clients may refuse participation in recreation activities" is a specification of the general principle of autonomy. Although rules and principles are conceptually different, the terms are often used interchangeably.

Rules and principles provide guidelines or "rules of thumb" for moral behavior. Rarely, however, are moral problems exactly alike. Situations involving similar rules and principles may be judged differently because of circumstances. For example, we treat lying by an adult differently than we do for children. A person who robs in order to feed her family is judged differently from a person who robs in order to feed a drug habit. Facts mediate moral situations; thus they must be weighed in the process of ethical reasoning. Therefore, both intellectual clarity and sound evidence are essential for effective ethical decision making.

While one may have strong feelings, opinions, or intuitions about moral problems, these alone are not enough. Justification of a moral decision requires giving sound reasons that can withstand question and criticism. Beauchamp and Childress (1994) present three methods of justification: deductivism, inductivism, and coherentism.

Deductivism means that particular judgments are made on the basis of preexisting theory. Take the example of truth-telling. An ethical theory based on duty would hold that a person is morally obligated to act in a prescribed way regardless of the consequences. One of our duties as moral agents is to tell the truth. The justification to tell the truth is thus deduced from an established theory based on the duty of a moral agent.

Moral justification, however, does not occur in a theoretical vacuum. Rather, it takes place in the context of particular moral experiences. As society examines and debates its moral experiences, rules and principles evolve that function as guides. As such, rules and principles are not eternal and universal. Instead, they are "rules of thumb" subject to change as new moral experiences accumulate. *Inductivism,* a second method of justification, means that rules and principles come from "the ground up," from the particular experiences people have, which are then formulated into general norms. Consider again the example of truth-telling. Imagine a group of people ignorant of ethical theories. Yet they discover through experience that their chances of achieving their individual needs and living harmoniously are improved if they are able to trust one another. Accordingly, telling the truth serves the vital function of promoting individual and social well-being. Out of shared particular moral experiences, then, a general principle of honesty emerges.

Coherentism, the third approach to justification, consists of a reflective balance between deductivism and inductivism. Coherentism takes into account the relevance of particular moral experiences while recognizing that these experiences can be organized and articulated as general, though not permanent, moral statements. According to Beauchamp and Childress (1994), "both general and particular considered judgments provide data for theory and are theory's testing ground" (p. 38). Over time, particular judgments can lead to the formulation of abstract principles. For example, particular judgments have led to the general conclusion that confidentiality is morally warranted because it is conducive to trust and privacy. Other particular judgments, such as the necessity of protecting innocent persons from harm, have led to reformulating confidentiality to include certain limits. Therefore, while the general principle of confidentiality is preserved, it takes into account other particular experiences, such as protecting the welfare of others. Coherentism incorporates the best features of deductivism and inductivism, justifying judgments on the basis of general moral principles that are responsive to particular moral experiences.

Other conceptual operations are useful in ethical reasoning. First, moral principles must be *specified*. Principles are often expressed at a level of generality that makes their practical application difficult. Specification involves developing the meaning and scope of principles, contributing much needed clarity and content so principles can be effectively applied to actual situations. Consider the principle of beneficence, which asserts that professionals are morally obligated to promote the well-being of their clients. Certainly, professionals are not directly responsible for the economic well-being of their clients. To what degree are they responsible for the emotional well-being of clients? Certain aspects of well-being are beyond the control and responsibility of professionals. The *NTRS Code of Ethics* (1990) provides an example of specification. Relative to well-being, it states:

> Professionals' foremost concern is the well-being of the people they serve. They do everything *reasonable* in their power and *within the scope of professional practice* to benefit them (emphases added).

The qualifiers "reasonable" and "within the scope of professional practice" help to specify the principle of well-being. It would be unreasonable to expect professionals to assume responsibility for clients' economic welfare. Moreover, professionals' responsibility to the well-being of clients is limited to the scope of therapeutic recreation, which warrants further specification. As such, specification seeks to clarify and articulate principles, such as well-being, so they can be shaped into realistic policy.

Second, moral principles must be *balanced*. Many moral situations involve more than a single principle. Consequently, their comparative merits must be evaluated. According to Beauchamp and Childress (1994), "balancing consists of deliberation and judgment about the relative weight of norms" (p. 32). Consider the following scenario: A young man who is receiving therapeutic recreation services has great difficulty making friends. In fact, he has never had a genuine friend. You have been working closely with him to help him improve his social skills so he will be able to establish and sustain personal relationships. In the course of working with him, you and he have developed a strong relationship. Indeed, he considers you his best—and only—friend. You have maintained your objectivity, so you see no harm in his perceiving you as his "buddy," especially since it has served to motivate him to improve his social skills. Your agency, however, has a policy prohibiting even the perception of friendship with clients. Among other reasons, friendship is discouraged because it has been found that clients are less likely to initiate outside relationships, remaining passively dependent on the staff. Therefore, you must decide what is ethically correct. Should you encourage the friendship and run the risk of creating dependency? Should you set limits on the relationship so the client will not perceive it as a friendship which may undermine his progress? Ideally, of course, you would want to promote friendship and autonomy. Sometimes, though, there is not a "middle ground," especially where unequivocal policies must be established.

Therefore, both specifying and balancing are essential functions, particularly when dealing with moral dilemmas. A *moral dilemma* occurs when there are good reasons supporting opposing courses of action. People generally agree that autonomy is an important value. They also generally agree that harm should not come to innocent people. There appears to be a dilemma or contradiction in agreeing on the one hand that women should be free to control their bodies and agreeing on the other hand that unborn children should not be aborted. There is an apparent dilemma in claiming that competent people should be allowed to live as they wish and holding that homeless people should be forcibly removed from the streets during extremely frigid weather. Further, the dilemma of choice is legendary in therapeutic recreation, whereby practitioners are pulled between promoting client freedom on the one hand and protecting clients from making choices that endanger their welfare on the other. Moral dilemmas leave us feeling pulled in opposite directions, making judgments all the more difficult.

Finally, *context* is an essential component of ethical reasoning. Traditional approaches to ethics have attempted to construct abstract, universal principles that apply equally to all moral situations. For example, if telling the truth is a universal principle of moral conduct, then everyone is obligated to tell the truth, regardless of the particular situation. Traditional approaches that stress universal principles leave little room for feeling, sentiment, and the context of moral situations. Committed to abstract principles, they fail to take into account the "flesh and blood" particulars of moral problems that typically weigh heavily on our judgments of what is right and wrong. For example, killing is wrong. But there are widely recognized contexts in which killing may be justified, such as in war or in self-defense. While some cultures value honesty, others prize loyalty to friends and family, even if it means lying to protect them. According to Agich (1993):

> Contextualism is the view that morality is properly concerned
> with the life of human beings who exist as finite, social creatures
> engaged in particular existential settings and projects. There is
> no absolute, privileged, or completely objective standpoint from
> which to settle ethical disputes once and for all. (p. 30)

In particular, feminist ethics typically incorporates a contextual approach. While principles have their place, they are by themselves incapable of accounting for the diversity and complexity of everyday moral situations (Sherwin, 1992). Therefore, "doing ethics" demands not only emotional sensitivity and intellectual rigor, but attention to situational factors, as well.

Virtue Ethics

Ethics has been dominated in the past two centuries by *principle ethics,* which is chiefly concerned with developing guidelines for making ethical decisions. Consequently, it emphasizes *doing* what is morally correct by following abstract rules. In recent decades, however, virtue ethics has achieved prominence in ethics. *Virtue ethics* focuses on the individual's character. It emphasizes not just doing what is morally correct, but *being* a virtuous person whose actions reflect a morally sound character (Pojman, 1999). Virtuous persons do not tell the truth, respect others, and show compassion simply because they follow rules. They do it because they *are* honest, respectful, and compassionate.

Proponents of virtue ethics consider character indispensable to ethical conduct because:

> A morally good person . . . is more likely than others to understand what should be done, more likely to attentively perform the acts that are required, and even more likely to form and act on moral ideals. (Beauchamp & Childress, 1994, p. 65).

Persons who abide by ethical principles yet lack character may not possess the conviction or courage necessary to fulfill their moral commitments. Virtuous individuals are more likely not only to follow ethical rules, but also to aspire to the highest ideals. For example, a therapeutic recreation specialist who is operating by principle ethics might abide by the principle of autonomy without considering how extreme forms of autonomy can compromise a sense of interdependence and community among people. A therapeutic recreation specialist with a virtuous character would be more responsive to the dynamic interplay between autonomy and community, aspiring to an ideal that respects and seeks to accommodate both values. Thus, virtue ethics would be conducive to multiculturalism, taking into account alternative values and ethics out of a deeply ingrained sense of respect for other world-views.

While virtue ethics has gained greater attention, it has not obviated principle ethics. Most theorists agree that virtues and principles have complementary roles (Kitchener, 1996; Beauchamp & Childress, 1994; Meara, Schmidt & Day, 1996). Professionals of impeccable character and high ideals still require principles to guide them in moral situations that are complex and confusing. Manning's (1997) concept of "moral citizenship" as the capacity to think, feel, and act for the good of the public aptly captures the partnership of virtues and principles. Therapeutic recreation professionals, therefore, need to understand principles of right conduct while possessing the kind of character that disposes them toward morally good action and the highest ethical ideals.

Multicultural Considerations for Professional Ethics

We have contended that therapeutic recreation lags behind other fields, such as education, social work, and counseling psychology, in its attention to multiculturalism. McGinn, Flowers & Rubin (1994) asserted that inadequate attention by professional ethics might explain why counseling psychology had failed to address multiculturalism. Accordingly, in this section we will explore the relation between several ethical principles and multiculturalism and offer recommendations for a multicultural approach to professional ethics.

Ethical Principles and Multiculturalism

Justice, welfare, competence, and autonomy are "pillar" principles in bioethics. While prominent in therapeutic recreation codes of ethics, they have not been examined from the vantage of multiculturalism.

The codes of ethics of both ATRA and NTRS include principles on justice and equality, an element of justice. Under Principle 3: Justice, The *ATRA Code of Ethics* (1998) states:

> Therapeutic Recreation personnel are responsible for ensuring that individuals are served fairly and that there is equity in the distribution of services. Individuals receive service without regard to race, color, creed, gender, sexual orientation, age, disability/disease, social and financial status.

The *NTRS Code of Ethics* (1990) states, Under Principle VI. The Obligation of the Profession to Society (B. Equality):

The profession is committed to equality of opportunity. No person shall be refused service because of race, gender, religion, social status, ethnic background, sexual orientation, or inability to pay.

It goes on to say:

The profession neither conducts nor condones discriminatory practices. It actively seeks to correct inequities that unjustly discriminate.

Both organizations thus endorse nondiscriminatory practice. Accordingly, failure to provide therapeutic recreation services on the basis of clients' cultural background would be unjust. Clients from diverse cultural backgrounds appear, then, to be procedurally protected from unjust denial of services. This, however, is only half of the picture.

In what has been the finest piece of political philosophy in the therapeutic recreation literature, Hemingway (1987) gave a full description of justice. In brief, he distinguished between *negative* justice, which protects the procedural rights of individuals, and *positive* justice, which addresses the content of rights. Where negative justice is concerned with procedures that allow equal access to services (protecting people *against* discrimination) positive justice is concerned with how the content of services enables people to achieve what is due them. Hemingway used the principle of capacity development to justify positive rights. Capacity development refers to the development and expression of a person's potentialities. He argued that the deprivation of capacity development is immoral because the person's moral growth is stunted and society is deprived of the person's contributions. Hemingway concluded that "all persons . . . . are equally entitled to the conditions in which the fullest possible capacity development becomes possible" (p. 13).

Positive justice, therefore, would entitle people to services that are sensitive and responsive to their cultural backgrounds, facilitating their capacity development. It is not enough to provide services to people of diverse cultural backgrounds. All aspects of therapeutic recreation service, including assessment, planning, interventions, evaluation, and ethics, should provide for capacity development that is culturally appropriate. While services may be equally available, the content of services may not be equally effective at facilitating capacity development for all clients. It is reasonable to assume, therefore, that therapeutic recreation is only partially meeting its ethical obligation of justice as it relates to people of different cultural backgrounds.

Justice is intended to safeguard the welfare of individuals. As such, welfare or well-being is among the highest ethical imperatives of professions. The

principle of well-being is frequently articulated as nonmaleficence and beneficence. Nonmaleficence obligates professionals to avoid doing harm to clients.
Beneficence holds professionals morally responsible for services that benefit
clients. Therapeutic recreation codes of ethics are explicit on these points. The
NTRS Code of Ethics (1990) states in Principle II.A Well-Being:

> Professionals' *foremost concern* is the well-being of the people
> they serve. They do everything reasonable in their power and
> within the scope of professional practice to benefit them. Above
> all, professionals cause no harm. (emphasis added)

The *ATRA Code of Ethics* (1998) states that Principle 1: Beneficence/Non-
Maleficence "serves as the guiding principle for the profession," which seeks
"to maximize possible benefits, and minimize possible harms." Lack of
multicultural awareness, knowledge, and skill, however, can seriously jeopar-
dize client well-being. Examples abound, but for the sake of illustration
consider two major areas of therapeutic recreation practice, assessment and
interventions.

Assessment uses a variety of means to gather valid and reliable information
about individuals in order to structure programs that meet their needs for health
and well-being. Accordingly, assessment should be sensitive to the cultural
context of an individual's life, because decisions are being made based on
assessment results that may significantly impact a person's life. Yet there is
ample evidence that therapeutic recreation assessments on the whole are not
culturally sensitive. For example, therapeutic recreation assessment tends to
equate independence with healthy functioning and dependence with dysfunction. But some cultures, such as Asian contexts, consider dependence normal
and necessary (Blankfield, 1987). Further, "leisure lifestyle" is widely promul-
gated in the therapeutic recreation literature as critical to the well-being of
individuals. Yet if assessment does not adequately attend to the cultural factors
that contribute to "leisure lifestyle," then people are placed at risk and denied
potential benefits, violating ethical principles of nonmaleficence and beneficence.

Therapeutic recreation interventions represent another vital area of therapeutic recreation practice where the well-being of persons from diverse cultural
backgrounds may be at risk. For example, assertiveness training is a common
intervention in therapeutic recreation. Peregoy and Dieser (1997) observed that
assertiveness training, while useful for clients who value independence and
individuality, can be detrimental to clients from cultures that value congeniality. Another example is the use of sacred rituals, such as American Indian pow-
wows, as interventions by individuals who are not members of that ethnic

group. According to Oles (1992), the misappropriation of Native American ceremonies as "tools" for adventure leadership programs desecrates holy and sacred cultural practices, which is certainly demeaning, potentially damaging, and highly unethical. The well-being of individuals from other cultures may also be impacted when interventions indigenous to their cultures are ignored by the dominant culture (Pedersen, 1997).

Detrimentally impacting people's well-being, either through harm or failure to provide benefits, can be partially attributed to lack of competence. As a result of a landmark 1973 conference of the American Psychological Association, it was concluded that it was unethical for counselors to work with clients from culturally distinct backgrounds unless they possessed the necessary cultural competencies (Burn, 1992). Each code of ethics in therapeutic recreation is explicit regarding competence. Principle 7 of the *ATRA Code of Ethics* (1998) states "Therapeutic Recreation personnel have the responsibility to continually seek to expand one's knowledge base related to Therapeutic Recreation practice." The *NTRS Code of Ethics* (1990) states in principle I.D Competence:

> Professionals function to the best of their knowledge and skill. They only render services and employ techniques of which they are qualified by training and experience. They recognize their limitations, and seek to reduce them by expanding their expertise. Professionals continuously enhance their knowledge and skills through education and by remaining informed of professional and social trends, issues and developments.

Regrettably, there is little research on the multicultural competence of therapeutic recreation professionals. Concluding that "therapeutic recreation specialists need to become culturally competent," Peregoy and Dieser (1997) lamented that "scant attention is placed upon multicultural competencies in pre-service and in-service training programs in therapeutic recreation education" (p. 185). Therapeutic recreation professionals, therefore, may find their ethics jeopardized due to the lack of multicultural competence.

Finally, autonomy has been a master principle in Western ethical theory. Embedded in Western values, its interpretation has been heavily oriented to independence and individualism. A culturally encapsulated understanding of autonomy, however, creates a moral conflict for persons from collectivist cultures that embrace communal values. Yet autonomy can still function as a vital principle using a multicultural approach to ethics. Individuals would be regarded as autonomous insofar as they can follow their plan for life *according to their cultural world-view.* As such, two individuals from different cultures, one who prefers to be self-reliant and one is more willingly reliant on others, would have their personal and cultural autonomy respected.

A Multicultural Approach to Professional Ethics

Before concluding this chapter with a couple of case studies, we wish to suggest three ways professional ethics can become more responsive to a multicultural society. First, therapeutic recreation's moral commitment to cultural diversity should be formalized in its codes of ethics. For example, the Preamble to the *NTRS Code of Ethics* (1990) should clearly espouse the organization's obligation to serve people from all cultures. Furthermore, multicultural aspects of professional ethics should be made explicit throughout the codes. The *ATRA Code of Ethics* (1998) states under Principle 5, Veracity/Informed Consent:

> Each individual receiving service has the right to know what is likely to take place during and as a result of professional intervention. Informed consent is obtained when information is provided by the professional.

Informed consent, however, is usually considered complete when information has been provided to and *understood* by the client. An interpreter or family member might be needed to achieve consent that is genuinely informed. Principles, like informed consent, should therefore include a multicultural perspective. Second, professional ethics must avoid cultural encapsulation lest the dominant group impose its values. Just as each ethical situation ought to be seen in its unique context, ethics should be viewed from the cultural context in which it occurs. For example, privacy is a cultural variable. Individualistic cultures tend to place more value on privacy than collectivistic cultures. Third, therapeutic recreation codes of ethics should make multicultural competence a moral responsibility of all professionals. It is morally untenable for technically skilled specialists to be unable to serve people from different cultures because they are culturally incompetent.

Case Studies

To provide the reader with practice in ethical reasoning, we conclude this chapter by presenting two ethical dilemmas. In the first one we will assist the reader in the process of moral reasoning. In the second one we will let the reader rely on his or her own resources.

"The Truth, the Whole Truth, and Nothing but the Truth?"

The setting is an adolescent residential psychiatric facility. The therapeutic recreation specialist has been working for six months with a 15-year-old male who has a behavior disorder that includes distorting reality. The care team has consistently confronted the boy whenever he has attempted to manipulate reality to his personal advantage, urging him to face the truth.

The therapeutic recreation program has an aggressive community integration component, and the boy has been placed on a local soccer team. He has been very happy with this development, demonstrating marked improvement since joining the soccer team. The league in which he is playing is extremely popular. In fact, demand is so great that some adolescents living in the community are not able to play because of the lack of resources. The league, however, has been a progressive force for integration, always reserving limited space for "special needs" participants. Consequently, some youngsters who are more qualified by ability are placed on a waiting list. The league is dealing with the problem, but will not be able to alter it until additional resources are available. One of the youngsters on the team has been teasing the boy, telling him that the only reason he is on the team is because he is a "psycho." The coach has attempted to address the situation with mixed success. After an especially tough practice, the boy asks the therapeutic recreation specialist, "Is it true I really didn't make the team on my own? The other kids tell me that I'm the 'charity' player and the team had to take me. I thought I made the team because I was good. You always told me when we used to practice that I was getting better and soon I'd be good enough to make the city team. Am I really only a 'charity' player?"

What should the therapeutic recreation specialist say? Should she tell the truth, explaining to the boy that the reason he is on the team is because spaces are reserved for special situations, thus translating in his mind to a "charity" player? Should she manipulate the truth, knowing that while she is committing the same behavior she and others have been discouraging him from, the truth is likely to undermine the gains he has made since making the team?

Before we examine this case, we wish to caution against a reaction typical of some students when they deal with moral dilemmas for the first time. A common response is to "fix the situation" in order to make the moral dilemma disappear. For example, most students call for reforming the soccer league. Before that can be done, however, the therapeutic recreation specialist is still faced with an ethical dilemma. Despite our best efforts to create an ethically unblemished world, moral dilemmas will always be present.

Let's see if an ethical dilemma actually exists. While the professional may not have explicitly told the adolescent he was skilled enough to make the local team on his own merits, the youngster was led to believe that he had earned a place based on his ability. In fact, the professional employed a technique recommended by *attribution theory* while working with the youth to improve his soccer skills. Theoretically, this approach is intended to achieve greater individual locus of control and perceived competence by having the individual attribute positive results to internal sources (ability) as opposed to external factors (luck or a socially engineered soccer league). Now the professional has been confronted by the boy regarding the true nature of his circumstances. Veracity, therefore, does appear to be relevant in this case.

On the other hand, there is clearly a number of benefits associated with participating in the soccer league. Perhaps most evident are the benefits of normalization and social inclusion. Yet these benefits probably would have resulted whether or not the truth was completely disclosed. There are psycho-social benefits, however, that the truth may affect, such as self-concept, self-esteem, social acceptance, and perceived competence. We could conclude, then, that there are good reasons for the principle of beneficence.

Our next step is to see whether guidance is available from the ATRA and NTRS codes of ethics. Both codes advocate veracity and beneficence (ATRA, Principles 3, Fidelity, and Principle 5, Veracity/Informed Consent, 1998; NTRS, Obligation I, Section B, Honesty, 1990). If the professional explains the situation truthfully, she jeopardizes the psychosocial benefits. Conversely, maximizing the psychosocial benefits may mean not being fully truthful.

Now that the principles have been outlined, we attempt to balance them by examining their pros and cons. Regarding the principle of veracity, there are several general advantages, such as the development of trust, respect, and autonomy. Furthermore, there is the more specific benefit of reinforcing the boy's care goal of truth-telling. The main disadvantage is that disclosure of the truth may undermine the psychosocial benefits associated with playing soccer.

We also need to consider any mitigating circumstances. One item that should be raised is the capacity of the boy to understand the truth and to cope with its ramifications. Could the truth possibly hurt the boy, in which case the professional would risk violating the principle of nonmaleficence? Since truth-telling is already one of his care goals, however, we can reasonably assume that the youngster is capable of understanding the nature and consequences of truth-telling.

In this scenario we would favor the principle of veracity. We believe that truth-telling is more compelling because the practice of truth is so fundamental to human relationships. The care team recognized this by including it as care goal. Furthermore, the psychosocial benefits would not necessarily be sacrificed. In the course of telling the truth, a stronger relationship might be fostered. While the boy now knows the truth, he can still work to earn a place on the team based on his ability.

You may disagree with our interpretation, which is not unusual with moral dilemmas. Reasonable people can disagree. If you do disagree, however, you must develop a rational case supporting your ethical judgment.

Professionalism

You have recently been employed in the physical rehabilitation unit of a hospital. One thing that you have noticed is that none of the staff works on weekends. There are plenty of volunteers on weekends, but several clients have complained that the quality of programs is subpar because there is no professional supervision. You talk with your supervisor about this situation. She explains that there is no professional staff assigned to weekends for several reasons. First, staffing during the week is more efficient, since allied professionals and support staff are available. Second, assigning professional staff to the weekend would deplete staff needed for weekdays. Third, the union has an agreement that only medical and other essential support personnel, such as nurses and physicians, are required to work on weekends. Finally, your supervisor informs you that therapeutic recreation was treated less professionally when it used to cover weekends because it was seen as offering just "diversional" programs, which volunteers could easily provide. To appear more professional, the therapeutic recreation department has done less "diversional" programming, concentrating instead on clients' rehabilitation goals. For these reasons weekend therapeutic recreation services are not offered, though activities such as television, table tennis, and board games are available to clients.

What ethical issues are involved? Is there an ethical dilemma? Can you specify and balance the relevant principles? What circumstances influence the context of this situation? What do therapeutic recreation codes of ethics have to say? What would you do?

Summary

We have only scratched the surface of professional ethics as it relates to therapeutic recreation. We urge the reader to explore the references we have relied on to create this chapter, including the ATRA and NTRS codes of ethics (see Appendices A and C). We further urge you to reflect on and to discuss professional ethics with your professors and fellow students. Above all, we recommend that you be aware of your own set of values, and the effect they have on others. Finally, we encourage you to act confidently. Knowledge, awareness, caring, and courage will be integral ingredients in your becoming an ethically competent professional.

Recommended Readings

Beauchamp, T. and Childress, J. (1994). *Principles of biomedical ethics* (4th ed.). New York, NY: Oxford University Press.

Collopy, B. (1996). Bioethics and therapeutic recreation: Expanding the dialogue. In C. Sylvester (Ed.), *Philosophy of therapeutic recreation: Ideas and issues Vol. 2* (pp. 10–19). Arlington, VA: National Recreation and Park Association.

Lahey, M. (1991). Serving the new poor: Therapeutic recreation values in hard times. *Therapeutic Recreation Journal, 25*(2), 9–18.

Meara, N., Schmidt, L., & Day, J. (1996). Principles and virtues: A foundation for ethical decisions, policies, and character. *The Counseling Psychologist, 24,* 4-77.

Shank, J. (1985). Bioethical principles and the practice of therapeutic recreation in clinical settings. *Therapeutic Recreation Journal, 19*(4), 31–40.

Shank, P. (1996). Doing ethics: Toward the resolution of ethical dilemmas. In C. Sylvester (Ed.), *Philosophy of therapeutic recreation: Ideas and issues Vol. 2* (pp. 30–56). Arlington, VA: National Recreation and Park Association.

Sherwin, S. (1992). *No longer patient: Feminist ethics and healthcare.* Philadelphia, PA: Temple University Press.

Sylvester, C. (1985). An analysis of selected ethical issues in therapeutic recreation. *Therapeutic Recreation Journal, 19*(4), 8–21.

Chapter

4

Models of Therapeutic Recreation Practice

Students studying therapeutic recreation typically have opportunities to observe therapeutic recreation services as part of their coursework. Many students volunteer or work part-time in therapeutic recreation agencies to gain firsthand knowledge of practice. In listening to each other describe their various experiences, students hear differences in the types of programs provided and the outcomes of service. The umbrella of therapeutic recreation covers a wide breadth of services and goals, sometimes making it difficult to locate the similarities across various programs. For the purpose of illustration, consider several typical volunteer experiences of therapeutic recreation students:

> *Scenario 1.* At an outpatient psychiatric clinic, a therapeutic recreation student assisted with a weekly family program for adolescents who receive individual and family counseling. One evening program included several activities. In one activity all the participants sat in a circle and played an old childhood favorite, Telephone. This involved a message being sent around the circle as each person whispered it to the next individual and the group compared the initial message to the final message. In another activity, family members were divided into pairs and instructed to sit back-to-back. One member was provided with a diagram and the other person was provided with a pencil and paper. The first person described the diagram in such a manner that the other person could draw a "duplicate" of the diagram. When the original was compared to the duplicate there was much laughter. Following these activities, the therapeutic recreation specialist led a discussion pertaining to communication (Atteberry-Rogers, 1993).

Scenario 2. At a local nursing home a therapeutic recreation student assisted with the development of memory wallets for residents with mild to moderate memory impairments. These memory wallets were designed to enhance the social interaction of individuals with dementia (Bourgeois, 1993). The typical memory wallet consisted of white index cards attached with two rings. The information in the memory wallets included six to twelve statements and ten to twenty photographs (e.g., name, daily routine, family members or friends who visit, past occupation, preferred activities) that were thought to trigger memories and information the older adult may use when engaged in social interactions. In order to develop a memory wallet with a resident the therapeutic recreation student interviewed the resident and his or her family members, asked the resident and family members to assist with selection of photographs, and asked the resident to construct the memory wallet.

Scenario 3. At a local recreation and park department a student is assigned to work with the therapeutic recreation specialist on the community integration program. The program entailed working one-to-one with children with physical disabilities to involve them in ongoing programs open to individuals with and without disabilities. The child the therapeutic recreation student worked with was integrated into a youth basketball program (Green & DeCoux, 1994).

These brief scenarios raise questions about the relationship between therapeutic recreation programs and the conceptual foundations of therapeutic recreation, the outcomes of programs and services, and the role of the therapeutic recreation specialist. These questions include:

- What is the scope of therapeutic recreation programming? Do individual programs that address the domains of (a) communication skills, (b) memory and social interaction skills, and (c) integration into community based programs all fall under the umbrella of therapeutic recreation? If so, how is such variety explained to clients, healthcare providers (e.g., physician, social worker, occupational therapist), administrators, and the public?

- What is the conceptual basis for therapeutic recreation? What does therapeutic recreation stand for? How does this conceptual basis provide the foundation for such different programs as depicted in the three scenarios?

- What are the roles of the therapeutic recreation specialist in relation to treatment, education, and recreation?

As therapeutic recreation specialists attempt to explain the similarities among diverse therapeutic recreation services, they usually begin by defining therapeutic recreation. Definitions are followed by conceptual diagrams, also called practice models, that depict the various components or types of therapeutic recreation services.

Therapeutic Recreation Practice Models

Therapeutic recreation practice models describe and explain the action of services. Austin (1991b) suggested that "a sound model for TR should identify the essential components for TR practice (i.e., it should describe); and, it should offer a theoretical basis for each of the parts of the model (i.e., it should explain)" (p. 129). Carter, Van Andel, and Robb (1995) explained that "Although all models have their limitations, they do provide a framework for visualizing the various components of a theory and often give us greater insights into the relationships of these components" (p. 15). Models typically include a written portion that describes and explains service delivery and a visual depiction of the relationship and action among the components of the model.

Practice models provide a blueprint of therapeutic recreation services, including the type of services provided, the client–therapeutic recreation specialist relationship, and the proposed outcomes (Voelkl, Carruthers & Hawkins, 1997). The identification of content and outcomes provides direction to therapeutic recreation specialists who design and implement programs. The outcomes identified in models articulate the intent of therapeutic recreation services to clients, administrators, the public, and third-party payers. They also generate dialogue among professionals, which promotes the professional development of therapeutic recreation.

Several therapeutic recreation practice models will be examined in this chapter. As you study them, carefully explore the assumptions underlying each of the models. Sylvester (1986) stated:

> Nearly all models are founded on unexpressed assumptions and values, presenting diverse implications and potent consequences

> depending on the context in which they are applied. It is para-
> mount, therefore, to step back and challenge our models, protect-
> ing against the creation of monoliths. This requires an attitude of
> critical wonder and the educated ability to ask "why?" (p. 8)

Understanding the conceptual foundations underlying the models helps clarify
the strengths and weaknesses of each model.

The models discussed in this chapter include (a) the Leisure Ability Model
(Peterson & Gunn, 1984; Peterson & Stumbo, 2000; Stumbo & Peterson,
1998), (b) the Health Protection and Health Promotion Model (Austin, 1991a,
1991b, 1998), (c) the Therapeutic Recreation Service Delivery and Outcome
Models (Carter, Van Andel & Robb, 1995; Van Andel, 1998), (d) the Self-
Determination and Enjoyment Enhancement Model (Dattilo & Kleiber, 1993;
Dattilo, Kleiber & Williams, 1998), and (d) the Optimizing Lifelong Health
Through Therapeutic Recreation Model (Wilhite, Keller & Caldwell, 1999).

Leisure Ability Model

Peterson and Gunn's (1984) Leisure Ability Model (see Fig. 4.1) is based on
the "leisure ability" philosophy espoused in their 1984 text and the philosophical statement adopted by the NTRS in 1982. The basic assumptions underlying
the model are that leisure is a basic human right and that many people encounter barriers to enjoyable leisure experiences (Stumbo & Peterson, 1998).
According to the Leisure Ability Model, "the purpose of therapeutic recreation
is to facilitate the development, maintenance, and expression of an appropriate
leisure lifestyle for individuals with physical, mental, emotional or social
limitations" (National Therapeutic Recreation Society, 1982). *Leisure lifestyle*
is defined as "the day-to-day behavioral expression of one's leisure-related
attitudes, awareness, and activities revealed within the context and composite
of the total life experience" (Peterson & Gunn, 1984, p. 4).

An appropriate leisure lifestyle is comprised of a number of behaviors
(Stumbo & Peterson, 1998). An individual must possess functional capabilities
that allow for engagement in leisure and recreation. An individual must also
possess social skills, decision-making abilities, knowledge of leisure resources,
and positive values and attitudes toward leisure. As a result of these skills,
attitudes, and behaviors, the individual perceives "choice, motivation, freedom,
responsibility, causality, and independence with regard to his or her leisure"
(Stumbo & Peterson, 1998, p. 91).

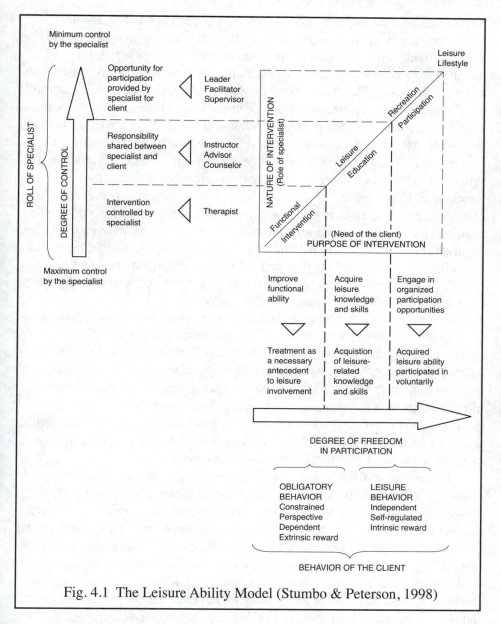

Fig. 4.1 The Leisure Ability Model (Stumbo & Peterson, 1998)

The theoretical underpinnings of the Leisure Ability Model are based on the concepts of learned helplessness, intrinsic motivation and locus of control, choice, and optimal experiences (Stumbo & Peterson, 1998). These concepts direct the design of therapeutic recreation programs. For example, individuals with health or functional impairments may learn to perceive themselves as helpless and unable to participate successfully in recreation. Therapeutic recreation programs are designed to provide such clients with opportunities for success. To ensure that the client attributes success to his or her abilities, the therapeutic recreation specialist talks with the client about how his or her actions (abilities) led to the positive outcome. Therapeutic recreation programs are also developed to promote clients' acquisition of leisure-related skills and knowledge, thereby enabling clients to choose the recreation activities in which they wish to participate. Lastly, based on Csikszentmihalyi's theory of optimal experience (1975; 1990), activities are designed so that clients perceive their skill level to be within the range of challenge offered by the activity. The matching of challenge and skill results in optimal experiences (*flow*) consisting of high levels of intrinsic motivation, enjoyment, and perceived freedom. For example, a client who enjoys kayaking would be most likely to have a positive experience (i.e., flow) when paddling on a river with rapids that she perceives as challenging but within her skill level. The same client may be bored when paddling a river with little perceived challenge and anxious when paddling a river that is more than she thinks she can handle.

The Leisure Ability Model depicts three components of service, including functional intervention, leisure education, and recreation participation (Peterson & Stumbo, 2000; Stumbo & Peterson, 1998). The purpose of the service, the role of the therapeutic recreation specialist, and the degree of control on the part of the client and the therapeutic recreation specialist are illustrated for each of the three components. The Leisure Ability Model espouses a client-centered, problem-oriented approach. Clients' needs are identified during the assessment process, and they are referred to programs from one or more of the three components based on these needs.

The purpose of the *functional intervention* component of the Leisure Ability Model is to improve clients' functional abilities (physical, cognitive, emotional, social). Adequate functional ability is a prerequisite to an independent leisure lifestyle. Peterson and Gunn further suggest that the medical model emphasizes the client's primary illness or disability with little attention paid to how the illness affects the client's daily living situation. Therapeutic recreation, on the other hand, addresses the client's functional deficiencies (i.e., secondary disability) that are a result of the primary illness or disability (e.g., depression following a spinal cord injury; poor self-esteem as a result of disfiguring burns). The therapeutic recreation specialist takes on the role of a therapist and is responsible for selecting activities that increase functional abilities. The activities selected are "not for their recreational or leisure potential, but rather for their specific inherent contribution to behavioral change" (Peterson & Gunn, 1984, p. 18). The functional intervention component is medically prescribed and clients have little or no freedom of choice.

The *leisure education* component is designed to facilitate clients' "development and acquisition of various leisure-related skills, attitudes, and knowledge . . ." (Peterson & Gunn, 1984, p. 22). The content areas for the leisure education component include leisure awareness, social skills, leisure skill development, and leisure resources (see Table 4.1). The therapeutic recreation specialist works with the client to identify the specific content areas (e.g., awareness, skill, resources) that require attention.

The third component of the Leisure Ability Model, *recreation participation,* provides clients with opportunities to engage in freely chosen recreation. The rationale for recreation participation services varies by setting (Peterson & Stumbo, 2000). For example, in community-based settings the rationale may be to integrate clients into general recreation programs. In hospital settings the rationale for recreation participation may be to respond to the rights and needs of all individuals for recreation, regardless of where they reside. Specific

Table 4.1 Leisure Ability Model: Leisure Education Content

Leisure Awareness:	Knowledge of leisure
	Self-awareness
	Leisure and play attitudes
	Related participatory and decision-making skills
Social Interaction Skills:	Communication skills
	Relationship-building skills
	Self-presentation skills
Leisure Activity Skills:	Traditional
	Nontraditional
Leisure Resources:	Activity opportunities
	Personal Resources
	Family and home resources
	State and national resources

examples of recreation participation include sports for individuals with disabilities, recreation facilities for free-time use by clients in a psychiatric facility, and social recreation activities in a long-term care facility. Clients' involvement is largely autonomous, with the therapeutic recreation specialist serving in a variety of capacities as needed, including resource guide, leader, or supervisor.

Critique of Peterson and Gunn's Leisure Ability Model

A strength of the Leisure Ability Model is its straightforward, common-sense approach to therapeutic recreation practice. The model logically lays out the components of service, the purpose of each component, and the roles of the client and therapeutic recreation specialist within each of the three components (Peterson & Gunn, 1984; Peterson & Stumbo, 2000). Although the model clearly defines and explains the three components of services, questions exist regarding the segmentation and sequential implementation of the components. Peterson and Stumbo (2000) indicated that any particular program is designed to produce outcomes for only one of the three components (functional intervention, leisure education, or recreation participation). This may not be necessary or practical. For example, one client may be participating in the gardening group to enhance her ability to following directions (functional intervention in cognitive abilities), while another client may be participating in the gardening group in order to learn a new leisure skill (leisure education). It is also possible that a client may simultaneously achieve outcomes stemming from two components while participating in one group. For instance, a client participating in a dance may attain outcomes in both the functional intervention (social skill to ask someone to dance) and leisure education (learning new dance steps) components. In day-to-day practice it is realistic to incorporate more than one component in any given activity. Therapeutic recreation specialists will be challenged, however, to provide an appropriate level of control for the client, since the client's autonomy is intended to increase as he or she moves across the continuum of components. As such, client freedom should be maximized as much as the situation permits.

Another issue with the Leisure Ability Model is its linear conceptualization. Little work has been done to substantiate empirically the need for clients to develop functional abilities before moving on to services oriented to leisure education or recreation participation. It is not clear how much functional ability is required before a client is ready to move on. Because medical settings tend to concentrate on dysfunction there is a risk that clients will be tethered to the functional intervention component longer than is warranted. Furthermore, given that the overall goal is an independent leisure lifestyle, the model may be strengthened if facilitating clients' leisure or "flow" experiences is incorporated into each of the components. Sylvester (1985) noted the irony of limiting freedom for the sake of functional improvement in a model whose overall goal of independent leisure lifestyle is freedom. Furthermore, using a recreation activity to facilitate functional abilities may lead to an overemphasis on instrumental outcomes at the expense of intrinsic benefits, such as enjoyment, friendship, and creativity.

Another objection to the model pertains to the roles assumed by the therapeutic recreation specialist. Austin (1991b) opposed the therapeutic recreation specialist taking the role of leader or supervisor in the recreation participation component, believing this role should be taken by community recreation professionals. Peterson and Stumbo (2000) provided several clinical and community-based scenarios, however, in which a therapeutic recreation specialist would provide recreation participation opportunities and act as a leader or supervisor. For example, residents in a nursing home often have few opportunities to engage in community-based recreation programs that require support of the therapeutic recreation specialist and the community recreation specialist. Residents also have periods of empty time in nursing homes that would benefit greatly from recreation participation. Clearly, the therapeutic recreation specialist can serve a vital role by facilitating recreation participation in this example. In recent years, federal legislation (e.g., 1992 Americans with Disabilities Act, 1987 Omnibus Reconciliation Act) has mandated recreation opportunities for individuals residing in a variety of settings and possessing a range of disabilities. Therefore, it is necessary for therapeutic recreation specialists to take on the role of supervisor along with their roles of therapist and educator.

The complexity of an independent leisure lifestyle is also problematic. An independent leisure lifestyle is multifaceted and calls for a multidimensional evaluation, making it difficult to measure the outcome of therapeutic recreation. At best, therapeutic recreation specialists evaluating the efficacy of services may select facets of the construct, such as social skills or leisure awareness. Furthermore, the concept "independent leisure lifestyle" does not accurately reflect the advantages of interdependence (Wilhite, Keller & Caldwell, 1999). Without diminishing the validity and importance of independence, recognition of interdependence—both in terms of its practical value for creating supports and its moral implications for the development of community—is warranted.

Finally, according to the Leisure Ability Model, the therapeutic recreation specialist is viewed as having a unique role in healthcare, since he or she addresses secondary disabilities and supports what other team members provide (e.g., physical therapy, occupational therapy, psychology). Given recent shifts and changes in healthcare, some therapeutic recreation specialists have advocated therapeutic recreation practice that is oriented to primary and secondary disabilities (Peterson, 1989). Yaffe (1998), however, raised potential benefits of embracing the Leisure Ability Model, due to its leisure philosophy and support of the role therapeutic recreation specialists have in addressing secondary disabilities:

> As even the medical field becomes more favorable to the mind, body, spirit connection, why would a profession with a dedicated history to this connection abandon its focus on this concept? As healthcare moves toward prevention and self-care, how will therapeutic recreation be affected? Since insurance companies may not even pay for physical therapy or other rehabilitation services, how could therapeutic recreation professionals believe that job security will come from a more restricted focus? The switch to a medical model appears to raise more questions than offering solutions. (p. 106)

Stumbo and Peterson (1998) acknowledged the medical community's change to a focus on prevention and wellness. Accordingly, they recommended attention to the interrelationships among health, wellness, and leisure ability in the continuing development of the Leisure Ability Model.

Health Protection/Health Promotion Model

According to Austin's Health Protection/Health Promotion Model (see Fig. 4.2; 1991b, 1998), the purpose of therapeutic recreation is "to assist persons to recover following threats to health (health protection) and to achieve as high a level of health as possible (health promotion)" (1998, p. 110). The model is built on the concepts of a humanistic perspective, high-level wellness, stabilizing and actualizing tendencies, and health. The humanistic perspective views people as being capable of change, being responsible for their health, and acting on an internal drive for personal growth. High-level wellness occurs when a person's physical, psychological, and environmental functioning leads to self-actualization. The stabilization tendency stimulates one's ability to adapt, cope, and keep stress within a manageable range. The actualization tendency stimulates growth and movement towards high-level wellness. Health is a dynamic state in which individuals are coping with change while simultaneously growing and developing.

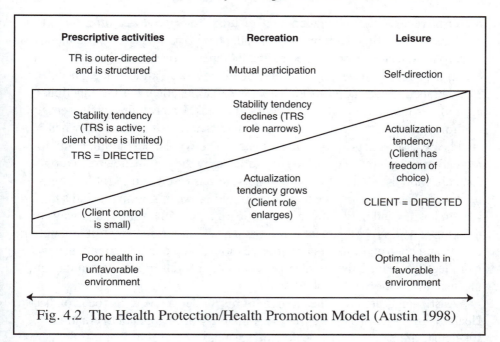

Fig. 4.2 The Health Protection/Health Promotion Model (Austin 1998)

The relationship between leisure and health is central to the Health Protection/Health Promotion Model. The characteristics of leisure, including perceived freedom, intrinsic motivation, and self-determination, are thought to be key factors in promoting health. Austin (1991a) stated:

> Leisure would seem to offer one of the best opportunities for people to experience self-determination because it offers a chance for individuals to be in control. The potential for control does not occur in. . . situations where external pressure exists. Leisure also provides occasion for achieving feelings of mastery or competence as challenging activities are conquered and positive feedback is received. (p. 6)

Although Austin recognizes that health benefits (e.g., competence, self-determination) may be derived from any recreation or leisure experience, he differentiates therapeutic recreation from general recreation services. The purposeful nature of therapeutic recreation makes it unique. Austin recommends that therapeutic recreation be called "clinical therapeutic recreation" since such terminology expresses the purposeful nature of the service.

The Health Protection/Health Promotion model includes three service components that move a client from health protection to health promotion:

prescriptive activities, recreation, and leisure. *Prescriptive activities* provide a stabilizing force. Stabilization (coping, adaptation) results from participation in an activity selected or prescribed by the therapeutic recreation specialist. For example, a client with depression may be given a bead kit to make a necklace. The therapeutic recreation specialist knows that the client has the functional capabilities to make a necklace. Making the necklace provides focus, sense of control, and ultimately, stabilization. *Prescriptive activities* are used when clients are assessed as needing to reengage in activities, but are not ready for recreation or leisure. *Recreation* is negotiated by the therapeutic recreation specialist and the client. Recreation interventions result in a client feeling refreshed. They also provide a middle ground between stabilizing and actualizing tendencies and may allow clients to learn new skills, values, and ways of thinking. The final component is *leisure*. The client has the greatest amount of choice and control during leisure interventions, and actualizing tendency is at its fullest. Therefore, the client experiences high levels of self-determination, intrinsic motivation, and wellness.

Austin suggested that the strength of his model is due to its focus on health. Health is important "because [the] vast majority of therapeutic recreation specialists are employed by healthcare agencies, the goal of therapeutic recreation should coincide with the purpose of these agencies" (1991b, p. 139).

Critique of Austin's Health Protection/Health Promotion Model

Austin's model lacks clarity as to how program content varies according to the three service components (Ross, 1998). The model shows the therapeutic recreation specialist's control lessening as the client moves from prescribed activities to leisure; however, it is not clear as to whether the same recreation activity may be used across all three types of services. For example, under what conditions would a bead kit used as a prescribed activity also be used as a recreation or leisure intervention? Does selection of the activity used in recreation and leisure interventions relate to client interest? Is prescribed activity a recreation activity? For instance, could folding towels constitute a prescribed activity that allowed a client to focus attention on a task he or she could control?

The model shows clients progressing from a state of stabilization to a state of actualization. Questions may be asked about the relationship between stabilization/actualization tendencies and leisure. For example, Austin (1991b) indicated that clients receiving prescriptive activities may occasionally experience recreation or leisure. He also stated, however, that "Clients, at this time of threat to health, are not ready for recreation or leisure" (p. 135). It seems, however, that if the overall outcome of the model is to move a client towards leisure experiences that foster actualizing tendencies and health, all three types of services may be strengthened by enabling opportunities for leisure experiences. Furthermore, there does not appear to be any empirical evidence that threats to health preclude recreation and leisure.

Another area of concern pertains to how the therapeutic recreation specialist or client can differentiate the client's experience in the three types of services (Lee, 1998; Ross, 1998). For example, how does the engagement in prescriptive activities differ from the refreshment or re-creation experienced in recreation? When individuals are fully engaged they typically feel refreshed (i.e., re-created) following the experience (Csikszentmihalyi, 1988).

Austin (1991a, 1991b) has undertaken a formidable task in attempting to articulate the link between health and therapeutic recreation services, bringing together a variety of literature. A present weakness of the model, however, is the lack of clarity regarding the interrelationships among these variables. In particular, clarification of the relationship between leisure and health is needed (Lee, 1998). What happens to leisure when the major thrust of the model is oriented to health? Sylvester (1985, 1989b) suggested that when health is the sole aim of therapeutic recreation, services may become narrowly utilitarian, diminishing the broader values of leisure, such as autonomy, community, and self-determination. As such, the subjective, expressive, and associational aspects of leisure that allow high levels of freedom and intrinsic motivation, promote the exercise of capabilities, and help to form social connections may not receive adequate attention in a model limited to health. Of course, Austin defines health broadly, possibly obscuring other desirable goals.

The Health Protection/Health Promotion Model conceptualizes health as the primary outcome of therapeutic recreation services. Engagement in prescriptive activities, recreation, or leisure is supposed to result in outcomes that enhance a client's level of health, such as perceived control, intrinsic motivation, and self-determination. Austin's observation that most therapeutic recreation professionals work in the healthcare system gives particular prominence to health as the goal of therapeutic recreation services.

Therapeutic Recreation Service Delivery and Outcome Models

Van Andel (1998) defined therapeutic recreation as "the specialized application of recreation and experiential activities or interventions that assist in maintaining or improving the health status, functional capabilities, and ultimately the quality of life of persons with special needs" (Carter, Van Andel & Robb, 1995; p. 10). He proposed a comprehensive two-part model (Carter, Van Andel & Robb, 1995; Van Andel, 1998). The first model, the Therapeutic Recreation

Service Delivery Model (see Fig. 4.3), outlines the types of services designed to achieve predetermined outcomes. The second model, the Therapeutic Recreation Outcome Model (see Fig. 4.4), describes the various outcomes of therapeutic recreation services. The Therapeutic Recreation Outcome Model serves as an extension of the Therapeutic Recreation Service Delivery Model.

Van Andel designed his model to create common ground for both the therapy and the leisure views of therapeutic recreation services. The theoretical grounding of the Therapeutic Recreation Service Delivery Model is based on Neulinger's conceptualization of leisure, which defines leisure as a subjective experience (Van Andel, 1998). Leisure experiences are differentiated from nonleisure or "therapy" experiences based on the client's state of mind. High degrees of choice, freedom, and intrinsic motivation foster leisure experiences. In contrast, nonleisure experiences occur when one perceives little choice, high constraint, and is extrinsically motivated. Van Andel suggested that whether a program promotes a leisure or nonleisure experience will depend on the type of service provided (e.g., treatment/rehabilitation, education), as well as the client's and the therapeutic recreation specialist's levels of control during the program.

The Therapeutic Recreation Service Delivery Model features four elements of service, including: (a) diagnosis or assessment of need, (b) treatment/rehabilitation, (c) education, and (d) prevention/health promotion. The *Diagnosis/ Needs Assessment* component entails a formal assessment or evaluation of a client's strengths and limitations. Assessment data are used to identify the components of services that will meet the client's needs. The *Treatment/*

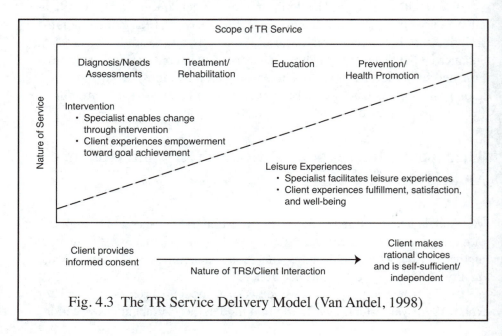

Fig. 4.3 The TR Service Delivery Model (Van Andel, 1998)

Rehabilitation component is designed to ameliorate the "primary or secondary effects of a disease process or injury . . ." (Carter, Van Andel & Robb, 1995, p. 21). Typically, therapeutic recreation programs within the treatment/rehabilitation component address functional abilities. Services within the *Education* component provide information that affects a client's knowledge, attitudes, and behaviors. The final component, *Prevention/Health Promotion,* is intended to promote a healthy lifestyle.

The particular activities used in any of the components depend on the goals of the program. For example, an aquatics program designed to increase clients' upper body strength would be classified as a treatment/rehabilitation intervention. In contrast, an aquatics program designed as an open swim would fall under the prevention/health promotion component. It is also possible for a client's involvement in one activity to fall within several of the components. Involvement in a gardening activity may allow for the therapeutic recreation specialist to further understand the cognitive functioning of the client in terms of following directions (diagnosis/needs assessment), while simultaneously allowing the client to learn a new leisure skill (education).

As indicated by the dotted diagonal line on the Therapeutic Recreation Service Delivery Model, the service components may be implemented for the

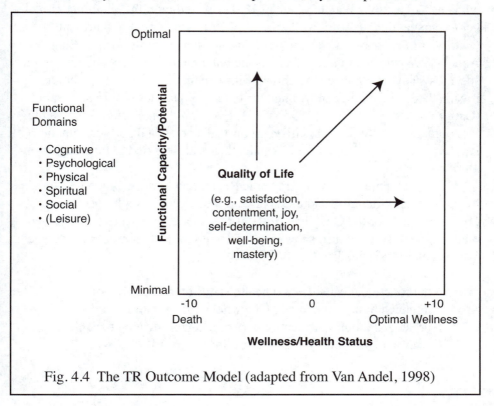

Fig. 4.4 The TR Outcome Model (adapted from Van Andel, 1998)

purpose of an intervention, a leisure experience, or a combination of the two. An intervention emphasizes the action of the therapeutic recreation specialist in moving the client through a program designed to achieve predetermined outcomes. Conversely, the leisure experience dimension emphasizes the client's autonomous experience of leisure. Van Andel (1998) indicated that whether the dotted diagonal line is moved up to focus on interventions or down to focus on leisure experiences will depend on the therapeutic recreation specialist's philosophy and the setting in which services are provided. For example, a therapeutic recreation specialist employed in a public recreation department with a mission to promote leisure and recreation opportunities for all residents may target leisure experiences. Lastly, Van Andel (1998) indicated that interventions and leisure experiences may occur simultaneously and be given equal focus by the therapeutic recreation specialist.

The second model, the Therapeutic Recreation Outcome Model, outlines three potential outcomes: health status, quality of life, and functional capability/potential. *Health status* is the interrelationship between physical, cognitive, emotional, social, and spiritual health. This perspective suggests that although an individual may have impairments in one domain he or she may still be capable of experiencing a high level of wellness. For example, an individual who has had a stroke may have adapted to impaired mobility, enabling him or her to pursue high levels of wellness in spite of a functional impairment. *Quality of life* assesses the client's psychological and spiritual well-being. Van Andel (1998) viewed quality of life as the outcome that therapeutic recreation specialists have the greatest potential of influencing given the role that leisure is capable of playing in confirming "the essential qualities of human nature" (Carter, Van Andel & Robb, 1995, p. 15). *Functional capabilities* involve the five domains of physical, cognitive, emotional, social, and spiritual functioning. Leisure is considered a sixth domain that is closely tied to functioning in all five domains.

The development of the Therapeutic Recreation Service Outcome Model is based on health literature and therapeutic recreation philosophy. Van Andel's (1998) premise for the Outcome Model is that as a client makes gains in one outcome he or she will also show improvement in the other areas of outcomes. Van Andel (1998) stated:

> the functional capacity and health status outcomes are not intended to be isolated from the whole but are interrelated, organized around the central core of a person striving to achieve a sense of wholeness, a quality of life... . (p. 10)

Quality of life assumes a central place in the Therapeutic Recreation Outcome Model, serving as a reminder to focus on the whole individual rather than focusing on only functional domains.

Critique of Van Andel's Therapeutic Recreation Service Delivery Model and Therapeutic Recreation Outcome Model

Van Andel recognized the influence of social change on the profession's foundations (Carter, Van Andel & Robb, 1995). His models were developed to respond to the need for healthcare professions to articulate their outcomes and scope of services. Van Andel endorsed the notion that leisure experiences and quality of life can be pursued as legitimate goals in healthcare while simultaneously seeking to improve functional abilities and health status (Van Andel, 1998).

Although Van Andel attempted to blend various definitions and philosophical perspectives of therapeutic recreation, the conflict among competing viewpoints is not readily resolved by their incorporation into a model. The flexibility of the Therapeutic Recreation Service Delivery Model seems to be both a strength and a weakness. For example, one may ask what role should leisure play in therapeutic recreation services? If one practitioner takes a reductionistic view of leisure by emphasizing functional improvements, is he or she providing a service that is at all similar to a practitioner who facilitates leisure experiences? Must leisure be the central phenomenon in order to say that services are therapeutic recreation? Such questions illuminate the difficulties the profession continues to have with defining and explaining recreation services.

Another consideration pertains to the scope of services in the Therapeutic Recreation Service Delivery Model. The model is flexible; one activity may be simultaneously addressing several service components. Although dealing with more than one component within a specific activity seems feasible, it makes it difficult to identify the appropriate level of interaction between the therapeutic recreation specialist and the client. The Therapeutic Recreation Service Delivery Model indicates that the client possesses increasing levels of control as they move from Diagnosis/Needs Assessment to Prevention/Health Promotion. If a gardening group is to be used with one client to promote the ability to follow directions (Treatment/Rehabilitation) and with another client to provide participation in a lifelong activity (Prevention/Health Promotion), how will a therapeutic recreation specialist deliver this program? Another consideration is the appropriateness of content for each component. At present, Van Andel suggests that activities fall within a component based on the short-term goal rather than the type of activity. Further clarity as to the scope of goals for each component and range of content would strengthen our understanding and implementation of the model (Coyle, 1998). Although exercise and stress management are examples of Prevention/Health Promotion programs, one may wonder if a nursing home resident's freely chosen engagement in a pottery class would constitute a Health Promotion intervention.

Concerns similar to those raised regarding Austin's Health Protection/ Health Promotion Model also warrant attention. The outcomes of health status and functional capabilities point to the utilitarian nature of therapeutic recreation services. The intrinsic, noninstrumental benefits of leisure may be diminished by the domination of functional outcomes. Carter, Van Andel and Robb (1995) claimed, however, that "affecting all three appears to be the unique role and function of TRSs as healthcare providers" (p. 19). Research is needed to examine how these three types of outcomes (health status, functional domains, and quality of life) may be interrelated. Attention must also be given to the development of measurement tools for documenting outcomes. The lack of valid and reliable assessment tools makes it difficult to document the effectiveness of therapeutic recreation services. The diversity of outcomes in this model suggests the need for additional assessment and evaluation tools (Coyle, 1998).

Van Andel's models provide an expanded map of therapeutic recreation services. Although greater conceptualization and development is needed, it is especially intriguing because of the attention it gives to quality of life. Further development is also needed to understand the relationship among key concepts, such as health, leisure, and functional capacity. Also, more needs to be said about the relationship between the two models. Therapeutic recreation specialists will be better able to plan effective programs as the link between the two models is developed and articulated (Coyle, 1998).

Self-Determination and Enjoyment Enhancement Model

The Self-Determination and Enjoyment Enhancement Model (see Fig. 4.5) was developed by Dattilo and Kleiber (1993) with later contributions by Williams (Dattilo, Kleiber & Williams, 1998). *Self-determination* occurs when an individual is the "primary causal agent in one's life . . . making choices and decisions free from external influence or interference" (Dattilo, Kleiber & Williams, 1998, p. 260). *Enjoyment* refers to the level of psychological absorption one has in an activity. The authors' definition of enjoyment is based on the work of Csikszentmihalyi (1975; 1990) and refers to a participant's involvement in an activity, rather than the degree of fun the person experiences. Based on their conceptualization of self-determination, enjoyment, and several related ideas, Dattilo, Kleiber, and Williams (1998) recently revised their model.

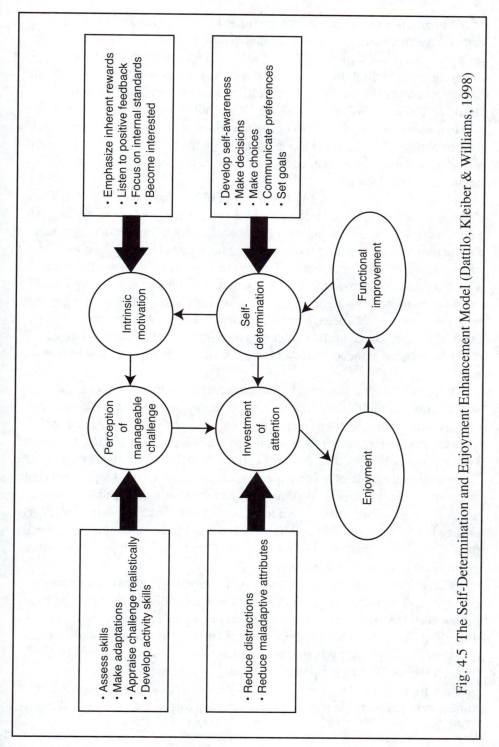

Fig. 4.5 The Self-Determination and Enjoyment Enhancement Model (Dattilo, Kleiber & Williams, 1998)

Drawing from materials jointly published by the ATRA and the NTRA, the authors asserted that the "purpose of therapeutic recreation is to treat . . . physical, social, cognitive, and emotional conditions associated with illness, injury, or chronic disability . . . through a variety of interventions . . . to create environments conducive to enjoyment [that] is consistent with that purpose . . ." (Dattilo, Kleiber & Williams, 1998, p. 260). Both *enjoyment* and *functional outcomes* serve as the objectives of the model, as well as the indicators of self-determination. Therefore, the model is based on the assumption that if clients experience enjoyment and functional improvements, they will display self-determination in leisure.

The Self-Determination and Enjoyment Enhancement Model differs from the linear and hierarchical structures of the models previously discussed. The Self-Determination and Enjoyment Enhancement Model is circular in nature. Self-determination, intrinsic motivation, manageable challenge, and investment of attention lead to the outcomes of enjoyment and functional improvement. The outcomes of improved levels of enjoyment and functional improvement "serve to reinforce experiences and lead a person on to greater challenges and to higher levels of self-determination" (Dattilo, Kleiber & Williams, 1998, p. 260). The significance of the model's circularity lies in the assumption that each intervention impacts the outcomes as well as components of self-determination.

The model outlines strategies for enhancing participants' experience of self-determination, intrinsic motivation, perception of manageable challenge, and investment of attention. Strategies to enhance *self-determination* may include providing participants with opportunities to make decisions, to become aware of their abilities, and to express preferences within the context of leisure. According to the authors, a participant's *intrinsic motivation* is tapped when an emphasis is placed on individual rewards and standards, rather than competition with others. Participants learn to recognize manageable levels of *challenge* as they become aware of their skill level and ways to adapt activities to match their skills. Lastly, participants' *investment of attention* is enhanced when the environment is free of distractions.

The strategies used to facilitate self-determination, intrinsic motivation, perception of manageable challenge, and investment of attention may be used during each therapeutic recreation intervention regardless of program content. Therefore, the same strategies may be used during a leisure education session or a community outing. Whether the emphasis is placed on one strategy rather than another is dependent upon the abilities, awareness, and needs of the participant. For instance, a participant may be intrinsically motivated to play horseshoes, but finds the number of children playing in the park to be distracting. In this example the therapeutic recreation specialist uses the strategies to promote investment of attention and therefore assists the participant in identifying times of day or other parks with fewer distractions.

Critique of Dattilo, Kleiber, and Williams' Self-Determination and Enjoyment Enhancement Model

The strong theoretical development of this model draws on theories of self-determination, intrinsic motivation, and enjoyment. The model is limited, however, by lack of knowledge on the linkages among the components. Neither previous research nor graphic depiction of the model explains how the components interact. Rather, the model suggests that each component builds on the previous component (e.g., self-determination leads to intrinsic motivation). Csikszentmihalyi's (1990) multifaceted conceptualization of optimal experiences (flow) supports the interactive and simultaneous use of the model's components and their strategies to produce the outcome of enjoyment.

Caldwell (1998) discussed the cultural bias of the model in terms of fostering primary control, whereby individuals from other cultures may feel more comfortable experiencing secondary control. An example of secondary control would be one adolescent watching two other adolescents playing Nintendo and being able to predict who would win the game. As such, control is experienced though observation rather than action.

Lastly, questions emerge as to the outcome of functional improvement. The authors did not address functional improvement in the original conceptualization of the model (Dattilo & Kleiber, 1993). Even in their recent work on the model (Dattilo, Kleiber & Williams, 1998), there is little discussion of functional improvement and its connection to the other constructs. The authors suggested that when participants experience high levels of enjoyment they will likely be motivated to enhance skills and thereby enhance functional abilities. The inclusion of functional improvement has been questioned since there is little evidence for the claim that an outcome of the model will be functional improvement (Caldwell, 1998; Mobily, 1999; Murray, 1998). As discussed in the previous critiques, an overemphasis on functional improvement may impede participants' experiencing of enjoyment and intrinsic motivation, which would be counterproductive to functional improvement and self-determination.

Optimizing Lifelong Health Through Therapeutic Recreation Model

Wilhite, Keller, and Caldwell (1999) developed the Optimizing Lifelong Health Through Therapeutic Recreation Model (see Fig. 4.6). The Optimizing Lifelong Health Through Therapeutic Recreation Model is a nonlinear model grounded in developmental psychology. More specifically, it was based on Baltes and Baltes' (1990) theory of selective optimization for explaining successful aging. Adapting the theory of selective optimization to therapeutic recreation suggests that as people age they experience changes in their abilities and resources. These changes require decision making and accommodations to maintain involvement in valued leisure activities.

Three key principles underlie the Optimizing Lifelong Health Through Therapeutic Recreation Model and guide therapeutic recreation practice

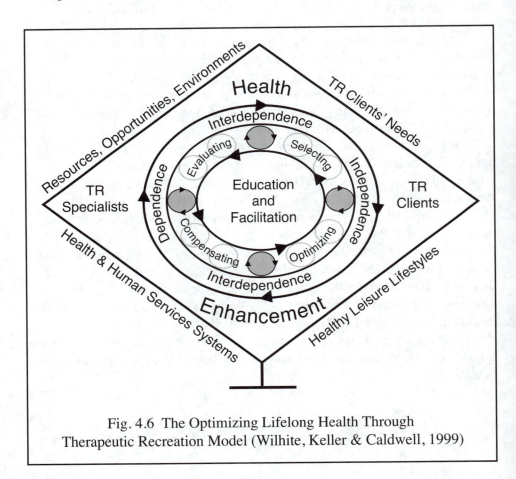

Fig. 4.6 The Optimizing Lifelong Health Through Therapeutic Recreation Model (Wilhite, Keller & Caldwell, 1999)

(Wilhite, Keller & Caldwell, 1999). First, a healthy leisure lifestyle is thought to reduce further illness, disability, or secondary consequences (e.g., depression in response to a spinal cord injury). Second, individualized resources and opportunities may enhance health and well-being. Third, individuals must be prepared to change or substitute leisure pursuits in response to personal and environmental changes.

The Optimizing Lifelong Health Through Therapeutic Recreation Model consists of four interrelated elements: selecting, optimizing, compensating, and evaluating. First, the client *selects* activities that match his or her interests, abilities, and resources. As part of the selection process, the client identifies achievable goals for his or her leisure. The client then *optimizes* those goals by engaging in activities that maximize use of personal and environmental resources. The client's activity engagement is influenced by his or her need to *compensate* for impaired abilities. For example, a musician who has developed severe arthritis and can no longer play the piano may compensate by selecting to attend musical concerts. Finally, the client *evaluates* the effectiveness of selecting, optimizing, and compensating in promoting or maintaining his or her healthy leisure lifestyle. Evaluating may result in the client continuing to engage in selected activities or making changes in the activities selected and the way activities compensate for impaired abilities.

The therapeutic recreation specialist serves as both educator and facilitator. As an educator the therapeutic recreation specialist designs and implements programs to deal with clients' awareness, skills, and knowledge. As a facilitator, the therapeutic recreation specialist designs and implements programs that provide clients with the opportunity to use what has been learned in the educational interventions and to experience leisure.

In contrast to other therapeutic recreation practice models, the Optimizing Lifelong Health Through Therapeutic Recreation Model proposes that as clients learn to optimize their abilities and compensate for impairments, they will vary in their levels of independence, ranging from dependency to interdependency to independence. Typically, therapeutic recreation specialists target independent leisure behavior as the outcome of therapeutic recreation services. Wilhite, Keller, and Caldwell contend that independence may not be a realistic outcome for some clients depending on their disabilities, resources, and environment. For some individuals, an interdependent relationship with a therapeutic recreation specialist, family members, or friends is necessary for optimizing leisure behavior. An example would be an older adult with dementia who needs verbal and physical cues to engage in her preferred activity of gardening. When the family member who serves as the caregiver provides these cues, the older adult with dementia can take an active role in weeding the family garden.

Although the authors of the other models would probably concur, Wilhite, Keller, and Caldwell explicitly acknowledge the reality of interdependence.

Critique of Wilhite, Keller, and Caldwell's Optimizing Lifelong Health Through Therapeutic Recreation Model

The Optimizing Lifelong Health Through Therapeutic Recreation Model provides the therapeutic recreation profession with a non-hierarchical practice model based on a healthy leisure lifestyle. Such a perspective allows therapeutic recreation practitioners to think broadly as to how their work with a client relates to the individual's lifelong interests and abilities. Further development of the life course perspective is needed, however, to clarify how the authors view age or life stage as influencing healthy leisure lifestyles (Freysinger, 1999).

Another strength of the Optimizing Lifelong Health Through Therapeutic Recreation Model is the potential for viewing the long-term relationship between optimal health and leisure. The model is limited, however, when used to guide therapeutic recreation interventions. Although Wilhite, Keller, and Caldwell presented the elements of selecting, optimizing, compensating, and evaluating as cyclical, with one element leading to the next, it does not seem possible to pull apart each step or element (Freysinger, 1999). Selecting activities that promote a healthy leisure lifestyle seem intertwined with optimizing and compensating. For example, an older adult who can no longer play the piano due to arthritis will select activities that optimize her resources and abilities, as well as compensate for lost abilities. It is doubtful that she would select an activity and then consider if it optimizes her resources.

Lastly, the Optimizing Lifelong Health Through Therapeutic Recreation Model supports the accommodation and substitution of activities as one's abilities and resources change. Freysinger (1999) pointed out that accommodation and substitution typically place the onus of responsibility on the individual. An individualized approach may foster passive acceptance on the part of clients instead of environmental change that accommodates individual leisure abilities. For example, over several years there is a significant decline in the number of people registering for the annual bridge tournament sponsored by a public recreation agency. The longtime participants are now older adults who due to changes in visual and physical abilities no longer drive. Many of the older adults have accommodated to these changes by seeking bridge players in their neighborhoods. One may question whether the environment, the public recreation agency, should also accommodate participants' changes by providing transportation for older citizens.

A Comparison of Therapeutic Recreation Practice Models

Examining the similarities and differences among the models allows readers to consider which model best represents their interpretation of therapeutic recreation. An overview of the models' characteristics is presented in Table 4.2, pp.104–105. The following questions will be used to guide analyses of the practice models:

- How do the assumptions underlying the models vary?
- What are the various components of therapeutic recreation services as outlined in the models?
- What are the similarities and differences in how the models conceptualize the client/therapeutic recreation specialist relationship? and
- What do the similarities among the models tell us about current therapeutic recreation practice?

How do the assumptions underlying the models vary?

The Leisure Ability Model and the Self-Determination and Enjoyment Enhancement Model are based on theories of leisure and enjoyment. The assumptions underlying the Leisure Ability Model include: leisure is a basic need and right of all individuals, and many individuals experience barriers to leisure. The Self-Determination and Enjoyment Enhancement Model is based on the assumption that when participants experience self-determination, intrinsic motivation, manageable levels of challenge, and investment of attention, their levels of enjoyment and functional abilities will be enhanced. Although the assumptions underlying these models differ in that one addresses leisure and the other addresses enjoyment, they do appear to be similar in that they are based on theories of intrinsic motivation, choice, and appropriate levels of challenge in promoting leisure and enjoyment. The Self-Determination and Enjoyment Enhancement Model also acknowledges functional outcomes, although little conceptual work is presented to support this assumption.

The Health Protection/Health Promotion Model, Therapeutic Recreation Service Delivery and Outcome Models, and the Optimizing Lifelong Health Through Therapeutic Recreation Model are based on concepts of health and leisure. Further, they all emphasize health as the outcome of therapeutic recreation. The Health Protection/Health Promotion Model is based on the assumption that activities, recreation, and leisure promote stabilizing or actualizing

Table 4.2 Therapeutic Recreation Practice Models

Peterson and Gunn's Leisure Ability Model

ASSUMPTIONS:
- Leisure is a need and right of all individuals
- Many individuals experience constraints and barriers to leisure
- TR services are designed to facilitate individuals' independence in leisure functioning

MISSION: Leisure

DEFINITION OF TR:
. . . the purpose of TR is to facilitate the development, maintenance, and expression of an appropriate leisure lifestyle for individuals with physical, mental, emotional or social limitations . . . (National Therapeutic Recreation Association, 1982)

Austin's Health Protection/Health Promotion

ASSUMPTIONS:
- Activity, recreation, and leisure interventions facilitate individuals' movement towards high levels of health and wellness
- People are motivated by stabilizing tendencies for managing stress, and actualizing tendencies for seeking growth and health
- Health is the focus because most professionals work in healthcare settings

MISSION: Health

DEFINITION OF TR:
. . . a means, first, to restore oneself or regain stability or equilibrium following a threat to health (health protection), and second, to develop oneself through leisure as a means to self actualization (health promotion) . . . (Austin, 1991a, p. 13)

Van Andel's TR Service Delivery Model and TR Outcome Model

ASSUMPTIONS:
- The focus of interventions differ in their degree of focus on intervention and leisure
- The outcomes of TR services are multidimentional in nature (e.g., health status, quality of life, functional capabilities)

MISSION: Quality of Life

Table 4.2 Therapeutic Recreation Practice Models (continued)

DEFINITION OF TR:

... the specialized application of recreation and experiential activities or interventions that assist in maintaining or improving the health status, functional capabilities, and ultimately the quality of life of persons with special needs ... (Carter, Van Andel, and Robb, 1995, p. 10)

Datillo, Kleiber, and William's Self-Determination and Enjoyment Enhancement Model

ASSUMPTIONS:

- Promoting self-determination, intrinsic motivation, manageable levels of challenge, and investment of attention results in the outcomes of enjoyment and functional abilities
- Increase in the level of enjoyment and functional abilities is associated with the perception of self-determination in leisure

MISSION: Self-determination and enjoyment

DEFINITION OF TR:

... the purpose of therapeutic recreation is to treat ... physical, social, cognitive, and emotional conditions associated with illness, injury, or chronic disability ... through a variety of interventions. (Dattilo, Kleiber, and Williams, 1998, p. 260)

Wilhite, Keller, and Caldwell's Optimizing Lifelong Health Through Therapeutic Recreation Model

ASSUMPTIONS:

- A healthy leisure lifestyle reduces further illness, primary disability, or a secondary disability
- Individualized resources and opportunities enhance health and well-being
- Over the life course people must be ready to adapt leisure in response to personal and/or environmental changes

MISSION: health enhancement

DEFINITION OF TR:

Therapeutic recreation (TR) service delivery is based on the assumed need for intervening with the intent of influencing the individual's personal and/or leisure functioning. (Wilhite, Keller and Caldwell, 1999, p. 98) tendencies that lead to health. The Therapeutic Recreation Outcome Model describes the outcomes of therapeutic recreation as multidimensional and, therefore, as a client's quality of life is enhanced, his or her functional capabilities and health status will be positively affected. Lastly, the Optimizing Life-long Health Through Therapeutic Recreation Model assumes that health enhancement occurs as a result of maintaining a healthy leisure lifestyle throughout the life course.

It is plausible that the time period in which each model was developed influenced the underlying assumptions. For example, the Leisure Ability Model emerging in the late 1970s while there was growth in the diversity of health and human services. In contrast, the Self-Determination and Enjoyment Enhancement Model, the Health Protection/Health Promotion Model, the Therapeutic Recreation Service Delivery and Outcome Models, and the Optimizing Lifelong Health through Therapeutic Recreation Model emerged in the early to mid 1990s when spending on medical/healthcare was sharply reduced through managed care, perhaps explaining the increased attention to functional outcomes and health.

What are the various components of therapeutic recreation services as outlined in the models?

Several of the practice models, including Leisure Ability, Health Protection/Health Promotion, and Therapeutic Recreation Service Delivery, indicate the areas of content addressed in therapeutic recreation services. For example, the Leisure Ability Model has specific content areas identified for each of the three components (functional intervention, leisure education, recreation participation). In particular, the content of the leisure education component has been developed extensively as is evident in programmatic manuals available to therapeutic recreation specialists (e.g., see Stumbo, 1992; Carruthers, Sneegas & Ashton-Shaeffer, 1986).

Recently developed models tend to outline client experience or treatment goals rather than program content to differentiate their components. A criticism of the components in the Health Protection/Health Promotion Model and the Therapeutic Recreation Service Delivery Model is the lack of clarity regarding content (Coyle, 1998; Ross, 1998). Austin (1998) suggested that the components in the Health Protection/Health Promotion Model differ in terms of the type of experience that the client has during the intervention or program. Difficulty differentiating these components may emerge since Austin stated that some clients may experience leisure or flow when engaged in a prescriptive activity (Ross, 1998). Van Andel (1998) suggested that the components of his model differ in terms of short-term goals identified for the intervention or program rather than the specific content or type of activity.

Several of the recent models are process-oriented rather than content-oriented. For example, both the Self-Determination and Enjoyment Enhancement Model and the Optimizing Lifelong Health through Therapeutic Recreation Model present cyclical processes that describe how clients move towards enhanced enjoyment, health, and leisure. The Self-Determination and Enjoyment Enhancement Model presents strategies that the therapeutic recreation specialist may use regardless of whether the program content is leisure education or a community reintegration program. The Optimizing Lifelong Health through Therapeutic Recreation Model presents a cognitive process (i.e., selecting, optimizing, compensating, evaluating) that clients go through to enhance and maintain healthy leisure lifestyles.

What are the similarities and differences in how the models conceptualize the client/therapeutic recreation specialist relationship?

All of the models provide the client with as much control during interventions as he or she is ready to handle. The Health Protection/Health Promotion and Leisure Ability Models indicate a decrease of the therapist's control and an increase of the client's control as the client moves through the sequential components of the model. Similarly, the Therapeutic Recreation Service Delivery Model emphasizes increasing clients' informed consent and independence as they are able. Van Andel acknowledges that client consent and control is greater in education and prevention/health promotion than in diagnosis/needs assessment or treatment/rehabilitation.

The two non-hierarchical models differ from other models in their temporal view of control. For example, the Optimizing Lifelong Health Through Therapeutic Recreation Model views variation in levels of client control from a life-course perspective. Wilhite, Keller, and Caldwell (1999) suggested that although providing the client with opportunities for independence is important, some clients may function best when engaged in interdependent or dependent relationships due to characteristics of a specific disability or cultural influences. On a program-to-program basis, the Self-Determination and Enjoyment Enhancement Model suggests that the therapeutic recreation specialist maximize clients' levels of choice and decision making (i.e., self-determination strategies).

What do the similarities among the models tell us about current therapeutic recreation practice?

Although we have discussed the differences among therapeutic practice models, their similarities are important since they provide us with insight into the agreed upon principles of therapeutic recreation practice. Underlying all the models is the assumption that therapeutic recreation services produce positive change in clients. Across all the models, services are designed to maximize client control in recreation. Key terms used in all the models (e.g., recreation, leisure, enjoyment, health, quality of life) direct us to the concepts central to therapeutic recreation practice. Continued development of the models in effort to articulate the interrelationship among these concepts is needed to strengthen our understanding of therapeutic recreation practice.

Multicultural Considerations for Therapeutic Recreation Models

Models of practice present many implications for a multicultural approach to therapeutic recreation programming. Belief systems and value orientations are inherent in all models. Of course, beliefs and values are products of culture. Therefore, it is essential to explore the cultural implications of models, ascertaining how open or closed they are to cultural diversity.

Dieser and Peregoy (1999) conducted a multicultural critique of three therapeutic recreation service models: the Leisure Ability Model (Peterson & Gunn, 1984; Stumbo & Peterson, 1998), the Health Protection/Health Promotion Model (Austin, 1997; 1998), and the Therapeutic Recreation Service Delivery Model/Therapeutic Recreation Outcome Model (Carter, Van Andel & Robb, 1995; Van Andel, 1998). They gleaned seven culturally biased assumptions from the literature, using them to scrutinize therapeutic recreation models of practice:

1. The definition of normal behavior is universal.
2. Individuals are the basic building blocks of a society.
3. Abstractions are universally recognized as the same (e.g., concepts like *health and leisure* have the same meaning in all cultures).
4. Independence is desirable and dependence is undesirable.
5. Clients are helped more by formal therapy than by their culturally-appropriate support systems.

6. All people employ linear thinking to understand the world.
7. Cultural history is not necessary for understanding contemporary issues.

Dieser and Peregoy (1999) were critical of all three models for their emphasis on Western values of independence and individualism. They concluded that the Leisure Ability Model and the Health Protection/Health Promotion Model were the worst offenders, having "very few cross-cultural assumptions" (pp. 62, 63). They noted, however, that the Therapeutic Recreation Service Delivery Model and the Therapeutic Recreation Outcome Model are partially sensitive to culture because they define quality of life according to the individual's worldview rather than dominant values.

Furthermore, the Self-Determination and Enjoyment Enhancement Model (Dattilo, Kleiber & Williams, 1998) is not attuned to cross-cultural differences. Drawing from humanistic psychology, it is particularly individualistic. Addressing gender differences, Caldwell (1998) criticized the model for stressing independent functioning at the exclusion of other patterns of functioning. While acknowledging a role for autonomy and self-determination, Caldwell (1998) claimed, "interdependence and cooperation might be a more comfortable way of operating for at least some, if not many women . . ." (p. 287).

Among the models of practice discussed in this chapter, the Optimizing Lifelong Health Through Therapeutic Recreation Model (Wilhite, Keller & Caldwell, 1999) contains the most cross-cultural assumptions. Specifically, it stresses interdependence, a nonlinear approach, and the key roles played by culture and environment. Wilhite, Keller, and Caldwell (1999) explained, "the OLH-TR model emphasizes all aspects of TR clients (i.e., mental, physical, social, psychological, cultural, spiritual) and the interdependence between clients, others, and their environments" (p. 105). Moreover, they concluded that "this perspective of TR service . . . is more conducive to accounting for diverse personal, social, and cultural needs . . ." (p. 5).

Nonetheless, Freysinger (1999) contended that the Optimizing Lifelong Health Through Therapeutic Recreation Model was still essentially individualistic. She stated:

> One of the tensions the field of recreation and leisure as a whole faces, and TR particularly, is reconciling how to think about concepts (i.e., leisure, recreation, development, health) that have been defined in North America and western cultures as essentially psychological and/or biological phenomena/processes with the fact that humans are social beings. Individual experiences cannot be separated from sociocultural and historical contexts. (p. 112)

While the Optimizing Lifelong Health through Therapeutic Recreation Model needs to work out the relationship among the individual, culture, and society, it is still an improvement over other models.

While a couple of therapeutic recreation service models demonstrate promise in terms of cultural appropriateness, most of them are culturally encapsulated. Yet models of practice always have the potential to change. Clearly, the next step in the evolution of therapeutic recreation service models is to become more informed and more inclusive of cultural differences. This will require extensive and penetrating analysis into the conceptual construction of models from a multicultural context. Creating culturally attuned conceptual materials for the construction or renovation of models will be a difficult challenge. Yet it is the only acceptable alternative if therapeutic recreation wishes to serve all people.

Summary

Therapeutic recreation practice models build on and contribute to conceptual principles of therapeutic recreation and explain the components of service delivery. The differences in the practice models are mainly derived from the profession's long-term identity crisis as to whether the field exists primarily as a medical specialty or as a human service field oriented to recreation and leisure. This conceptual difference was found to have ramifications in terms of goals and service components.

In this chapter we reviewed and critiqued five practice models. The number of models that have been developed to conceptualize and explain services has grown over the past decade. The increased number of models speaks to the growth of our profession. Continued examination of practice models in relation to therapeutic recreation practice, research, and philosophy is an ongoing endeavor.

Recommended Readings

Austin, D. R. (1998). The Health Protection/Health Promotion Model. *Therapeutic Recreation Journal, 32*(2), 109–117.

Dattilo, J., Kleiber, D., and Williams, R. (1998). Self-determination and enjoyment enhancement: A psychologically-based service delivery model for therapeutic recreation. *Therapeutic Recreation Journal, 32*(4), 258–271.

Dieser, R. B. and Peregoy, J. J. (1999). A multicultural critique of three therapeutic recreation service models. *Annual in Therapeutic Recreation, 8,* 56–69.

Freysinger, V. J. (1999). A critique of the "Optimizing Lifelong Health Through Therapeutic Recreation" (OLH-TR) Model. *Therapeutic Recreation Journal, 33*(2), 109–115.

Mobily, K. E. (1999). New horizons in models of practice in therapeutic recreation. *Therapeutic Recreation Journal, 33*(3), 174–192.

Peterson, C. A. and Stumbo, N. J. (2000). *Therapeutic recreation program design: Principles and procedures.* Boston, MA: Allyn and Bacon.

Stumbo, N. J. and Peterson, C. A. (1998). The Leisure Ability Model. *Therapeutic Recreation Journal, 32*(2), 82–96.

Van Andel, G. (1998). TR Service Delivery and TR Outcome Models. *Therapeutic Recreation Journal, 32*(3), 180–193.

Wilhite, B., Keller, M.J., and Caldwell, L. (1999). Optimizing lifelong health and well-being: A health enhancing model of therapeutic recreation. *Therapeutic Recreation Journal, 33*(2), 98–108.

Section

Theoretical Aspects of Therapeutic Recreation Programming

Whether creating a program for a group of participants or developing a care plan for an individual client, therapeutic recreation specialists use the steps in the therapeutic recreation process to guide their actions. The specialist begins with assessment of client interests, strengths, and weaknesses. Assessment is followed by planning, implementation, and evaluation. In recent years there has been growth in the technical aspects of practice, as is evident in publications that provide examples of assessment tools and content for leisure education programs (burlingame & Blaschko, 1997; Stumbo, 1992). Therapeutic recreation specialists are challenged, however, to explain why they prefer one assessment tool or counseling approach over another. To answer these challenges, therapeutic recreation specialists must possess knowledge of the theories that guide practice. The theoretical underpinnings of therapeutic recreation practice are thus presented in Section Two.

Chapter 5 discusses the importance of using formal assessment procedures. Several assessment paradigms are examined in terms of how human behavior is measured. For example, psychometric techniques measure constructs that are not directly observable in clients, such as emotions and dispositions. Behavioral techniques examine observable behaviors such as social skills (e.g., eye contact, initiating conversations). Finally, we review means of establishing the quality of the assessment tools that are used in therapeutic recreation practice.

Chapters 6 and 7 present counseling and learning theories that guide the development of programs that facilitate client growth and change. Readers are encouraged to consider why they would adopt one theory over another when designing programs and how each theory influences leaders' behavior. Chapter 7 provides a basic understanding of learning theories.

One of the main goals of therapeutic recreation is to help people to make successful returns to their communities. Chapter 8 presents information on principles of and barriers to recreation inclusion. Several models of including people with disabilities into community leisure programs are also reviewed.

Section Two concludes with a chapter on program evaluation. Program evaluation allows practitioners to examine the effectiveness, efficiency, and ethical aspects of therapeutic recreation practice. More specifically, program evaluation can be used to assess the effectiveness of interventions in helping clients to change. Such examination also leads to professional accountability.

Chapter

Introduction to Assessment in Therapeutic Recreation

Virtually any human condition for which change is sought through a human service provider could appropriately begin with an assessment of the current status of a patient or client. For example, if you experienced a fever and found it necessary to see your physician, chances are your visit began with an assessment of your condition. How high is your fever? Do you also have a headache? Are you also congested? Does evidence of an ear infection exist? Answers to such questions lead to an understanding of a condition and point to appropriate forms of treatment.

Therapeutic recreation assessment is similar to this example. In treatment settings, therapeutic recreation specialists encounter clients who present some attribute that is in need of change. In a manner analogous to the assessments conducted by physicians, therapeutic recreation specialists must identify the attributes of the person and collect evidence on the status of the individual with respect to those attributes. Therapeutic recreation specialists collect information on select realms of clients' functioning and integrate those data to develop a treatment plan or evaluate the effectiveness of an intervention.

Therapeutic recreation assessment, however, presents a much more complex challenge than medical assessment and other forms of assessment in human services. Therapeutic recreation specialists serve individuals with a broad array of physical, psychological, and social challenges. The sphere of their service includes not only direct implications of the specific illness or disability, but also vital indirect effects on families, occupations, activities of daily living, and leisure behavior. Further, the factors that are considered to be within the scope of the therapeutic recreation specialist are a function of the treatment model that has been adopted by the hospital, treatment center, or agency with which the therapist is affiliated. One organization might focus its assessment and its services entirely on the functional skills of the patient while another might include attention to a broad array of social, leisure, familial, and occupational outcomes associated with the client's condition (See Chapter 4). Finally, the scope of instruments available for assessment is much better developed for physicians and for other human service providers than for therapeutic recreation specialists. Whereas physicians have at their disposal a number of devices ranging from stethoscopes and thermometers to complex, high technology procedures, therapeutic recreation specialists lack tools that can provide insight into recreation and leisure-related concerns and challenges of their clients.

We begin the chapter with a central question: "Why is formal assessment in therapeutic recreation needed?" From there, we examine different "paradigms of assessment," each with its own assumptions about the perspective that the professional should take in understanding his or her clients' challenges and needs. The focus of that section is on two dominant and promising assessment paradigms: the psychometric paradigm and the behavioral paradigm. Two approaches to integrating assessment results are then provided, and the chapter concludes with multicultural considerations and some thoughts on the future of assessment in therapeutic recreation.

Why Is Formal Assessment Needed?

Formal assessment refers to use of standard techniques, procedures, and instruments to generate information about clients to assist in structuring therapeutic recreation interventions. Formal assessment might be contrasted with informal assessment where a therapist uses his or her best judgment. Given this distinction, at least three reasons that formal assessment procedures are needed in therapeutic recreation may be considered. First, a professional mandate exists for formal assessment. The two main accrediting bodies of healthcare organizations in the United States, the Commission on Accreditation of Rehabilitation Facilities (CARF) and the Joint Commission on Accreditation of Healthcare Organizations (JCAHO), both specify that assessment is the first step in patient care for all disciplines.

As important as professional mandates are, an even more significant reason for providing formal assessments in therapeutic recreation is that, *appropriately used,* they vastly improve the quality of service that therapeutic recreation specialists can provide to clients. Formal assessments can provide rich insight into clients' recreation and leisure-related needs within the context of their illness, disability, or social circumstances. Assessment results also provide important insight into the effectiveness of interventions. Armed with such knowledge, the therapeutic recreation specialist is prepared to adjust his or her approach and, hopefully, provide services that are more effective in bringing about desired change.

Formal assessments are also invaluable in helping therapists avoid certain biases that may affect their interpretation of clients' needs and circumstances. Examples of these biases are the *confirmatory bias,* the *availability heuristic,* and the *representativeness heuristic* (Achenbach, 1985). The confirmatory bias describes our human tendency to selectively attend to information that is supportive of our beliefs. Suppose, for example, that your upbringing had convinced you that most problems that youth face today are a result of dysfunctional families. If the confirmatory bias were operative, as you worked with a youth who was exhibiting problems with substance abuse, you would take special note of all cues that pointed to family dysfunction as being the root of the problem. You might note, for example, that the youth's parents are occasional drinkers, that the father travels extensively on business, and that the parents have intense discussions about financial concerns of the family. The confirmatory bias would also encourage you to ignore the fact that the youth has three siblings who are highly popular and successful honor students who are apparently not using substances, and that the intense discussions that the parents have are reasoned, respectful, thorough, and trust-promoting. Your bias toward family origins of personal dysfunction would thus lead you to selectively attend to information that supports your beliefs while ignoring disconfirming evidence.

The availability heuristic is another device that frequently leads to inappropriate assumptions about human conditions. This results from our tendency to understand new phenomena that we encounter in terms of some information that is readily available to us, perhaps as a result of recent exposure to that information. You may recognize the availability heuristic under its more common name, the "medical student disease." The availability heuristic is well represented by this "disease." As medical students engage in rigorous study of the symptoms of particular diseases a number of those students may begin to notice the presence of those symptoms within themselves. Students begin to believe that they have actually acquired the condition about which they are learning. If the condition being investigated involves a slight fever and an itchy skin, students may report feeling a slight fever and itchy skin. The availability heuristic could also be operative in the example of the troubled youth. A therapeutic recreation specialist might, for example, have recently read a book or journal article on the etiology of substance abuse that points to the significance of self-esteem as a factor. With the recency or availability of that information, the specialist might become overly attentive to the self-esteem status of the troubled youth. In focusing on self-esteem, the therapist might overlook more fundamental issues that require resolution in order to address the substance abuse problem.

A third example that has potential to create bias in understanding clients' challenges is the representativeness heuristic. According to Achenbach (1985) this heuristic has to do with the probability that "A [is] representative of X, in the sense of being typical of X" (p. 23). More concretely, if a given client is a member of a particular group known or assumed to have a high incidence of a particular condition, the therapist might inappropriately conclude that any member of that group has the condition. Thus, if a therapeutic recreation specialist believed that substance abuse is widespread among inner-city youth, the representativeness heuristic would tend to lead the therapeutic recreation specialist to expect substance abuse among *any* inner-city youth with whom the specialist worked.

Although biases such as these will be present to some degree in any assessment context, formal assessment provides a first line of defense against making inappropriate judgments about clients' characteristics or circumstances. With formal assessment techniques, individuals use standard approaches that yield scores and observations that are less susceptible to bias. These standard approaches may involve formal questionnaires, structured or semistructured interviews of clients and significant others, behavioral observations, or rating scales. The approach used should follow from the ethical position that the organization endorses, and the position that the agency takes on the scope of considerations that are relevant to assessment and intervention. In the following section, we explore different assumptions and assessment procedures that follow from those assumptions.

Assessment Paradigms

A *paradigm* is a conceptual model used to represent or explain the relevant features of a complex phenomenon. Achenbach (1985) illustrated four paradigms that are relevant to assessment of child psychopathology: medical, psychodynamic, psychometric, and behavioral. A brief discussion of the medical and psychodynamic paradigms follows. The psychometric and behavioral paradigm are addressed in greater depth due to the prominence of those models in therapeutic recreation assessment. A summary of the paradigms discussed here is presented in Table 5.1.

The medical paradigm establishes that assessment is directed at identifying an "underlying organic abnormality" (Achenbach, 1985, p. 30) based on signs and symptoms that patients present. Typically, a medical assessment begins with an interview and physical examination, followed up with laboratory tests,

Table 5.1 Summary of Major Assessment Paradigms in Human Services

Paradigm	Focus/Assumption	Key Concepts	Examples of Assessment Techniques
Medical	Organic dysfunctionality	Organic dysfunctionality Illness	Clinical interviews Medical diagnostic devices
Psychodynamic	Repressed energies create dysfunctions	Projection Associated techniques Construction techniques Completion techniques Choice or ordering techniques Expresive techniques	Word association Create stories about pictures Interpret pictures Sentence completion Sociodramatic play Ink blots
Psychometric	Underlying Constructs	Constructs Reliability Validity Content-related evidence Criterion-related evidence Construct validity	Objective tests Questionnaires Rating scales Structured interviews
Behavioral	Observable Behaviors	Molar behaviors Molecular behaviors Continuous recording Discrete recording Time sampling Whole interval recording Part interval recording Momentary recording Interrater agreement	Counts of incidence Measurement of duration Examination of patterns

x-rays, and other high-technology diagnostic procedures as necessary. Based on the results of these procedures, physicians produce a diagnosis that represents their best judgment of the nature of the organic abnormality (e.g., cancer, broken bone, pneumonia). With knowledge of the nature of the organic dysfunction, physicians are in a position to plan and implement appropriate medical interventions.

Despite the fact that its origins lie in the medical paradigm, the psychodynamic paradigm includes different assumptions about the nature of human disorder. The psychodynamic paradigm is founded in Freudian theory. Freud assumed that thoughts that are not considered acceptable may be repressed to subconscious levels, such that individuals are not aware of those thoughts. Despite the lack of awareness, the thoughts remain active at a level at which the individual is not conscious. The energy associated with these repressed thoughts is assumed to lead to a variety of dysfunctions. Freud's approach to assessment followed directly from these assumptions. He encouraged his patients to engage in methods of "free association" through projective techniques. The method involves exposing individuals to ambiguous stimuli (e.g., words, phrases, pictures, ink blots) and encouraging them to project their own thoughts upon those stimuli. Through such procedures, repressed thoughts are thought to be "projected" on the ambiguous stimuli and the therapist is thus able to identify repressed thoughts and the associated tensions or energies. These repressed thoughts and their associated energies then become the focus of psychodynamic therapy.

Projective techniques have three essential characteristics (Rabin, 1981): (1) ambiguity of the stimulus to which people respond; (2) the response involves "quantity, variety, and richness" (p. 11) with little attention to the purpose for which the data will be used; and (3) the task of the assessment specialist is particularly complex, requiring a sound understanding of the multidimensional nature of the data. Techniques widely recognized as being consistent with these characteristics include association techniques (e.g., What word comes to mind when you see the word play?), construction techniques (e.g., creating stories about pictures), completion techniques (e.g., completing sentences), choice or ordering techniques, and expressive techniques (Rabin, 1981). Through responses to such tasks, therapists may make inferences about characteristics of their clients and about repressed energies that may be creating psychological challenges.

Although many leaders argue that therapeutic recreation services ought to be directed at alleviation of specific medically based conditions, therapeutic recreation assessment techniques have not evolved from either the medical paradigm or the psychoanalytic paradigm. Perhaps the discipline could benefit from greater attention to development of assessment and treatment approaches within these paradigms. For example, in play therapy, therapists observe patterns and themes of sociodramatic play of children (e.g., creating stories using dolls, action figures). Through those themes, therapists derive an understanding of repressed tensions and energies that may be operative in clients' lives. Similarly, many therapeutic recreation specialists have found techniques that involve selection and interpretation of photographs or artifacts from clients' personal histories to be very useful in understanding critical factors in people's lives. With such techniques, clients may, for example, indicate their preference from among collections of photographs and then proceed to explain how the photographs selected represent something significant in their lives. As illustrated by these examples, therapeutic recreation settings do provide environments rich in the ambiguity necessary for projection. Lacking, however, are therapeutic recreation specialists who are well-schooled in the psychodynamic theories that underlie effective, efficient, and appropriate use of such methods.

In the following sections, two paradigms that have played a more prominent role in therapeutic recreation assessment, the psychometric paradigm and the behavioral paradigm, are introduced.

Psychometric Paradigm

The *psychometric paradigm* assumes that it is useful to explain human behavior in terms of characteristics of people which are not directly observable, called constructs. Constructs are inferred from observable behaviors. For example, we infer a person is sad when we see him or her frown and cry. Categories of constructs include feelings, emotions, moods, beliefs, knowledge, opinions, dispositions, and attitudes. Examples of specific constructs within these categories include self-concept, self-esteem, self-confidence, social skills, alertness, happiness, intrinsic motivation, commitment to recreation, recreation experience preference, and boredom.

These diverse constructs have several common elements. First, they pass the tests of intuitive importance and ubiquity. For example, we often hear or read about experts who are concerned about low self-esteem of at-risk youth or self-concept problems of students who have been exposed to tragic failures. We speak of being bored or inspired by a lecture or a classroom experience. Our friends' behaviors are described through the use of constructs when we refer to them as being moody, optimistic, energetic, thoughtful, compassionate, loving, or rude.

A second important characteristic of constructs is variability; different people seem to have different quantities of constructs. Thus, we may speak of people as being highly optimistic or highly pessimistic, socially outgoing or socially introverted, involved or detached to an activity, or well-informed or not well-informed on an issue.

Another element common to constructs is that they have no real, tangible existence. A surgeon cannot extract an attitude, belief, emotion or any other type of construct from a person and subject it to evaluation through a microscope, x-ray, or the like. How then, is it possible to assess clients' status with respect to constructs? Or, in the context of assessment, if constructs have no real existence, how is it possible to make judgments about such matters as clients' activity preferences, degrees of independence in leisure, levels of motivation, distress, joy, or any other construct?

Constructs are analogous to ghosts. Like ghosts, constructs have no real, tangible, objective existence. Those who believe in ghosts must infer their existence based on observable changes in the environment. If a heavy object seems to float across a room, if chains rattle in a haunted house, or if a blood-curdling scream pierces a quiet evening, one might assume that a ghost is present. Similarly, if we observe a person chatting happily and enthusiastically moving from conversation to conversation at a party, we might interpret that behavior as the construct "extroversion." The chatting person at the party is assumed to have high quantities of that construct whereas the less visible individual quietly but intensely involved in a lengthy discussion with another individual might be assumed to have a lesser degree of extroversion. Thus, like with ghosts, we assume the existence of constructs based on behavior that we actually observe in an environment.

It is important in this process to rely on theory and sound reasoning to define the construct of interest and identify appropriate component parts. The necessity for such construction follows from the fact that constructs have no tangible existence. In the absence of physical properties, it is necessary to create symbolic models. As such, we might define a construct named "self-concept" as having elements of self-esteem (Am I a good person?), physical self-image (How does my body appear to others?), and social self-image (What do other people think about me socially?).

Let's review two more examples of constructs. What comes to mind when someone mentions "boredom?" In day-to-day usage, that term typically suggests a transient state that most of us experience while, for example, we wait in line or endure an eternal lecture of our least popular professor. In this sense, boredom comes and goes and is usually of little consequence relative to our overall healthiness, sense of well-being, or satisfaction with life. But other constructions of boredom are also possible. Iso-Ahola and Weissinger (1990), for example, constructed a leisure boredom construct in which boredom was defined as a relatively stable characteristic of individuals' lives. Iso-Ahola and

Weissinger's construction of leisure boredom describes the extent to which different people are *typically* bored with the leisure portion of their day-to-day lives. That construction of boredom has been shown to have highly significant relationships to such variables as depression, substance abuse, and educational success and aspiration (Iso-Ahola & Crowley, 1991; Weissinger, Ellis, Compton, Rosegard & Haggard, 1996; Widmer, 1993). Similarly, the Leisure Diagnostic Battery (Witt & Ellis, 1989) defines "perceived freedom in leisure" as a general set of beliefs that people hold about their ability to successfully participate in forms of recreation of their choice. Perceived freedom commonly refers to a more transient and fleeting state in which one is relatively free from constraints in day-to-day life (Mannell, Zuzanek & Larson, 1988). A key to understanding this characteristic of constructs is that no "right" or "wrong" definition exists. Rather, in working with constructs, it is absolutely essential to understand how the construct is being defined.

Measurement of Constructs

Measurement is the systematic assignment of numbers to represent the exist-ence, level, magnitude, frequency, or quantity of a characteristic. As applied to constructs, measurement is no different from measuring our foot length and width when we buy shoes or our waistlines when we buy pants. Like foot size and waist girth, when we measure constructs, we are attempting to assign a number to represent how much of a construct is characteristic of a particular client. How strong, for example, is client X's preference for participation in natural resource-dependent forms of recreation? To what extent does client Z experience interpersonal constraints with respect to leisure (Crawford, Jackson & Godbey, 1987)? Constructs, however, are far more elusive than feet or waistlines. The challenge of measuring constructs is of sufficient complexity that a branch of social science has emerged to address the issue specifically. That branch is "psychometrics" and people who are involved in test develop-ment are often referred to as "psychometricians." Two of the more prominent challenges faced by psychometricians are reliability and validity. These chal-lenges are of central concern to practitioners in therapeutic recreation because they establish the extent to which scores from measurement tools (e.g., tests, questionnaires, scales) can be interpreted as representative of clients' status on a construct. With pants and shoe sizes, the results of our measurement are readily evident; the pants are too big, too little, or a good fit. How, though, do we know if a measure of, say, preference for natural resource-based recreation fits a particular client? Psychometric theory addresses this problem.

How Is It Possible to Measure a Construct?

Please reconsider a question that was posed in the previous section of this chapter: "If constructs have no real existence, how is it possible to make judgments about such matters as clients' activity preferences, degrees of independence in leisure, levels of motivation, or any other construct?" The answer was that we make inferences about the existence, level, magnitude, or frequency of a construct through systematic recording and interpretation of behaviors that we actually observe. Measurement of a construct, therefore, involves collections of observations of behaviors and interpretation of those behaviors. In many cases, these behaviors involve marking responses to questions on scales that we create. Three questions from Iso-Ahola and Weissinger's (1990) sixteen item Leisure Boredom Scale, for example, are as follows:

> For me, leisure time just drags on and on.
> Leisure time is boring.
> I do not have many leisure skills.

1	2	3	4	5
strongly disagree	disagree	neutral	agree	strongly agree

In response to each question, examinees circle a number to show the extent to which they agree or disagree, ranging from 1 (strongly disagree) to 5 (strongly agree). A fundamental assumption of one of the dominant measurement theories within psychometric theory (classical test theory) is that the underlying construct influences examinees to respond in particular ways. Consistent with this assumption, if I am an examinee with a high level of leisure boredom, that construct will influence me to circle the number "5" for each of these three items. Similarly, if you are an examinee who is low in the leisure boredom construct, you would be expected to circle "1" in response to each of these three items. Because classical test theory assumes that the construct affects all items equally (Suen, 1990), we can derive a total boredom score by simply summing across the item scores. In the current example, our high leisure boredom examinee would receive a score of 15 across the three items and our low leisure boredom examinee would receive a score of three across those items.

This process is summarized graphically in Fig. 5.1 (p. 126). Leisure boredom is represented by a circle, which signifies it is a construct that is not directly observable. Leisure boredom is assumed, however, to directly influence our responses to the three items depicted in the figure. Those items are represented with a different symbol, a rectangle. The effect of the construct in the circle on each item in the rectangles is assumed to be constant; we expect each examinee to have similar responses to all items that measure leisure boredom.

A variety of paper-and-pencil tests are used to generate the sets of behaviors needed to make psychometric inferences. Students readily recognize the traditional true-false and multiple-choice examinations. Essay scores may also be used to measure a construct related to academic achievement. Measures of attitudes, beliefs, intentions, moods, and the like often follow some variation of the "strongly agree" to "strongly disagree" format above. Other approaches within the psychometric paradigm include rating scales (Cronbach, 1990; Ellis & Niles, 1989; Kloseck & Crilley, 1997), direct observation of behavior in controlled situations, and structured interviews.

Quality of Measurement in Psychometric Theory: Introduction to Reliability and Validity

Any assessment tool within the psychometric paradigm may be evaluated in terms of reliability and validity of inferences from scores produced by the instrument. Manuals that accompany psychometric tests invariably include significant attention to these criteria as well as attention to important matters of scoring, interpretation, and use. It is vital that therapeutic recreation specialists have a basic understanding of reliability and validity. A brief introduction to each follows. For a more thorough treatment of the topic, a variety of excellent resources are available (Cronbach, 1990; DeVellis, 1991; Messick, 1989; Suen, 1990).

Reliability

Reliability is a statistical tool that provides an estimate of the consistency of scores on an assessment tool. Reliability is a necessary (but not sufficient) consideration in determining the extent to which a valid inference may be made about an individual's status on a construct, based on test scores. To develop an understanding of the reliability concept, consider a set of scores that might be collected by administering a test to a group of clients. If you administered the three items from the Leisure Boredom Scale above to one hundred people, all one hundred examinees would probably not get the same score. Some would have higher scores, some would have lower scores, and most would have

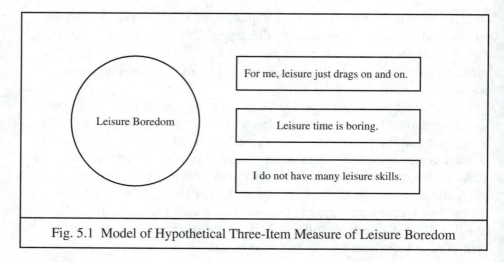

Fig. 5.1 Model of Hypothetical Three-Item Measure of Leisure Boredom

scores clustered around an average. In other words, scores would *vary* across these 100 examinees. You would thus find *variance* in your set of 100 scores. Variance is a highly desirable feature of tests. In assessment, the therapist may be attempting to identify people with extreme scores (e.g., high self-esteem, low leisure boredom) in order to identify clients in greatest need of focused intervention. If scores from a particular test or measurement tool do not vary across examinees, that test or measurement tool does not provide the therapeutic recreation specialist with useful information in planning a treatment or intervention.

However, all variance among a set of scores is not desirable. Scores can vary across examinees because people differ in the quantity of a construct that they possess or because they marked answers differently for reasons unrelated to the effects of the construct. In test theory, a construct is assumed to affect examinees' responses to create "true score" variance across a set of scores. Variance that results from the effect of all factors other than the construct is called "error variance." Statistically, the sum of true score variance and error variance is the total variance of the scale. In evaluating psychometric tests and understanding the concept of reliability, it is vitally important to distinguish between true score and error of variance.

Most students can readily understand the distinction between true score and error variance when they consider the last multiple-choice exam that they took. As you read each question, many factors influenced your response. For many questions, you probably had some feel for the correct answer. That "feel" represents the effect of the construct. Across all test takers that day, that "feel" created true score variance in the total test scores. But many other factors also affected examinees' responses as well. Certain questions were unclearly worded. Some questions had more than one "correct" answer, depending upon the perspective from which the item was viewed. Some examinees had more incentive or desire to succeed than others. Some examinees were ill, some were unmotivated, some were fatigued, some were uncomfortable in the seating provided, some were experiencing test anxiety, some lacked needed reading ability, some were lucky, some were distracted by recent events in their personal lives, and some were disadvantaged culturally. All of these factors played an important role in determining the final scores that were obtained. Collectively, these factors other than the construct created "error variance" in the set of test scores.

Given a set of test scores from a group of examinees, the "total variance" is the sum of true score variance and error variance (see Fig. 5.2, p. 128). The ideal assessment tool would generate only "true score" variance, equal to total variance, with error variance being zero. Test construction specialists work to approximate that goal through careful wording of items, including sufficient numbers of items to represent the construct, standardizing the administration protocol, and many other methods. In practice, however, all tests contain some degree of error variance and hopefully some degree of true score variance. The ratio of true score variance to total variance defines the *reliability* of the test. The larger the portion of the variance that is true score variance, the smaller the error, and the larger the reliability. Reliability values range from 0 (no true score variance) to 1.0 (100% true score variance). These "reliability estimates" or "internal consistency estimates" are routinely published in manuals that accompany psychometric measurement tools. For assessment purposes, a useful rule of thumb is that a measure should have a reliability of no less than .85 (85% true score variance, 15% error variance).

If you have developed an insatiable appetite to learn more about reliability, additional readings can readily be found in books and journal articles on educational and psychological tests and measurement and in methods of behavioral research. Through such readings, you will find that numerous approaches have been taken to the actual calculation of reliability estimates. Among these are approaches that require the test to be administered on two occasions (test-retest method), methods that require creating two tests from the single test (split-halves methods with Spearman-Brown "prophecy" corrections), and methods that estimate true score and error based on patterns of similar responses to the items on the test (e.g., Cronbach's alpha, standardized item alpha, and Kuder-Richardson formulas). Although these approaches seem to be radically different, all of them share the common purpose of estimating the fraction of total variance in the measure that is true score variance.

Validity

Validity may be defined as an "integrative judgment of the appropriateness of inferences made about constructs based on scores from tests" (Suen, 1990, p. 134). Reliability plays an essential role in determining the appropriateness of inferences. In the absence of "true score variance" (i.e., reliability = 0), an inference about an individual's status on a construct would be inappropriate. But reliability alone is not a sufficient condition for establishing validity; it is very possible for a measure to be developed that produces large "true score" variance in a set of scores, but fails to provide an appropriate measure of the intended construct. Such a measure would likely provide a reliable measure of some construct, but not the construct that was intended.

As an extreme example of how this might occur, consider the following questions from a true-false examination on the content that we have just explored:

1. Examinee fatigue is an example of a factor that produces error variance in a set of test scores.
    True   False

2. Reliability is the percentage of true score variance in a set of scores.
    True   False

An individual who carefully read this chapter would likely recognize that the response "true" would be correct for both of these items. If one point was given

Person	Observed Test Score	True Score	Error
Kim	15	13	+2
Kyle	12	11	+1
Karen	12	8	+4
Kathryn	5	8	-3
Kent	4	6	-2
Karla	8	4	+4

Fig. 5.2 True Score and Error

for each correct response, that reader would receive two points for this two-item test. A less careful reader might record a response of "false" to either or both of these questions and thereby receive a score of 1 or 0 on the two item test. Now, assume that the two-item test is perfectly reliable (which it is not). Would it be appropriate to make an inference about our examinees' leisure boredom based on these two items? Of course not! These items are designed to measure knowledge of material in a section of this chapter. They produce a reliable test, but they do not produce scores from which it is appropriate to make an inference about examinees' leisure boredom. Reliability is necessary but not sufficient for valid inference making.

How then, can we determine the extent to which inferences from test scores are appropriate? To do this, we may draw on various *construct-related* sources of evidence (see Table 5.2, p. 131). Although the measurement litera-ture has identified such types of evidence in a number of categories (e.g., concurrent validity, predictive validity, construct validity, and face validity), these validity checks can be categorized into two principle sources of evidence: content-related evidence and criterion-related evidence (Messick, 1989; Suen, 1990). Content-related evidence of validity is concerned with the extent to which the questions adequately represent the construct of interest. Of concern are the relevance and representativeness of the content. Thus, content-related evidence of validity is present if the questions and components of the test are sufficiently representative of the construct. As a test of leisure boredom, the two-item true-false test above clearly fails the content-related evidence of validity test. The items are not relevant to the concept nor are they representative of the scope of questions that we need to ask to derive an adequate measure of leisure boredom. As a measure of knowledge of assessment, the two-item true-false test also fares poorly. Although the two items are arguably content-relevant, many more items would be needed to provide a good measure of the extent to which you understand the concepts that are introduced in this chapter.

In test development, content-related evidence of validity is assessed by asking experts to review the test in terms of how the construct is "constructed." They examine the definition of the construct, the component parts of the construct, and the wording, clarity, readability, and response format associated with the items. It is important to involve experts who are familiar with theory from which the construct is derived, the population of people with whom the test will be used and with test development in general. In other words, an expert panel comprised of theory experts, population experts, and test develop-ment experts is needed to generate content-related evidence of validity.

Criterion-related evidence of validity requires a different set of procedures. For criterion-related evidence of validity the test developer examines similari-ties between patterns of scores on the new test and scores on tests of similar constructs. Of interest are the correlations between scores on the instrument under development and instruments that have been designed to measure related constructs or variables. A good example of this process is Widmer's (1993) measure of ethical behavior in leisure among adolescents. Widmer sought to develop an "Aristotelian Ethical Behavior in Leisure Scale" (AEBLS) that would be useful in understanding the recreation and leisure behavior of at-risk youth. The construct was created from Aristotle's ethics. Ethical behavior was considered to be based on the following dimensions: intellectual and creative activity, close personal relationships, and moral behavior. Questionnaire items were written representing each of these dimensions and the set of items was reviewed by a panel of experts for content-related evidence of validity. For criterion-related evidence of validity, Widmer reasoned that behaviors involving tobacco use, alcohol use, and illegal drug use were incompatible with two dimensions of the AEBLS: moral behavior and intellectual activity. As such, people whose lifestyles are characterized by ethical behavior as defined by Aristotle would be expected to not be as involved in substance use as people whose lifestyles are characterized by lower levels of Aristotelian ethical behavior. This hypothesis was tested by administering the AEBLS and a self-report questionnaire concerning substance use to a group of adolescents. Consistent with the hypothesis, high scorers on the AEBLS were adolescents who used substances to a lesser extent than low scorers. This study thereby provided criterion-related evidence of validity for the AEBLS.

This discussion is intended to provide a general understanding of the nature of content and criterion-related evidence of validity. Procedures for generating such evidence can become quite extensive, involving sophisticated experiments and statistical analysis. Fundamentally, however, all such efforts center on the conduct of expert reviews (content-related evidence) and scientific investigations (criterion-related evidence) to test hypotheses about relationships between scores on the instrument under development and measures of theoretically or conceptually related constructs and variables.

Case Study: Psychometric Paradigm

Tate and Dieser (1997) provide a case study that illustrates the use of the psychometric paradigm in therapeutic recreation. The case involved a 17-year-old male high school student, Jon, who was receiving treatment for drug addiction. An overdose by a girlfriend at a party had convinced Jon to seek treatment at an outpatient treatment facility. Based on clinical evaluations and the DSM-IV (American Psychiatric Association, 1994), the treatment team at the hospital diagnosed Jon as having polysubstance abuse, moderate conduct disorder, and Attention Deficit Hyperactivity Disorder.

Table 5.2 Validity: Essential Concepts

Definition of Validity: An integrated judgment of the appropriateness of inferences made about constructs based on scores from tests (Suen, 1990)

Sources of Evidence of Validity of Inferences

Source of Evidence	Description	How Obtained
Content-related Evidence	Extent to which test items (or other indicators) are appropriate and adequately representative	Review of content and format by measurement experts, population experts, and theory experts
Criterion-related Evidence	Extent to which scores on the correlation research test are (1) correlated with scores on tests of theoretically related concepts, and (2) not correlated with measures of constructs with which the measure theoretically ought not be related	Tests of the construct of interest are administered to representatives of the population of interest, along with measures of variables that theoretically should be related and measures of variables that theoretically should not be related to the construct of interest
Construct-related Evidence	Extent to which scores may be interpreted as measures of the constructs that are of interest. All evidence of validity is construct-related	Integrative assessment of content-related and criterion-related evidence of validity

Extensive leisure assessment using many different methods followed the preliminary diagnosis, including review of historical data, interview, direct observation, and standardized testing. Historical data revealed considerable resentment at being "forced to go" places and a "very controlling" mother. The interview results also revealed issues related to control. Jon reported that his "free time [was] not really free" and that "the only time that [he felt] free was when [he was] high [on substances]." Recorded comments during structured observation also revealed five loss of control statements made in a span of five minutes.

Standardized testing was also used to assess perceptions of freedom and control. Instruments used were the Children's Nowicki-Strickland Locus of Control Scale (CNSLCS) (Nowicki & Strickland, 1973) and the Leisure Diagnostic Battery (LDB) (Witt & Ellis, 1989). The CNSLCS includes 40 yes/ no questions. Individuals with high scores believe that their efforts, abilities, and initiatives can bring about change in their circumstances whereas low scorers believe that changes result from luck or fate. Reliability coefficients ranging from 0.43-0.70 have been reported for the CNSLCS. Criterion-related evidence of validity is provided through statistical relationships that have been found between CNSLCS scores and measures of academic achievement and perceived competence.

The LDB includes 95 items comprising five separate scales as well as a total score. The five component measures are perceived leisure competence, perceived leisure control, leisure needs satisfaction, depth of involvement in leisure experiences, and playfulness. Individuals who score high on the instrument are assumed to have a stable set of beliefs that promote a sense of freedom with respect to their recreation and leisure behavior. Reliability coefficients of 0.86 and higher have been reported for the individual scales and a reliability coefficient of 0.90 has been reported for the entire scale. Evidence of validity of inferences that can be made from scale scores includes correlations with locus of control, depression, self-esteem, and attribution style (Morris & Ellis, 1993; Witt, 1990).

Consistent with personal history, interview, and observation data, Tate and Dieser (1997) found strong evidence of low degrees of personal control for Jon through their use of the standardized assessment tools. Both the CNSLCS score and the LDB perceived leisure control scale produced scores indicative of lack of control. In response, a six-session intervention based on self-control therapy was implemented. Session One focused on leisure lifestyle awareness, Session Two focused on "helping Jon resolve leisure behavioral concerns" (p. 263). Session Three involved teaching two relaxation techniques, and Sessions Four through Six focused on assertiveness training, positive reinforcement, modeling, and visualization. Upon conclusion of the intervention, the CNSLCS and the LDB were administered. Results revealed a "large increase" (Tate & Dieser, 1997, p. 263) in Jon's internal locus of control and his perceived leisure control. Jon's overall perceived freedom in leisure score also improved significantly.

Behavioral Paradigm

For a substantial number of clients who may be served by therapeutic recreation specialists, the notion of a construct may not be particularly useful or appropriate. Such clients might include individuals with severe illnesses and disabilities who are unable to respond to psychometric testing strategies, and for whom we could find no evidence of the relevance of certain constructs. In other instances, circumstances demand attention to specific client behaviors that are clearly damaging to the client or to other people who may come into contact with the client. Such might be the case when a client is overly aggressive toward others or when suicidal tendencies are evident. In such instances, the focus of assessment and intervention must be on actual, observable behaviors rather than complex and elusive constructs.

Behaviors may be classified as being molecular or molar. A molecular behavior is a single, well-defined, observable action. For example, an upward curvature at the corners of the mouth describes a smile, a curve of fingers about the hand describes a clenched fist, orientation of eyes toward a communicator describes looking behavior, and teeth clinched around an object other then food represents a molecular perspective on biting. In each of these examples, a single, precisely defined observable phenomenon is described. The behaviors are being considered at their basic, molecular level. Collections of molecular behaviors comprise molar behaviors. As such, aggression might be defined as a circumstance in which an individual clinches fists, strikes another with a body part, and/or yells at another person. Interest behavior might include directing the eyes at a communicator, asking questions, and/or responding in a manner that is appropriate.

A hypothetical case illustrates the focus on observable behaviors. Consider the case of an individual with Alzheimer's disease who attends an adult day-care program. Of interest to the therapeutic recreation specialist is the extent to which this client shows involvement in programs that are provided. The therapist might proceed by defining involvement in terms of specific, observable behaviors. In this case, let us assume that involvement is defined as a molar behavior. Involvement is present when the client (1) directs her eyes on the activity, (2) responds appropriately to questions about her participation in the activity, (3) initiates conversation about the activity, (4) provides comment or information about the activity, (5) smiles or frowns when appropriate to events that occur during the course of the activity, or (6) engages in physical actions required of the activity.

Note that a number of the molecular behaviors within this definition could be more precisely defined. What, in terms of directly observable behaviors, is a smile? What are appropriate responses to questions? What is information? Precise definitions of these terms is necessary for sound measurement of observable behaviors. Given this molar definition of involvement and the associated molecular components, the therapist would select specific observation schedules. In our example, these observation schedules might include sessions from reminiscence, crafts, and pet visitation programs.

Within a particular observation session one can observe the behavior continuously or select sample intervals (Suen, 1990, p. 176). Continuous observation for the entire session provides the most precise measure, but is not always feasible. When continuous observation over the entire session is possible, the therapist may use either real-time or discrete recording. With real-time recording, the therapist records the exact clock time that the behavior is initiated and terminated over the course of the entire session. In our example, if a pet visit occupied a thirty minute period of time, the therapist would observe the client over the entire period and record the clock time of initiation and termination of involvement behaviors. Discrete recording is used to record the number of times that the behavior of interest is initiated during the entire observation session. No attempt is made to measure the length of time that the behavior is present or absent.

Because it may not be feasible to observe a client's behavior over an entire observation session, time sampling procedures are often used instead of real time or discrete recording. With time sampling, particular intervals within the session are chosen, with measurements taken within these intervals. In our example, the therapist might choose intervals of 15 seconds each, beginning on each third minute, for the duration of the activity. Behavior would be measured within each of these 15-second intervals, using one of three approaches: whole interval recording, partial interval recording, or momentary recording (Suen, 1990). If whole interval recording were used, the therapist would record the presence or absence of involvement behavior if that behavior were present during the entire 15-second interval. If partial interval recording was used, the therapist would record the existence of involvement behavior if that behavior occurred during any time throughout the course of the interval. Momentary recording would lead to a situation in which the presence or absence of the behavior was recorded at the last instant of the interval, in our case at the 15-second point of each interval. In each case, a score of "1" would be used to indicate the presence of the behavior and a score of "0" could be used to indicate the absence of the behavior.

Results of an assessment of the hypothetical Alzheimer's client are presented in Fig. 5.3 (p. 136). Observation sessions are represented on the horizontal axis. Three sessions are nested within each day, with one session corresponding to each of the three programs: reminiscence, crafts, and pet visitation. In Chart A, the vertical axis is the number of minutes that the involvement behavior was present, a measure made possible by the "real time" recording of behaviors. In Chart B, the vertical axis is a count of the number of sampled intervals during which the involvement behavior was present, as recorded through either whole interval, partial interval, or momentary recording. In both cases, it is clear that the desired behavior (involvement) is increasing over time. The client seems to be improving, perhaps as a result of the intervention.

Behaviors and Constructs

Although the behavioral paradigm seems to involve a very different set of assumptions than the psychometric paradigm, the difference is a matter of interpretation. When behaviors are interpreted as a sign of a construct, the therapist is working within psychometric theory and concerns of reliability and validity apply. For studies that directly address behaviors, without inference to constructs, the behavioral paradigm is being applied. The relevant issue becomes the extent to which different raters agree on the presence or absence of behaviors. Statistical tools for measuring agreement are described by Suen (1990).

Case Study: Behavioral Paradigm

Williams and Dattilo (1997) conducted a research project that is representative of the behavioral paradigm. The authors studied the effects of a leisure education program on the self-determination, social interaction, and positive affect of four young adults (ages 20–27) with mental retardation. Self-determination was defined in terms of choices: ". . . a discrete act by the participant without prompting from another person and was socially responsible" (p. 247). Social interaction was recorded when a client engaged in one of the following behaviors:

- Faced and spoke to a person with whom no conversation had preceded for at least three seconds,

- Addressed a person by name or a second person pronoun while not facing that person when no conversation had preceded for at least three seconds, and
- Asked a question of another person either facing the other person or using [her or his] name or a second person pronoun when no conversation had immediately preceded for at least three seconds.

Positive affect was defined in terms of smiles and positive vocalizations. Smiles were defined as upward turns at the corners of the mouth and positive vocalizations were laughs, chuckles, giggles, and squeals (p. 248).

The investigators videotaped all four clients during a recreation period and used continuous, discrete recording to count the number of times the behaviors were initiated during each observation session. Observations were made before an intervention (baseline), during a leisure education intervention, and at a follow-up after the intervention. Results of the behavior observation suggested that after the intervention the "frequency of positive affect behaviors was consistently higher than at baseline and at intervention stages" (p. 252).

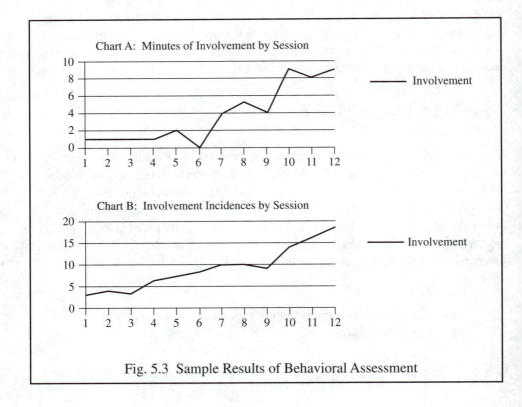

Fig. 5.3 Sample Results of Behavioral Assessment

Multicultural Considerations for Assessment

Like all aspects of therapeutic recreation programming, assessment takes place in a cultural context. Yet among the 35 problems of therapeutic recreation assessment identified by Peterson and Stumbo (2000, pp. 237–238), none explicitly mentions culture. We contend that multiculturalism is perhaps the most pressing improvement needed in therapeutic recreation assessment because of the effect culturally uninformed assessment can have on people's beliefs, values, and ways of life. In particular, validity requires culturally sensitive assessment. For example, therapeutic recreation assessment tends to equate independence with healthy functioning and dependence with dysfunction. But some cultures consider dependence normal and necessary (Blankfield, 1987). Therapeutic recreation assessment also tends to be individualistic. Activity inventories often do not reflect ethnic, gender, or sexual differences. Validity and reliability, however, are just the beginning of the cultural shortcomings in therapeutic recreation assessment.

Ridley, Li, and Hill (1998) conducted an extensive critique of multicultural assessment in the field of counseling psychology. The following are suggestions they made for counselors to consider that are also relevant for therapeutic recreation assessment:

1. *Use emic criteria*: An *emic* approach conceptualizes functioning from the perspective of the individual's culture rather than from an *etic* approach, which stresses external cultural standards. For example, instead of interpreting independence as a universal standard of healthy functioning and dependence as a sign of dysfunction, dependence would be recognized as normal and acceptable in other cultures.

2. *Use standardized instruments in culturally appropriate ways:* Ridley, Li, and Hill (1998) identified a host of common problems, including "bias in test content, inappropriate standardization samples, examiner and language bias, inequitable social consequences, measurement of different constructs, differences in test-taking skills, lack of appropriate norms for various cultures, misinterpretation of test data, and problems in test administration" (p. 836). Standardized assessments in therapeutic recreation, such as the Leisure Diagnostic Battery and the Leisure Competence Measure, must be evaluated for cultural appropriateness. The design and development of future instruments should incorporate cross cultural considerations as standard practice.

3. *Use nonstandardized methods:* Projective techniques, narratives, and journal work have been recommended as nonstandard ways to collect

information that are not as culturally limited as standardized methods. Nonstandardized methods are particularly conducive to therapeutic recreation assessment, because practitioners should be intent on learning where individuals are coming from, including their cultural context.

4. *Use culture-specific instruments:* While culture-specific instruments exist in other fields, such as the *Handbook of Tests and Measurements for Black Populations* (Vols. 1-2) (Jones, 1996), we are unaware of any culture-specific instruments in therapeutic recreation.

5. *Use the Diagnostic and Statistical Manual-IV (DSM-IV) with cultural sensitivity:* Although therapeutic recreation specialists typically do not use the DSM-IV to evaluate clients, they may use it as an assessment resource. Therefore, they should be sure to use the culturally relevant features of the DSM-IV, which includes discussion of cultural variations in disorders, a glossary of culture-bound syndromes, and an outline for cultural formulation.

6. *Assess the client's psychocultural adjustment:* Experts recommend including the following constructs in the assessment process:
   - Acculturation (the incorporation of new cultural patterns into original cultural patterns),
   - Ethnic/racial identity (self-acceptance and acceptance of the social implications of one's ethnic/racial group identity),
   - Biculturalism (ability to function in more than one culture and reconcile for oneself various cultural influences), and
   - Worldview (the perspective people use to interpret their worlds).

7. *Clarify the purpose of assessment:* While the goals and process of therapeutic recreation assessment should be explained to all clients, it is critical when clients are culturally different from professionals. This is especially important where professionals and clients may have different understandings and expectations of assessment.

8. *Conduct a behavioral analysis:* In this case, specific behaviors are targeted and monitored in the individual's environment. This method recognizes the importance of the individual's environment, which includes culture, and avoids the inference of underlying states. It is also subject to the cultural attitudes and values of the individual conducting the assessment, so care must be exercised in using behavioral analysis.

9. *Negotiate the explanatory model:* Because clients and professionals sometimes conceptualize and explain problems in different ways, a discrepancy may exist. This discrepancy needs to be addressed to

reduce misunderstanding and misinterpretation. For example, a therapeutic recreation specialist might consider external locus of control a problem, whereas the client views sharing control with others (external) as a sign of solidarity and health. Also, individuals who lived during the Depression may view leisure as an absolute problem rather than as a way to solve their problems.

10. *Establish credibility:* Clients who are not members of the dominant culture may distrust professionals, seeing them as members of an oppressive establishment. Credibility, therefore, is a necessary condition of assessment.

11. *Validate the client's cultural belief system:* Validation of the client's cultural belief system can increase rapport and encourage discussion from a cultural perspective.

12. *Develop cultural self-awareness:* Self-awareness is a key element of multicultural competence. With respect to assessment, Solomon (1992) stated that professionals "must examine their own prejudices and biases so that assessment procedures can better reflect the reality of clients' experience" (p. 377).

13. *Use a broad-based strategy:* Due to the complexity of assessment, a broad-based approach is recommended. Ibrahim and Arredondo (1986) asserted that "Counselors need to use multisource, multilevel, and multimethod approaches to assess the capabilities, potentials, and limitations of the client" (p. 350).

14. *Use interpreters/translators:* The importance of language to successful assessment should be fully evident. While observing that interpreters can obviously improve communication, Ridley, Li, and Hill cautioned that "miscommunication still can occur if translators are inadequately trained or clinicians are inexperienced in working with the client." (p. 848).

15. *Involve the family network:* Immediate families, relatives, friends, and associates are invaluable resources for cross-cultural understanding, especially for clients from collectivistic cultures.

The recommendations of Ridley, Li, and Hill provide an excellent starting place. Because differences exist between counseling psychology and therapeutic recreation, however, therapeutic recreation must conduct far more inquiry of its own to make assessment multiculturally sound.

Summary

This chapter provided an overview of assessment in therapeutic recreation. Readers were introduced to reasons for formal assessment and to paradigms within which assessment is conducted. Constructs and their measurement were also explored, as well as the measurement of observable behaviors.

Although valuable paradigms exist, very few assessment tool development specialists or well-developed tools for assessment in therapeutic recreation exist. Many of the available instruments were developed by individuals who are not therapeutic recreation specialists for use in settings other than therapeutic recreation. As a result, the quality and integrity (validity) of the assessment is often severely compromised. Additionally, a common error that practitioners make in devising a strategy for assessment is to begin the process with an attempt to find and select measurement tools on the basis of their reported reliability, validity, rigor of development, or popularity. Although the intentions of such individuals are clearly laudable, those efforts are misdirected. Selection of an assessment strategy ought to begin with the question, "What do I (the therapeutic recreation specialist) want to know about my clients?" The best of assessment tool in terms of reliability, validity, or efficiency is of little use if it measures constructs or behaviors that are irrelevant to the intervention or purpose of treatment.

Finally, it seems appropriate to comment on the future of assessment. In educational measurement, a revolution seems to be occurring in terms of assumptions about testing and about how testing can be accomplished. Using a relatively new set of assumptions called "item response theory" test development specialists are creating computer software that administers tests in a fraction of the time required of conventional tests and produces more precise estimates of individuals' abilities (Hambleton, Swaminathan, & Rogers, 1991; van der Linden & Hambleton, 1997). This "adaptive testing" represents a radical departure from dominant assumptions in psychometric theory. Another frontier for therapeutic recreation assessment is to apply item response theory to the therapeutic recreation context in an attempt to develop assessment approaches that are more efficient and precise.

Recommended Readings

DeVellis, R. F. (1991). *Scale development: Theory and applications.* Newbury Park, CA: Sage Publications.

Horvat, M. and Kalakian, L. H. (1996). *Assessment in adapted physical education and therapeutic recreation* (2nd ed.). Madison, WI: Brown & Benchmark.

McDonald, R. P. (1999). *Test theory.* Mahwah, NJ: Lawrence Erlbaum Associates.

National Therapeutic Recreation Society, (1989, October). *The best of assessment.* Ashburn, VA: National Recreation and Park Association.

Stumbo, N. (1997). Issues and concerns in therapeutic recreation assessment. In D. Compton (Ed.), *Issues in therapeutic recreation: Toward the new millennium* (2nd ed.) (pp. 347–371). Champaign, IL: Sagamore.

Suen, H. K. (1990). *Principles of test theories.* Hillsdale, NJ: Lawrence Erlbaum Associates.

Chapter 6

Therapeutic Recreation Interventions: The Integration of Counseling Theories

The helping relationship is one of the key factors in the therapeutic recreation process. The desire to help, however, is not enough. Knowledge and skills are paramount in creating an effective helping relationship. In this chapter we will discuss theories, strategies, and skills typically used by the therapeutic recreation specialist to establish helping relationships (Egan, 1994; Okun, 1997).

Helping Relationships

Helping relationships differ from the social relationships we have with friends and family in that they focus solely on the needs of the client. Social relationships meet our personal needs, such as the needs for understanding and companionship. In contrast, a helping relationship is intended to assist clients to achieve specific goals related to their health, leisure, and quality of life, not to meet the personal needs of the professional. Of course, helping others to achieve their goals can be immensely gratifying, meeting such needs as accomplishment and service to others. Nonetheless, even though personal needs may be satisfied through professional helping relationships, they must not take priority over helping clients to meet their needs.

The benefit of establishing an effective helping relationship with a client can be observed during the assessment process. Ideally, the development of a trusting relationship during assessment will enable the client to discuss openly the barriers he or she is experiencing in leisure. A helping relationship may also facilitate clients' full participation in group activities and their willingness to process their experiences with the therapeutic recreation specialist and other group members.

The characteristics of an effective helper include positive attitudes towards other people (Combs, 1989; Okun, 1997), self-awareness (Combs, 1989; Corey, 1996; Egan, 1994; Okun, 1997), knowledge and skill (Corey, 1996; Okun, 1997), and ethical behavior (Okun, 1997). In the following sections we will explore the characteristics of an effective helper under the three broad categories of (1) self-awareness, (2) knowledge, and (3) communication skills.

Self-Awareness

Effective helpers are aware of their own attitudes, values, and feelings, particularly in relation to self-growth, relationships, and leisure and recreation. Awareness of attitudes and values allows a helper to recognize how his or her values may influence interactions with clients. For instance, when devising a client's care plan, awareness of one's own values can enable the helper to honor the values of the client. Consider a scenario in which a therapeutic recreation specialist is working with a client who shares that he has difficulty finding people with whom he can play pickup basketball. The client belongs to an ethnic group different from that of the therapeutic recreation specialist. The therapeutic recreation specialist recently moved and was faced with making new friends and finding companions for leisure pursuits. As such, the therapeutic recreation specialist began to explain how she had found friends and suggested the client follow the same steps. Although the therapeutic recreation specialist may have had good intentions, she did not acknowledge how her life situation was different from that of the client. As a therapeutic recreation specialist becomes self-aware, he or she is better able to differentiate his or her experiences from the client's. This self-awareness allows a therapeutic recreation specialist to better understand a client and use strategies that are in line with the client's cultural background.

Knowledge

To function as effective helpers, therapeutic recreation specialists must possess knowledge of helping relationships, counseling theories, leisure theory, and the therapeutic use of recreation activities. Knowledge and skill in developing helping relationships with clients is important for fostering positive experiences and promoting therapeutic outcomes for a client. Knowledge of leisure theory and therapeutic recreation is what sets a therapeutic recreation specialist apart from professional helpers in other fields, such as social workers or mental health counselors. Therapeutic recreation specialists must also understand the influence of cultural variables on social relationships and leisure behavior. Lastly, therapeutic recreation specialists must understand the ethical principles underlying therapeutic recreation practice and how to apply those principles in their day-to-day practice.

Communication Skills

This section examines the basic elements of verbal and nonverbal communication skills. Mastering these skills requires considerable practice and further study. We recommend that students take specialized courses in communication and counseling as part of their degree program.

Nonverbal communication skills are used by the therapeutic recreation specialist in virtually all interactions, including assessment interviews, implementation of groups, and general interactions with clients following group activities. To highlight the role of nonverbal communication in interpersonal relationships, consider the nonverbal communication of a teacher who creates a positive learning environment in the classroom. How does he or she communicate interest in learning and learners via body posture? Eye contact? Facial expression? General appearance? In contrast, what is the nonverbal communication of a teacher who expresses lack of interest in learning or learners? Our personal experiences and observations can assist us in better understanding the impact of nonverbal communication. Consider the following means of nonverbal communication in Western culture that are used to express interest and are essential in establishing relationships with therapeutic recreation clients from similar cultural backgrounds. When listening to clients we use eye contact to communicate attentiveness and facial expressions to communicate understanding of what is being said. Direct eye contact, rather than looking aside or to the floor, typically expresses interest as well as comfort in relating to another person. Eye contact also conveys that one is carefully listening to the other person. Closely aligned with eye contact is the use of facial expressions. Facial expressions allow us to express joy at seeing another person, puzzlement or difficulty in understanding what another is saying, or sadness in response to what a client is relating.

A handy device for enhancing our attending and listening skills is contained in the acronym SOLER (Egan, 1994). "S" stands for sitting squarely, rather than slouching or turning away from a client. "O" stands for open posture, sitting comfortably and relaxed. "L" stands for leaning appropriately forward to indicate careful listening of what is being stated and felt by a client. "E" stands for using eye contact to communicate attentiveness. Lastly, "R" stands for relaxed listening, without tense posture or fidgeting that communicates disinterest or discomfort. When a helper uses SOLER, individuals perceive that the helper is listening, which increases the effectiveness of the helping relationship (Egan, 1994).

Verbal communication skills are central to establishing and building relationships with clients. Several verbal responses have been recognized as particularly effective, including minimal verbal response, probing, paraphrasing, reflecting, clarifying, checking out, interpreting, confronting, and summarizing (Austin, 1997; Okun, 1997).

Minimal Verbal Response: Listening to another person, we frequently encourage him or her by nodding and saying "uh-huh," "yeah," or "yes." These behaviors constitute a minimal verbal response that indicates to the client attentive listening on the part of the therapeutic recreation specialist. For example:

> Client: I feel so tense when I have to go downtown. It's so hard.
> TRS: Yeah. (nods head while speaking)

Probing: While interacting with a client, the therapeutic recreation specialist may use an open-ended statement to facilitate his or her elaboration on a topic. Probes enable the therapeutic recreation specialist to gain more information. Instances of probing verbal responses include, "Tell me more about your experiences at the community recreation center" or "Let's talk about the outing you went on." For example:

> Client: There is never enough time! Last weekend I was cleaning and working when I realized that I just wanted to sit out in the sun.
> TRS: What happens when you think, "I just want to go sit in the sun?"

Paraphrasing: Paraphrasing involves rewording the content of a client's statement. For example, a client says "That picnic was really fun—we even had marshmallows!" In response the therapeutic recreation specialist rephrases the client's comments by saying "What a good day, including the treats!" Paraphrasing allows a client to hear what he or she just said in different words that do not directly parrot what the client said. It conveys understanding on the professional's part and may promote elaboration on the client's part. The therapeutic recreation specialist typically attempts to paraphrase in fewer words than the client's comments, which encourages clarity and concreteness.

Client:	I have to learn how to play better before I sign up for basketball at the rec center.
TRS:	You'd like to improve your game.

Reflecting: Reflecting responses permit the therapeutic recreation specialist to convey back to the client the feelings that he or she is expressing verbally and nonverbally. Again, this type of verbal response allows the client to hear the feelings he or she is expressing and to further explore those feelings. The client might say "I hate him—he teases me constantly!" The therapeutic recreation specialist would attempt to reflect back the client's emotion by stating "He makes you angry." As another example:

Client:	It was great fun. We just laughed and laughed.
TRS:	It sounds like you had a good time together.
	-OR-
	What a great time!

Reflecting responses are especially important because they help to uncover feelings. Understanding how we feel about a situation is often the initial step toward comprehending its dynamics and deciding what action to take. Getting in touch with one's feelings is an important part of coming to understand the situations we constantly encounter in life, and reflecting responses can be an effective means in encouraging the exploration of feelings.

The expression, "It sounds like . . . ," is associated with reflecting responses. Overuse of this expression may result in responses that sound mechanical and superficial. We encourage students to use the expression, "It sounds like . . ." as they learn reflective responding. Once the skill has been learned, reflective responses can be expressed in ways that sound more natural and authentic. For example, instead of saying to an adolescent "It sounds like you're excited to go to the concert!" you could simply say "Man, you're excited!" The latter sounds more natural and is more effective at conveying emotion.

Clarifying: At times, a therapeutic recreation specialist may be unsure or have difficulty understanding what a client is stating. Accordingly, a therapeutic recreation specialist may use clarifying responses, such as "I'm not sure I understand what happens when you hang out with your friends; could you explain it to me again?" As another example:

Client:	When she is around I just keep a low profile.
TRS:	I'm not sure I understand what happens when she is around. Could you explain it to me?

Checking Out: Checking out provides the therapeutic recreation specialist the opportunity to ensure that he or she understands what a client is saying. The therapeutic recreation specialist may use statements such as "It sounds like you don't like team sports such as volleyball or basketball; do I have that right?" Another example:

Client:	I love bowling, but they are so much better than me. So, I keep practicing whenever I can.
TRS:	So you want to bowl as well as they do before you join the league; do I have that right?

Clarifying and checking out responses are sometimes confused. Clarifying is used to reduce confusion. Checking-out is used to explore a hunch or impression the therapeutic recreation specialist may have that has not been explicitly expressed by the client. In the example of a clarifying response, the therapeutic recreation specialist was not clear about what another individual was doing that caused the client to keep a "low-profile." Hence, she sought more information for the sake of clarity. In the example of a checking-out response, the therapeutic recreation specialist suspects that what may be preventing the client from joining a bowling league is her lack of confidence. Therefore, the therapeutic recreation specialist explores her hunch by using a checking-out response.

Interpreting: Occasionally a therapeutic recreation specialist may add something to what a client is saying. For example, a client may say "My family is all excited about me coming home from the hospital. They have all sorts of plans and projects in mind for me. I don't know if I want to do that stuff." The therapeutic recreation specialist might interpret the client's words by saying "It seems like all of the commotion makes you anxious." Another example:

Client:	It's scary to think about going back to where I used to hang out.
TRS:	Are you afraid that you may relapse?

The key element regarding interpretation is that it adds something to the communication. In the preceding example, the client had said nothing in reference to relapsing. The therapeutic recreation specialist contributed it on the basis of his interpretation of what had transpired in the course of their discussion. Interpretation is a more advanced skill, and should only be used after the therapeutic recreation specialist has established trust and rapport with the client.

Confronting: A confronting response is useful for dealing with issues and inconsistencies in what a client says or does. For example:

Client::   I just don't want to do it. I can't explain it.
TRS: We've been through this before. I think you know why.

Confronting responses can help a client move from a helpless state to one of understanding his or her thoughts and behaviors. Confronting responses are an advanced skill and should only be used by experienced specialists.

Summarizing: Summarizing is frequently used at the end of a discussion or session with a client. The therapeutic recreation specialist will verbally summarize the key points covered in the session, including both the content and affect expressed by the client. The strength of summarizing is that it communicates that the helper has listened to the client and provides a final opportunity for the client to clarify aspects of their discussion. The following example occurred at the end of a discussion between a therapeutic recreation specialist and a client:

TRS: Well, we have hit on all sorts of topics. I know that you have a meeting in ten minutes. Let me see if I can summarize what we have talked about. We discussed what you like to do when you have time with your family, some of the frustration you feel when plans don't work out, and how difficult it is to get your teenagers to keep you informed of their schedules.
Client: We did talk about a lot of things.
TRS: Did I cover all the issues we discussed?
Client: Yeah, I think so.
TRS: Okay. We'll talk again. We may also talk about some of these challenges in the Leisure Awareness Group.

Verbal and nonverbal communication skills are essential for developing helping relationships with clients. Readers should observe trained individuals using these helping skills, and should practice them through role-plays and other structured activities. In Table 6.1 (p. 151) you will find an exercise for practicing the use of appropriate verbal responses.

Multicultural Considerations for Communication

Working in a multicultural society, therapeutic recreation specialists must understand cross-cultural communication. The following discussion, which relies on Ting-Toomey's (1999) excellent study, is intended to alert readers to some of the major aspects of multicultural communication.

Language is shaped by culture and reflects each culture's worldview. For example, in some Asian cultures the family name comes before the personal name, indicating the priority given to family. One of the most evident examples of the power of language in Western culture is gender bias, a form of linguistic sexism. Ting-Toomey (1999) observed that "the male generic language in English—terms such as *chairman, fireman, businessman*, or *mankind* used in Western society—tends to elevate men's experience as more valid and make women's experience less prominent" (p. 99). In order to empower women, gender-neutral language should be used.

Another example of the power of language that should be familiar to students of therapeutic recreation is how negative terminology devalues persons with disabilities. Words like "spaz," "psycho," "retard," "cripple," "invalid," and "deaf and dumb" signal that persons with disabilities are less able, less worthwhile, and less deserving (see Datillo & Smith, 1990). Understanding language, therefore, reveals much about culture and society, including beliefs, values, attitudes, social status, and power relations.

Knowing how language is expressed verbally and nonverbally across cultures is also vital. Ting-Toomey (1999) discussed five cross-cultural verbal communication styles:

1.   *Low-context and high-context communication*: In low-context communication meaning is expressed directly and explicitly. High-context communication involves indirect talk, status-orientation, self-efface-ment, and the significance of nonverbal behavior, including silence. According to Sue and Sue (1990), while the United States is generally a low-context culture, "Asian Americans, Blacks, Hispanics, American Indians, and other minority groups in the United States . . . emphasize [high-context] cues" (p. 58). They further noted that where in United States culture a single invitation followed by a "yes" or "no" often suffices, other cultures expect several invitations as a sign of being sincere. The therapeutic recreation specialist who believes he or she is respecting autonomy by accepting an initial refusal from a

Table 6.1 Communication Skills: Verbal Responses

In response to each of the following client statements, take on the role of the therapeutic recreation specialist and provide the requested verbal response. Following completion of this excercise, share your responses with several classmates and discuss the accuracy of the statement in relation to the verbal response requested.

Client: The birthday party was great fun. We even had balloons and sang Happy Birthday!

> Minimal Verbal Response:

> Paraphrasing:

Client: I have always hated crafts. All that tedious stuff!

> Interpreting:

> Confronting:

Client: That was a waste. I'm never going back to that place.

> Probing:

> Clarifying:

Client: At first it is okay. Then after a while I feel sorta tired, like I don't fit in.

> Reflecting:

> Checking out:

client to attend a program may instead be failing to show sincerity by not inviting the individual several times. In short, words alone do not account for the whole message in high-context communication. Nonverbals and shared understandings about the situation must be included to get the whole message.

2. *Direct and indirect verbal interaction styles*: In the direct verbal style statements are forthright in intention and tone. In the indirect verbal style statements are more veiled and nuanced. Westerners tend to be more direct, while Chinese are less forthright.

3. *Person-oriented and status-oriented verbal styles*: Person-oriented verbal styles stress informality and the suspension of roles. Status-oriented verbal styles are more formal and stress power differential. Americans tend to be more informal and casual in communication, whereas Japanese are generally more formal.

4. *Self-enhancement and self-effacement verbal styles*: Self-enhancement encourages communication about one's abilities and achievements, while self-effacement stresses modesty. Ting-Toomey (1999) noted that "While a moderate self-enhancement verbal style is reflective of many Western individualistic cultures, a self-effacement verbal style is reflective of many Asian collectivistic cultures" (p. 109). In light of the difference in verbal styles, consider the following example. Attribution theory, in which individuals attribute personal success to their abilities, is recommended in therapeutic recreation as a way of building locus of control and perceived competence. A person from a culture that favors self-effacement, however, might consider personal attribution too self-enhancing or conceited. A therapeutic recreation specialist, therefore, would need to modify his or her intervention to suit the individual's cultural style.

5. *Silence*: Silence performs a variety of functions in communication, and in certain cultures is desirable, expressing respect or social position. Generally, European Americans prefer talk, while Chinese Americans prefer silence. Accordingly, the activity environment characteristic of therapeutic recreation, in which people can be constructively silent if they wish, may be a welcomed alternative to talk-oriented Western interventions.

Several areas of nonverbal behavior are vital to understanding cross-cultural communication, including proxemics, haptics, chronemics (Ting-Toomey, 1999), and kinesics (Sue & Sue, 1990).

Proxemics studies interpersonal space. What one culture considers invasive another culture treats as appropriate. In terms of personal space, Arabs, who favor a distance of 9-10 inches, consider European Americans, who prefer a distance of about 20 inches, cold and aloof. Conversely, European Americans generally find the personal space favored by Arabs as rude and invasive.

Haptics examines touch behavior as communication. In Arab and Latin American cultures, males linking arms is a friendly and common practice. In the United States, physical contact between males is rare, though not between women. Ting-Toomey (1999) explained "while Chinese view opposite-sex handshakes as acceptable, Malays and Arabs view contact by opposite-sex handshakes as taboo" (p. 130). Because contact is inherent in some recreational activities (e.g., dance) and has therapeutic applications (e.g., trust circle) therapeutic recreation specialists need to be well versed in the cultural implications of touch.

Chronemics explores people's understanding of time. Cultures are organized around two basic temporal patterns, monochronic and polychronic. Clock time, appointments, segmentation, task orientation, and an achievement-oriented tempo characterize monochronic time. Conversely, polychronic time is more situational, flexible, simultaneous, experiential, and relationship-oriented. Imagine the difficulty a practitioner would face reconciling the mechanical, task-oriented precision of managed care (monochronic) with the temporal orientation of a client who disdains scheduled appointments, wishing instead to relate with others at an unhurried pace (polychronic).

Kinesics refers to bodily movements associated with communication, such as facial expression, posture, gestures, and eye contact (Sue & Sue, 1990). Eye contact, for example, is typically considered a positive interpersonal behavior in Western culture. Conversely, lack of eye contact is often interpreted as passive and uninterested. In some non-Western cultures, however, avoiding eye contact is considered proper. Young people, for example, are expected to avoid eye contact with older persons as a sign of respect for their authority. Some cultures are not demonstrative, believing that controlling strong feelings is indicative of maturity and wisdom (Sue & Sue, 1990). On the other hand, being emotionally demonstrative is normal in other cultures.

The importance of cross-cultural communication cannot be overstated. Acting on our knowledge multicultural communication "signals our desire to understand, respect, and support the other's cultural identity and way of communicating—and to do so with sensitivity and mindfulness" (Ting-Toomey, 1999, p. 141).

Counseling Theories

Counseling theories provide explanations of behavior, feelings, and cognition, as well as strategies for change. The following section discusses four prominent counseling theories that are used in therapeutic recreation practice: existentialism, person-centered, behavioral, and cognitive-behavioral.

As a therapeutic recreation specialist gains knowledge of the various counseling theories, it is important that he or she selects a theory that fits his or her beliefs about human behavior and behavior change. For instance, some theories are based on the tenet that specific behavioral change leads to changes in health and lifestyle (behavioral theory). Other theories suggest that changes in perception alter the way one experiences life (person-centered theory). If we apply these two different belief systems to a leisure education program, it becomes apparent how the integration of a counseling theory into a therapeutic recreation program will influence content and process. In the first case, with the emphasis on behavior, the therapeutic recreation specialist may initially engage the client in skill development sessions and specific recreation groups. Following that, the client will receive positive reinforcement from the therapeutic recreation specialist to strengthen development of healthy behaviors. In the second case, with the focus on attitudes and feelings, the therapeutic recreation specialist will involve the client in one-on-one and group sessions addressing perceptions regarding leisure. Such sessions will be followed by the client being able to make decisions regarding his or her use of leisure. These brief scenarios exemplify how counseling theories provide grounding and direction for therapeutic recreation interventions.

The counseling theories presented in this section—existentialism, person-centered, behavioral, and cognitive-behavioral—include discussion as to why an individual displays dysfunctional behavior. For each theory, the principles regarding the client-therapist relationship and techniques that promote change in clients are also presented. Examples of the application of the theory to therapeutic recreation practice are also provided. As you read this section, we encourage you to consider how well each of the theories fits your understanding and view of human behavior. You may find it helpful to think about how each theory explains why problems in human functioning occur and the methods for fostering change. Furthermore, consider the application of each theory in therapeutic recreation. Following the presentation of each counseling theory, you will have the opportunity to apply each theory to two therapeutic recreation scenarios presented in Table 6.2, page 156.

Existentialism

Existential therapy provides a philosophical approach to working with clients as they experience the struggles inherent in human existence (Corey, 1996; May & Yalom, 1995). Existentialists explore issues of meaning, isolation, and death. As individuals struggle with existential issues (e.g., death, freedom, isolation, meaninglessness), they question the basic reasons for their existence. People who are able to explain "why" they exist are thought to be able to handle the struggles that occur in life. As stated by Nietzsche: "He who has a why to live for can bear with almost any how" (Frankl, 1992, p. 121).

The ultimate existential issues that people deal with are death, freedom, isolation, and meaninglessness. Each of these concerns produces tension and anxiety. Tension occurs as one wishes to continue to live while recognizing that *death* is the inevitable end point of life. Consideration of *freedom*, how to free oneself from external structures to make responsible decisions in line with internal standards, may also lead to feelings of tension and anxiety. For example, a student whose parents want him to major in business may feel anxious as he struggles to free himself from the external expectations of his parents when he declares philosophy as his major. The acknowledgment of *isolation*, that one is ultimately alone in the world, also results in feelings of anxiety for many people. Feelings of isolation are heightened, for example, when a woman with a terminal illness recognizes that no matter how many intimate people exist in her life, her departure from life will be done alone. The final existential concern, *meaninglessness*, speaks of the struggle facing individuals as they consider what aspects of life provide meaning given the knowledge that they are ultimately alone in life and in facing death. A woman who has lost her spouse may express a sense of meaninglessness in her life. As part of the struggle with meaninglessness she may begin to consider roles other than spouse (e.g., friend, mother, teacher, painter, quilter) that provide meaning, identity, and purpose in her life.

Anxiety and tension are thought to be normal responses to dealing with existential concerns (May & Yalom, 1995; Yalom, 1980). Frankl (1992) posited that tension is an essential ingredient in mental health. Some individuals, however, experience neurotic anxiety in response to dealing with existential concerns. Neurotic anxiety limits one's ability to act and lessens his or her creative energy (May & Yalom, 1995). Existential psychotherapists work with clients to address the reasons for their existence, including aspects of life that are meaningful.

Table 6.2 Individual and Group Therapeutic Recreation Scenarios

---

Scenario A: Mike is 19 years old and currently an inpatient in a psychiatric unit. He has been depressed and resistant to attending any group activities. Yesterday he refused to go on the afternoon unit outing, stating that no one likes him and he has no friends among the other patients. You are the therapeutic recreation specialist who is working with Mike. For each of the three counseling theories, consider how you would approach Mike. Specifically, what would you say?

Scenario B: Self-Determination in Leisure (Dattilo and Murphy, 1991). You have developed a leisure education program to enhance participants' self-determination in leisure. The plan for the first session includes a goal, behavioral objectives, content and process.

GOAL:
Demonstrate knowledge of the importance of personal responsibility for leisure participation.

BEHAVIORAL OBJECTIVE:
Upon request, client will state four possible reasons why personal responsibility for leisure is important with 100% accuracy on three consecutive occasions.

LEARNING ACTIVITY:
Content: We must take personal responsibility to learn the skills that are required for leisure participation. On the board I have listed six different activities. We are going to list the skills that we would need to learn for each one. Then, we will discuss why it is our responsibility to develope these skills if we want to participate in these activities.

Process: Explain the activity. Write the activities on the board and leave space for skills to be recorded under each activity. List activities appropriate for the participants. Some possible activities include: swimming, gardening, playing volleyball, bowling, walking, playing softball.

Debriefing Content: How can lack of skills prevent us from participating in recreation activities? How can we take responsibility and learn skills needed to experience leisure? If we can learn the skills needed to particpate in a desired recreation activity are we more determined to participate in an activity? If not, why? What could happen if we do not take responsibility to learn leisure skills?

Debriefing Process: Conduct debriefing using questions listed above. Encourage all participants to respond to at least one of the questions. For each counseling theory, consider how it may be incorporated into the content, process, or both. Revise/rewrite the program plan and highlight statements or directions that represent the specific counseling theory.

Existential psychotherapy provides a framework of the concerns to be addressed in therapy. The four ultimate concerns of death, isolation, freedom, and meaninglessness are thought to be the causes of client suffering. Techniques specific to existential psychotherapy have not been developed or identified.

Many therapists draw on other counseling theories for specific techniques as they explore existential concerns with a client.

Victor Frankl developed a form of existential therapy called "logotherapy." Frankl was a psychiatrist who survived the Nazi concentration camps of World War II. In the first half of his book, *Man's Search for Meaning*, he shares his experiences as a prisoner in a Nazi concentration camp and how he sought meaning in such a dehumanizing, brutal environment. Upon entering the camp, Frankl had a book manuscript confiscated by the guards. Consequently, much of his energy was directed at finding paper scraps on which he wrote down his thoughts, observations, and theories pertaining to existential therapy.

Logotherapy is presented in the second half of *Man's Search for Meaning*. Logotherapy focuses on the discovery of personal meaning in one's life. The intent is to move clients from a state of boredom, an "existential vacuum," to being able to identify aspects of life that provide direction, challenge, and personal meaning. The therapist cannot create or identify meaning for a client. Rather, the role of the therapist is one of "widening and broadening the visual field of the patient so that the whole spectrum of potential meaning becomes conscious and visible" (Frankl, 1992, p. 115). Meaning is thought to emerge from work, life experiences, personal relationships, and one's attitude towards the inevitable aspects of suffering encountered in life.

Use of Existential Therapy in Therapeutic Recreation

Recreation activities have the potential to provide meaning and a sense of identity for participants (Richter & Kaschalk, 1997). For example, a young woman who takes up painting may start to identify herself as a "painter" and find meaning in the self-expression of painting. A therapeutic recreation specialist drawing from existential therapy is concerned with the meaning and identity that clients experience in recreation activities.

Richter and Kaschalk (1997) identified the therapeutic recreation specialist as the only member of the medical treatment team who is concerned with clients identifying activities that are motivating and affirming of their abilities. The therapeutic recreation specialist is seen as the existential therapist on the treatment team. "The therapeutic recreation specialist is the professional who can help people realize that what remains when they face disability and treatment is a life worth living." (Richter & Kaschalk, 1997, p. 87).

In therapeutic recreation practice, Murray (1998) used journal writing to create existential outcomes (e.g., meaning, identity) for adults with physical disabilities. For Kimberly, one of the clients Murray worked with, journal writing "became an existential outcome where she revitalized her biography as a woman with an amputation" (Murray, 1998, p. 278). The importance of reflective writing in Kimberly's search for meaning is evident in the following excerpt from her journal:

> I was tryin' to explain the part of my life that was goin' on so I drew the pictures to make it more real. Making the journal . . . Helped me to look at and think about things . . . It made me think more . . . it made the time go faster . . . Writing and drawing gives you something to do . . . I kinda noticed the nurses sayin', 'What has she been doin' in her little workshop [bed]?!!' because I had ink all over the sheets . . . I couldn't even sleep when I was in the hospital [making the journal], I don't know what you call it, something flowing! . . . it gave me somethin' else to do besides sit around and mope . . . It was therapeutic. (Murray, 1998, p. 278)

Journal writing provided Kimberly with the opportunity to think about and deal with her amputation. Journal writing became part of her identity as she noted staff watching her work in the journal. From an existential therapy framework, the importance of therapeutic recreation interventions lies in the sense of meaning and identity that emerges from the experience. The scenarios from Table 6.2 further our understanding of the link between existential therapy and therapeutic recreation practice.

Scenario A. Mike has refused to go on the outing that is planned for this afternoon. You enter the common day area to join Mike where he is sitting. Mike looks up and says: "Guess you heard that I don't want to go out." Drawing from existential therapy, what might you say? How would you handle this interaction with Mike? Here is how one therapeutic recreation specialist approached the interaction.

Mike:	Guess you heard that I don't want to go on the outing.
TRS:	Yes, that is what the nursing staff said. What is going on?
Mike:	Well, I was hanging out with Rob, but he went home. I don't know anyone.
TRS:	Have any of the folks going on the outing been in group therapy sessions with you?
Mike:	Well, yeah. But I don't hang out with them. I don't like doing things unless I know them . . . I feel sorta like I don't fit in.
TRS:	Are there other times that you have felt this way?

Mike:	Yeah, I sorta felt that way when I came here.
TRS:	How did you and Rob get to know each other?
Mike:	We started playing cards at night and just hanging out.
TRS:	Did you feel comfortable with Rob right away?
Mike:	Well, once we started playing cards we just had fun.
TRS:	So doing something together helped you out as you got to know Rob. Many people talk about feeling sorta uncomfortable or lonely when they first spend time around people they do not know. But I think you have a good idea—doing something with other people can let you get to know them. Maybe going ahead on the outing will let you get to know some new folks. You may not feel so lonely afterwards.
Mike:	Yeah, I guess so.

Scenario B. An important component of existential therapy is client responsibility. Clients are encouraged to seek and define meaning for themselves in activities and relationships. The Self-Determination in Leisure group activity addresses the responsibility one has for learning leisure skills. A therapeutic recreation specialist drawing on existential therapy when developing the group activity may ask each participant to identify three recreation activities that are meaningful in his or her life, rather than listing six recreation activities for the group to discuss. This would allow each participant to further investigate meaningful recreation activities and the responsible actions that allow participation. Therefore, the content of the group activity may be as follows:

TRS:	We must take personal responsibility to learn the skills that are required for leisure participation. For each of us to consider our responsibility for engaging in recreation that is meaningful to us, I would like you to write down three recreation activities that are important in your life. We will then discuss the activities and how we are responsible for our participation.

Therapeutic recreation specialists who draw from existential therapy are concerned with having clients discover meaningful activities in their lives. For example, in the first scenario, the influence of existential therapy is evident in the way the therapeutic recreation specialist talks with Mike about feelings of loneliness in groups and the actions he can take to develop meaningful connections to other people. In the second scenario, the therapeutic recreation specialist asks clients to identify recreation activities that are personally meaningful and discuss their responsibility for maintaining participation in such activities.

Person-Centered Therapy

In the 1940s Carl Rogers began developing and writing about a counseling theory known today as person-centered therapy. Until his death in 1987 he actively worked as a counselor and studied the role of the counselor in creating a therapeutic environment that would foster clients' growth. Rogers' view of people and their potential for change and growth draws from humanistic psychology. He believed that people possess an innate ability to grow, develop, and seek self-actualization. In the process of growth, people are viewed as struggling with several basic questions. In the words of Carl Rogers:

> It seems to me that at the bottom each person is asking, 'Who am I, really? How can I get in touch with this real self, underlying all my surface behavior? How can I become myself?' (Rogers, 1961, p. 108)

The person-centered therapeutic process is designed to allow people to discover and develop their "real selves." The ways of experiencing life that are frequently displayed by real people include an openness to experience, the ability to tolerate ambiguity, and a lessening of rigidly held beliefs. Real people demonstrate trust in themselves and draw on an internal sense of evaluation to guide their behavior. Ultimately, the real or authentic person strives to live each moment fully. An example is Tom, who is a teenager out with friends on a Saturday night. Tom and his friends become bored and decide to do something exciting. When the group begins to talk about spray painting graffiti on the headstones in the city cemetery, however, Tom reflects on his need for excitement along with options with which he is comfortable. Since Tom is not interested in spray painting public property, he suggests that the group consider going swimming in the park lake. Such an activity would be fun and would not cause any damage to public property. As is evident in this example, an individual who has evolved according to Rogers' theory will be able to reflect on his or her own needs and interests.

Professionals who adopt a person-centered approach strive to create an atmosphere that fosters client movement towards living an open, real life. Person-centered therapists typically demonstrate three attributes that create an atmosphere of growth: (1) congruence, (2) unconditional positive regard, and (3) empathic understanding.

Congruence occurs when an individual is genuine and open to how he or she is feeling in the moment. A therapeutic recreation specialist is congruent when his or her actions and feelings are in accord with each other. A genuine person is congruent in word, emotion, and deed. This quality in turn creates an authentic environment that encourages the client to seek congruence and genuineness in his or her life.

Consider interactions you have had with an individual who has not been congruent. For example, have you ever sought assistance from a faculty member who says he or she would be glad to discuss an issue with you and then rushes the conversation, continually looking at the clock? The lack of congruence does not create an environment conducive to discussion of an issue or problem. Congruence fosters a sense of connection between a client and therapist and provides the client the opportunity to encounter fully how he or she feels and thinks, seeking a life characterized by genuineness and consistency.

Unconditional positive regard is expressed by displaying a warm and accepting attitude. A client is accepted completely rather than conditionally. A therapeutic recreation specialist may display unconditional positive regard for a client when discussing a client's difficulty in engaging in recreation during free time over the weekend. For example, a therapeutic recreation specialist and a client may have agreed on a number of activities the client would engage in on a Saturday. During their next leisure education session the client reports that he felt tired over the weekend and the thought of calling friends was overwhelming. Unconditional positive regard may be demonstrated by allowing the client to discuss his weekend experience without being judgmental. In contrast, conditional positive regard would occur if the therapeutic recreation specialist made judgmental statements (e.g., "We can only work together if you abide by my instructions and right now you're not living up to your end of the bargain."). Another example involves a teenager talking about the difficulty she has in spending time with her family. When she becomes frustrated with her family, she begins to make fun of and physically strike out at her younger brother. Although the therapeutic recreation specialist would not condone the client's treatment of her brother, he or she accepts the client as a unique individual capable of making constructive changes. As a result, the therapeutic recreation specialist will not judge the behavior, but will ask the client to discuss her feelings of frustration. Eventually they would explore other means for handling frustration. Rogers suggests that displaying unconditional positive regard permits the client to explore difficult feelings or behaviors, rather than trying to avoid sharing such material in the therapeutic relationship.

Empathic understanding occurs when the therapeutic recreation specialist is able to experience deeply the feelings that the client is expressing. The therapeutic recreation specialist does not judge or evaluate what the client is saying or experiencing, but instead focuses on listening and observing a client to understand fully the client's perceptions. The ability to listen and understand a client allows the therapeutic recreation specialist to acknowledge the client's experiences. In turn, the client is able to better understand him or herself through the process of hearing another person's perception of what he or she is experiencing. Empathic understanding has been described as "walking in the psychological moccasins of the other person." It is the capacity to step into the other person's perceptual world, sensing deeply his or her emotional and cognitive perspective on life.

Use of Person-Centered Therapy in Therapeutic Recreation

Much of Rogers' early work occurred in traditional counseling situations, such as individual or group therapy. As the theory implies, the focus and direction of the therapeutic process lies within the person. Therefore, a therapeutic recreation specialist using the person-centered approach encourages the individual to lead the interaction. For example, following participation in a recreation activity, the client would be asked to discuss his thoughts and feelings. The therapeutic recreation specialist acts mainly as a "mirror," reflecting the client's thoughts and feelings so the client can explore his or her perceptions. Consider the scenarios in Table 6.2 (p. 156).

Scenario A. Mike has refused to go on the outing that is planned for this afternoon. You enter the common day area to join Mike where he is sitting. Mike looks up and says: "Guess you heard that I don't want to go out." Drawing from person-centered therapy, what might you say? How would you handle this interaction with Mike? Here is how one therapeutic recreation specialist approached the interaction.

Mike:	Guess you heard that I don't want to go on the outing.
TRS:	Yes, the nursing staff told me that you had decided not to go.
Mike:	I don't know. I know that I said I'd try it. (silence)
TRS:	Well, that was at the beginning of the week when we talked about some new activities.
Mike:	Yeah, back on Monday I felt pretty good. Rob and I were hanging out together and playing cards.
TRS:	So, when you agreed to go on the outing you were hanging out with other people.
Mike:	Now Rob is gone. It's back to sitting around. No one to hang out with.
TRS:	It sounds like it's sorta hard when there is no one around to hang out with.
Mike:	Yeah. I don't like it when no one is around. Now they're talking about me going home and no one is around at home except at night.

TRS: Going out, either on our outing or back home, isn't always easy. It is different than having Rob around to be there.

Mike: They keep asking me what I will do. I know that they want me to do things, hang out with people. But it is hard. I did talk with Rick, that new kid for awhile. I wonder if he would go on the outing.

TRS: He may. You might want to ask him. Mike, it sounds like right now you feel more comfortable having people to do things with. Think about what you just said: 'I wonder if he would go on the outing.' Seems like asking people to do things helps you to be active.

Scenario B. As the therapeutic recreation specialist implementing a "Self-Determination in Leisure" program, you are considering how to incorporate person-centered therapy into the content and process. One approach may be to consider the debriefing process.

Debriefing Content
- How can a lack of skills prevent us from participating in recreation activities?
- How can we take responsibility and learn skills needed to experience leisure?
- If we learn the skills needed to participate in a desired recreation activity, are we more determined to participate in an activity?
- What could happen if we do not take responsibility to learn new leisure skills?

Debriefing Process
- Conduct debriefing questions listed.
- Encourage all participants to respond to at least one of the questions.

Person-Centered Counseling
- Respond to participants by paraphrasing content or reflecting affect.
- Use responses to ensure people perceive that the TRS understands meanings/feelings. For example, "You felt comfortable going to the weekend softball games once you had tried out your old skills during that practice game."

The person-centered approach enables the therapeutic recreation specialist to respond to a client in terms of where he or she is at that moment. For example, in the first scenario the therapeutic recreation specialist uses reflective and paraphrasing verbal responses to ensure that she understands how Mike feels and communicates her acceptance of his experience. In the second scenario, the therapeutic recreation specialist prepares to use verbal responses to communicate empathy and genuineness. Drawing from person-centered therapy, the therapeutic recreation specialist creates an environment in which the client may express himself or herself. These types of therapeutic interactions move clients towards acceptance of themselves and the ability to live an open life.

Behavioral Approach

Behaviorism views people's behavior as resulting from rewards they receive in daily life. People learn to increase or decrease the frequency of particular behaviors based on positive and negative rewards that they receive in response to the behavior (Chambless & Goldstein, 1989; Nemeroff & Karoly, 1991). Consider the following situations:

> *Situation A*: You are working on a course assignment and realize that you need some questions answered by the instructor. When you stop by his office he informs you that his office hours are over for the day. He stands in the doorway and responds curtly to your questions. As a result of this unsatisfactory interaction, you decide that next time you have a question you will stop by during his posted office hours.

> *Situation B*: You have agreed to baby-sit for your nephew. When you arrive at your brother and sister-in-law's home they tell you that if your six-year-old nephew misbehaves by talking back or refusing to pick up his toys, you should have him take a time-out for three minutes in his room. You ask him to take a time-out when he starts throwing his toys around the family room and refuses to pick them up. During the time-out you peek in his room and observe him playing happily with legos. You begin to wonder how effective this time-out may be; he seems to be having fun and shows no interest in leaving his room.

> *Situation C*: You have a part-time job that ends at 5:00 p.m. three evenings a week. When you leave your job each evening you encounter traffic jams and congestion. One evening you decide to take the longer, less congested route. The longer route is quite

enjoyable. You swing around town nonstop with the windows down and the music blaring. What a great way to end the work day! You plan to use the longer route on a regular basis.

These situations exemplify how we learn from our experiences. Some experiences, such as the interaction with the instructor, shape our future actions. Other experiences that are meant to influence behavior, such as your nephew's time-out, do not appear to be very effective. Knowledge of behaviorism will give us a better understanding of the rewards impacting the behaviors depicted in the three scenarios.

In the early part of the twentieth century a number of psychologists, including Pavlov, Thorndike, and Watson, examined how the environment shaped the behavior of animals and humans (Spiegler, 1983). Their work laid the foundations for psychologists in the 1950s who began to doubt the effectiveness of psychoanalysis as the preferred treatment for individuals with psychological diagnoses. In the 1960s and 1970s there was tremendous growth and development of behavioral therapies. The influence of behaviorism is seen today in the many of the settings where therapeutic recreation specialists are employed. This section will cover basic principles of behavior change and provide examples of the application of the behavioral approach in therapeutic recreation practice.

Traditional behavioral therapies target clients' observable behaviors and do not address emotions or cognitions. The focus of the behavioral approach is to help clients learn new behaviors and revise maladaptive patterns of behavior. The methods of behavioral change are based on principles of classical conditioning and operant conditioning. Classical conditioning emerged from Pavlov's early work (Crider, Goethals, Kavanaugh & Solomon, 1983; Kazdin, 1994), and involves learned or conditioned responses that become paired with reflexive or unconditioned responses. Typically, some stimulus in the environment is used to invoke learning to pair the unconditional and conditional responses. For example, Pavlov noted that hungry dogs responded to food by salivating. Pavlov rang a bell each time he presented food to the dogs. After twelve sessions in which ringing the bell was paired with providing food, the dogs would salivate when they heard the bell even if food was not paired with the bell.

Operant conditioning developed from the work of Thorndike and Skinner (Kazdin, 1994; Spiegler, 1983). Operant conditioning involves increasing or decreasing specific behaviors based on positive or negative rewards. Positive reinforcement is used to increase the odds of the specific behavior being displayed again. Positive reinforcers include primary reinforcers that meet a basic biological need (e.g., food, water) and secondary reinforcers which we learn to experience as rewarding (e.g., money, praise, social interaction). Secondary reinforcers are frequently used in therapeutic recreation practice. For example, when a client displays a targeted behavior of initiating social interaction with another person, the therapeutic recreation specialist might say "You did a great job!" Another example would be a client who is rewarded with a two-hour pass for attending all group activities.

Negative reinforcement involves the removal of something undesirable following display of the desired response. For example, an individual interested in playing in a softball league will submit the application by the deadline in order to avoid being excluded from the league. Another example would be a teenager with a spinal cord injury who decides to participate in an after-school wheelchair basketball league in order to avoid dealing with pressure from peers to use drugs.

The Premack Principle provides further insight into ways that positive rewards operate. Premack found that when individuals were given the opportunity to select a high-frequency behavior as reinforcement for a low-frequency behavior, their engagement in the low-frequency behavior increased (Kazdin, 1994; Spiegler, 1983). For example, a child may participate in after-school soccer games with his friends on a frequent basis. However, he seldom engages in the activity of cleaning his room. Using the Premack Principle, playing soccer would be contingent on cleaning his room. After cleaning his room each day he would be free to play soccer with his friends. According to the Premack Principle, we should observe an increase in the frequency of his cleaning his room because it is reinforced by the reward of playing soccer.

Some behaviorists also use punishment or positive reinforcement withdrawal (Nemeroff & Karoly, 1991). Such tactics include response cost and time-out. Response cost involves taking away a reinforcer when an inappropriate or undesirable behavior is displayed. For example, a client in an inpatient psychiatric unit may have acquired a daily off-unit pass. Upon displaying behaviors deemed inappropriate (e.g., refusing to attend group therapy), the off-unit pass would be revoked. Time-out involves removing a client from a positive environment when he or she exhibits inappropriate behavior. The length of the time out varies depending on the age of the client and policies of the setting. Therapeutic recreation specialists using time-outs must ensure that the time-out environment contains no positive reinforcers such as solitary activities that the client enjoys. If positive reinforcers exist in the time-out environment, the client may seek time-out periods.

Behaviorists draw on a variety of reinforcement schedules when working with clients to increase the occurrence of targeted behaviors (Dattilo & Murphy, 1987a; Nemeroff & Karoly, 1991). A fixed interval reinforcement schedule rewards the first occurrence of the targeted behavior within each timed interval. For example, if the interval schedule is five minutes, then the first time the behavior is displayed during the five minute interval it is rewarded. The behavior will not be rewarded again until its first occurrence in the next five minute interval. A variable interval reinforcement schedule consists of intervals of varying lengths. The first occurrence of the behavior in each interval is rewarded. A fixed ratio reinforcement schedule reinforces the target behavior after a fixed number of occurrences. For example, every fifth occurrence of the target behavior is reinforced. Lastly, the variable ratio reinforcement schedule reinforces the target behavior at a ratio that varies around an average number of occurrences.

The frequency of displayed targeted behaviors is influenced by the type of reinforcement schedule (Nemeroff & Karoly, 1991). Generally, people respond to the fixed interval schedule by emitting the specific behavior at the beginning of the interval and then decreasing the occurrence of the behavior until the beginning of the next interval. The variable interval and fixed ratio schedules generally result in consistent display of the specific behavior. The variable ratio schedule produces the most consistent and highest frequency of specific behaviors. The strength of the variable ratio reinforcement schedule lies in the fact that the individual can never know when the next reinforcement will be given and, therefore, they continue to engage in the behavior that may bring a reward. The use of slot machines provides an excellent example of variable ratio reinforcement schedules (Nemeroff & Karoly, 1991).

Behaviorists draw on several strategies to assist clients to learn new behaviors. A therapeutic recreation specialist will frequently find that a client is unable to perform the target behavior initially. Therefore, it will be necessary to reinforce an approximation of the target behavior. This procedure is called *shaping*. The therapeutic recreation specialist initially reinforces an approximation of the behavior and as the client consistently displays this approximation, the therapeutic recreation specialist then begins to provide reinforcement for a closer approximation of the targeted behavior. For instance, for a client who is working to master the behavior of initiating social interactions, the therapeutic recreation specialist may initially reinforce the client's attendance at a group activity. As the client demonstrates the ability to attend a group activity consistently, the therapeutic recreation specialist may begin to provide reinforcement whenever the client verbally responds to the question posed by another group member. Slowly, over time, the therapeutic recreation specialist and client work towards the client being able to attend groups independently and initiate verbal interactions with other group members.

Another strategy used to assist clients in learning new skills is *chaining*. Many recreation activities require skills that consist of several steps (e.g., taking a turn bowling, kicking a soccer ball). To assist a client in learning these skills the therapeutic recreation specialist will break the skill down into steps. As the client demonstrates ability in one step, the subsequent step will then be added or "chained" to the first step. Initially, demonstration of one step of the skill is rewarded. Over time, rewards are given only when the client demonstrates the ability to carry out several sequential steps of the skill. For example, a client who is learning to bowl may at first be rewarded for releasing the bowling ball down the alley. Systematically, the next step would be for the client to learn to chain together swinging his arm back and then step forward to release the ball. The client would then receive rewards when he completes, or chains together, the swinging of his arm back and stepping forward as his arm swings forward to release the ball.

Use of the Behavioral Approach in Therapeutic Recreation

Research shows that adults with depression engage in few pleasant activities that serve as positive reinforcement in daily life. Adults who engage in a high number of pleasant activities each day report higher levels of affect and lower levels of depression than those who engage in few pleasant activities (Lewinsohn & Graf, 1973; Lewinsohn & Libert, 1972; Wasserman & Iso-Ahola, 1985). Drawing on the findings of Lewinsohn and his colleagues, as well as behavioral principles, Hickman (1992) designed a leisure counseling group for women with depression that addressed engagement in pleasant leisure activities and development of social skills to facilitate involvement in activities. Fifty-two women with depression participated in the program. Each participant was assigned to one of four groups: (a) pleasant activities, (b) social skills training, (c) pleasant activities and social skills training, and (d) relaxation. All of the women, regardless of group assignment, showed significant change in perceived freedom in leisure, depression, and self-esteem. The women who participated in the combined Pleasant Activities and Social Skills Training group had a significantly higher mean level of perceived freedom in leisure than those in the relaxation group. See Table 6.3 (page 170) for an example of one session of Hickman's leisure counseling group that focused on pleasant activities.

Many therapeutic recreation specialists instruct clients on how to use relaxation techniques when faced with a difficult leisure situation. Relaxation techniques are central to systematic desensitization. Systematic desensitization draws from principles of classical conditioning and assists clients in desensitizing their anxiety responses in specific situations (Chambless & Goldstein, 1989; Corey, 1996). Clients who suffer severe anxiety when in the company of a large group of people are believed to have learned their response. Systematic desensitization involves relearning a neutral response when presented with a situation involving a large group of people. Typically, relaxation techniques and guided imagery are used to assist clients in learning new responses to challenging situations. Although therapeutic recreation specialists do not typically conduct systematic desensitization interventions, they do use techniques such as relaxation to assist clients in approaching challenging situations. For example, a therapeutic recreation specialist might employ a relaxation group that instructs participants on relaxation and breathing exercises. They can then apply what they have learned about relaxation to leisure and everyday life in general, including situations that might be stressful.

The scenarios presented in Table 6.2 (p. 156) provide us with another opportunity to consider the application of behavioral approaches to therapeutic recreation practice.

Scenario A: Mike has refused to go on the afternoon outing. You enter the common day area to join Mike where he is sitting. Mike looks up and says, "Guess you heard that I don't want to go out." As a therapeutic recreation specialist drawing from behavioral principles, what might you say? How would you handle this interaction with Mike? Look at how one therapeutic recreation specialist approached the situation.

Mike:	Guess you heard that I don't want to go out.
TRS:	Yes, the nursing staff told me that you had decided not to go. We had agreed that you must attend three group activities on the unit and one outing each week in order to have a weekend pass.
Mike:	I'm sick of doing all this stuff.
TRS:	We can discuss this at Monday's team meeting, but for this week you will not have weekend privileges.

Scenario B: As the therapeutic recreation specialist who implements the Self-Determination in Leisure Program, you are considering how to incorporate the behavioral approach into the content and process. One approach would be to consider adding it to the content at the beginning of the session. Further, you may decide to include a Leisure Action Plan that requires participants to write out leisure plans and indicate the rewards they will receive as a result of carrying out their leisure plan.

Content: "We must take personal responsibility to learn the skills that are required for leisure participation. On the board I have listed six different activities. We are going to list the skills that we would need to learn for each

Table 6.3 Examples of a Leisure Counseling Session*

PLEASANT ACTIVITIES
Session 1: Importance of Pleasant Activities

INTRODUCTION
Introduce class members to each other as they arrive for the first time. Pleasant Activities will be the topic for this eight-week workshop. The purpose of this workshop is to increase your pleasant activities. You may have important issues to discuss and we will try to discuss important issues and we will try to have group discussion that is constructive and specific but the most important part of the workshop is to increase your pleasant activities.

EXERCISE
Hand out pencils and paper.
Write down Twenty Things I Love to Do.
Define pleasant activities. In terms of discretionary time, what do you like to do when you do not have to do something.
Read the 320 activities from the Pleasant Event Schedule (MacPhillamy and Lewinsohn, 1982)
Write next to each activity on your list the last time that you did it.
Put the letter A after the activities you like to do alone; the letter P after activities you enjoy doing with people; and AP next to those you enjoy doing either alone or with people.
Put the letter M next to the activities which cost money.

DISCUSSION
Ask class members what they discovered from activities they love to do. List responses on a chalkboard.
Does a low number of pleasant activities cause us to feel depressed, or does feeling depressed cause us to be inactive?

HOMEWORK
Hand out 3"x5" cards.
Record pleasant activities for the next week.

* Hickman (1992).

one. Then, we will discuss why is it our responsibility to develop these skills if we want to participate in these activities. We will conclude today's session by having each of you develop a personal plan for your leisure this week."

Debriefing Content
- How can a lack of skills prevent us from participating in recreation activities?
- How can we take responsibility and learn skills needed to experience leisure?
- If we learn the skills needed to participate in a desired recreation activity, are we more determined to participate in an activity?

- What could happen if we do not take responsibility to learn new leisure skills?

Debriefing Process
- Conduct debriefing questions listed.
- Encourage all participants to respond to at least one of the questions.

Content
Now I would like each of you to develop a plan for the next week. I have Leisure Action Plan Forms for you to complete. First, you write down the leisure activity that you want to participate in this week. Next you indicate what resources and skills you have that will allow you to participate. Third, you write down when you will participate. Last, I would like each of you to write down what rewards you would gain by taking responsibility for participation.

Process
Provide time for participants to complete the four items on the Leisure Action Plan Forms. Agree on a time to meet next week.

The actions of the therapeutic recreation specialist in each scenario demonstrate the use of behavioral principles. In the first scenario, Mike's care plan listed the groups he must attend to be rewarded with a pass to leave the unit. When Mike did not attend the community outing, his weekend pass was revoked. Scenario A provides an example of positive reinforcement withdrawal. In Scenario B, clients developed leisure action plans that identified the positive reinforcement they would experience as a result of participation in leisure activities. As is evident in the examples used throughout this section, behavior therapy focuses on observable behavior. The use of positive and negative reinforcement serves as a powerful means of increasing clients' engagement in appropriate behaviors and decreasing their engagement in inappropriate behaviors.

Cognitive-Behavioral Approaches

As an outgrowth of the behaviorism of the 1950s and 1960s, a number of psychologists began to consider the interplay between cognition, or how people think, and their behavior (Beck, 1976; Ellis, 1973). The premise underlying cognitively based therapies is that people create their psychological problems because of how they think about events and feelings experienced in daily life. For example, a client may be asked to attend an evening dance. During this event, he does not dance or talk with others. At the end of the evening he tells the therapeutic recreation specialist that he is terrible at social events and feels depressed. The experience of not dancing or socializing was interpreted using old messages such as "People don't like me" and "I am no good at socializing or making friends." As a result of these cognitive interpretations he does not feel good about himself and reports feeling "blue."

Cognitive-behavioral approaches focus on the present, tend to be brief in duration, and involve therapists actively engaging with clients (Corey, 1996). This group of counseling theories is aimed at assisting clients in recognizing maladaptive or irrational thinking, restructuring those thoughts, reengaging in behaviors using new cognitions, and examining subsequent behaviors and feelings. To better understand cognitive-behavioral approaches, we will examine Beck's Cognitive Therapy (CT) Ellis's Rational Emotive Behavior Therapy (REBT).

Beck's Cognitive Therapy

CT focuses on identifying and changing maladaptive thoughts. As a result of altering one's thoughts, individuals will change their behavior and emotional reaction to events or behaviors. A basic tenet of CT is that "to understand the nature of an emotional episode or disturbance, it is essential to focus on the cognitive content of an individual's reaction to the upsetting event or stream of thoughts" (Corey, 1996, p. 337). Beck (1976; 1985) indicates that clients can learn to identify their cognitive content by becoming aware of "automatic thoughts." People are thought to engage in self-talk throughout daily experiences. As they continually reengage in activities they are less aware of their internal dialogues. However, with heightened awareness of the potential impact of such internal thoughts, clients can begin to identify the cognitive content.

Not everyone develops cognitive messages or self-talk that foster maladaptive behaviors or emotions. Beck (1976; 1985) has found, however, that some people tend to engage in a variety of cognitive errors that do foster negative outcomes. Examples of cognitive errors reported by clients include:

- *Selective abstractions*. An individual comes to a conclusion based on an isolated detail of an experience (e.g., "After group this morning some of us stood around talking. Whenever Janie spoke she looked at everyone but me. Janie just doesn't like me. I don't understand.").
- *Arbitrary inferences*. An individual comes to a conclusion that is not based on relevant or supporting evidence. This cognitive error may involve "catastrophizing" or thinking of the worst possible outcome. (e.g., "No one spoke with me at the dance. No one ever likes me; I am always left out. That's never going to change.").

- *Overgeneralizations*. Based on a single experience an individual comes to a general conclusion (e.g., "That dance was terrible. No one spoke to me or wanted to dance with me. I hate groups. I never feel comfortable and it doesn't matter what kind of group it is. I am not attending any more groups, or trying that community recreation thing that you keep talking about.").
- *Personalization*. An individual attributes an event to himself or herself when in reality the event may be related to another factor, such as another person or the environment (e.g., "No one likes me, even that girl who offered me some punch. She couldn't even look at me when she asked." The client attributes this experience to the fact that he is not a likeable person rather than the possibility that the other participant is struggling to learn new interaction skills.).
- *Magnification and minimization*. An individual credits an event with too much or too little importance (e.g., "Yeah, I went to that dance. No one talked with me. Sat around, had some punch some girl offered me, watched people dance. It was terrible, no one spoke to me or asked me to dance." His interaction with the girl who offered the punch is glossed over by the client as he discusses the experience of not dancing or socializing with anyone.).
- *Polarized thinking*. An individual sees events in extreme (e.g., "Since no one asked me to dance, no one likes me.").

When reviewing clients' cognitive self-talk, the therapeutic recreation specialist and client may identify one or more of the cognitive errors reviewed.

The CT process involves three steps. First, clients are instructed to identify their automatic thoughts. Clients are encouraged to identify the thoughts that filter through their minds as an event occurs. Thoughts may take the form of self-talk or visual images. Clients are typically given the following instructions: "Whenever you experience an unpleasant feeling or sensation, try to recall what thoughts you had been having prior to this feeling" (Beck, 1976, p. 33). The second step involves the therapeutic recreation specialist and the client recognizing the cognitive errors within these automatic thoughts. Although the therapeutic recreation specialist may not use the labels for the various types of cognitive errors, it is during this step that the therapeutic recreation specialist and client work together to identify faulty thinking. The therapeutic recreation specialist is active in asking the client about the validity and truth inherent in his or her cognitive messages. For example:

Client: Since no one asked me to dance, I just know that no one likes me.

TRS:	Well, let's think through this. No one asked you to dance. Could there be any reasons other than "no one likes me?"
Client:	That is all I can think of.
TRS:	How long have you been attending the weekly dances?
Client:	You know that was my first weekly dance.
TRS:	Yes. We may also want to consider how many people from the unit went down to the dance.
Client:	Only Sarah. But she knows all those folks from 2 East, so she didn't talk to me until we got back to the unit.
TRS:	So, no one asked you to dance and you did not know anyone except for Sarah. What may be going on here?
Client:	Oh. So you think that no one asked me to dance because they don't know me? I don't know.
TRS:	That may be another way to think about last night rather than "no one likes me."

Lastly, the third step involves reality testing by working with the client to examine the validity of the automatic thoughts. The therapeutic recreation specialist and client may agree on specific activities the client will engage in and evaluate the evidence supporting the cognitive error and subsequent emotions. In the example given above, the therapeutic recreation specialist and client might agree that the client attend the dance again, along with others from the unit, and then reevaluate reasons why he may or may not be asked to dance.

The client-therapist relationship in cognitive therapy draws on the work of Carl Rogers. The cognitive therapist must be genuine and display unconditional positive regard and empathetic understanding for the client. These characteristics, however, are not viewed as sufficient in fostering client change. Client change will occur through the process of the therapeutic recreation specialist and client working together to identify cognitions and reexamine the validity of those cognitions. As a client begins to learn that some of his or her cognitions are faulty, he or she may feel more willing to try out new behaviors. Throughout this process the therapist uses open-ended questions and builds a collaborative relationship with the client (Corey, 1996).

Ellis's Rational Emotive Behavior Therapy

Ellis believes that people are born with the capacity to think rationally or irrationally about themselves, others, and the environment. Irrational thinking, as well as rational thinking, affects the behavior and emotions of people. People who develop difficulty in functioning have learned to think irrationally in terms of their expectations or beliefs about themselves, others, and the environment.

Rational emotive behavior therapy (REBT) uses an ABC framework for understanding emotional disturbances or maladaptive functioning (Dryden & Giuseppe, 1990; Ellis, 1985). *A* stands for the *activating* event or experience. *C* stands for the emotional and behavioral *consequences* of the activating event. *B* stands for the *beliefs* that one holds about *A* that result in *C*. For example, a client who resides in a group home and is working on assertiveness in social situations may be responsible for asking other residents for ideas for outings during the weekly house meeting. *A* represents the actual or imagined weekly meeting in which the client must seek input from other residents. *C* represents anxiety and avoidance of the weekly meeting. *B* represents the irrational belief such as "I must be perfect and get everyone to share where they want to go" and "Everyone must think that I did a good job."

In REBT, the therapeutic recreation specialist works with a client to dispute irrational beliefs (B). One of the basic premises of REBT is that irrational beliefs must be replaced with rational beliefs, and these rational beliefs will result in positive emotional and behavioral consequences. In order to facilitate change in irrational beliefs (B), the therapeutic recreation specialist may interact with the client during either a one-on-one or group setting and assign the client home work to track irrational beliefs, try out new behaviors, and track subsequent consequences (C; see Table 6.4, p. 178). Initially the focus is on identifying the activating event and consequences. This is followed by the therapist working with the client to identify irrational beliefs and understand the linkage between activating events, beliefs, and consequences. The next step is confronting irrational beliefs and supporting the client in the development and use of rational beliefs.

REBT is an educational process. Collaborative work with a therapist teaches a client the tools of REBT; that is, how to dispute irrational beliefs and replace them with rational beliefs that foster positive emotional and behavioral consequences. The therapist is directive and confrontational in REBT. Ellis has indicated that many qualities professed by therapists, such as unconditional positive regard or empathetic understanding, lead to the client developing a dependent relationship with a therapist (Ellis, 1962; Weinrach, 1995). In contrast, REBT prepares clients to dispute irrational beliefs independently.

Use of Cognitive-Behavioral Therapy in Therapeutic Recreation

Therapeutic recreation specialists frequently use cognitive-behavioral techniques with clients. An innovative therapeutic recreation program that draws on cognitive-behavioral therapy, "I Believe In Me: Project IBIM," was developed by Karen Floyd and Sandra Negley (1989). Floyd and Negley developed this self-esteem program after observing that many clients who had completed a leisure education program during hospitalization in a psychiatric facility returned to the community and demonstrated no change in their leisure experiences. Project IBIM was designed to enhance participants' self-esteem and prepare them to make changes in their leisure behavior and overall functioning. Project IBIM consists of ten modules. The cognitive-behavioral therapy component is evident in Module 2: Moving From the Negative to Positive . . . With My Thoughts (see Table 6.5, pp. 180-181).

Another opportunity to consider the integration of cognitive-behavioral therapy in therapeutic recreation is provided in the exercise presented in Table 6.2, page 156.

Scenario A. Mike has refused to go on the outing that is planned for the afternoon. You enter the common day area to join Mike where he is sitting. Mike looks up and says: "Guess you heard that I don't want to go out." As a therapeutic recreation specialist drawing from cognitive-behavioral therapy, what might you say? How would you handle this interaction with Mike? Consider how one therapeutic recreation specialist approached the interaction.

Mike:	Guess you heard that I don't want to go out.
TRS:	Yes, the nursing staff told me that you had decided not to go.
Mike:	I don't know. I know that I said I'd try it. (silence)
TRS:	Well, that was at the beginning of the week when we talked about some new activities.
Mike:	Yeah, back on Monday I felt pretty good. Rob and I were hanging out together and playing cards. Now it's like no one is around, no one likes to talk with me.
TRS:	So, if no one is around it is because no one likes to talk with you?
Mike:	Well, Rob went home so there is no one to hang out with.
TRS:	If there is no one to hang out with, is it because no one likes you or could there be other reasons?
Mike:	Yeah, I don't really know any of the new people.
TRS:	Rather than people not liking you, perhaps not having anyone to hang out with is because you are just getting to know the new folks.

Scenario B. As the therapeutic recreation specialist who implements the Self-Determination in Leisure Program, you are considering how to incorporate cognitive-behavioral therapy into the content and process. One approach may be to consider the Debriefing Process.

Debriefing Content
- How can a lack of skills prevent us from participating in recreation activities?
- How can we take responsibility and learn skills needed to experience leisure?
- If we learn the skills needed to participate in a desired recreation activity, are we more determined to participate in an activity?
- What could happen if we do not take responsibility to learn new leisure skills?

Debriefing Process
- Conduct debriefing questions listed.
- Encourage all participants to respond to at least one of the questions.

Cognitive-Behavioral Therapy
Respond to participants by questioning irrational beliefs. Acknowledge and support rational beliefs.

Cognitive-behavioral theory provides specific strategies for promoting changes in clients' thinking, feeling, and actions. The therapeutic recreation specialist in the first scenario paraphrased Mike's statements so that he could hear the link between his experiences (behavior) and feelings (consequences). Such an interaction allowed Mike to begin to question whether it was rational to believe that people did not talk with him because they did not like him. In the second scenario, the therapeutic recreation specialist planned to confront irrational thinking expressed about learning and using leisure skills.

Therapeutic recreation specialists who use cognitive-behavioral theories will initially focus on clients' thoughts. The ultimate outcome, however, is for clients to replace irrational thoughts with rational thoughts that promote positive feelings and behavior.

Multicultural Considerations for Counseling

All of the theories discussed in this chapter—existential, person-centered, behaviorist, and cognitive—are based on Western values, especially independence and individualism. Consequently, there are situations in which they

---

Table 6.4 Example of a REBT Homework Assignment *

Recreation Experience Form

How do you feel about the recreation activities in which you participate? Do you look forward to recreation in your day-to-day life? These are a few of the questions that we are discussing in our Recreation Education Group. This form is designed to assist you in examining your recreation experiences. Please complete this form prior to our next Recreation Education Group.

Activating event or recreation participation:

Consequences - feelings and behaviors as a result of activating event:

Beliefs - irrational beliefs that lead to consequences listed above. Circle all that apply.

- I MUST do well or very well.

- I am a BAD or WORTHLESS person when I act stupid.

- I MUST be approved or accepted by all people.

- I am a BAD, UNLOVEABLE PERSON if I get rejected.

- People MUST treat me fairly and give me what I NEED.

- My life MUST have few major hassles or troubles.

- I CAN'T STAND really bad things or very difficult people.

- It is AWFUL and HORRIBLE when major things don't go my way.

Select one of the irrational beliefs circled above. As we have done in group, attempt to dispute the selected irrational belief.

Now you are ready to replace your irrational belief with a rational belief.

Good job! See you in group.

---

* Adapted from Dobson, 1988.

would not be appropriate for persons from cultures that are interdependent and collectivist. Jafari (as cited in Tjeltveit, 1999) argued that Western therapy conflicts with the Islamic worldview. Islam affirms:

the goodness of righteous benevolence rather than (Western) self-fulfillment, the goodness of a holistic (i.e. individual and collective; mental, physical, and spiritual) rather than a materialistic outlook, the goodness of bounded rather than unbounded freedom, and the goodness of repentance rather than rationalizing guilt away. (p. 219)

Furthermore, Western counseling generally favors self-exploration, self-disclosure, and expressiveness (verbal, emotional, and behavioral). Other cultures, however, may negatively view these Western preferences as self-absorption and lack of proper restraint.

The efficacy of techniques also varies among cultures. For example, after reviewing the literature, Sue and Sue (1990) reported, "American Indians, Asian Americans, Black Americans, and Hispanic Americans tend to prefer more active-directive forms of helping than nondirective ones" (p. 69). The attending and listening techniques discussed earlier in this chapter are generally more conducive to a Rogerian or nondirective approach to helping. As such, a therapeutic recreation specialist might need to adjust or even discard some of these techniques when working with people from non-Western cultures. One of authors learned a relevant lesson about this when he was just starting in the field of therapeutic recreation. Using the Rogerian skills he had acquired as an undergraduate, the author repeatedly laced a conversation between a client and himself with the expression, "I hear you saying . . . ." Growing annoyed and exasperated, the client finally said to the author, "You know darn well what I'm saying. Get the wax out of your ears!" In other words, the client was pleading with the author to be direct rather than reflective. Things improved once the author realized that not everyone communicates like Carl Rogers.

Clearly, no single theory or set of techniques will be universally effective. Accordingly, Sue and Sue (1990) recommended that helpers be open, flexible, and eclectic, adjusting their helping styles to the cultural backgrounds of their clients.

Table 6.5 I Believe In Me: Project IBIM*

Module 2: Moving from the Negative to Positive...With My Thoughts Introduction: We discussed the effects that your negative beliefs can have on you and how they may stop you from risking and experiencing life. Negative self-talk comes from those negative beliefs and stops you from continuing your journey. It becomes necessary to understand and realize how much control you actually have over your thoughts. You can think anything you choose to think, and the key word in that statement in choose. Any kind of emotion that you experience, whether negative or positive, is a direct result of what you have chosen to think.

Everyone, at one point or antoher, has negative thoughts about themselves. But, in some people those thoughts are much stronger than in others.

Each of you have an ongoing conversation inside your head, that is called self-talk. Self-talk can give you strength or it can dissolve your strength depending on whether it is possitive or negative.

Activity: This activity will help you to realize what kind of negative self-talk you experience.
Compare your mind to a tape recorder. Different situations arise during the day which influence the type of tape you play in your mind. At times you may find your negative tape playing. These thoughts stop you from taking risks, trying new things, and make you feel like you can't do anything right. These are critical, negative, devaluing thoughts that play in your mind. This is the kind of self-talk that contributes to lack of self-worth. What are some examples of your negative self-talk?

Sometimes you may be reinforced by others in negative statements about yourself, whetehr it's from peers, family, parents, teachers, or others. And that reinforces your belief in that negative chatter.

Let's do an experiment together: We have talked briefly about negative thoughts, now close your eyes and let's do a quick imaginary excercise. Visualize a tape recorder. Next to the recorder is your negative self-talk tape. Visualize yourself putting that tape into the recorder and pushing the "play" button. Start thinking of all the things you say about yourself that are negative. Allow the tape to play over and over again. (Allow 15-20 seconds to pass).

STOP! What happened when I shouted STOP? The analogy that I want to draw from this quick experiment is that you can and do contro, what tape is playing in your mind. You have the control to stop the "garbage thoughts" from continuiing to play. The first step in stopping the negative thoughts is to recognize when your thoughts are negative and sel-destructive. The second step is to consciously STOP the tape from playing. Every time a negative thought about yourself enters your mind say to yourself loud and clear: "STOP!" Thirdly, acknowledge the thought for what it is. Avoid harsh judgment regarding the dicovery of your negative thought. Focus on ways of changing the behavior and letting it go. The fourth step is to change the negative thought to a positive one. We're going to do an excercise together to help build a vareity of positive thoughts.

Activity: have the group divide into smaller groups of three to four people. If your numbers are too small keep the group together and brainstorm as one group. You will need the Positive Vocabulary Worksheet for each group memebr and a chalkboard or dry erase board for you. The objective is to brainstorm together as many positive self-esteem words as possible (e.g., A=attractive, affectionate, B=bright, brave). Provide the group 10 to 15 minutes to generate positive words. Assign a spokesperson for each group and combine all ideas on one main list on the chalkboard. Each member will select at least ten positive self-esteem words that they can use to subsitute for their negative words.

Table 6.5 I Believe In Me: Project IBIM* (continued)

Discussion:

    1. Effects of positive self-statements.
    2. The need for practice and support from others.

Follow Up: Throughout next week, listen for "I can't" or other forms of negative self-talk. Seek and encourage support from each other in switching negative thoughts to positive thoughts.

* This activity is from: Floyd, K. and Negley, S. (1989). I Believe In Me: Project I.B.I.M. Salt Lake City, Utah. (pp. 4-6)

Summary

Therapeutic recreation services are designed to enhance clients' quality of life. Therefore, therapeutic recreation specialists frequently work to facilitate change in clients' daily experiences and behaviors. Helping skills and counseling theories provide us with knowledge and competencies needed to establish meaningful and fruitful relationships with clients. Furthermore, counseling theories assist therapeutic recreation specialists in identifying how their actions and words guide clients in growth and change. Readers are encouraged to continue to learn about these therapeutic tools through additional coursework in communications, psychology, and counseling, as well as practical experience.

Recommended Readings

Corey, G. (1996). *Theory and practice of counseling and psychotherapy*. Pacific Grove, CA: Brooks/Cole Publishing Co.

Burns, D. D. (1989). *The feeling good handbook*. New York, NY: Penguin Group.

Corsini, R. J. and Wedding, D. (1995). *Current psychotherapies*. Itasca, IL: F. E. Peacock Publishers, Inc.

Dattilo, J. and Murphy, W. D. (1987). *Behavior modification in therapeutic recreation*. State College, PA: Venture Publishing, Inc.

Egan, G. (1994). *The skilled helper: A problem-management approach to helping*. Pacific Grove, CA: Brooks/Cole Publishing Company.

Floyd, K. and Negley, S. (1989). *I Believe In Me: Project I.B.I.M.* Salt Lake City, UT: Authors.

Frankl, V. E. (1992). *Man's search for meaning: An introduction to logotherapy*. New York, NY: Simon and Schuster.

Kazdin, A. E. (1994). *Behavior modification in applied settings*. Pacific Grove, CA: Brooks/Cole Publishing Company.

Kirschenbaum, H. and Henderson, V. L. (1989). *The Carl Rogers reader*. Boston, MA: Houghton Mifflin Company.

Lewinsohn, P. M., Munoz, R. F., Youngren, M. A. and Zeiss, A. M. (1978). *Control your depression*. New York, NY: Prentice Hall Press.

May, R. and Yalom, I. (1995). Existential psychotherapy. In R. J. Corsini and D. Wedding (Eds.), *Current psychotherapies* (pp. 262–292). Itasca, IL: F. E. Peacock Publishers, Inc.

Negley, S. (1997). *Crossing the bridge: A journey in self-esteem, relationships and life balance*. Beachwood, OH: Wellness Reproductions & Publishing, Inc.

Okun, B. F. (1997). *Effective helping: Interviewing and counseling techniques*. Pacific Grove, CA: Brooks/Cole Publishing Company.

Yalom, I. D., (1998). *The Yalom reader: Selections from the work of a master therapist and storyteller*. New York, NY: Basic Books.

Chapter

Introduction to Learning and Teaching in Therapeutic Recreation

This chapter is about human learning and its role in therapeutic recreation practice. Promoting and facilitating human learning is a fundamental goal of therapeutic recreation service. Therefore, therapeutic recreation specialists are at least as much educators as they are therapists. As such, therapeutic recreation specialists should develop an understanding of the nature of learning, approaches to teaching that have been successfully used in therapeutic recreation, and major perspectives on teaching and learning. This chapter is intended to provide an introduction to these topics.

What is learning and what does it have to do with therapeutic recreation?

Although everyone seems to know when learning occurs, development of a precise and universally acceptable definition is much like attempting to herd cats. Suppose I spend a week carefully and completely digesting the cover-to-cover contents of an exceptionally thorough book on how to fly airplanes while you spend a day taking flying lessons from an expert instructor. At the conclusion of these events, who would have learned more about flying? Also, have you noticed that you tend to smile when you greet a friend or loved one? Although you probably never read a book on that topic and probably never took a class on smiling when you greet someone, surely that response is "learned." The dog of one of the authors will happily roll onto his back and lie quietly in response to the question, "would you rather study at [a competitor university] or be a lazy dog?" Most would agree that the dog learned that response. In these three examples, we encounter much of the complexity of the problem of arriving at a universal definition of learning. We can see that: (1) learning is not a phenomenon that is unique to humankind, (2) learning can be deliberate (learning to fly an airplane) or it can be unintended (smiling when we greet a friend or loved one), (3) learning involves a change in something, (4) learning often results from one or more encounters with a person, place, or thing in the environment, and (5) the change that occurs may be a change in observable behavior (smile, an ability to fly an airplane, or turning on one's back in response to a question) or a change in knowledge (learning written material from a book on how to fly airplanes).

These and other observations about such common features of learning provide a basis for a tentative, though quite limited, definition of learning:

> Learning is a relatively permanent change in behavior or knowl-
> edge that is the result of experience (cf., Kimble, 1961; Bourne
> & Ekstrand, 1973; Deaux & Wrightsman, 1988; Woolfolk, 1998).

The limitations of this and related definitions of learning are summarized by Cantania (1998). First, we fail to adequately describe how permanent a change must be in order to qualify as learning. Who among us has marched into a midterm exam classroom with sharpened pencils and great optimism, only to draw a total blank on material that we were certain that we had learned? Second, the definition does not sufficiently delimit the types of experience that ought to be associated with learning. Standing for more than a few seconds on a hot piece of charcoal that has fallen from your grill will certainly change your behavior (manner of walking) in a way that is relatively permanent, but we do not ordinarily think of that change as learning.

Despite its limitations, the preceding definition is sufficient for our purposes. Therapeutic recreation specialists are in the business of attempting to bring about "relatively permanent changes in behavior or knowledge" of their clients. The National Therapeutic Recreation Society definition establishes that therapeutic recreation services "help people . . . develop and use their leisure in ways that enhance their health, independence, and well-being" (NTRS, 1994). Both "development" and "use" imply learning. Clients must learn to use, and they tend to learn as they develop. The American Therapeutic Recreation Association definition of therapeutic recreation establishes that "recreation services" are provided "in order to improve health and well-being" (ATRA, 1988). Improvement of health and well-being would certainly involve learning new skills and new lifestyles.

Examples of specific learning that is facilitated by therapeutic recreation specialists may further underscore the point that therapeutic recreation specialists are centrally involved in human learning. The scope of learning that therapeutic recreation specialists promote is expansive, including:

- Helping young people with developmental disabilities learn behaviors that will empower them to successfully negotiate the transition from public school to involvement in the work force (The Institute for Career and Leisure Development, 1993),
- Helping people with newly acquired disabilities to learn the skills necessary to participate in health-promoting forms of recreation that are of interest to them (Austin, 1998),
- Helping youths with anger management problems to develop knowledge and behaviors that will empower them to more effectively manage conflicts with their peers,
- Helping people with disabilities learn skills that will empower them to more effectively access community leisure resources (e.g., ride buses, visit libraries, attend movies and sporting events),
- Helping individuals whose families are dysfunctional to learn new leisure activities that might promote the development of a more healthy family, and
- Helping individuals learn to develop and express their intellectual and creative abilities, to establish and maintain close personal relationships with other people, and to behave in morally appropriate ways. (Widmer & Ellis, 1998)

Learning is thus central to therapeutic recreation practice. With this foundation, we may proceed to an investigation of leisure education and to models of learning and teaching.

Leisure Education

The centrality of learning to the mission of therapeutic recreation is reflected in leisure education, which has been defined as:

- A total developmental process through which individuals develop an understanding of self, leisure, and the relationship of leisure to their own lifestyles and society (Mundy & Odum, 1979, p. 2),
- A broad category of services that focuses on the development and acquisition of various leisure-related skills, attitudes, and knowledge (Peterson & Gunn, 1984),
- A process whereby people:
  - recognize the use of leisure (discretionary) time as an avenue for personal satisfaction and enrichment
  - know the array of valuable opportunities available in leisure time

- understand the significant impact that leisure time has and will have on society
- appreciate the natural resources and their relationships to discretionary time and quality of life
- are able to make decisions regarding their own leisure behavior (Zeyen, et al., 1977), and
- Educating for the wholesome use of discretionary time in order to enhance the quality of one's life. (Brannon, Chinn & Verhoven, 1981)

Significant attention was devoted to leisure education in the 1970s and 1980s. Among the notable contributions during that period were the Leisure Education Advancement Project (LEAP), the development of a leisure education subcommittee of the Society of Park and Recreation Educators, and the publication of influential books on leisure education. The LEAP project was conducted by the National Recreation and Park Association through financial support from Lily Endowment of Indianapolis (Zeyen, et al., 1977). One of the notable outcomes of that project was the development of a curriculum for teaching leisure education in public and private school classrooms. The curriculum, *Kangaroo Kit*, provided teachers with educational objectives, rationale, and learning experiences for teaching students in grades K-12 about recreation and leisure behavior.

One of the educational goals within the *Kangaroo Kit* was to help students "understand that almost any life experience can be a leisure experience—it's a matter of personal choice and attitude" (Zeyen, et al., 1977, p. 121). Following from that educational goal is the need to understand different forms that leisure may take. A *Kangaroo Kit* lesson plan was designed which asked students to prepare a list of their present and past leisure experiences and then categorize those experiences in terms of the position of each experience on five continua: performer/participant vs. audience, physical vs. mental, individual vs. social, structured/planned vs. nonstructured/spontaneous, and momentary vs. long-term. Following this evaluation of forms that their leisure takes, students were asked to identify the forms of leisure that they wished to expand. Teachers were asked to help students find ways of accomplishing that expansion within students' existing profiles of leisure interests. A student who enjoyed playing softball informally on the playgrounds, for example, might indicate that his or her current form of that activity was performer, physical, social, spontaneous, and long-term. The teacher might suggest ways of expanding that activity through joining a formal league (increase structured/planned form), reading books about softball (increase mental form), or attending local softball tournaments (increase audience form).

The LEAP project was an ambitious effort that reflected the considerable attention that the recreation profession provided to leisure education during the 1970s and early 1980s. A variety of written materials also emerged from that era, including Mundy and Odum's (1979) *Leisure Education: Theory and Practice*, Brannon, Chinn, and Verhoven's (1981) *What is Leisure Education? A Primer for Persons Working with Handicapped Children and Youth*, Brightbill and Mobley's (1977) *Education for Leisure Centered Living*, and Corbin and Tait's (1973) *Education for Leisure*. These and related works emphasized the importance of leisure education for promoting the health of individuals, families, and society.

In terms of therapeutic recreation, perhaps the most influential work was Peterson and Gunn's attention to leisure education in their textbook on therapeutic recreation program design (Gunn & Peterson, 1978; Peterson & Gunn, 1984). In the first edition Gunn and Peterson (1978) emphasized leisure education as a focus of therapeutic recreation service. They presented a hypothetical case in which the therapist "no longer acts as a therapist, but rather as a teacher and counselor" (p. 19). In the second edition Peterson and Gunn (1984) identified four major components of leisure education content: leisure awareness, social interaction skills, leisure resources, and leisure activity skills.

Leisure awareness is comprised of four subcomponents: knowledge of leisure, self-awareness, leisure and play attitudes, and related participatory and decision-making skills (Peterson & Gunn, 1984). Among the educational activities to help students master this content are examining the meaning of leisure to the individual, analyzing similarities and differences between leisure behavior and other behavior, examining areas for future development of leisure skills, and exploring problem solving skills (Peterson & Gunn, 1984). The second major content area, social interaction skills, was concerned with learning appropriate and effective communication skills in different groups and for different types of activities. The third major content area, leisure resources, was divided into five parts: learning about activity opportunities, personal resources, family and home resources, community resources, and state and national resources. The fourth area, leisure activity skills, helps learners to develop a repertoire of activity skills that engender a sense of freedom through the availability of "options and alternatives" (p. 35).

In a more recent formulation of leisure education content, Dattilo and Murphy (1991, p. 23) proposed seven components. These components include the following:

- Awareness of self in leisure,
- Appreciation of leisure,

- Understanding of self-determination in leisure,
- Ability to make decisions concerning participation in leisure,
- Knowledge and utilization of resources for leisure participation,
- Knowledge of effective social interaction skills, and
- Recreation activity skills.

Dattilo and Murphy provide precise educational goals associated with these components, specific learning objectives, and educational activities designed to meet those objectives. In addition, detailed curricula are provided that can be used to implement comprehensive leisure education programs through select recreation activities: swimming, walking, gardening, bowling, softball, volleyball, canoeing, camping, cooking, and painting (Dattillo, 1999).

The early work on leisure education content and curricula spawned implementation of a number of leisure education programs. Table 7.1 (pp. 192-193) provides a summary of some recent studies on leisure education. Studies selected for inclusion in the table were published in *Therapeutic Recreation Journal* between 1991 and 1999. All of the studies included "leisure education" in either the title of the article or in the "key words" listed with each article. The purpose of this review was to (1) illustrate the content of leisure education programs, (2) identify the scope of populations to which leisure education has been applied, (3) identify approaches that have been taken to the study of leisure education, and, (4) provide some evidence of the extent to which leisure education programs produce the types of learning that are desired. No attempt was made to be comprehensive and readers will find examples of excellent research published in sources other than the *Therapeutic Recreation Journal*.

The eight studies summarized in Table 7.1 warrant closer examination. The pioneering works of the LEAP project (Zeyen, et al., 1977), of Jean Mundy and Linda Odum (1979), and of Carol Peterson and Scout Gunn (Gunn & Peterson, 1978; Peterson & Gunn, 1984) have been extended in more recent leisure education curricula. In addition to leisure education content that has been recommended by those works (e.g., leisure awareness, social interaction skills, leisure resources, leisure activity skills), contemporary leisure education models have included values clarification exercises (Zoerink & Lauener, 1991), substitutability of activities (Bullock & Howe, 1991), decision-making training (Mahon & Bullock, 1992), self-determination (Williams & Dattilo, 1997), community tenure (Mahon, Bullock, Luken, & Martens, 1996), and leisure constraints (Searle & Mahon, 1993).

Table 7.1 also indicates that leisure education programs have been implemented with a variety of populations. The eight studies reviewed included young adults (Williams & Dattilo, 1997), older women (Dunn & Wilhite,

1997), individuals with "severe and persistent mental illness" (Mahon, Bullock, Luken, & Martins, 1996), high school students in special education classes (Bedini, Bullock, & Driscoll, 1993), elderly patients in a day hospital (Searle & Mahon, 1993), adolescents with mental retardation (Mahon & Bullock, 1992), young adults with physical disabilities (Bullock & Howe, 1991), and adults with traumatic brain injury (Zoerink & Lauener, 1991). The diversity of populations to which leisure education programs has been applied is quite impressive. This diversity, and the fact that leisure education has not proven harmful with any of these populations, suggests that therapeutic recreation specialists might consider implementing a leisure education curriculum with virtually any population served.

Table 7.1 also summarizes approaches that have been taken to study the effects of leisure education. These approaches range from experimental studies of groups, to single subject studies, to qualitative designs. In experimental studies of groups in leisure education (e.g., Searle & Mahon, 1993; Zoerink & Lauener, 1991; Bedini, Bullock, & Driscoll, 1993), students are assigned to either a "treatment" group, which receives the leisure education program, or a "control" group in which students receive either no instruction or another form of instruction. Single case designs (Mahon & Bullock, 1992; Williams & Dattilo, 1997; Dunn & Wilhite, 1997) involve taking measures of leisure education effectiveness over time and evaluating the extent to which behavior changes (or learning occurs) after the leisure education program has been implemented. Qualitative designs involve classification, analysis, and synthesis of a variety of types of information. The qualitative component of the Bedini, Bullock, and Driscoll (1993) study was accomplished through systematic examination of data from interviews and progress notes.

Only five of the eight studies produced evidence of a positive effect of leisure education on at least one facet of learning studied. Further, significant effects on all types of learning studied were observed in only four of the eight studies. Given the history of interest and the ambitious development projects that have been completed, these results are rather disappointing. The lack of consistent results might be attributed to any of a variety of factors, including small sample sizes, diffusion of treatment effects by students in the same groups, failure of the profession to develop a precise definition of leisure education from which standard techniques may be derived, instructor effectiveness, lack of sensitivity of measures of learning, and insufficient time for learning to occur.

It is possible that treatment effects are compromised by the absence of sufficient attention to specific methods of teaching, based on existing knowledge about human learning. The studies reviewed consistently point out the duration of the leisure education program in terms of numbers of hours per

Table 7.1 Summary of Select Leisure Education Research

Authors	Population/Sample	Program Content	Outcome Measures	Design	Results
Searle and Mahon, 1993	Elderly patients in a day hospital, $N=44$	Eight weeks, one hour per week. Definition and meaning of leisure, leisure needs, constraints, preferences, goal setting, community resources, decision making, action plan	Perceived Leisure Control Perceived Leisure Competence	Experimental: Leisure Education group v. control group	Gains in leisure competence noted in an earlier study were sustained. No lasting effects on the other variables
Mahon and Bullock, 1992	Four adolescents with mild mental retardation	Twice per week, one hour. Decision-making training and leisure awareness training	Self-Esteem Leisure Awareness via independent self-instruction TR-assisted instruction	Single case AB design	All four students displayed an increase in both outcome variables
Bullock and Howe, 1991	Seven individuals with physical disabilities	Transitional community reintegration program. Eleven sessions address activity identification, motivations, activity adaptation, substitutable activities, goal setting, identification of resources, recreation skill development, coping with barriers	Data from internal records Client forms Peer evaluation forms	Case study	Positive effects noted on recreation participation, social interaction, self-concept, initiative, positive affect, behavioral functioning, adjustment to disability, autonomy, and quality of life
Zoerink and Lauener, 1991	Adults with traumatic brain injury ($N=14$)	Values clarification, designed to augment other transitional living services. Included either 90-minute sessions, one per week for 8 weeks. Didactic and experiential. Identifying and choosing activities, making decisions, evaluating alternatives, exploring past events, building pattern of consistent action, examining benefits and alternatives, barriers, planning	Leisure ethic Leisure satisfaction Perceived freedom in leisure	Experimental: Pretest, post-test, control group	No treatment effects were observed. The investigator noted increased awareness of leisure opportunities by participants in the treatment group
Williams and Dattilo, 1997	Young adults with mental retardation	TRAIL Curriculum: leisure appreciation, self-determination, social interaction, 24 lessons, 3x per week, 8 weeks	Choice-Making Social Interaction Positive Affect	Single case multiple baseline	No effect on choice making or social interaction. Smile frequency and positive vocalization increased

Table 7.1 Summary of Select Leisure Education Research (continued)

Authors	Population/Sample	Program Content	Outcome Measures	Design	Results
Dunn and Wilhite, 1997	Older women	Community reintegration program: Awareness skills, knowledge. Also addresses physical, mental, and social benefits. Eight weeks, 2 one hour sessions per week	Psychosocial well-being Leisure Participation	Single case, multiple baseline	Frequency and duration of leisure participation increased. Psychosocial well-being was not increased by the program
Mahon, Bullock, Luken, and Martens, 1996	Program consumers with severe and persistent mental illness (N=21) Family members of consumers Service Providers	Reintegration through recreation curriculum: Community accept-ance, social support, leisure interests, problem solving, life satisfaction, self-esteem, action on choices	Attitude toward the program as applied to individuals with severe and persistent mental illness	Survey	Consumers, family members, and service providers found the program to be socially valid
Bedini, Bullock, and Driscoll, 1993	High school students in special education classes, N=45	Leisure awareness, self-awareness, leisure opportunities, community resource awareness, barriers, personal resources and respon-sibility, planning an outing, evaluation of outing	Student survey Teacher questionnaire Parent questionnaire Leisure inventory	Experimental (pretest, postest, control) and qualitiative analysis of in-depth interviews, case studies, and progress notes	Quantitative data showed no significant effect. Although parents and teachers indicated that leisure education was a good idea, more time was spent on content related to work than content related to leisure

week and numbers of weeks. The contents of the curricula are also well-described. Absent from those discussions, however, are descriptions of specific teaching methods used. We thus know little about the extent to which lectures, discussion, simulations, role-playing, homework assignments, or other techniques were used. We also know very little about the nature of discussion questions that might have been presented to students, nor do we know sufficient details about the frequency and type of reinforcement or feedback that students may have been provided. If you reflect upon the good and bad educational experiences that you have had, you will likely agree that skillful use of such techniques by teachers does matter. Many effective teaching techniques are deeply rooted in knowledge and theory about human learning, the topic to which we now turn.

Theories about Human Learning

At the beginning of the chapter, we briefly explored the challenge of defining learning. As that review revealed, learning is a vital, yet complex and elusive concept. Part of the challenge of defining learning has to do with the complexity of the behavior or knowledge that is learned. Any given behavior that a person exhibits can be interpreted in a variety of ways. Suppose, for example, you are leading a basketball game among a group of youth. One participant, Denise, believing she was fouled on a shot, shoves an opponent, and shouts obscenities. That incident is consistent with a pattern of behavior that Denise typically exhibits during participation in recreation activities with other people. How many different ways can you describe the things that a therapeutic recreation professional might help Denise to "learn?" Myriad answers to this question might be advanced, two examples of which are: (1) the therapeutic recreation professional might help Denise learn to not shove opponents during recreation activities, and (2) the therapeutic recreation professional might help Denise learn coping skills that will enable her to control her anger and participate in recreation with others more effectively and appropriately.

Notice how these answers differ. The first implies a direct action that we could objectively define and observe. Shoving, for example, might be defined as an action of extending one or more arms and hands against another person's body with sufficient speed and force to disrupt the balance of that other person. Based on this definition, the therapeutic recreation specialist could design strategies to help Denise learn to not shove other participants. In contrast, coping skills may include cognitive processes that no one else can observe. Instead of interpreting the foul as a direct, intentional affront, the therapeutic recreation specialist might help Denise learn to interpret actions differently.

When fouled by an opponent, Denise might, for example, learn to interpret the event as follows:

> She fouled me, but it was only because she was off balance. Besides, the fact that she believes that she blocked my shot this time may help her be more confident when she plays on my team during the next game.

Both of these examples demonstrate learning, because both are relatively permanent changes in behavior that are the result of experience. The first involves learning a behavior (shoving) that is directly observable. The second example involves cognitive learning (developing thinking skills) that enable one to interpret situations in different ways. Both approaches could be effective in working with the troubled client. In the following section, we explore theories of learning that relate to each of these examples.

Select Behavioral Perspectives on Learning

Behavioral theories of learning seek to explain changes in observable actions that result from events and conditions that are external to the individual. In contrast to cognitive theories of learning, behavioral theories avoid the complexities that are inherent in attempting to understand thoughts, emotions, beliefs, and attitudes, focusing instead on what people actually do or learn from in particular sets of circumstances. A behavioral perspective on working with Denise (from the example above) would emphasize that the problem is that Denise shoves people during recreation activities. No inference would be made concerning abstract notions such as her motives, her anger, her awareness of consequences, or her intentions. From a behavioral perspective, Denise needs to learn to not engage in that form of inappropriate behavior. Other behavioral outcomes that recreation therapists working with Denise might pursue include making choices (e.g., Williams & Dattilo, 1997), participating in activities rather than sitting passively (e.g., Dunn & Wilhite, 1997), attending to assigned learning activities, initiating conversations, or other behaviors that are appropriate leisure education processes and outcomes.

Behavioral theories can be divided into those theories that emphasize contiguity and those that emphasize reinforcement. Contiguity theories emphasize that learning is a result of co-occurrence of events or environmental conditions. Many elementary school students have, for example, learned to stop talking to their friends when their teacher flashes the classroom ceiling lights on and off. In contrast, reinforcement theories emphasize that the important factor in learning is the presence of consequences, such as rewards or punishments, of engaging in particular behaviors. An example would be the "token economy" systems used in some mental health institutions. If you are a patient in such an institution, you earn tokens for specifically described behaviors, such as dressing appropriately, avoiding aggressive behavior, or choosing to participate in recreation programs. Tokens may then be exchanged for special privileges or other items of value.

Behavioral Learning: Contiguity Theory

Contiguity theories are traceable to the works of Ivan Pavlov (1849-1936), a Russian physiologist, and John Watson (1878-1958), a psychologist. Pavlov's initiation to a contiguity perspective on learning was rather serendipitous. As a Nobel prize winning physiologist, he was involved in an investigation of the length of time it took for dogs to secrete digestive juices after being fed. The research involved rather difficult surgery to enable measurement of the time at which digestive juices were secreted. Surgery went well, but Pavlov encountered a problem. He noticed that the time that juices were secreted changed mysteriously. Secretions occurred not only when food reached the stomach, but also when dogs chewed or even saw food. Fascinated by this observation, Pavlov devised a new method for studying this form of learning in dogs that involved inserting a duct into dogs' salivary glands and counting the fall of saliva drops into a beaker as a result of different environmental conditions. Using this method, Pavlov found that he could train dogs to salivate by pairing the presence of food with virtually any object perceptible to the dog. After the sound of a bell was presented concurrent with the food for a period of time, for example, presence of the bell sound alone was sufficient to elicit salivation by the dogs. Obviously, the dogs had no interest in eating the bells; rather, they had learned to associate the sound of the bell with food.

This form of learning is now referred to as "classical conditioning" or "Pavlovian conditioning." Pavlov created names for the various elements involved in this form of learning. He referred to the stimulus (e.g., the food) that normally elicited the response of interest (e.g., the salivation) as the "unconditional stimulus" because that stimulus requires no conditioning in eliciting the response. He named the other element (e.g., the bell) the "conditioned stimulus" because that element does not produce the response until it is paired with the unconditional stimulus. The extent to which a bell elicits salivation is thus conditional on whether or not it has been paired with the food.

What happens if the unconditional stimulus is removed and a conditional stimulus is repeatedly presented to a person who has learned to associate that stimulus with a particular response? For example, suppose a dog has learned to salivate in response to the sound of a bell because that sound has been repeatedly accompanied by the presence of food. For a period of time the sound is then presented without the food. What will happen? Due to the physiological workings of the cortex, as described by Pavlov, the animal will stop salivating in response to the bell alone. This process is referred to as "extinction" of the behavior.

In addition to extinction, other learning processes that emerged from Pavlov's pioneering work were generalization and discrimination. Generalization and discrimination have to do with the extent to which an animal may learn to elicit a given response as change occurs in the conditional stimulus. Assume, for example, that an animal has learned to salivate when it is exposed to the tone of a middle C from a violin. Conditioning could also be used to help the animal learn to salivate when exposed to a middle C from a piano (generalization) or not to salivate in response to a middle C on a piano (discrimination).

Psychologist John Watson was a contemporary of Pavlov. Watson objected to the fascination of psychologists of that era with elusive characteristics of the mind, such as thoughts, sensations, and the like, referring to those matters as "mentalisms." Watson's position was that mentalisms are abstract constructions that are not directly observable and, as a result, they do not provide a sound foundation for the development of an understanding of human behavior. As such, observable acts ought to be the focus of human psychology. That premise led Watson to build his own contiguity theory of learning. That theory was based on the notion of innate reflexes, such as sneezing as a result of irritation of the inner lining of the nose. Learning, to Watson, is a process through which new and increasingly complex behaviors and series of behaviors are connected to these basic reflexes. By structuring the way in which behaviors are paired with external stimuli, Watson believed that people could learn to do virtually anything (Watson, 1930).

This discussion of salivary glands, dogs, extinction, and reflexes probably seems far removed from therapeutic recreation practice. Careful reflection on the basic principles, however, reveals that contiguity theories provide useful direction for teaching strategies in a variety of situations, as indicated by the following examples.

Several years ago, a graduate student of one of the authors was involved in research on the "galvanic skin response" (skin conductance) of recipients of therapeutic recreation services. Galvanic skin response is a measure of the extent to which small, imperceptible electrical currents can pass through skin. From galvanic skin responses, one can infer the level of alertness, interest, or physiological arousal that an individual has at a given point in time. Educators are very interested in physiological arousal because conditions of heightened physiological arousal can be conducive to learning. (Law enforcement officials use physiological arousal as a basis for lie detection.)

Special educators at a local school learned of the skin conductance research and approached the student about using the galvanic skin response device to identify stimulation that would produce arousal in an elementary school girl with a level of mental retardation so severe that she was unable to communicate. A variety of sensory stimulation activities had been attempted. She had been exposed to recorded animal sounds, different pleasant aromas, and a variety of pictures and drawings to view. Both her overt behaviors (e.g., posture, eye contact) and her galvanic skin response suggested little interest in any of these activities. The graduate student and the special education teachers were baffled. Then, the girl's brother happened to pass along the hallway and one of the teachers present astutely suggested that the brother be invited into the room. Immediately, the girl's galvanic skin response soared. She was clearly alerted by the presence of her brother. No other stimulation produced a comparable response.

How could that event and your knowledge of contiguity theory be used in future educational efforts with the girl? Clearly, one could not expect the brother to be present to heighten the girl's arousal level at all times. From a classical conditioning perspective, we might think of the girl's arousal level (as indicated by the galvanic skin response) to be an unconditional behavioral response to the unconditional stimulus of her brother's presence. Using classical conditioning principles, we might present a particular object, perhaps a plush bear or other toy, along with the brother's presence over a few occasions, until the girl begins to show arousal in response to the plush animal. The plush animal would thus become a conditional stimulus that could be presented to the girl in future special education efforts. We would also need to pair the presentation of the plush animal with the actual presence of the girl's brother periodically in order to avoid extinction of the behavior. Additional forms of learning might then be built upon this foundation of physiological arousal.

The scope of possible classical conditioning applications far exceeds this isolated example. A philosophy of education professor once shared the following observation with one of his doctoral students:

> An elite tennis player, viewing a novice opponent from across the net can use his superior skills in either of two ways. He can use his superior skills to carefully place shots that optimally challenge the learning opponent so that the opponent can develop skills and enthusiasm for the activity. Or, he can destroy the opponent.

How might this advice be interpreted in terms of classical conditioning? Let's assume that we are working with a client who has no history of playing tennis, but has shown interest in learning how to play that sport. With this client, we wish to not only teach essential skills and strategy, but also to help the client learn to experience pleasant feelings when playing tennis or, by generalization, thinking about playing tennis. We assume that these pleasant feelings will help the client pursue the activity as a part of his or her lifestyle. As such, from a classical conditioning perspective, we may direct our teaching activities at helping our new tennis student to learn to associate pleasant feelings with stimuli associated with tennis (e.g., ball, racquet, and tennis court).

In this example, items that the student will encounter when playing tennis, such as tennis courts, tennis racquets, and tennis balls, might be considered conditional stimuli. These characteristics of the tennis environment are conditional for individuals who have never played tennis, because first time players have no history of behavioral or experiential outcomes that result from involvement with tennis courts, racquets, or balls. Our challenge is to condition these stimuli such that when the individual encounters them directly or indirectly (perhaps through generalization to television or watching others play), he or she experiences positive feelings.

The remaining elements of this hypothetical scenario are the physiological response of pleasure (e.g., Smith, 1985) and the conditioning of the pleasure response to the stimuli. The mechanism for conditioning is the level of challenge that the teacher introduces into the instruction. Levels of challenge commensurate with individuals' skills are thought to elicit pleasurable responses (e.g., Csikszentmihlayi & Csikszentmihalyi, 1988). Thus, as a leisure educator, the teacher must use her or his skills to design learning experiences that involve using the court, ball, and racquet to present optimal challenges. Optimal challenge will be expected, in turn, to produce a pleasure response for the student. If challenges are optimal, the beginner will learn to associate the tennis context with physiological pleasure. In contrast, if the teacher introduces levels of challenge that are too complex or too simple, the pleasure response and will not occur nor will the desired conditioning result. Too much or too little complexity introduced by the teacher will thus "destroy" the student's pleasure and future participation in tennis playing.

Thus, an important teaching principle that follows from classical conditioning is to design learning experiences that are optimally challenging to participants. Leisure educators may further build upon this principle by encouraging generalization. How, for example, might a therapeutic recreation specialist use classical conditioning principles to promote development of a broadened repertoire of activities of clients? Accomplishing this goal may begin by simply pointing out common features of existing and new activities. Our novice tennis player might also enjoy racquetball. Both sports involve racquets, balls, and both sports have singles and doubles versions. Softball and baseball have similar elements of striking a ball with an object, running, and being outdoors. In attempting to expand a student's leisure repertoire, these similarities and differences could easily be pointed out by the astute leisure educator with an understanding of classical conditioning. Existing research clearly suggests that teaching actions as simple as pointing out such similarities lead to generalization of learning (Wise, 1999).

In addition to generalizing positive feelings, classical conditioning can be used to alleviate physiological stress, fear, and anxiety. A common problem in children's baseball, for example, is young batters being terrified of being hit by a pitched baseball. How might classical conditioning principles be used to alleviate that fear while helping the young player develop a healthy respect for safety? Leaving you with that challenge, we now turn to a second significant behavioral theory of learning: reinforcement theory or operant conditioning.

Behavioral Learning: Reinforcement Theory

Among the contemporaries of Watson and Pavlov was Edward Thorndike (1874-1949). Cat lovers will be pleased to know that those noble beasts played a significant role in Thorndike's pioneering research on the role of reinforcement in behavioral learning. Hungry cats were placed in boxes with transparent sides that enabled them to view a piece of fresh fish that was tantalizingly positioned just outside the box. Being cats, the animals frantically attacked all corners, top, and bottom of the box, eventually pulling a looped piece of string that opened the box and provided access to the piece of fish. In subsequent trials, cats similarly attacked all corners of the box, but began to pull the string a bit sooner than on earlier trials. Eventually, the cats learned to pull the string immediately.

This and subsequent work led Thorndike to advance his "law of effect," which proposed that if a stimulus (a string dangling in a box) is followed by a response (pulling the string) and then by a "satisfier" (a delicious fish dinner), the connection between the stimulus and response is strengthened. Conversely, if an "annoyer follows the stimulus and response" the connection is weakened. Subsequent research on satisfiers and annoyers convinced Thorndike that satisfiers are much more influential determinants of learning than are annoyers.

Thorndike's work offered a significant departure from the work of Pavlov, Watson, and others involved in the study of classical conditioning. In classical conditioning, certain environmental conditions elicit a particular response. In contrast, Thorndike's approach involves individual's acting, or operating, on an environment in order to receive a satisfier. Our novice tennis player might work hard to successfully execute a particular type of stroke and then be rewarded by the leisure educator with verbal praise or some other satisfier. This type of behavioral learning involves operating on the environment in order to receive a satisfier. It is thus referred to as operant conditioning.

While Thorndike pioneered operant conditioning, B. F. Skinner spent much of his career developing the approach. Skinner (1950) emphasized that actions we take (behaviors) must be understood in terms of the conditions that preceded the behavior (antecedents) and the events that result from the behavior (consequences). This sequence has been illustrated as A-B-C: antecedents, behavior, and consequences. Because consequences of one behavior naturally become antecedents of a subsequent behavior, learning can occur by changing either the antecedents or the consequences of a particular behavior.

Central to operant conditioning is understanding the nature and application of reinforcement. A reinforcer is any consequence that strengthens the behavior it follows (Woolfolk, 1998). Thus, if the verbal praise that the leisure educator provides to the novice tennis player strengthens the correct execution of a particular stroke, the verbal praise is a reinforcer. Many types of reinforcers may be considered in different therapeutic recreation settings, including verbal praise, granting of special privileges, candy, awards, and stickers. Reinforcements can be classified as being either positive or negative. Positive reinforcers are illustrated by the preceding examples. When positive reinforcers are provided, the link between the stimulus and the response is strengthened.

Not to be confused with punishment, negative reinforcement results from the removal of an aversive consequence. The leisure educator might use negative reinforcement by telling the novice player, "Let's play a little game. When you execute an appropriate serve, I will give you a point. If your serve is not correctly executed, we will volley until one of us wins the point. The first person who accumulates five points is the winner. I must caution you that I will volley using the very best of my skills." In this example, the aversive consequence, aggressive volleying by an opponent with superior skill, is removed if the behavior (correct serving) is correctly executed. In contrast to negative reinforcement, punishment occurs when a negative reinforcer is presented in response to a behavior. Suppose one of the novice tennis players is happily and deliberately launching tennis balls over the fence, putting them as close to orbit as possible. The leisure educator might use punishment to eliminate that behavior. "For every ball you his out of the court," the instructor might say, "you must sit for five minutes while everyone else plays." Thus, punishment involves an attempt to suppress a behavior while negative reinforcement attempts to strengthen a particular behavior.

Most of Skinner's work addressed positive reinforcers. He noted that negative reinforcement and punishment are less effective and may lead to a variety of undesired and unanticipated behaviors. Consistently, research in education indicates that among most populations of students, teachers can improve student behavior by praising students who follow the rules while ignoring those who are rule-breakers (Woolfolk, 1998).

A wealth of literature related to operant conditioning exists and much has been learned about reinforcers, punishment, antecedents, and consequences. One of the valuable results of that work has been identification of different schedules of reinforcement and the effects of such schedules. For learning a new behavior, a continuous reinforcement schedule is most effective. With such a schedule, reinforcement follows each occasion on which the behavior is exhibited. Our tennis instructor thus might choose to provide praise following each successful serve that the novice produced. Another approach is to provide an intermittent reinforcement schedule. Intermittent schedules are designed such that each and every desired behavior is not followed by a reward. Two types of intermittent reinforcement schedules may be considered. In an interval schedule, the behavior is rewarded each time a certain interval of time has passed between reinforcers. In a ratio schedule, reinforcement is provided following a certain number of desired responses between reinforcements.

Suppose a leisure educator is interested in helping students increase their awareness of leisure opportunities in the community. Students meet two times per week over a six week period. During that time, the leisure educator asks her students to spend some time each day thinking of one new activity that they could do in their community and to write a short paragraph about (1) why they might or might not like that activity and (2) what they would need to do to be in that activity. The leisure educator is interested in ensuring that the students complete the behavior of writing these paragraphs, in order that they may more fully explore community leisure opportunities.

The leisure educator could choose any of a variety of types of reinforcement and reinforcement schedules. Reinforcement options include verbal praise, providing prizes for progress, or awarding tokens that collectively lead to a desired outcome (e.g., a trip to a movie). These positive reinforcements could be provided on any of five different "schedules," as presented in Table 7.2 (p. 204). Information in that table is based on the assumption that the leisure educator was working with young children, who could be rewarded for completing homework assignments by being given a colorful sticker. Each of the schedules would be expected to produce a different result in terms of the rate at which the learning to complete the assignment occurs and the rapidity of extinction of the behavior following removal of the reinforcement. If a continuous reinforcement schedule were used, students would receive positive reinforcement each day they completed the assignment. That continuous reinforcement schedule would likely lead to the most rapid learning of the response (i.e., completing the homework), but the learning would also likely disappear quickly after the reinforcement was no longer provided (e.g., after the program, students might be less likely to think about community recreation possibilities). In contrast, a variable-ratio schedule could be expected to produce a very high response rate and greater persistence following the end of the program or termination of the reinforcement.

This section provided readers with a brief introduction to behavioral theories on human learning. Optimal use of behavioral learning theories by therapeutic recreation specialists would certainly involve intensive study of the theories and techniques, followed by actual practice. Nonetheless, the scope and complexity of that material should not dissuade therapeutic recreation specialists from attempting to incorporate basic ideas of both contiguity theory and reinforcement theory into their work. In the next section, we turn to an introduction to learning theories that embrace cognitive processes and address forms of learning other than behavior change.

An Introduction to Cognitive Learning

Cognitive learning theories seek to identify, model, and make use of capacities that are (perhaps) uniquely human. In this process doors are opened to a variety of phenomena that are intimately connected to learning. Cognitive perspectives include study of short-term and long-term memory, emotions, motivation, language development, creativity, culture, personality and individual differences, human development, and a myriad of related concerns. Given the enormity of the topic, our attention to the topic will be brief. We seek to introduce the reader to the nature of cognitive learning and suggest some teaching strategies that follow from an example of a cognitive learning theory.

Earlier, we provided a widely accepted definition of learning and pointed out its limitations. That definition established that learning has to do with a change in behavior or knowledge. The changes in behavior that were described in the previous sections are much less elusive than changes in knowledge. Given appropriate behavioral definitions of relevant behaviors, it is relatively easy to determine if a person has shoved someone else, executed a tennis serve, or has written in a daily journal. Because of our inability to observe cognitive knowledge directly, cognitive knowledge is much more difficult to understand and assess than behavior.

Because cognitive knowledge is not observable, we must construct conceptual models to understand it. In other words, knowledge is a construct. In

Table 7.2 Reinforcement Schedules and their Effects*

Reinforcement Schedule	Description	Example	Comments
Continuous	Every appropriate response is followed by reinforcement	A sticker is provided each time the student completes the homework	Facilitates rapid rate of learning. Rapid extinction when reinforcement is discontinued
Fixed-Interval	Reinforcement is provided after the passage of a predetermined and constant amount of time	A sticker is provided to students who did their homework at the end of the second class meeting each week	Desired responses increase in frequency as time for reinforcement approaches. Rapid extinction when reinforcement is discontinued
Variable-Interval	Reinforcement is provided after varying lengths of time	A sticker is provided to students who completed their homework after meetings 1, 4, 5, 7, and 11	Slower rate of learning. More resistant to extinction than continuous or fixed-interval reinforcement
Fixed-Ratio	Reinforcement is provided after a fixed number of desired responses have been provided	Completion of every three homework assignments is reinforced with a sticker	Facilitates rapid rate of learning. Rapid extinction when reinforcement is discontinued
Variable-Ratio	Reinforcement after a changing number of responses	Stickers are provided after students have completed 1, 3, 7, and 10 homework assignments	Facilitates rapid rate of learning. Form of reinforcement that creates greatest resistance of response to extinction

* Adapted from Woolfolk, 1998, p. 213.

investigating cognitive learning we consider examples of how the construct (knowledge) has been developed by learning theorists and educators. Two examples will be given, each of which seem to have great relevance to therapeutic recreation specialists when they are in their leisure educator roles. One of these models is the result of work by Farnham-Diggory (1994) and the other is from Merrill's (1983) component-display theory.

To provide a context for this discussion, recall our earlier question about learning. We asked readers to consider the difference between learning that would result from careful scrutiny of a book on how to fly airplanes and actual training. This example illustrates two different types of learning, both of which are included in both Farnham-Diggory's (1994) model and in the component-display theory (Merrill, 1983). As we describe these two models, see if you can relate the airplane example to types of learning described in the models.

Cognitive Learning Theory:
Types of Knowledge and Instructional Tactics

Farnham-Diggory (1994) identified five distinct types of knowledge that have emerged from research on learning between 1930 and 1960:

Declarative Knowledge   "Knowledge that can be declared, usually in words, through lectures, books, writing, verbal exchange, braille, sign language, mathematical notation, and so on (p. 468)."

Procedural Knowledge

"Procedural knowledge that is in the form of action sequences (p. 469)." When we learn the steps necessary to play a new game, complete our tax returns, process a group discussion, or drive an automobile, we are using procedural knowledge.

Conceptual Knowledge

"Mental representations of complex ideas, like knowledge, for example. Includes categorizing and development of schemata. Categories are groupings of common features. Schemata are more complex arrangements, like maps and scripts (p. 469)."

Analogical Knowledge

"Sometimes called imagery, [analogical knowledge] preserves specific correspondence between what is in the outside world and what is in the head . . . this type of learning is . . . something like a sensory imprint (p. 469)." Many successful athletes, for example, generate mental pictures or mental movies of an action (making a free throw in basketball, kicking a field goal in football, ball hitting the pocket in bowling, sinking an object ball in billiards) before actually attempting that action.

Logical Knowledge

"System of causal implications, a mental model of what is connected to what and what leads to what (p. 469)." These are the causal connections. For example, what results occur, when we flip light switches, rub matches across an abrasive surface, turn an automobile ignition key, or implement a leisure education program?

Each of these different forms of knowledge "dictates different knowledge acquisition strategies and objectives" (Farnham-Diggory, 1994, p. 469). Careful study of material in a book describing how to fly an airplane would certainly be useful in the acquisition of *declarative knowledge*. Acquisition of knowledge of specific sequences of actions needed to fly the airplane, however, would require quite different knowledge acquisition strategies. Learning these sequences of action, or *procedural learning*, would almost certainly be needed to fly an airplane. Perhaps lack of recognition of the need for different knowledge acquisition strategies accounts for the unimpressive results of leisure education efforts that were described earlier. Little evidence exists of instructors using teaching strategies to help learners develop mental images of how to participate in activities to facilitate the development of *analogical knowledge* (e.g., Gallwey, 1971) or of actual cause-and-effect exercises and learning experiments that might facilitate the acquisition of the *logical knowledge* necessary for problem solving and leisure decision making.

Further, in the leisure education literature, little evidence exists of instructors seeking to match teaching strategies appropriate to the different forms of learning to appropriate teaching tasks. Farnham-Diggory (1994, p. 470) points out that, in most teaching contexts, four basic "Teaching Tactics" may be used:

Talking	Lecturing, telling, reading from notes, presenting information verbally, talking . . . questioning, and so on.
Displaying	Modeling, showing, demonstrating.
Coaching	Pointing out cues, suggesting changes, guiding (all this while the student is doing something)
Arranging the learning environment	Case studies, simulations, experiments that students conduct

In planning strategies for teaching leisure education, therapeutic recreation specialists may find it useful to construct a matrix of the type of knowledge they seek to create by teaching tactic that can be used. In teaching leisure decision making, for example, a leisure educator might use the talking tactic to teach analogical knowledge by asking students to create a mental picture of (and perhaps artistically draw) a set of circumstances that might result from choosing one option instead of another. The teacher might also design a case study (arranging the learning environment) to help learners acquire logical knowledge of the effects of decisions that they make. Arranging information about teaching tactics and knowledge type in this way may be useful in reminding leisure educators to consider which teaching tactics will work more successfully in creating which type of learning.

Cognitive Learning Theory: Component-Display Theory

A foundation for Merrill's (1983) *component-display theory* is a matrix of learning performance by learning content. As can be seen from review of Table 7.3 (p. 208), three levels of performance are specified. One can *find* knowledge, one can *use* knowledge, or one can simply *remember* knowledge. Remembering knowledge is the simplest of these procedures. For example, you may recall that John Watson was one of the pioneers of contiguity theory and you may be able to describe how classical conditioning works. But does reading the chapter alone make you a better therapeutic recreation specialist? Can you use that knowledge as a therapist or leisure educator? Using knowledge indicates that you can apply the knowledge that you have learned. Finally, finding knowledge is the most complex form of learning implied by the performance by content matrix. Finding knowledge does not mean locating information, as you might find an answer to an algebra problem in the back of the book. Rather, finding knowledge points to the discovery of knowledge. In the context of the current chapter, if you are able to discover new and innovative approaches to reinforcement and punishment when you are teaching leisure education lessons, you would be performing at the find level of cognitive performance.

In addition to level of learning performance, Table 7.3 specifies "learning content" that students might acquire. The learning performance by learning content matrix identifies four types of knowledge: facts, concepts, procedures, and principles. Each of these corresponds rather well to one of Farnham-Diggory's (1994) types of knowledge. Facts correspond to declarative knowledge. To remember a fact, one needs only to search one's memory to reproduce or recognize the information that was previously stored (Merrill, 1983, p. 287). Concepts correspond to Farnham-Diggory's (1994) conceptual knowledge. Merrill points out that "concepts are groups of objects, events, or symbols that all share some common characteristics and are identified by the same name" (Merrill, 1983, p. 287). Tennis, racquetball, badminton, and squash may thus all be combined into the concept of racquet sports. Procedures in Merrill's performance-content matrix correspond to Farnham-Diggory's procedural knowledge. This form of knowledge has to do with the sequence of steps necessary to accomplish a given outcome. How does one produce a ceramic pot? What are the correct steps for serving a tennis ball? How does a sailor execute a "quick stop recovery" person-overboard maneuver? What steps should one follow when one encounters an interpersonal conflict? Finally, principle in the performance-content matrix corresponds to Farnham-Diggory's logical knowledge. As such, principles "are explanations or predictions of why things happen in the world . . . [they] are those cause-and-effect or correlational relationships that are used to interpret events and circumstances" (Merrill, 1983, p. 288).

The performance content matrix provides a foundation for learning objectives and suggests appropriate teaching tactics. Different learning objectives and different teaching tactics are appropriate to each combination of performance and content. Learning objectives and teaching tactics appropriate for learning a fact (Learning Objectives 3.1 and Teaching Tactics 3.1) would differ significantly from learning objectives and teaching tactics associated with finding a principle (Learning Objectives 1.4 and Teaching Tactics 1.4). Given the goal of increasing awareness of community leisure opportunities, for example, the following learning objectives might be established:

- Students will demonstrate their ability to access community resources by riding the bus to three different recreation destinations over the next three weeks (Cell 2.3 in Table 7.3—level of performance: use, type of content: procedure),
- When asked, students will name four different public parks that they could visit by the end of the leisure education unit (Cell 3.3 in Table 7.3—level of performance: remember, type of content: procedure),
- When asked, students will describe what leisure means to them and the significance of leisure in their lives (Cell 1.2 in Table 7.3—level of performance: find, type of content: concept), and
- By the end of the program, students will demonstrate the use of a conflict resolution strategy (Cell 2.3 in Table 7.3—level of performance: use, type of content: procedure).

Collectively these learning objectives represent the goal of increasing awareness and utilization of community leisure opportunities for a particular client. Accomplishment of that goal may require objectives from any number

Level of Performance	Type of Content			
	Fact (1)	Concept (2)	Procedure (3)	Principle (4)
Find (1)	Learning Objectives 1.1 Teaching Tactics 1.1	Learning Objectives 1.2 Teaching Tactics 1.2	Learning Objectives 1.3 Teaching Tactics 1.3	Learning Objectives 1.4 Teaching Tactics 1.4
Use (2)	Learning Objectives 2.1 Teaching Tactics 2.1	Learning Objectives 2.2 Teaching Tactics 2.2	Learning Objectives 2.3 Teaching Tactics 2.3	Learning Objectives 2.4 Teaching Tactics 2.4
Remember (3)	Learning Objectives 3.1 Teaching Tactics 3.1	Learning Objectives 3.2 Teaching Tactics 3.2	Learning Objectives 3.3 Teaching Tactics 3.3	Learning Objectives 3.4 Teaching Tactics 3.4

Table 7.3 Merrill's (1983) Performance-Content Matrix*

* Adapted from Merrill, 1983, p. 286.

of cells in Table 7.3. In the current example none of the cells associated with fact or principle were considered important for this hypothetical group of learners. Procedures, however, were the focus of three of the objectives because utilization (remembering and using a procedure) was central to the overall goal of the program.

Applying component-display theory is a very complex matter of implementing particular teaching tactics ("displays") in sequences specified by the theory (Merrill, 1983). Simple awareness of the performance by content matrix however, is sufficient to help leisure educators identify teaching strategies that may be effective. The objective above concerning conflict resolution could probably not, for example, be taught with only "talk" methods. In order to "use" a procedure, learners must actually practice that procedure. More effective learning would likely follow from techniques within the families of arranging the learning environment (perhaps a simulated interpersonal conflict) and displaying (providing an actual example of conflict resolution procedures through a simulated conflict).

In working with cognitive learning theory, we must begin by constructing models of knowledge such as those of Merrill (1983), Farnham-Diggory (1994), or others (e.g., Bloom, Englehart, Furst, Hill, & Krathwohl, 1956; Gagne, 1970) before we may proceed to develop a theory of how knowledge may best be acquired. There are many cognitive theories of learning. We complete our glimpse of cognitive learning theories with an example of a constructivist approach, which emphasizes that successful learners must actively grapple with information, interpret it in unique ways that make sense to them, and make it fit with existing mental arrangements of previous information that they have encountered, processed, and classified (Hill, 1997).

Cognitive Learning Theory: Reciprocal Questioning

King (1990) conducted a study that compared two approaches to promoting student comprehension of a lecture. Two groups of students were formed: a discussion group and a "reciprocal questioning" group. Both groups listened to the same lecture but following the lecture they engaged in two very different learning activities. The discussion group was asked to divide into groups of two to three students each and then engage in a discussion of the lecture, with the intent of helping other students to comprehend the material discussed in the lecture. In contrast, members of the reciprocal questioning group generated a set of discussion questions using a set of question stems provided by the researcher and then discussed answers to those questions in groups of two to three students each. At the conclusion of the discussion and reciprocal question period, all students completed a test of comprehension. Results revealed that the students who participated in the reciprocal questioning exercise had significantly greater comprehension of the lecture than the students who participated in the discussion group.

The study was based on several assumptions of cognitive learning theory. Constructivist theory emphasizes the vital importance of social interaction in developing knowledge. Those theories assume that significant learning arises from resolution of differing perspectives of different students. These differences result from both different amounts of information retained by different students and from differing opinions about that information. As King (1990) points out, ". . . these theories emphasize the cognitive advantages of peer interaction . . . cognitive discrepancies arising in a social context are seen as having *greater* cognitive benefit for an individual than the conflict of ideas that an individual might experience alone" (p. 666).

In addition to constructivist approaches to cognitive learning, King (1990) pointed out that the reciprocal questioning strategy was also consistent with information processing theories of learning. These theories emphasize the importance of connections between information that learners encounter. Making connections between new information facilitates learning. That connection can either be between old information that we have stored in our memory or between elements of different types of new information. We better understand the assassination of President John Kennedy, for example, if we contrast that tragic event with the equally tragic assassination of President Abraham Lincoln. Information processing theory suggests that successful teachers actively include in their teaching methods strategies that help students to make these connections.

The reciprocal question stems were specifically designed to promote such connections. Examples of the question stems used are as follows (King, 1990, p. 669):

1. How is _____ related to _____ that we studied earlier?

2. What is the difference between _____ and _____ ?

3. How are _____ and _____ similar?

4. In your opinion, which is better, _____ or _____ ? Why?

5. How would you use _____ to _____ ?

6. How does _____ affect _____ ?

7. Explain why _____ .

8. What do you think would happen if _____ ?

Notice that all of these questions require the learner to make cognitive connections between information that has been learned. Further, these questions imply knowledge that is at higher levels than declarative (Farnham-Diggory, 1994) or *fact* (Merrill, 1983). Identification of similarities and differences, as required by questions one, two, three, and four involves conceptual knowledge (Farnham-Diggory, 1994; Merrill, 1983). Questions five through eight involve learning about cause and effect, which Farnham-Diggory refers to as logical knowledge and Merrill (1983) refers to as a principle.

The examples of cognitive learning provided here are only a fraction of a wealth of literature available to therapeutic recreation specialists. These limited examples, however, are sufficient to provide guidance to the leisure education process. As they plan curricula and lessons for teaching leisure education, therapeutic recreation specialists should consider the type of knowledge (e.g., Should I teach a fact? A concept? A procedure?), the teaching tactic (Farnham-Diggory, 1994), and the method (e.g., How can I help learners make connections between information that I teach?). Attention to these theory-based techniques of teaching have great potential to significantly increase the effectiveness of leisure education programs.

Multicultural Considerations for Learning and Leisure Education

Teachers of multicultural education often begin with implicit assumptions about the purpose and specific techniques of instruction. Below are some examples of assumptions associated with leisure education:

> *Assumption 1:* The long-term goal of the leisure education program is to promote individual freedom and independence.

> *Assumption 2:* Individual achievement should be emphasized rather than group achievement.

> *Assumption 3:* Good communication is reflected by the extent of eye contact maintained during leisure education lessons.

Assumption 4: Issues of spirituality and religion are highly sensitive matters that should be avoided or excluded.

All of these assumptions have been held in therapeutic recreation practice. The assumption that the long-term goal of leisure education is to promote independence is entirely consistent with philosophy and purpose statements of the National Therapeutic Recreation Association (NTRS) and the American Therapeutic Recreation Association (ATRA). An emphasis on individual achievement pervades our educational system, reflected in activities from assignment of individual grades to the establishment of class rankings. Many people consider consistent eye contact to be a hallmark of good communication in teaching, suggesting that the individual is an interested and active learner. Finally, the separation of church and state discourages learning that has religious or spiritual content. (One of the authors has occasionally heard professionals contend that spirituality is not an appropriate "outcome" for therapeutic recreation.)

Yet assumptions are not always correct. With respect to promoting independence and emphasizing individual achievement (assumptions 1 and 2), some minority groups instead emphasize a collectivist orientation. Nonetheless, the NTRS and ATRA assert that therapeutic recreation should primarily focus on individualist values such as independence, personal freedom, and self-esteem (Peregoy & Dieser, 1997). With respect to Assumption 3, avoiding eye contact with authorities is a sign of respect in some cultures (Peregoy & Dieser, 1997). Thus, lack of eye contact might in no way suggest detachment from learning. Avoiding spirituality (Assumption 4) could seriously compromise serving clients from Hispanic backgrounds where "espirituismo," or spiritualism, is a significant value (Gloria & Peregoy, 1996). Finally, important learning style differences exist among people of different ethnic backgrounds (Banks, 1994). Cultural variation in values and learning styles are thus significant concerns in designing appropriate and effective leisure education experiences.

The literature on multicultural learning has expanded appreciably, covering a wide variety of topics and issues. In this section, we wish to stress the importance of a multicultural approach to leisure education and briefly address the basics of what Gay (2000) described as *culturally responsive teaching*.

Several characteristics of culturally responsive teaching are relevant to leisure education, including:

- Acknowledging the legitimacy of multiculturalism for teaching and learning,
- Incorporating multicultural information, resources, and materials, and
- Using a wide variety of teaching strategies that are appropriate to diverse learning styles. (Gay, 2000)

We have previously emphasized the legitimacy of multiculturalism in general and for teaching and learning in particular. Furthermore, therapeutic recreation professionals must be sufficiently knowledgeable of the cultural backgrounds of their clients to incorporate multicultural information, resources, and materials. Besides offering leisure education curricula appropriate for persons of diverse backgrounds (e.g., class, gender, ethnicity, sexual orientation), therapeutic recreation professionals must consider learning styles.

A learning style is "the process one habitually uses for cognitive problem solving and for showing what one knows and is capable of doing" (Gay, 2000, p. 150). Culturally responsive teaching necessitates understanding how cultural socialization influences the learning style of culturally diverse individuals. Gay (2000) described eight key dimensions of learning styles that provide an interactive composite for planning culturally compatible teaching:

- *Procedural* pertains to the preferred ways of approaching and working through learning tasks (pacing rates; distribution of time; variety versus similarity; novelty or predictability; passivity or activity; task-directed or sociality; structured order or freedom; and preference for direct teaching or inquiry and discovery learning).
- *Communicative* refers to the organization, sequencing, and presentation of thoughts in verbal and written forms, such as "elaborated narrative storytelling or precise responses to explicit questions; as topic-specific or topic-chaining discourse techniques; as passionate advocacy of ideas or dispassionate recorders and reporters; whether the purpose is to achieve descriptive and factual accuracy or to capture persuasive power and convey literary aestheticism."
- *Substantive* refers to how content is preferred "such as descriptive details or general pattern, concepts and principles or factual information, statistics or personal and social scenarios; preferred subjects, such as math, science, social studies, fine or language arts; technical, interpretative, and evaluative tasks; preferred intellectualizing tasks, such as memorizing, describing, analyzing, classifying, or criticizing."
- *Environmental* pertains to physical, social, and interpersonal settings for learning, including the individual's preference for "sound or silence; room lighting and temperature; presence or absence of others; ambiance of struggle or playfulness, of fun and joy, or of pain and somberness."
- *Organizational* relates to preferences for structural arrangements, "including the amount of personal space; the fullness or emptiness of learning space; rigidity or flexibility in use of and claims made to space; carefully organized or cluttered learning resources and space locations; individually claimed or group-shared space; rigidity or flexibility of the habitation of space."

- *Perceptual* addresses preferences for sensory stimulation, "including visual, tactile, auditory, kinetic, oral, or multiple sensory modalities."
- *Relational* refers to preferences for interpersonal and social approaches to learning, "including formality or informality, individual competition or group cooperation, independence or interdependence, peer-peer or child-adult, authoritarian or egalitarian, internal or external locus of control; conquest or community."
- *Motivational* refers to preferences for incentives that promote learning, "including individual accomplishment or group well-being, competition or cooperation, conquest or harmony, expediency or propriety, image or integrity, external rewards or internal desires."
(pp. 151-152)

A brief scenario depicting how a therapeutic recreation specialist might approach leisure education in a culturally responsive manner follows. While reading this example, keep in mind that the influence of culture must be treated as a set of *tendencies* that run from weak to strong rather than as inflexible laws that lead to stereotypes.

Imagine that a therapeutic recreation specialist works in a culturally diverse psychiatric facility. The therapeutic recreation specialist covers community leisure resources as part of a leisure education program for a group of clients who will be discharged soon. Committed to multiculturalism as socially just and programmatically effective, the specialist initially makes certain that the information, resources, and materials she uses reflect her clients' cultural backgrounds. While selecting material that addresses where clients can join community celebrations during holidays, she includes holidays that reflect her clientele, incorporating information on Hanukkah, Kwanza, and Christmas. Furthermore, she provides information on community celebrations that honor historically significant events, such as Cinco de Mayo and the local Stonewall Celebration, which commemorates the struggle for gay and lesbian rights.

Besides assessing content, the therapeutic recreation specialist prepares a process for culturally responsive teaching using Gay's (2000) eight dimensions of learning styles. In the *procedural dimension,* the therapeutic recreation specialist recognizes that her older clients require a predictable routine while her younger clients respond better to novelty. Further, she determines that most of her African-American clients tend to prefer active and social learning (Bennett, 1995). Consequently, she incorporates music and dance into leisure education sessions. Looking at the *communicative dimension,* she discerns that her older clients generally prefer using narratives. Her European American clients relate better to literal narratives while her American Indian participants respond well to metaphorical stories. In the *substantive dimension,* the therapeutic recreation specialist has learned that male clients tend to prefer content that emphasizes factual information and analytic tasks. Conversely, female clients usually prefer content oriented to social scenarios and tasks that allow them to interpret their subjective experiences. Of course, she has male and female clients who resist categorization, and therefore makes suitable adjustments for their individual needs. In constructing the *environmental dimension,* the therapeutic recreation accommodates various styles. For instance, she does not assume that reflection on spirituality and leisure is necessarily done in silence and solitude by all of her clients. Accordingly, she creates an environment where people can reflect together or by themselves. Similarly, she uses the *organization dimension* to provide for individual and group space. In planning for the *perceptual dimension,* the therapeutic recreation specialist incorporates multiple sensory modalities suited for a variety of learning styles. For example, her male clients tend to respond to stimuli along class lines. Those from blue-collar backgrounds show a preference for visual, verbal, and tactile learning; thus she uses "show, tell, and touch" presentations of community leisure programs, such as fishing and woodworking. Conversely, white-collar male clients prefer gathering information through oral presentations and written materials. The *relational dimension* is integral to leisure education. The therapeutic recreation specialist has found that European Americans prefer to learn independently whereas Asian-American males show equal preference for independence and interdependence, depending on the context. Her male and female Latino clients are more interdependent, reflective of the cultural value placed on communalism. Finally, the therapeutic recreation specialist makes certain to create a *motivational dimension* responsive to cultural differences. She has found that class is generally a better predicator of incentive than ethnicity for most of her clients. Individual rewards such as certificates of achievement seem to work best with clients from white-collar backgrounds. On the other hand, blue-collar clients of color are more motivated by the therapeutic recreation specialist's acknowledgement of group accomplishments. By her commitment and careful attention to content and process, the therapeutic recreation specialist has made progress toward providing a culturally responsive leisure education program.

Obviously, a policy of one size fits all, especially where it exclusively follows European-American culture, is inappropriate in a multicultural environment. Equally evident is the formidable challenge of providing multicultural leisure education. Yet it is the only ethical choice for therapeutic recreation professionals. While this section has provided elementary guidance, readers should consult a variety of resources as they prepare culturally rich and responsive leisure education programs.

Case Study: Forms that Leisure May Take

In this chapter, we have introduced an enormous scope of topics about human learning and its relationship to leisure education. From this overview it seems reasonable to propose a few general principles for teaching. Those principles are presented in Table 7.4 (p. 220). Included are principles that follow from behavioral learning theory, cognitive learning theory, and multicultural concerns.

These principles provide an opportunity for us to observe how theories about human learning may be put into practice. Earlier in the chapter, we provided a brief description of a lesson from the *Kangaroo Kit*, a leisure education curriculum that was developed in the 1970s for use in public schools (Zeyen, et al., 1977). The lesson involved investigation of different forms that leisure may take. Readers may recall that in the lesson students are asked to prepare a list of their present and past leisure experiences and categorize each in terms of five continua:

- Performer/participant vs. audience,
- Physical vs. mental,
- Individual vs. social,
- Structured/planned vs. nonstructured/spontaneous, and
- Momentary vs. Long term.

Let's assume that a lesson on this topic is in progress in a public school classroom. We can eavesdrop on that lesson and look for evidence of the principles in the instructional approach. As you review the dialogue, try to identify ways in which techniques used are consistent and inconsistent with the learning theories introduced.

> TEACHER: *(As an exciting, active game draws to a conclusion)* What great fun that was! I hope that you enjoyed that warm-up activity as much as I did. I am impressed with how excited all of you are to be talking about recreation today.
>
> JOHNNY: Susie pinched me just after we started the game.
>
> SUSIE: I did not. I fell against you when I was trying to hop.
>
> TEACHER: Let's start our lesson about recreation. Who can remember the activity that we did last time we talked about recreation?

JENNIFER: I can! We made lists of three places that we can go in our neighborhood and we drew maps of how to get there from our school.

TEACHER: Excellent, Jennifer! You have an outstanding memory!

JACOB: We also made a list of what hours of the day we could visit those places and how much it would cost for us to go. We even put in how much it would cost to ride a bus to those places.

SHIRLEY: I think that Susie tried to pinch me, too.

TEACHER: Superb, Jacob! I can see that you put a lot of work into your map and that you remember what we did very well! Today, we are going to do another activity that involves listing things and then providing more information about each. You might recall that when we talked about places in our communities that we could go for recreation, we discovered that there are several ways that you can get to those places. What were some ways of getting to places where we do recreation?

TYLER: You can ride a bus.

SUSIE: We said that one already, Tyler.

TEACHER: Thank you for reminding us that we can ride a bus to recreation places, Tyler.

TIMOTHY: I like to ride my bicycle to places where I do recreation.

TEACHER: Good suggestion! Anyone else have an idea?

AMY: I did that once and had my bike ripped off.

SETH: You can walk. My older sister sometimes drives me to skating rink, if I promise to do the dishes for her for a week.

TEACHER: Excellent suggestion, Seth! Sometimes we can find other people who are happy to help us.

AMY: Yeah, it helps to bribe people. But I hate doing dishes.

SUSIE: I make my mom take me.

TEACHER: Thank you, Susie. I'm pleased that your mom loves you so much that she finds time to take you to special places for recreation.

SUSIE: Sometimes the places are not that special. We go to the mall aaaallll the time. . .

TEACHER: Thank you for all of these wonderful ideas! Today, we are going to talk about forms of participation in activities. To start, I would like for you to think about whether you agree or disagree with this statement: 'Any recreation activity can be done in different ways. *(The teacher points to that statement, which is written on a white board)*

JOHNNY: I disagree. If you play softball, there is only one way; by the rules.

SUSIE: But people can break rules.

SHIRLEY: You bet they can, you break rules all the time, Susie.

MAX: You can also play softball either fast pitch or slow pitch. And if you want to be sure who is on what team, you can play shirts or skins.

MARK: You only play shirts and skins in basketball.

SARAH: Yeah, and girls never play on the skins team.

TEACHER: Thank you for these ideas about rules and doing activities in different ways. You are good listeners and quick thinkers. Now, here is what I would like you to do. Please find two other people to work with, so that we end up with teams of three people per group. In each group, I would like for you to do the things listed on the board over here. *(She gestures to the white board)* First, choose one person in your group. Find out two activities that she or he likes to do in her or his free time. On your group's space on the white board, list at least three ways that those activities are similar and three ways that they are different. Then, for both activities, list three ways that the activity could be done differently. Repeat this for all people in your group. Finally, review all of your work and see if you can describe five general ways that recreation activities can be done differently. Be ready to share with the rest of us what you have found. Thank you again for your involvement today, you really are a great group of kids!

What evidence of use of learning theory can you find in this dialogue? Can you relate the use of the active game to start the session with contiguity theory? Why did the teacher begin the lesson by asking students to reflect on their previous lesson? In what ways is that approach consistent with both contiguity theory and cognitive learning theory? Did you notice that, consistent with reinforcement theories, the teacher ignores inappropriate responses (such as "Susie pinched me") and reinforced every appropriate response with a positive comment? Why did the teacher ask the students to form into cooperative learning groups for the exercise? Why did she ask students to compare and contrast activities and forms of participation? Would her motives lie in the notion of social construction of meaning? Why did she not enumerate for the students the five forms that she was trying to teach? Might this have something to do with a learning objective about discovery of a concept? Careful review of the dialogue will reveal other applications of learning theory to this teaching environment and it will uncover missed opportunity to capitalize on learning opportunities as well. We encourage you to engage in this exercise.

Table 7.4 General Principles/Teaching Tips

1. Plan opportunities for students to associate new stimuli (e.g., equipment, setting, strategies) with conditions that naturally create physical arousal and pleasure.

2. Help learners develop new skills, point out similarities between the new activity and activities with which learners are familiar.

3. Provide continuous reinforcement of appropriate behaviors when teaching a new skill to a novice.

4. Provide reinforcement on a variable-ratio schedule when working with a learner who is experienced in a particular topic or activity.

5. Identify a variety of types of reinforcement that might be used with learners with whom you work.

6. Plan strategies that are appropriate to the type of content (e.g., fact, concept, procedure, principle) *and* level of performance (remember, use, discover) that you desire learners to attain.

7. Keep in mind that certain teaching tactics may work better than others when you teach particular types of content at particular levels of performance. Techniques that help learners remember a fact, for example, will likely be much different than techniques that help learners use a procedure.

8. Search for ways to help learners find similarities, differences, and other types of associations between existing knowledge and new knowledge.

9. Include in your instructions opportunities for cooperative learning, in which learners work together to solve problems related to the content that you teach.

10. Maintain awareness of differences in learning styles and cultural values of students with whom you work. Design learning experiences that are appropriate to these learning styles and values.

Summary

This chapter provided an introduction to learning as related to therapeutic recreation. Learning may tentatively be defined as a relatively permanent change in knowledge or behavior that follows from experience. Given the mission of therapeutic recreation as stated by professional organizations, therapeutic recreation specialists are at least as much educators as they are therapists and recreation specialists. They create experiences that bring about relatively permanent changes in knowledge and behavior. Based on the results of a review of leisure education research, we proposed that leisure education efficacy might be enhanced through greater attention to learning theory. We then provided an introduction to behavioral learning theory and to cognitive learning theory. This chapter provided only a very basic, introductory treatment of an infinitely fascinating topic, human learning. Students are encouraged to undertake a much more thorough study of human learning and how it is related to the science and craft of teaching.

Recommended Readings

Dattilo, J. (1999). *Leisure education program planning*. (2nd ed.) State College, PA: Venture Publishing, Inc.

Farnham-Diggory, S. (1994). Paradigms of knowledge and instruction. *Review of Educational Research, 64,* 463-467.

Gay, G. (2000). *Culturally responsive teaching: Theory, research, and practice*. New York, NY: Teachers College.

Hill, W. F. (1997). *Learning: A survey of psychological interpretations* (6th ed.). New York, NY: Longman.

National Therapeutic Recreation Society. (1993). *Leisure Education*. Ashburn, VA: National Recreation and Park Association.

Peregoy, J. J. & Dieser, R. B. (1997). Multicultural awareness in therapeutic recreation: Hamlet living. *Therapeutic Recreation Journal 31*, 174-188.

Chapter

Recreation Inclusion

The main goal of rehabilitation is quality of life. For that reason, comprehensive rehabilitation has become more oriented to the community (Sandstrom, Hoppe & Smutko, 1996). Furthermore, leisure has been acknowledged as a powerful resource for involving people in their communities (Hutchison & McGill, 1998). Therapeutic recreation's contribution to rehabilitation should also be judged by its capacity to help people to become involved in community leisure opportunities for the purpose of improving their quality of life. The remainder of this chapter presents basic principles and practices of community integration and recreation inclusion.

Foundations of Recreation Inclusion

With respect to community integration, *recreation inclusion* refers to empowering persons who have disabling conditions to become valued and active members of their communities through sociocultural involvement in community-based leisure opportunities. Persons with disabilities should have the same chances for quality of life as persons without disabilities.

A compelling argument can be made for including persons with disabilities in community leisure activities and programs. Experts agree that quality of life can best be achieved in the community, where people have access to key resources, such as work, leisure, education, and relationships (Galambos, 1995). Sylvester (1992) argued that well-being, a ubiquitous goal in therapeutic recreation, "requires some measure of leisure" making the right to leisure "an indispensable corollary of the right to well-being" (p. 16). The *National Therapeutic Recreation Society Code of Ethics* (1990) features the right to leisure in its preamble, declaring it "essential to health and well-being" (see Appendix C) The *National Recreation and Park Association Position Statement on Inclusion* (1999) also embraces the right to leisure, stating that "the value of inclusive leisure experiences in enhancing the quality of life for all people, with and without disabilities, cannot be overstated" (see Appendix E). Referring to the rights of life, liberty, and the pursuit of happiness contained in the Declaration of Independence, Schleien, Ray, and Green (1997) assert, "*All American citizens have these rights*" (p. xiv). "All Americans" must also apply to persons with disabilities, since a disabling condition does not disqualify an individual from citizenship. The Americans with Disabilities Act has institutionalized these principles and commitments into law, making it illegal to discriminate against persons with disabilities in employment, transportation, government agencies, telecommunications systems, and goods, services, and facilities offered to the public by private agencies (see Dattilo, 1994). Donna Shalala, former Secretary of Health and Human Services, said, "No person should have to live in a nursing home or other institution if he or she can life in his or her community," adding further that "unnecessary institutionalization of individuals with disabilities is discrimination under the Americans with Disabilities Act" (quoted in Pear, 2000, p. 20). In partnership with our Canadian colleagues and human service professionals worldwide, therapeutic recreation has the opportunity and responsibility to assume prominent leadership in securing the right to leisure for all persons.

Although more studies on the benefits of recreation inclusion need to be performed, the existing research is encouraging. Programs associated with recreation inclusion have contributed to improved decision making (Bedini, Bullock & Driscoll, 1993), confidence, risk-taking, and self-esteem (McAvoy, Schatz, Stutz, Schleien & Lais, 1989), and increased social interactions (Schleien, Ray, Soderman-Olson & McMahon, 1987). Furthermore, it can be inferred from the existing evidence that persons with disabilities can benefit from recreation and leisure participation comparable to persons without disabilities (see Driver, Brown & Peterson, 1991).

Another reason for inclusion relates to the concept of self. The existence of a "self," especially in the forms of self-concept and self-esteem, depends on the presence of other human beings. People acquire their perceptions of who they are (identity) and what makes them worthwhile (esteem) through experiences they have and messages they receive from family, friends, peers, neighbors, coworkers, teammates, and teachers. Without culturally based appraisals of valued identities and esteemed behaviors, individuals would have no basis for developing self-concept and self-esteem. In short, they would have no idea of who they are. The work ethic is a prime example of how social views become sources of individual identity. Autonomy, a key aspect of European-American identity and a prominent cultural value in America, also requires involvement with other human beings. "Sociality," as Agich (1993) explained, "is an essential feature of human existence. Indeed, social life makes autonomy . . . possible because without the social life there would be no space for agency" (p. 88).

Agency, in turn, is a requisite for self-determination, one of therapeutic recreation's cardinal goals.

In the case of persons with disabilities, the issues of worth, identity, and inclusion are expressed on at least two fronts. First, without access to social spheres, persons with disabilities remain socially invisible to persons without disabilities, which breeds fear, mistrust, intolerance, prejudice, and discrimination (see Hutchison & Lord, 1979). Second, even where they are physically integrated into society, without opportunities to acquire the identities that are valued in society—parent, partner, lover, student, friend, athlete, worker—they are limited to the monolithic identity of disabled person. This is not meant to suggest that a disability is not *a* part of a person's identity. All characteristics constitute a person's identity. Yet it is no more the entirety of one's being than is age, gender, religion, or ethnicity. Therefore, having opportunities to participate in community life is essential to the humanity of persons with disabilities.

Another compelling reason for recreation inclusion is for the sake of community. This is especially true for persons from cultures that hold collectivist values. Even American society, with its predominant ethos of individualism, has a discernible communitarian tradition (Bellah, Madsen, Sullivan & Tipton, 1985). An early advocate of community as a core value of therapeutic recreation, Sylvester (1989b) wrote:

> Community is not just the final destination along the mainstreaming continuum; it is an essential element of quality of life. . . . Despite the folklore of individualism, we are more interdependent than independent. . . . "Independent living," then, is not our aim. We wish to create opportunities for "community living"—sharing in and contributing to the goods of life, of which one is belonging. (p. 20)

Recreation inclusion in a community of one's choosing is essential. It affords opportunities for individual growth and development and because community is a core value of quality of life. As such, community integration and recreation inclusion must be central goals of rehabilitation.

Principles of Recreation Inclusion

The practice of recreation inclusion is based on a group of key principles. One principle is the concept of *normalization* (Wolfensberger, 1972). Normalization is sometimes misconstrued to mean that persons with disabilities are expected to comply with society's standards of normality, making them "normal" or "average." Normalization actually refers to using appropriate cultural norms to measure the suitability of services delivered to persons with disabilities. Services should reflect such *positive* cultural norms as choice, autonomy, dignity, interdependence, the rights to work and leisure, and living according to the typical rhythms and patterns of life. In other words, services and opportunities for persons with disabilities should be similar in form and content to what is available to nondisabled persons. Further, normalization should be incorporated in institutional settings to the greatest degree possible. Institutions are too often designed for bureaucratic efficiency at the cost of normalized experiences. For example, residents of institutions are usually required to eat and sleep at specified times. Their waking activities are precisely scheduled and tightly controlled. Persons who are in hospitals, residential facilities, and other types of treatment institutions should have choice, dignity, meaningful leisure expression, and other normative opportunities in their lives. The more institutional settings are normalized, the higher the quality of life and the better prepared clients will be for inclusive experiences.

Another principle is *self-determination*. Closely associated with choice, freedom, and autonomy, self-determination suggests living according to a life-plan that is freely conceived and initiated by the individual. It means that if we are truly masters of our own lives, then we must be at liberty to choose and act on the goals that define who we are and what we wish to become (see Mahon, 1994). A corollary of self-determination is *empowerment*, which refers to the process of gaining or regaining control in all aspects of one's life (Hutchison & McGill, 1998). Self-determination is impossible without empowerment. As such, it requires that persons with disabilities be afforded the supports and opportunities they need to exercise choice and ability.

A third principle is *social role valorization* (Wolfensberger, 1983, 1985). Social role valorization pertains to the value society attaches to people and social practices. Discussing the implications of social role valorization for therapeutic recreation, Rancourt (1989) noted that disability and leisure are less valued in society. She urged professionals to "demonstrate the worth of that which is presently culturally deemed as worthless" (p. 52), giving people with disabilities roles that are prized in society. Clearly, the best way to achieve social valorization is by accepting persons with disabilities as worthwhile members of society and by affording them opportunities to express their worth. Bullock and Howe (1991) suggested that recreation inclusion can be effective at helping people with disabilities to achieve socially valued roles, contributing to their self-esteem.

The final principle is *optimal environment*. Persons with disabilities should be permitted to function in environments that are optimally conducive to their growth and development. As an analogy, college students would rightly resent being treated like elementary school students, because it constrains their growth and development. Similarly, persons with disabilities should be able to participate in environments that maximize choice, ability, and growth. In the past, *least restrictive environment* has been used to convey this idea. Hutchison and McGill (1998) argued, however, that the principle of least restrictive environment has tended to keep people in more restrictive environments, hindering integration. Therefore, we suggest the principle of optimal environment as a starting point. The initial assumption will be that people are capable of functioning in mainly integrated settings. Only when there is evidence clearly contradicting this assumption, and when all conceivable supports have been exhausted, would *temporary* restrictions be considered. The same assumption would be applied in clinical settings where restrictions already exist. The legitimacy of those restrictions, however, should also be reviewed. Clearly, programs that involve sex offenders or persons with histories of violence must employ restrictions for the health, safety, and well-being of everyone. On the other hand, restrictions that fail tests of legitimacy should be challenged and removed when proved invalid. For example, the contention that some people with disabilities prefer segregated settings is spurious. Far too often persons with disabilities "choose" segregated settings due to lack of support and insufficient experience in integrated settings. Thus, their capacity to choose has not been optimized, effectively restricting their options.

The principles of normalization, self-determination, social role valorization, and optimal environment provide conceptual guideposts for the practice of recreation inclusion. The challenge of recreation inclusion, however, lies in the flesh-and-blood experience of assisting persons with disabilities to become participants in community recreation activities and leisure opportunities. The following discussion of recreation inclusion practices is intended to inform readers of the barriers to recreation inclusion and to provide them with tools to dismantle them.

Barriers to Recreation Inclusion

Schleien, Ray, and Green (1997) designated barriers as individual (related to the person's particular disability) and external (related to the environment). Of the two classes, "external . . . barriers are the leading factors that inhibit accessible and inclusive recreation services" (Schleien, Ray & Green, 1997, p. 52). External barriers include:

- *Financial constraints*. Persons with disabilities often have additional expenses associated with their conditions, such as medications or specialized equipment. Agencies may also incur expenses, such as purchasing adapted equipment or hiring interpreters. In this regard, however, the costs of inclusion ought not be viewed as "additional expenses," but rather the price for serving the entire community which includes persons with disabilities. Several strategies for dealing with financial obstacles include sliding fees based on income for persons with disabilities, donations of resources, and grants for agencies. Cooperation between clinical and community programs can also be an effective means of reducing costs. For example, clinical programs can loan adaptive equipment to community programs while community programs can offer discounts to clients who are using community services prior to discharge.

- *Lack of qualified staff.* Staff must be knowledgeable of disabling conditions and be able to make necessary arrangements and accommodations in all areas of programming and leadership. There should be enough staff to meet the needs of persons with disabilities and to train other staff and volunteers. Moreover, it is critical that recreation inclusion not be viewed as the exclusive province of therapeutic recreation specialists. Because of their specialized training, they will assume much of the leadership, but inclusion *is the responsibility of all staff,* including leaders, planners, supervisors, managers, and maintenance staff. As such, training in recreation inclusion should be viewed as an indispensable aspect of ongoing professional development.

- *Lack of transportation.* The Americans with Disabilities Act (ADA) is explicit that people with disabilities cannot be discriminated against in the area of transportation. Nonetheless, problems persist even as communities make accommodations for the transportation needs of persons with disabilities. For example, some communities structure public transportation around the typical workday. Consequently, persons with and without disabilities who rely on public transportation are restricted during their leisure hours. This is also a good example of social role valorization. Where persons with disabilities and leisure opportunities are valued, efforts will be made to serve people in all of their life domains.

- *Inaccessible facilities.* Lack of accessibility results from physical barriers, both constructed (e.g., curbs, stairways) and natural (e.g., hills, debris, mud). An accessibility survey should be conducted to determine the type and extent of barrier. There are several sources for accessibility surveys, such as the Americans with Disabilities Act Accessibility Guidelines and the Architectural and Transportation Barriers Compliance Board (see Schleien, Ray & Green, 1997, pp. 44–45). To achieve compliance with the requirements of the ADA, local, state, and federal agencies, as well as some private entities, are developing accessibility plans.

Communities may have individuals who serve as "accessibility specialists." It is advisable that all employees of leisure service agencies, from part-time to maintenance to administrative staff, be knowledgeable of accessibility issues and be capable of informing the public. Moreover, at least one person should serve as the agency "expert." This person should be able to assist clinically-based professionals and persons with disabilities in minimizing barriers and developing strategies to deal with delicate problems, such as accessibility to pristine natural areas (see Dattilo & Murphy, 1987). He or she should also provide ongoing training and consultation. No matter who assumes primary responsibility for accessibility, it is imperative that persons with disabilities be included in planning and surveying areas and facilities. Omitting involvement by persons with disabilities may doom the best-intentioned project to failure because nondisabled planners were not sensitive to small details that can turn into insurmountable obstacles.

- *Poor communication.* Persons with hearing, speech, and visual impediments will require the assistance of trained professionals. Key staff should have communication skills sufficient to welcome and assist persons with visual or hearing impairments, and interpreters should be available when needed. Appropriate signage and telecommunications systems should also be present. People must be able to "get the message" through whatever medium is most effective. Agencies must establish communication networks with the disabled community for the purpose of understanding their needs and issues. Due to a variety of barriers, persons with disabilities can easily become isolated. Their "voice," however, must be heard. Clinical and community therapeutic recreation services must establish effective lines of communication and to use them regularly. Advisory boards, comprised of individuals who are instrumental in the process of inclusion, are highly recommended for enhancing communication. Professionals, volunteers, parents, legislators, advocates, and persons with disabilities must be able to communicate clearly, regularly, and completely. No different than any other situation people face, communication is the difference between success and failure.

- *Ineffective service systems.* Service systems must evaluate how they encourage or inhibit inclusion. Schleien, Ray, and Green (1997) observed that "ineffective service systems may result from a combination of obstacles in the environment, including barriers of omission, and rules and regulations barriers" (p. 59). Barriers of omission include everything that service systems neglect to include, such as failure to have program offerings available in Braille and audio format. Prohibitive rules and regulations include such things as placing people in wheelchairs in aisles at theaters and sports arenas, which violates fire regulations. Service providers must conduct self-studies to determine what aspects of their systems impede inclusion, as well as to plan preventively for future services. The more that agencies see persons with disabilities as a part of their constituency, the more likely they will consider them in planning services.

- *Negative attitudes.* Negative attitudes are probably the root of all other barriers, contributing to stereotypes, prejudice, and discrimination. There are different ways of impacting attitudes, including education and positive interactions between nondisabled individuals and persons with disabilities (Hamilton & Anderson, 1991). Bedini (1998) recommended a variety of techniques, including: (a) exposure and direct contact, (b) persuasive communication and sensitivity training, (c) simulations and role-play, and (d) combination of a, b, and c. Dattilo and Smith (1990) urged attention to language, including terminology that focuses on the person rather than the disability, communicates dignity and respect, and emphasizes strengths and abilities. Perhaps well-planned inclusive experiences, where persons with and without disabilities can share their common humanity on common ground, are the best means of attitude change.

Besides external obstacles, internal barriers, or those that relate to the individual's disability, also require attention. They include:

- *Skill limitations.* Skill limitations include functional deficits attributable to the disability, as well as developmental deficiencies caused by a lack of physical, social, cognitive, and emotional opportunities. It also includes lack of skills and knowledge needed to participate in leisure activities. Leisure education is thus essential, including social and physical skill development. The functional assessment that is conducted as part of transition planning should indicate what social, physical, cognitive, and psychological areas require attention. Individuals should then be taught core competencies that are required for participation. Individuals must have acquired the competencies, with supports, to participate in community leisure activities. Otherwise, they are doomed to fail.

- *Dependence.* Everyone requires supports of one sort or another to participate in activities that meet their needs and interests. Without transportation systems, whether bikes, trails, roads, or cars, most of us would be severely isolated. Without materials such as computers and books learning would be inhibited. Above all, people depend on each other. Beyond the supports necessary for the achievement of their needs, however, persons with disabilities should be free to make and act on their own decisions. Dependency is created by making decisions for persons with disabilities without their consent and by providing unnecessary assistance, robbing them of dignity and respect. Even if they ultimately fail, as all people do at one time or another, persons with disabilities should be allowed to assume control over their own lives as much as possible. In this respect, practitioners should consider the eloquent words of the late Paul Haun (1966), a pioneer in therapeutic recreation, who cautioned that "it is tragically easy to take away the all-important sovereignty the person with a disability must exercise over his own tillable acreage . . . and with the best of intentions make him truly a pauper" (p. 95). Dependence should not be confused, however, with interdependence, which more accurately reflects our social condition. People are reciprocally dependent on one another, creating a condition of interdependence. Where people are forced to remain dependent, however, they lose not only the opportunity to help themselves, but to support others, including persons without disabilities. People should be sufficiently autonomous to decide for themselves how they wish to behave in a world that mixes the values of independence and interdependence.

- *Health and fitness.* Careful attention must be paid to fatigue, circulation, memory, and coordination as they affect participation. Persons who have health complications due to disabling conditions may concurrently suffer poor physical fitness, affecting strength and endurance. Professionals should be thoroughly informed regarding the individual's health and fitness as well as any special precautions and medications. A recent physical exam is imperative and in most cases a fitness appraisal is recommended.
- *Lack of knowledge.* It is essential to provide all pertinent information regarding programs and services as well as supports required for participation. Information should be readily available in a variety of forms (e.g., audio tapes for blind). A resource book of all leisure services in a community, containing information such as accessibility, available supports, and contact persons, is an excellent aid.

Howe-Murphy and Charboneau (1987) cited social, political, and cultural elements that can be either barriers or assets. Social policies, organizational structures, and program philosophies should be scrutinized to determine if they are potential barriers to recreation inclusion and community integration.

The barriers we have just visited are not easily eliminated, but without a concerted effort to surmount them, recreation inclusion is impossible. In our view, recreation inclusion is the most important and difficult challenge facing therapeutic recreation. Rehabilitation should be measured not by sheer functionality alone, but by the quality of life that it facilitates. Successful return to as culturally normal a life as possible should be the ultimate test of therapeutic recreation. Especially in light of the trend toward briefer hospital stays, professional practices must be developed that result in successful inclusion of persons with disabilities in leisure programs and activities that reflect their needs and interests. Toward that end, the next section presents several approaches to recreation inclusion.

Selected Approaches to Recreation Inclusion

Models of therapeutic recreation practice were extensively discussed in Chapter 2. Approaches to recreation inclusion have also been developed; some as generic models, others as methods and applications designed for specific settings such as mental health and physical rehabilitation. The following examples are featured in this section to demonstrate the range of approaches to recreation inclusion. Readers should also consult other approaches to tailor an approach to recreation inclusion that best fits their particular circumstances.

General Approaches

Schleien and Green (1992) reviewed three general approaches for integrating persons with disabilities into community recreation. In the *zero-exclusion* approach, programs are planned from the beginning to include everyone, disabled and nondisabled. The zero-exclusion approach demands high levels of collaboration and commitment, accurate assessment of needs, interests, and skills of individuals, and aggressive recruitment of all participants. In the *reverse mainstreaming* approach, segregated programs for persons with disabilities are structured to include nondisabled persons. The five-step process generally used in the reverse discrimination approach is as follows: (1) identification of segregated programs appropriate to the interests of persons without disabilities; (2) assessment of the needs, interests, and capabilities of potential participants; (3) comparison and prioritization of the needs of participants with and without disabilities; (4) training of segregated program leaders to meet the needs of individuals with and without disabilities; (5) program modifications to entice and keep the interest of all individuals (pp. 56–57). The third approach, and probably the most popular, is the *integration of generic recreation pro-*

grams. Generally, a six-step strategy is used to integrate persons with disabilities into existing community recreation programs, including: (1) assessment of individual recreation preferences and needs; (2) selection of age-appropriate community recreation activity; (3) inventory of the environmental constraints and demands of the activity; (4) assessment of individual skill levels and personal skill deficits relative to the identified demands of the activity (discrepancy analysis); and (5) development of intrinsic and extrinsic strategies to facilitate the social inclusion of the individual with a disability by overcoming individual deficits and environmental barriers, including negative attitudes of nondisabled participants; and (6) implementation of strategies by integration specialists (p. 55). Consider the application of the integration of generic recreation programs approach to the following example.

Kate is a 50-year-old woman with a diagnosis of schizophrenia. She has been hospitalized on and off for the past 25 years. She is preparing to return to the community after a recent three-week hospitalization. The therapeutic recreation specialist who is employed in the hospital where Kate was treated has prepared a discharge and transition plan. She and one of the therapeutic recreation specialists employed by the community are working together on Kate's case.

- *Assessment of individual recreation preferences and needs.* Kate's recreation preferences and needs were assessed when she entered the hospital for her most recent treatment. The results were reviewed with Kate prior to discharge to determine if there were changes. In particular, Kate enjoys art and music. She started a fitness program while in the hospital and, although she is sensitive about her weight, she would like to continue with aerobics. Kate enjoys other people, but can become isolated when she experiences relapses. Everyone agrees that it is important for Kate to remain socially connected.

- *Selection of age-appropriate community recreation activity.* Kate is fully capable of interacting with the adult public. Therefore, community programs offering art, music, and fitness for adults would be suitable.

- *Inventory of the environmental constraints and demands of the activity.* An inventory of barriers identified several constraints, including:

1. Kate was not familiar with the bus route to the ceramics class she wanted to take.
2. Kate's budget did not allow her to pay in full the registration fee for the ceramics class.

3.   Kate wished to continue guitar lessons she had started in the hospital, but her former roommate had left with her guitar while Kate was hospitalized.

4.   Kate was interested in an aerobics class at the local YMCA, but was apprehensive because she is self-conscious about her weight.

- *Assessment of individual skill levels and personal skill deficits relative to the identified demands of the activity.* Initially, an activity analysis was done to determine the knowledge and skills needed to participate in the activities Kate had identified. Activity analysis will be discussed fully in Chapter 10. Activities of interest to Kate were examined along social, physical, cognitive, and emotional domains to determine the levels of functioning they required for successful participation. Kate possesses the knowledge and skill required to participate in the ceramics and guitar classes. Her fitness level suggests that Kate may not be physically prepared for the aerobics class she initially identified. A couple of potential problems also surfaced. Kate will smoke when she becomes anxious and talk loudly when she gets excited. When directed to speak more quietly, however, she feels rejected and retreats socially.

- *Development of intrinsic and extrinsic strategies.* The following strategies were employed to overcome barriers:

1.   *Barrier*: Kate's lack of familiarity with bus route to ceramics class.
     Strategy: Kate called the transportation authority, which prepares individualized route directions on request. Bus operators will assist riders until they become familiar with the route.

2.   *Barrier*: Kate cannot pay the registration fee for the ceramics class in full.
     Strategy: The community recreation department has several means to accommodate financial need. Because Kate has a part-time job, an installment plan she can afford was used.

3.   *Barrier*: Kate does not own a guitar.
     Strategy: The class has guitars available for on-site use, but they cannot be taken home. A local music store offered to rent Kate a used guitar for $2.00 a week, which can be applied to the purchase.

4.   *Barrier*: Kate is apprehensive about joining an aerobics class because she is self-conscious about her weight.
     Strategy: Initially, it was suggested that Kate sign up for a class designed for larger participants. Kate vetoed the idea because she did

not want to be "segregated" on the basis of her weight. It was decided that Kate would participate in the YMCA aerobics class with the support of an "advocate." Unlike a "leisure companion," an advocate is a volunteer who is available to assist persons with disabilities as the situation demands. In Kate's case, her advocate would help to make her feel at ease and generally provide support. Furthermore, because of everyone's interest in helping Kate to establish permanent relationships, the advocate facilitate connections between Kate and other members of the class.

Regarding skill levels and personal skill deficits, the following strategies were employed:

- Kate was not physically prepared for the class she originally identified. *Strategy*: Because this was a problem for other participants in the past, the class is being taught at several levels simultaneously to accommodate all abilities.
- Kate occasionally smokes and talks loudly.
Strategy: Kate will be reminded when she talks too loud or is tempted to smoke a cigarette in the building. Kate's advocate admits to chewing gum in class and singing out of key to the music. Kate has agreed to remind her advocate when she commits those offenses.

Admittedly, this example was idealized for the sake of illustration. It was intended simply to give readers a glimpse of systematic integration and the types of problems and responses that may occur.

Community Reintegration Program

A specific example of the integration of generic recreation programs approach is the *Community Reintegration Program* (CRP). According to Bullock and Howe (1991), the CRP:

> provides a continuation of therapeutic recreation services to recently discharged rehabilitation patients during the period of transition from hospital to home to community. Its purpose is to enhance the quality of life for persons with disabilities by providing a continuation of treatment through transitional [therapeutic recreation services]. (p. 8)

Following principles of normalization, social role valorization, and least restrictive environment, the CRP Model consists of three components. The first component calls for assessment of the individual and the community. This assessment identifies the individual's strengths, interests, needs, skills, and resources, as well as his or her deficits. It also appraises barriers and resources. The second component provides transitional therapeutic recreation services to assist clients to make optimal transitions in their home communities. This element mainly consists of leisure education for the purpose of helping people to acquire core competencies, such as managing money, using public transportation, developing social relationships, and acquiring leisure activity skills. The third component involves evaluation of treatment and leisure education goals. Evaluation of the CRP has produced encouraging results, prompting Bullock and Howe (1991) to conclude that perhaps "the future of [therapeutic recreation services] lies not with inpatient settings, but in home and community based services . . ." (p. 16)

Community Integration Program

Originally designed to meet the needs of rehabilitation clients, the *Community Integration Program* (CIP) (Armstrong & Lauzen, 1994) was developed by the therapeutic recreation department of Harborview Medical Center in Seattle, Washington. The overall goal of the CIP is "to provide opportunities and experiences for the patient that promote the development and application of new knowledge, skills, and attitudes necessary for successful participation in daily community living" (p. 5). The following goals detail this purpose:

- To provide opportunities for the integration of diverse physical, social, emotional, and cognitive skills,
- To provide information and related community resources for patient review and use,
- To provide opportunities for patients to use and evaluate the community resources available,
- To facilitate and increase patient participation in everyday activities and leisure pursuits,
- To provide experiences that require the use of independent thinking, problem-solving and organizational skills,
- To encourage and assist patients in their adjustment to their injury and newly defined physical, cognitive, and emotional limitations,
- To provide opportunities to perform independently without the assistance of family or therapists,

- To provide opportunities for the patient to demonstrate the ability to direct others in helping with their care needs,
- To provide opportunities in new social settings that will increase self-confidence,
- To provide an atmosphere of acceptance and positive attitude toward patients and their rehabilitation process, and
- To provide opportunities to improve social interaction skills within an atmosphere of *fun* and *good humor*. (pp. 5–6)

The CIP is organized by modules that cover a particular community or leisure experience. The modules are grouped into the following six domains:

- Community environment (environmental safety, emergency preparation, basic survival skills),
- Cultural activity (theater, library, sporting event),
- Community activity (shopping mall, grocery store, bank),
- Transportation (taxi, city bus, train, air travel, personal travel),
- Physical activity (aquatics, wheelchair sports), and
- Independent activity (leisure activity of client's choice).

Module selection is determined after an initial therapeutic recreation assessment. While each of the modules addresses a variety of skills, the following questions are typically covered in each module:

- *Prearrangements*: What is the basic information a client will need to know before leaving on the activity? (When are performances scheduled? Are reservations necessary? Is special dress required? Are interpreters available for persons who are hearing impaired? Is a library card required?)
- *Transportation*: How will the client travel to and from the activity? (Is handicapped parking readily available? Do the busses accommodate evening activities?)
- *Accessibility*: What will the client need to know regarding architectural barriers? (Is the building accessible? Is assistance available? If a trail is accessible, how difficult is it?)
- *Emergency/Safety*: What issues related to mobility and health may occur during the activity? (What medications are needed? Does the client know where the first-aid station is located? If a fire alarm were to sound, does the client know the proper procedures?)
- *Equipment*: What equipment and supplies will the client need? (What clothes and supplies are needed?)

The CIP employs three basic steps. First, a *pretest* is conducted to determine the client's capacity to discuss the steps needed for successful community integration. Second, a *field trial* is conducted to assess the client's functional skills necessary for integration. Third, a *post-test* is performed to appraise the client's recollection of how to solve problems that occurred on the outing.

The Harborview Medical Center Community Integration Program is a good example of one facility's successful effort. The CIP is flexible and can be adapted to meet the needs of different populations and facilities. The reader is encouraged to consult the CIP directly for useful examples drawn from actual experiences of the therapeutic recreation staff as they modified it for the individual needs of clients. Of course, a variety of approaches should be studied in preparing to develop a program that will serve the needs of clients in their particular context.

Community Development Approach

The final approach to community integration and recreation inclusion highlighted in this section challenges several key principles and practices of therapeutic recreation. Because of healthcare reforms, therapeutic recreation has had to reevaluate its traditional role in healthcare settings, giving greater consideration to community-based services (Wilhite, Keller & Caldwell, 1999). In particular, shorter hospitalizations have resulted in more people being released back into their communities before they have fully recovered, requiring further care. Furthermore, many persons who have received treatment and rehabilitative services are not cured of their conditions. Instead, they spend the remainder of their lives coping with their disabilities. Therefore, experts have suggested that therapeutic recreation reorient its central focus and resources from acute care to community-based care (Bullock and Howe, 1991; Wilhite, Keller & Caldwell, 1999).

Hutchison and McGill (1998) take this perspective dramatically further, arguing for a more revolutionary transformation of therapeutic recreation. Rather than viewing persons who require further care after having been discharged into the community as *patients*, Hutchison and McGill suggest that they be primarily regarded as *citizens*. The difference between the roles is significant. The patient role assumes that individuals with disabilities require care in segregated environments before they are functionally ready for independent lives and full membership in the community. This assumption is consistent with the continuum model that has been popular in community integration (see Hutchison & McGill, 1998, pp. 104–105). Based on the concept of *least restrictive environment*, it holds that the functional abilities of individuals need to be upgraded in segregated and semi-segregated programs before they are ready to participate more fully in the community. The tendency was to develop segregated and more restrictive environments rather than integrated and least restrictive options (Hutchison & McGill, 1998, pp. 104–105). On the other hand, the citizen role suggests that many people with disabilities are already sufficiently prepared to participate interdependently in their communities with opportunity and adequate support. According to Hutchison and McGill, "the continuum model has confused the need to develop competencies with the real and more important issues of support and intensity of service" (p. 106). Reflecting for a moment on the idea of supports, it is apparent that everyone, disabled and nondisabled, requires support of one sort or another to function and enjoy community life. Parks, schools, libraries, fire and police, communication and transportation systems, and recreation programs and facilities are only a few examples of supports. Without them our lives would be severely handicapped and impoverished. Hutchison and McGill argue that the idea of supports needs to be expanded so persons with disabilities are included. They contend that the problem of integration and inclusion is less a matter of functional ability than one of persons with disabilities being socially devalued and disenfranchised.

Hutchison and McGill shift the paradigm. Instead of a treatment-rehabilitation paradigm that seeks to make individuals more functionally competent, they boldly propose an approach that endeavors to rehabilitate communities, making them more accommodating of persons with disabilities. They do acknowledge that some persons with disabilities who are discharged from hospitals will continue to require some level of rehabilitative care in managing their disabilities. Nonetheless, they argue that far more attention and resources should be devoted to changing physical, social, economic, and political environments that handicap persons with disabilities. In short, rehabilitated, barrier-free environments would do wonders in enabling people of varying abilities to live and thrive in their communities.

Oriented to community living and quality of life, Hutchison and McGill's approach is consistent with earlier ecological perspectives that stress social and political change (Howe-Murphy & Charboneau, 1987; Rusalem, 1973). First of all, Hutchison and McGill insist that the insidious phenomenon of *devaluation* must be addressed. Devaluation refers to the systematic relegation of persons with disabilities to a poorly esteemed status by society, resulting in isolation, segregation, powerlessness, disenfranchisement, and poor self-concept and self-worth. Devaluation can be dismantled by reconstructing society's view by promoting awareness and by empowering persons with disabilities to participate fully in society.

Adopting a person-centered approach, Hutchison and McGill propose a framework for integration based on social role valorization. Social role valorization aims to create, support, and defend "valued social roles and life conditions for people who are at risk of social devaluation" (Hutchison & McGill, 1998, p. 110). Along with other social roles (e.g., wife, husband, partner, worker, citizen), leisure offers a rich variety of socially valued roles, such as singer, dancer, volunteer, and mountaineer. Furthermore, individuals with disabilities can be enhancing personal competencies at the same time they are experiencing valued social roles. Everyone—disabled and nondisabled—is in the process of growing and developing. Therefore, everyone requires esteemed social roles to reach their potential. According to Hutchison and McGill, this is more likely to happen using a community development approach. The very notion of community speaks to the importance of including persons with disabilities in a wide range of activities where people form relationships. Leisure experiences afford a resource for including persons with disabilities, offering opportunities for social role valorization and community membership that stresses close, meaningful relationships.

The approach recommended by Hutchison and McGill is based on community building. As it pertains to persons with disabilities, *community building* concerns promoting relationships and interdependence between citizens who are disabled and citizens who are nondisabled. It consists of two components: community development and community organizing. *Community development* is "a process of working with groups to increase their confidence and cooperation in order to build a stronger sense of community, strengthen membership, and increase group effectiveness" (Hutchison & McGill, 1998, p. 348). It aims to prepare citizens to make decisions and take action that will improve the quality of their lives. Hutchison and McGill identify five community development functions in recreation:

- *Research/Reconnaissance*: Citizens study the social, economic, cultural, and political makeup of the community, identifying their needs and concerns in relation to leisure.
- *Education*: Beginning with self-awareness and values clarification, citizens "explore all the opportunities and resources available to them, as well as the barriers that prevent them from satisfying their personal needs" (p. 171).
- *Group Development*: This function entails moving from individual empowerment to community empowerment by learning how to make decisions, achieve consensus, and achieve cooperation.

- *Leadership Development*: Persons with disabilities develop confidence and skills to assume visible and influential roles as facilitators of change and distributors of power.
- *Forming Partnerships*: Alliances and networks are explored with other community groups and agencies for the sake of additional resources and more effective interventions on issues of shared concern.

Where community development is about involving and educating people, "community organizing is about taking action" for the purpose of social change (Hutchison & McGill, 1998, p. 173). Community organizing involves dealing directly and sometimes dramatically with injustice. Its strategies include educating, negotiating, lobbying, advocating, protesting, and whistleblowing. Community organizing is a controversial role for therapeutic recreation professionals, who may find themselves in conflicts of interest, challenging the policies and practices of the agencies that employ them. For this and other reasons, Hutchison and McGill have suggested that "it is sometimes the best role for people working in the system to act as allies and not become directly involved in [community] organizing" (p. 193). They recommend that professional allies assume a role in community organizing through such efforts as taking a stand on an issue from inside the system, supporting groups that are seeking justice and change, and teaching people to help themselves.

Community building is a role that too often exceeds the traditional boundaries of therapeutic recreation programming. Unless persons with disabilities can be included in the sociocultural fabric of their communities, all of the best clinical programs are for naught. Even though community organizing is beyond the job description of most therapeutic recreation specialists, it points to the need for systematic change in how professions do their business. Empowerment is not simply teaching a social skill or a new leisure activity. It literally means *power to the people*, which implies that people with disabilities must be supported in assuming more control over their lives, not just in terms of biopsychosocial functioning, but socially, culturally, and politically as well. This will require new thinking, models, and practices of therapeutic recreation.

Case Examples

We wish to conclude this chapter with a pair of case studies. Regardless of the particular model or approach used, recreation inclusion requires systematic assessment, meticulous planning, constant communication, attention to barriers, and adequate supports. The first case, admittedly idealized, provides a simple, straightforward example. The second case attempts to convey some of the broader social problems of recreation inclusion suggested by the analysis of Hutchison and McGill (1998).

Dewey

Dewey is a 32-year-old male. Six months ago he suffered a spinal cord injury in a rockclimbing accident, paralyzing him below the waist. He is married, has two children, and works as a computer analyst. A transition plan was developed in anticipation of Dewey's imminent discharge. First, a summary of his progress was shared with appropriate parties, including his family and a community therapeutic recreation specialist. Second, a functional abilities assessment was conducted. Dewey's physical and social functioning were superior. He has experienced bouts of depression, however, expressing concerns related to his athletic and sexual abilities. Dewey's leisure interests and needs were also assessed. He has a variety of interests, including basketball, rockclimbing, skiing, biking, reading, travel, and environmental issues.

Next, recommendations were prepared. Dewey was referred to a wheelchair basketball team with the help of the community therapeutic recreation specialist. Because he had no prior experience, and did not wish to appear a "klutz" his first time out, he was provided instruction prior to discharge. Dewey was also referred to an organization that specializes in outdoor recreation for persons with disabilities. Especially keen to continue skiing and biking, an appointment was made for a recreation equipment specialist to visit Dewey prior to discharge.

Dewey's most sensitive concern is maintaining a satisfying sexual relationship with his wife. His worries regarding performance have been largely alleviated in the course of sexual counseling. What he lacks, however, are materials he needs to engage in sexual relations. The therapeutic recreation specialist, who has received training in sexual counseling, has arranged to introduce Dewey and his wife to the requisite materials.

A follow-up was conducted six weeks after discharge by the therapeutic recreation specialist. Dewey had revived his athletic career with a successful transition to wheelchair basketball. Further, he had purchased an adapted tandem bike that he can ride with his five-year old son. Dewey had also made contact with an organization that specializes in ecotourism, which was eager to adapt their programs to his disability. Lastly, when queried about the effectiveness of the adapted sexual materials, Dewey just grinned.

This fictitious story was obviously a smooth success. Admittedly, most recreation inclusion efforts prove to be far more difficult. For the sake of illustration, consider one more case study woven from the experiences of one of the authors.

Lucy

Lucy is a 35-year-old single woman diagnosed with chronic schizophrenia and mild mental retardation. She has spent over half her life in a variety of psychiatric hospitals. Lucy had a relapse after failing to take her medications, resulting in a three-week hospitalization. During this period, the therapeutic recreation specialist focused on recreation inclusion as the key piece in her return to the community.

A functional assessment was conducted. Back on her medications, Lucy is fully oriented to person, place, and time. Although she chain-smokes and is overweight, Lucy functions physically. Socially, she can be argumentative and stubborn. Due to mild retardation, Lucy has difficulty with abstract thinking; instructions must be clear and simple.

Despite being kept busy in her previous hospitalizations, Lucy has developed few leisure skills and interests, with a couple of exceptions. She is accomplished at needlepoint, which she will sit alone and do for hours. She also has a passion for music, particularly oldies. Further assessment reveals familiarity, but only limited experience with recreation activities. Lucy has spent much of her adult life in and out of hospitals, sewing, smoking, and listening to oldies by herself. Lucy has made it clear that one thing she would like to have is a friend who is not "crazier than me."

The transition plan calls for Lucy to be integrated into a couple of community recreation programs: a weekly needlepoint and quilting club and a weekly social dance class. The clinical and community therapeutic recreation specialists have spoken a couple of times by phone with the leaders of both programs. All parties have expressed their commitment to making Lucy's involvement a success.

The results were disastrous. First, Lucy repeatedly left the community center for smoke breaks. The smell of smoke was offensive to other participants. Also, Lucy attended the social dance class immediately after her part-time job at a fast-food restaurant. She arrived unshowered in her food-stained uniform. Needless to say, she was not the most attractive candidate for a cha-cha. When gently approached by the leader about her smoking and hygiene, Lucy accused her of being "mean," lacing her comments with expletives. To make matters worse, a supervisor with the community recreation department happened to be enrolled in the class. Never an enthusiastic supporter of integration, he opined openly that perhaps "special interest" people like Lucy would be happier and more successful in their own programs. Finally, leaving the community center, Lucy took the wrong bus. Ending up in an unfamiliar section of town, she was forced to call the clinical therapeutic recreation specialist for help getting home.

It has been said that the road to hell is paved with good intentions. Good intentions were certainly abundant in this case. Lacking, however, were systematic planning and adequate supports for successful integration. Before reading on, take a moment to think of some of the mistakes that were made.

Lucy was not properly prepared for recreation inclusion. Bullock and Howe (1991) wrote about the importance of assessing and teaching "core competencies," which pertain to a range of functional skills, such as budgeting, transportation, personal hygiene, and social relations. Several mistakes were made in this respect. Lucy received no guidance in controlling her smoking habits, changing and showering before arriving, and how to catch the return bus. Furthermore, a functional assessment revealed that Lucy has difficulty controlling her temper. Consequently, she should have received assistance managing her anger, including role-playing to test her progress.

Just as seriously, the community programs were not adequately prepared. In particular, rather than question the presence of "special interest" people, the assistant manager should have been prepared to intervene as an advocate. His failure suggests that recreation inclusion was viewed as the job of the therapeutic recreation specialist rather than the responsibility of the entire recreation department. Readiness involves both the individual and the environment. More serious than any of Lucy's limitations was the lack of community supports. Hutchison and McGill (1998) argued that individual limitations often are blamed where inadequate supports are actually the difficulty, mistakenly making the person's impairment the problem in need of a fix rather than the disabling environment.

Successful recreation inclusion requires systematic planning, comprehensive support, painstaking implementation, and the lessons of trial and error (see Armstrong & Lauzen, 1994, for instructive discussion on how recreation integration is improved with experience.) Recreation inclusion begins with transition planning at the onset of care. It must also prepare communities to be supportive of persons with disabilities. Ultimately, achievements with recreation inclusion will be the measure of the field's success. Therefore, it must begin in clinical settings and extend into well-prepared community environments. Functionality alone is not enough. Because quality of life is the goal of rehabilitative care, it requires opportunities in an environment most conducive to choice, autonomy, growth, relationships, and self-determination. In the vast majority of cases that place is the community.

Summary

Because improving quality of life is the ultimate goal of rehabilitation and therapeutic recreation, effective community integration and successful recreation inclusion are vital components of therapeutic recreation practice. Recreation inclusion is justified on the basis of continuity of care, individual growth and development, and achieving a sense of community, all of which are integral to quality of life. The principles of normalization, self-determination, social role valorization, and optimal environment provide conceptual guidelines for recreation inclusion. The success of recreation inclusion, however, rests on the degree to which barriers can be alleviated, individual knowledge and skill can be enhanced, and supports can be provided. A variety of models and approaches have been successfully used in recreation inclusion and community integration. A community development approach proposed by Hutchison and McGill (1998) was highlighted as a complement to rehabilitation. In the end, therapeutic recreation's success should be measured by how well it helps people to return to, become involved in, and enjoy the benefits of community life.

Recommended Readings

Armstrong, M. and Lauzen, S. (1994). *Community integration program* (2nd ed.). Ravensdale, WA: Idyll Arbor.

Bullock, C. and Howe, C. (1991). A model therapeutic recreation program for the reintegration of persons with disabilities into the community. *Therapeutic Recreation Journal, 25*(1), 7–17.

Galambos, D. (1995). *Planning to have a life: Individualized planning for quality of life.* Oakville, ON: Sheridan College.

Hutchison, P. and McGill, J. (1998). *Leisure, integration, and community.* Toronto, ON: Leisurability Publications.

National Recreation and Park Association. (1997). *National Recreation and Park Association Position Statement on Inclusion.* Ashburn, VA: National Recreation and Park Association.

Schleien, S., Ray, M., and Green, F. (1997). *Community recreation and people with disabilities: Strategies for inclusion* (2nd ed.). Baltimore, MD: Paul H. Brookes.

Wolfensberger, W. (1983). Social role valorization: A proposed new term for the principle of normalization. *Mental Retardation, 21*, 234–239.

Chapter

9

Introduction to Program Evaluation in Therapeutic Recreation

Evaluation may be defined as a procedure through which information is collected and analyzed to generate knowledge concerning the ethics (appropriateness), efficacy (effectiveness), efficiency, or equity of something. Knowledge that is gained from an evaluation may be used by a decision maker to assess the relative desirability of different options and to select a particular course of action. To increase your familiarity with this definition, please join me in a brief exercise. Think about all of the things that you have evaluated today. How long is your list? Given time and patience, it is perhaps sufficient to say that our list could occupy several pages. My list includes an evaluation that immediately follows the first breath I take following the demise of blissful sleep. Maintaining my love-hate relationship with my alarm clock, I quickly generate knowledge concerning the time of day and determine the desirability of getting my lazy carcass in action in order to reach work on time. In this process, I am evaluating my behavior of lying in bed, given the time of day and expectations of me. I then gain knowledge about my physical appearance using a mirror. Have those annoying whiskers grown again? If so, perhaps I should shave. How about the hair? Can it go another day without combing? Probably not. Evaluation continues as I proceed through evaluation of exercise considerations (Do I have time? How far? How fast? How intense?), other personal hygiene considerations, nutrition and appetite considerations (Am I hungry? Should I eat healthy fruit or unhealthy but delicious sausage?), transportation to work (How fast am I driving?), and on and on over the course of a day. Two points follow from this simple exercise: (1) evaluation is ubiquitous; it is so much a part of our stream of daily activities that we hardly notice it, (2) it is an attempt to generate knowledge, using information that we actively acquire from sources and techniques available to us.

Evaluation is also a companion that follows us to work, whether our job site is a university, construction site, or therapeutic recreation setting. At such sites, we are faced with another array of circumstances requiring evaluation. (How effective are the programs that we are providing? Could our leisure education program be improved if we adopted a new curriculum? To what extent is progress evident in our attempts to serve a particular client or client group? Which candidate for our vacant therapeutic recreation specialist position should we hire?) Answering these questions requires gathering and synthesizing information through evaluation procedures. Evaluation is thus as pervasive in our professional lives as in our personal lives, involving a diversity of purposes and methods. In our professional lives, evaluation techniques range in scope a casual glance at an ongoing service to such complex and systematic procedures as experiments, surveys, focus groups, and other techniques of generating knowledge. In this chapter, we illustrate systematic approaches to evaluation of recreation services and assumptions about knowledge on which those approaches are based.

Knowing and Evaluation

We have defined evaluation as "procedures through which information is collected and analyzed to generate knowledge concerning the ethics, efficacy, efficiency, or equity of something." Before launching into an exploration of different evaluation procedures, it is necessary to first grapple with the most deceptively difficult of the concepts embedded in that definition: knowledge. What, specifically, does it mean to have knowledge? Consider the following things that a therapeutic recreation specialist might "know:"

- Verbal persuasion messages that help clients internalize successes they experience (e.g., "You are good at that.") build more confidence than verbal persuasion messages that do not directly promote personalization (e.g., "Good work."),
- Developing an internship program in cooperation with a local university can reduce staffing costs for a therapeutic recreation department,
- An effective way of making a group become more cohesive is to present that group with a common challenge or common enemy,
- How to administer a questionnaire to assess recreation activity preferences,
- How to sail a small boat, and
- How to conduct a performance evaluation of volunteers in a therapeutic recreation department.

Note the difference between the first three of these statements and the last three. The last three statements represent a skill-based form of knowledge that requires active participation to learn. In contrast, the first three statements involve declarative statements for which the question of their degree of being true or false is relevant. The type of knowledge that is associated with statements that can be assessed in terms of being true or false is called *propositional knowledge* (Earle, 1992). Evaluation is primarily directed at generating propositional knowledge.

A person is assumed to have propositional knowledge when he or she holds a justifiable belief about the object or entity (e.g., program, service, client, decision) being evaluated (Earle, 1992). More specifically, the person has knowledge when the following three conditions are met: (1) he or she believes the object being evaluated has certain characteristics, (2) it is true that the object has those characteristics, and (3) he or she can justify her or his belief about the presence of the characteristics. Philosophers consider all three of these conditions to be necessary for demonstrating knowledge (Earle, 1992).

Now, imagine that you are a wealthy philanthropist and that a manager of a nonprofit organization that provides high adventure outdoor recreation experiences for at-risk youth is visiting you. In an introductory letter to you, this manager points out that she has created a program in which at-risk youth participate in climbing, rappelling, whitewater rafting, and challenge experiences that are carefully engineered to promote prosocial behavior among at-risk youth. Prosocial behavior implies such skills, abilities, and dispositions as compassion, helping behavior, ability to resolve conflicts, altruism, empathy, and ability to take the perspective of other people in situations faced. After introductions and other pleasantries are exchanged, the manager exclaims, "I am quite certain that our program promotes prosocial behavior of the troubled youth who participate. But, we are running seriously short of funds to continue. Will you please contribute $50,000 to allow us to continue the program?"

What would you do? Probably, you are suspicious; something seems to be missing. Knowledge, you recall, is *justified* true belief (Earle, 1992), and the statement that the manager has provided is seriously lacking in being justified. She has demonstrated her belief in the effect (condition 1), but has failed to provide evidence in support of that belief (conditions 2 and 3). In short, the manager has not demonstrated that her belief is justified; she has not produced a single shred of evidence to demonstrate the truth of the assertion. She has thus failed the test of knowledge and, if you are a wise and concerned philanthropist, she has likely not yet won your support.

Being very concerned about the at-risk youth population, you decide to probe further. Perhaps evidence of the effectiveness of the program does indeed exist, yet this manager has failed to share it with you. What evidence would you find compelling? According to Earle (1992), "doxastic" justification may be present when "an ideally rational human, undistracted by passion or interest" (p. 40) would acquire a belief based on the evidence that is provided. Thus, in order for an individual to gain knowledge, information that is generated and synthesized through evaluation must have not been produced in a manner that allows the evaluator or sponsor's passion, interest, or other bias to significantly influence the information. The information must also have been produced through use of procedures that a rational person would accept as evidence in support of a position. Given this perspective on justification, the adventure recreation manager's assertion about the effects of her program on prosocial behavior would be problematic because: (1) the assertions are rich in opportunity to have been influenced by passion or interest (e.g., the manager's self-interest in continuation of the program) and (2) no evidence exists of the assertion being based on an acceptable method of generating evidence.

What form of evidence, then, might you find compelling? Suppose the manager supplied you with copies of letters from parents who had seen improvement in their children following participation in the high adventure program. Would you be convinced or would you likely wonder about all of the other parents who chose to not write letters? Or, perhaps the manager had conducted an experiment in which a group of youth participated in the program and another group did not. If, following the program, participants' prosocial behavior was shown to be superior to that of nonparticipants, would you be convinced of the program's efficacy? What if the program had the endorsement of a famous athlete or an influential politician? Or, would it be possible that the manager's testimonial about the program was so totally energetic and full-spirited that you were convinced and willing to shell out $50,000 to support the program?

Consideration of these questions reveals that huge areas of uncertainty surround the problem of identifying the types of evidence that should convince a "fully rational" human that knowledge exists. In this chapter, we do not attempt to resolve this problem. Rather, we provide examples of approaches that are commonly accepted in research and evaluation of human services, which seem to minimize the influence of "passion and interest." The approaches were selected to illustrate techniques that minimize the influence of "passion and interest" as well as other biases.

Therapeutic Recreation Program Evaluation

Programming involves creating and delivering services. A given service within an agency's repertoire can be considered a "program." A camp for a select population of participants might, for example, create and deliver programs in arts and crafts, sports and games, music and rhythmic movement, high adventure, natural resource-based activities, and other program areas. In this section we review methods that might be used in evaluation of a program. We illustrate three "Es" of evaluation: ethics, efficacy, and efficiency analysis. Each of these implies different evaluation questions, different types of evidence of interest, and different procedures for collecting and interpreting evidence that is collected.

The First E: Ethical Analysis

Ethics is the branch of philosophy "that attempts to determine what is good for people and what is right for them to do" (Honer, Hunt & Okholm, 1992). With respect to evaluation of programs, ethics play a central role that is far too often overlooked. Far too often, programs are offered because of tradition, precedent, popularity, demand, or other reasons, without due consideration of the extent to which these outcomes are "good for people" or "right for them to do." The task of sorting out what is "good for people" is deceptively complex. Few people, for example, would provide a second glance in consideration of the ethics of a program that was engineered to increase physical fitness, promote prosocial behavior, or enhance self-esteem. Yet such a program may involve activities and consequences that people find ethically unacceptable.

Consider an example of a program that presents clear ethical challenges. In the last few years numerous organizations have developed services to promote such goals as enhancing sense of social responsibility and self-esteem of youth offenders through intensive, wilderness therapy programs. Youth who are sent to these programs for rehabilitation often include very violent offenders who, without intervention, may be destined for a future involving deliberate destruction of lives of other people. Wilderness therapy programs present youth with highly intensive challenges, such as endurance hikes in highly remote areas. These activities are designed to push participants near, and sometimes beyond, their physical and psychological limits. Such programs have led to the death of some participants and to severe emotional trauma of others. An obvious ethical question that emerges from such programs is, "Does the means justify the end?" Are occasional deaths and emotional traumas brought about by the demands of such programs tragic but necessary components of programs that seek to bring about dramatic changes in people who are deeply troubled? More fundamentally, however, are questions of the "goodness" or "rightness" of the outcomes that these programs, or any programs, seek to achieve.

An example of the complexity of this "goodness" or "rightness" is the set of outcomes related to individuals' beliefs about themselves that frequently are promoted as outcomes of recreation participation or therapeutic recreation service. Many of these have to do with perceptions of personal worth, value, or efficacy. Two examples are self-esteem and perceived freedom in leisure. Self-esteem implies value of one's self. As such, an individual with high self-esteem would be expected to consider himself or herself to be a person with special and admirable skills, talents, values, worth, and potential. These attributes are thought to be a precursor to success in life. Children with high self-esteem are thought to be superior learners to their low self-esteem peers. They are also assumed to be in a better position to resist experimentation with drugs and more resilient to negative events in their lives. Self-esteem development is often touted as a fundamental purpose of recreation and recreation services (e.g., Leitner, Leitner & Associates, 1996; MacLean, Peterson & Martin, 1985, p. 18; Pacific Northwest Regional Council, 1994). Similarly, perceived freedom in leisure (Ellis & Witt, 1984) is a set of beliefs that individuals hold about themselves that includes perceptions of personal competence and ability to control outcomes of recreation experiences. Individuals with high degrees of perceived freedom in leisure tend to have higher degrees of self-esteem and life satisfaction, greater ability to find satisfaction with daily events, and lesser degrees of depression.

At a glance, self-esteem, perceived freedom, and similar concepts appear to be "good" outcomes that are very much "right" outcomes of recreation programs. Appearances, however, can be deceptive. Discussions of services directed at enhancing individuals' beliefs about their personal worth, competence, and value almost never take into account the potential of such services to produce self-centered and egotistic individuals whose perceptions of self may border as much on self-idolatry as self-esteem. Significant to this possibility is the observation that the dominant religion in United States culture is Christianity. Written Christian dogma emphasizes the importance of humility and clearly cautions against development of enhanced beliefs about one's worth, competence, and value. It teaches that: (1) a Christian should "deny themselves," ([Matthew 16:24, Mark, 8:34, Luke, 9:23] Barker, 1985, pp. 1466, 1510, 1557); (2) the Christian who exalts him or herself "shall be humbled" and that the Christian who humbles him or herself "shall be exalted" ([Matthew 23:12, Luke, 14:11] Barker, 1985, p. 1475, 1568); (3) all people are unworthy sinners who require redemption and justification from a Savior; and (4) Christians should, "in humility, consider others as being better than [themselves]" ([Philippians, 2:3] Barker, 1985, p. 1805). One of the most influential individuals in Christian history, Paul, chose to be crucified with his head toward the ground due to his personal inadequacy. Humility is a Christian virtue, and it stands in contrast to concepts that reflect high levels of self-regard. Given this perspective, significant doubt can be reasonably cast on the inherent, unquestionable goodness and rightness of programs that are directed at enhancing individuals' beliefs of their worthiness, competence, and value.

This example serves to illustrate the vital importance of a thoughtful and rigorous ethical analysis of program content and outcomes. Perhaps such analyses are uncommon because they rarely, if ever, lead to universally acceptable and indisputable positions. The rightness of any position can be argued from numerous ethical positions. Honer, Hunt, and Okholm (1992) illustrate these positions through use of an "ethical continuum." The continuum ranges from subjectivism (i.e., all values are relative to what the individual values) to absolutism (i.e., fundamental laws that are universal and immutable laws apply to all circumstances), with positions such as cultural relativism (i.e., social authorities of a culture determine what is right and good), egoism (i.e., right and good are that which benefits the individual), and rational choice (i.e., right and good are reasoned judgments, perhaps leading to Kant's position that anything that one asserts to be good must be good for everyone) at various locations along the continuum. A given outcome, activity, or program, therefore, might be defended as being "good" or "right" from one of these ethical perspectives and be judged to be equally "wrong" from another. As suggested in the previous paragraph, self-esteem might, for example, be deemed a "good" and "right" outcome from a cultural relativism perspective but perhaps not from an absolutist perspective.

Where does this leave the therapeutic recreation professional faced with the challenge of making a decision about the goodness or rightness of a program? If left to his or her own devices, the committed professional might search each ethical position, from subjectivism to absolutism, and ultimately arrive at a position that, for whatever reason, was most preferred by that professional. The existence of a profession, however, can simplify this process somewhat. All professions develop ethical statements that define the purpose and process of services that are delivered by practitioners within that profession. As a result of the existence of these ethical statements, what is good and right becomes a special case of cultural relativism. The relevant culture becomes the culture of that profession and the leaders of that organization become the social authorities who determine what the profession values.

An example of a position with ethical content in therapeutic recreation is the American Therapeutic Recreation Association Definition Statement (ATRA, 1996). According to that statement, therapeutic recreation has two arms of service. The treatment arm seeks to restore, remediate, or rehabilitate in order to improve functioning and independence [and] to reduce or eliminate the effects of illness or disability. The recreation services arm seeks to provide recreation resources and opportunities in order to improve health and well-being [of persons with illnesses or disabling conditions]. A professional who adheres to ATRA's philosophy, therefore, is charged with the responsibility of assessing the extent to which services offered are consistent with the goals of treatment or recreation services. Programs that do not conform to these goals must be considered either services that are beyond the scope of therapeutic recreation or are not "right" or "good."

The existence of these ethical statements is helpful to the professional, but professional statements of ethics do not fully solve the problem of ethical evaluation. Careful scrutiny of virtually any program will reveal many conflicts in terms of values related to the nature of the activity and the outcomes produced. Dance, for example, is an activity that clearly promotes health through physical fitness. As such, a therapeutic recreation program involving dance activities would seem to fit ATRA's recreation services arm in that it is the provision of services that "improve health and well-being" (ATRA, 1996). Members of certain religions, however, disapprove of particular forms of dance and would consider involvement in that activity to be threatening to members' spiritual health and well-being. Similarly, many people believe that art activities surrounding holiday celebrations promote family unity and well-being, while other groups consider such activities to be an ultimately destructive form of idolatry. Great diversity exists in peoples' values within modern society. Complex questions arise from this diversity. Should therapeutic recreation programs that are directed at increasing health and well-being of families include families of same-sex couples? Should they include couples of different racial and ethnic backgrounds? Families that are polygamous?

In considering such questions, values of professionals are sometimes in conflict with values of professions and key elements of ethical statements are interpreted in different ways to defend different positions. How, exactly, should "health and well-being" be defined (ATRA, 1996)? What, exactly, does it mean to "restore, remediate, or rehabilitate?" What forms of recreation are acceptable under the "recreation services" mission? Should organized sports and games be included? If so, should the importance of winning and losing be emphasized or deemphasized? Is a program based on classical music acceptable in terms of anticipated effects on health and well-being? Can rap music be used in a program to restore, remediate, or rehabilitate? Is gambling acceptable as a therapeutic recreation program theme?

Ethical analysis of programs and services is clearly among the most challenging and most important of the phases of evaluation. The first step of evaluation of a program or set of programs is to undertake inquiry into these matters. All therapeutic recreation departments and organizations are challenged to produce statements of mission and policy that interpret the profession's values at a level of detail sufficient to provide guidance in the ethical evaluation of programs. Absolute solutions will not be found, but such efforts are necessary to ensure that services provided are, to the best of the professional's ability, consistent with what is right and what is good. (See Chapter 3 for an extensive discussion of professional ethics.)

The Second E: Efficacy Evaluation

After a program has been considered ethically acceptable, attention might turn to the efficacy of the program in achieving its specified objectives. In short, did the program accomplish what it intended to accomplish? At this phase of evaluation the challenge is to draw upon methods of knowing that minimize the effects of "passion and interest" and produce evidence that a reasonable person would accept as being indicative of a program's effect or lack of effect. A plethora of approaches are possible, with three approaches being represented here. These approaches were selected because they are directly or indirectly connected to science, a way of generating knowledge that is considered by most people to be less susceptible to the threats of passion or interest than other ways of knowing. Approaches briefly illustrated include a field experiment, a correlational study, and a naturalistic approach. The context within which these approaches are presented is a hypothetical day camp for children with disabilities provided by the therapeutic recreation division of a municipal parks and recreation department. We will assume that the branch offers two, two-week sessions of the camp, with approximately fifty children and youth, ages 9–15 in each session.

Efficacy Evaluation: Field Experiments

An *agent* is something that brings about a change or creates an effect on something. When we swallow an aspirin because of a headache, the aspirin is an agent in alleviating our subjective experience of pain. In social science, agents called independent variables play a pivotal role in experiments. Experiments are methods in which carefully selected and defined reactions (dependent variables) of people (or plants, animals, parks, cells, materials, or other entities) to agents (independent variables) are observed under controlled conditions. One form of an experiment is a "between groups" experiment. In that form, one group of people is exposed to a particular agent of change while other people are exposed to either different agents or to no agent. After being exposed to the agent for an appropriate period of time, outcomes are measured and comparisons are made between people who were exposed to the agent of interest and people who were either not exposed to the agent of interest or were exposed to other agents.

In an experiment designed to assess the effects of the aspirin agent on headaches, an investigator might test a hypothesis that people who were exposed to the agent (aspirin) will report that their headaches were less painful than the reported headache pain of the people who were not exposed to that agent (aspirin).

An alternative form of an experiment involves exposing the same group of people to an agent at one point in time, not exposing them to that agent at another point in time and comparing differences on outcomes. This may be referred to as a "repeated measures" or "within-subjects" experiment. An example might be a study designed to assess the impact of two types of activities on enjoyment. For example, enjoyment experienced during challenge initiatives focused on individual attainment might be contrasted with enjoyment experienced during challenge initiatives focused on group attainment. In such an investigation, participants would engage in activity sessions corresponding to each of the two types. At the conclusion of each session, measures of enjoyment would be taken. Two groups might be used to counterbalance the evaluation study (e.g., control for the effect of order). One group would participate in the individual initiatives first and the other group would participate in the group initiatives first. Enjoyment means would be calculated for both treatment conditions (individual initiatives and group initiatives).

Some experiments have features of both within-group and between-group experiments. An example would be to include gender as a variable in the study of the effect of initiative type on enjoyment. Further, compromises in some of the features of an experiment that we must make for many evaluation settings produce studies described as "quasi-experiments" (near-experiments) and our outcomes would be called dependent variables. The term quasi-experimental is often used to describe studies in which participants were not randomly selected from a well-defined population and/or were not randomly assigned to treatment conditions. Both of these steps are necessary for application of inferential statistical techniques, which enable a researcher to make inferences about relationships between variables in well-defined populations based on data from samples. For our introductory purposes, however, we shall ignore these details.

For our hypothetical day camp, assume that the therapeutic recreation branch of the municipal parks and recreation department has conducted its ethical analysis and has determined that the scope of programs and services provided by the camp are "right" and "good." Further, that analysis affirmed that select portions of the overall camp program were clearly within the framework of ATRA's "treatment" arm, with services directly intended to remediate, rehabilitate, and restore function (ATRA, 1996). Other services offered by the camp primarily served the "recreation services" arm and were appropriately directed at providing resources necessary for recreation that promoted health and well-being. Directors of the camp were very interested in determining the extent to which the "treatment" arm services were, in fact, serving to restore function. Specifically, they were interested in the effects of their program on campers' physical strength, flexibility, endurance, and range of motion.

Given this scenario, a between-groups experiment might proceed as follows. The evaluator begins by writing the following evaluation research hypotheses:

> Participants in the camp will report greater strength (hypothesis one), flexibility (hypothesis two), endurance (hypothesis three), and range of motion (hypothesis four) than nonparticipants.

These hypotheses suggest that two groups are needed. One of the groups will be exposed to the agent (the camp) and the other group will have not been exposed to that agent. It is thus convenient to the evaluator that two sessions of the camp are scheduled (although these nonequivalent groups constitute one of the compromises of our evaluation example, as compared to a *true* experiment). On the last day of the first session, children who have participated in the program will have received the agent, and children who have not yet attended the camp will not have been exposed to the agent. That occasion presents a grand opportunity to measure strength, flexibility, endurance, and range of motion, which are assumed to be the outcomes that are affected by the agent (camp). Thus, at the end of the first session and prior to the beginning of the second session, measures of strength, flexibility, range of motion, and endurance would be taken from individuals from both groups. These measures might be taken using any of a variety of physical tests, such as quantity of weight lifted (e.g., strength), angle to which a given joint can be bent (e.g., range of motion), ability to stretch muscles (e.g., flexibility), and length of time to reported exhaustion in a demanding physical activity (e.g., endurance).

Results of the test of hypothesis four, regarding physical endurance, are presented in Table 9.1 (p. 260). Assume that all participants were wheelchair users and the endurance test involved repeatedly maneuvering a wheelchair up a steep ramp until participants indicated that they were exhausted and had to stop. Perhaps the most vital of the statistics is the *mean*. The mean is simply the arithmetic average of the minutes each child participated in the demanding physical activity before stopping due to reported exhaustion. As can be seen from review of Table 9.1, participants in the camp, on the average, continued the demanding activity for 12.5 minutes, whereas the children who had not yet participated in the camp reported exhaustion and discontinued their involvement in the activity after only 8.3 minutes. The *standard deviation* is a measure of how much variation exists in the scores. The fact that the standard deviation is substantially larger for the group that participated suggests the possibility that the camp/agent substantially improved endurance of some campers while other campers may have either been unaffected or even declined in endurance.

A *repeated measures* design might also be used. In that approach, measures of strength, flexibility, range of motion, and endurance would be taken at two times from the same group of campers: before the camp began and after the camp had ended. That approach would yield scores on the outcome variables from the same people on two occasions. Of interest would be differences in means (and, perhaps to a lesser extent, standard deviations) across those two occasions (see Table 9.1). Variations of this basic design are frequently used in evaluation practice. It is important to note, however, that the specific approach described here is severely limited because some factor other than the camp experience could have led to any increases in the physical performance that were observed on the second occasion. Perhaps, for example, people tend to be more active during the summer months and increases in physical performance occur naturally as a consequence of this activity increased level, not as a function of participation in the camp.

Table 9.1 Hypothetical Results: Field Experiment

Hypothetical data from a Between-Participants Experiment

Group	Mean (Minutes)	Standard Deviation
Participants	12.5	6.2
Not yet participants	8.3	3.1

Hypothetical Data from Within-Participants (Repeated Measures) Experiment

Time	Mean (Minutes)	Standard Deviation
Before Participation	8.3	3.1
After Participation	12.5	6.2

Efficacy Evaluation: Correlational and Descriptive Studies

It is not always possible, feasible, or ethical to conduct experiments by systematically exposing people to agents that are of interest. An extreme example of a situation for which an experiment would not be appropriate or possible would be a test of the effects of seat belt use (the agent) on severity of head injuries (the outcome) among motorists. To conduct an experiment on that topic, it would be necessary to recruit a group of volunteers willing to crash an automobile in such a way as to cause a head injury. Some would wear seat belts and some would not. Any volunteers? Although this is an extreme example and no experimenter would consider even attempting to conduct such a study, it is important to note that a number of agents in which we could be interested are not appropriate for manipulation. An example might be participation in the wilderness therapy programs described earlier in this chapter.

In addition to dangerous agents are agents that do not lend themselves to experimental manipulation. Studies that involve examination of the effects of personality, type of disability, juvenile offender type, gender, and a myriad of other variables must be conducted in a manner that does not involve systematically exposing people to agents. A popular option in these circumstances is to find people who have been exposed to an agent previously or people who have a particular characteristic and then compare those groups with people from other relevant comparison groups. Thus, in our seat belt example, we might identify a group of people who have been involved in automobile accidents and then form groups by figuring out which people were wearing seat belts during their accidents and which people were not. We could then compare the two groups in terms of head injury severity. Studies of this nature, in which the effect of agents has already occurred or existing characteristics are assessed and outcomes are observed may be referred to as *correlational studies*.

Results of a hypothetical correlational study involving our camp are presented in Table 9.2. The hypothetical data in that table are based on a design

Table 9.2 Hypothetical Results: Correlation Study		
Group	Mean (Minutes)	Standard Deviation
Participant, last 5 years	12.5	6.2
Nonparticipant, last 5 years	8.3	3.1

in which the evaluator identified two groups of participants: (1) those who participated in the camp at any time over the past five years and (2) those who had never participated in the camp. The investigator measured the physical performance variables on both groups and organized the data into Table 9.2. Data in the table are the same as in Table 9.1. The only difference is the method in which the data were collected.

Occasionally, an evaluator is interested in individual variables instead of an agent and an outcome. Studies of this type can accurately be referred to as *descriptive studies*. An evaluator, might, for example, be interested in campers' responses to the single question, "On a scale of zero to ten, with ten being the best experience possible and zero being the worst camping experience possible, how would you rate your camp experience?" A positive camping experience would be indicated by higher scores on that scale (eight to ten, perhaps) and negative experiences would be indicated by lower scores on the scale. Both correlational studies and descriptive studies are often, but not always, conducted using surveys, questionnaires, and interviews.

We have chosen to illustrate a particularly useful and versatile form of descriptive study. This technique is referred to as *importance by performance analysis* (Martilla & James, 1977; see also Havitz, Twynam & DeLorenzo, 1991). The technique involves identifying important features of a service or product and then asking participants to rate each in two ways: (1) importance of that feature to the participant and (2) performance, or the effectiveness of the organization in providing the service. Ratings might be completed on a five point scale. With respect to importance, a one might represent low importance and a five might be used to represent high importance. A similar response format might be used for performance ratings. A one might indicate very poor performance and a five might represent superb performance. Ratings of two, three, and four could be used to represent varying degrees of importance and performance.

After surveying campers and securing their ratings on key attributes of the camp, evaluators might, for example, learn that the campers considered arts and crafts, quality food, comfortable cabins, and an evening program to be very important features of the camp. They might also learn that the campers considered the camp counselors to have performed their jobs very well, that staff were very good about letting campers know about activities in which they could choose to participate, and that the archery program was not conducted well. But the magic of importance by performance analysis is not so much in these responses to the importance and performance dimensions. Rather, importance by performance analysis becomes even more useful when the information is organized such that importance and performance are used to create a two dimensional space. Using average (mean) ratings, attributes can then be positioned in that two dimensional space (see Fig. 9.1).

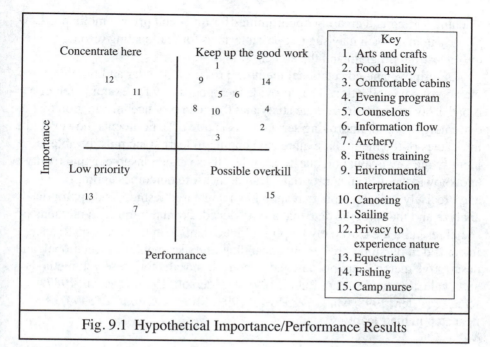

Fig. 9.1 Hypothetical Importance/Performance Results

As can be seen from review of Fig. 9.1, each space within the chart carries a highly intuitive interpretation:

Area	Action Needed
• High Importance/High Performance:	Keep up the good work
• High Importance/Low Performance:	Correct these problems now, high priority
• Low Importance/High Performance:	Possible Overkill
• Low Importance/Low Performance:	Low Priority

The naming of the respective areas provides very useful information for improving the program. The technique identifies important features of the program that should be maintained, it targets features that should become priorities for action by managers of the program, and it suggests features that might be eliminated or that might be ripe for reallocation of resources to more important features and features for which performance has been good.

Review of Fig. 9.1 for our hypothetical camp clearly illustrates this situation. The figure reveals that the campers believe that staff are doing an excellent job in providing such programs and services as physical fitness training, interpretation of the natural environment in which the camp is located, arts and crafts, providing comfortable sleeping arrangements, and canoeing. The chart also shows that high priority actions (high importance/low performance) are teaching sailing and creating opportunities for quiet and private moments. Low priority items, which may suggest possible areas for reallocating resources, are the equestrian program and the archery program.

Descriptive and correlational methods provide a popular and flexible method of data collection. They provide the opportunity for examination of a broad array of issues in a single study and they can produce information that is extremely useful in improving services. As is true of experiments, however, the intricacies of the method are quite challenging to learn. One must be able to identify the key evaluation questions, relate those questions to existing theory and knowledge, use an appropriate design, measure outcomes appropriately and precisely, select people to respond in a nonbiased fashion, and appropriately analyze and interpret the data that are produced. Formal training in methods of social research are extremely helpful, if not essential, in this process. Readers interested in pursuing greater understanding of experimental, correlational, and descriptive methods are encouraged to consult introductory research methods and evaluation books (e.g., Babbi, 1998; Henderson, 1995; Herman, 1987; Kraus & Allen, 1998; Malkin & Howe, 1993; Mitra & Lankford, 1999) as a next step in their learning.

Efficacy Evaluation: A Naturalistic Approach

Consider for a moment some of the ways that experiments, correlational studies, and descriptive studies are similar. In each case, it is vitally important to carefully define the variables (agent and/or outcome) and to figure out a way to measure that variable. In an experiment involving self-esteem, for example, it would be essential to define and measure self-esteem in a way that is similar for all groups involved in the study. In defining and operationalizing variables in a common way, we are essentially reducing a large and complex phenomenon to a smaller and more refined variable. The process of reducing complex phenomena into refined units is called *reductionism*. Using a reductionist approach, we might observe a totally gleeful, exuberant, and joyful child who is happily singing in a warm summer breeze and record only that the child "exhibited a curvature at the corners of the mouth" (i.e., smiled). Consistent with this example, many evaluators would argue that a reductionist approach results in a situation in which the richness, complexity, and true significance of the phenomenon as it is expressed is lost.

Naturalistic methods provide an approach that stands in contrast to reductionism. Using naturalistic methods, evaluators are able to study phenomena in a broad sense and from the "phenomenological" perspective of the people who are a part of the phenomenon under investigation (e.g., Bullock, 1993; Denzin & Lincoln, 1994; Lincoln & Guba, 1985). Evaluators using naturalistic methods approach the acquisition of knowledge through collection of many types of information. Their data may be words from conversations, observations, pictures, music, physical traces, interviews, or any other type of information that provides insight into the phenomenon being examined. An analysis of such data involves classification, systematic searches for common themes and elements, and triangulation of data, theory, and method to determine the trustworthiness of the data and the evaluator's interpretations of the data.

As with experiments, correlational studies and descriptive studies, naturalistic studies involve great complexity. Readers interested in pursuing greater understanding of this approach to evaluation and knowing might consult the excellent introduction by Bullock (1983). Bullock's chapter and similar sources provide readers with a fundamental understanding of naturalistic approaches and provide a foundation for understanding more advanced concepts related to naturalistic inquiry (e.g., Denzin & Lincoln, 1994; Lincoln & Guba, 1985).

For our introductory purposes, an example will have to suffice. Returning to our hypothetical day camp, an evaluator using a naturalistic approach might start with a very general question: "What benefits result from participation in this camp?" With that question as a point of departure, the evaluator might proceed to collect a variety of types of information. He or she might interview participants and parents, observe participants' behavior during select activities of the camp, conduct tests of strength, endurance, and flexibility, or use questionnaires to measure select psychological variables. For example, arts and crafts projects completed as part of the camp experiences might be examined. Are projects more elaborate as the camp progresses? Do the themes depicted or implied by the artwork reflect more positive and optimistic orientations toward self and others? Human service providers at schools and other agencies might be consulted for observations related to changes in participants that they have witnessed. Field notes kept by program leaders might be examined and journals kept by participants might be reviewed. Additional questions might emerge as the data collection and analysis proceeds. Are participants using community recreation services with greater frequency? Are friendships being formed? How are parents and families benefiting from their children's participation? As children develop greater skills in activities, what changes occur in the ways that they view themselves? The process of collecting data, synthesizing data, identifying themes and new questions, and collecting more data would continue until the investigator achieved an understanding of the camp benefits phenomenon.

An example of hypothetical results of a naturalistic evaluation of our camp benefits is presented in Fig. 9.2 (p. 266). Intrapersonal benefits included strength, flexibility, endurance, psychological gains in confidence, and interest in new activities. Confidence and interest in new activities seemed to lead to greater participation in community leisure services, which in turn led to increases

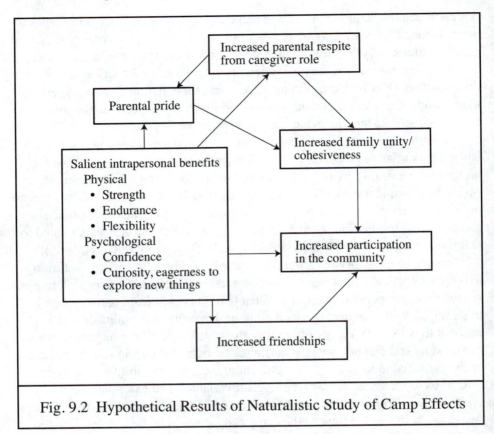

Fig. 9.2 Hypothetical Results of Naturalistic Study of Camp Effects

in parents' pride in their children and confidence in their children's abilities to succeed. Increased time away from the demands of parental supervision seemed to follow from increased community involvement and as a result family units seemed to be significantly strengthened. As this example reveals, the naturalistic approach allowed for identification of many benefits and suggested some possible linkages among those benefits. It is significant to note that a number of these benefits would likely have not been identified through reductionistic methods.

Naturalistic methods provide an interesting contrast to the reductionist approaches. Naturalistic methods take advantage of the richness of the context and allow for the evaluation to proceed in directions totally unexpected by the researcher. The effectiveness of these approaches, however, is highly dependent upon the investigative skills of the evaluator. Unfortunately, such methods are often perceived as being much more open than reductionist methods to being influenced by passion or self-interest. The discussion of the *confirmatory bias* in Chapter 5 is relevant here. That bias describes a tendency of people to attend selectively to data that are supportive of existing beliefs while ignoring or devaluing data that is not supportive of those beliefs. A highly skilled investigator is needed to acknowledge preexisting biases in naturalistic inquiry and to work effectively with those biases in conducting an investigation.

The Third E: Efficiency Analysis

Two approaches to efficiency analysis are briefly introduced in this section: cost-benefit analysis and cost-effectiveness analysis. To begin, it is useful to understand the concept of efficiency and how that concept is related to cost-benefit analysis and cost-effectiveness analysis. *Efficiency* may be defined as the ratio of return to input for a given time period. Classes that are thought to be efficient with respect to achievement of high grades are popular with some students. In such classes, minimal input of effort leads to maximum output, or easy grades. Cost-benefit analyses are efficiency analyses in which both the return (benefits) and input (investment) are expressed in monetary units. In contrast, cost-effectiveness analyses are analyses in which inputs are expressed in monetary units and benefits are expressed in units of some other variable.

Two hypothetical examples might clarify the similarities and differences between these two approaches. A cost-benefit analysis reveals that for each $100 that a community invests in after-school programs for at-risk youth, a savings of $250 in social benefits (e.g., reduced vandalism, reduced juvenile justice costs, increased community service) is realized. In contrast, a cost-effectiveness study might reveal that each $1,000 spent on the at-risk youth program produces an increase in students' mean standardized achievement test scores of 0.5 points.

Fundamental to cost-benefit analysis and cost-effectiveness analysis is the ratio of benefits to inputs or costs. To understand that ratio, consider this example: You are presented with an opportunity to invest in either widgets or wadgets. If you invest in widgets, you might expect a return of $10 for every $1 that you invested after a one year period. Your cost-benefit ratio for widgets would be $10/$1=10. For wadgets, your $1.00 investment would yield $1.50 after the one year period and your cost/benefit ratio for wadgets would be $1.50/$1.00, or 1.5. In terms of efficiency, the ratio for widgets is far superior.

When applied to evaluation of human services and social policies, difficult questions such as "Whose costs and whose benefits?" quickly arise. The evaluator must be clear as to whether he or she is addressing benefits to the service recipient, benefits to the agency that provides the service, and/or benefits to society as a whole (Rossi & Freeman, 1993). Calculating tangible and intangible, direct and indirect, fixed and variable, and present and future costs and benefits associated with a program can be both enormously challenging and politically sensitive. Analyses of the sensitivity of results to variations in assumptions used in estimating costs and benefits must be undertaken. Measurement error is a problem in efficiency analyses (see Chapter 5). For cases that involve human life and death outcomes, the difficult ethical issue of representing the value of human life in monetary units arises. As with the previous treatment of experimental and correlational evaluation designs, attention to efficiency analyses is limited to a brief introduction to the concept. For more complete understanding, consult Boardman, Greenberg, Vining, and Weimer (1996). Loomis and Walsh (1997) provide an interesting application of efficiency analysis in a park and recreation context, and Rossi and Freeman (1993) introduce efficiency analysis in a very thorough, yet concise chapter.

Sample Efficiency Analysis: A Hypothetical Cost-Effectiveness Analysis

Imagine that your county park and recreation department has been working with your local school district to address at-risk youth problems over the past year. The program, titled, "Enrichment through Recreation" (ETR) has two primary goals:

- To increase the percentage of high school students who report that they intend to pursue university education following graduation from high school, and
- To decrease the number of arrests of high school students in the communities in which the program is conducted.

Three different formats of the program have been implemented in different communities: (1) an after school program, from 3:00–6:00 on weekdays; (2) a weekend program, that includes Friday evenings, Saturdays, and Sundays; and (3) a recess-only program. An assumption common to all programs is that the therapeutic recreation specialists who are leaders in the program serve as significant role models and leisure educators who teach youth participants about socially acceptable and growth-producing forms of leisure behavior. The park and recreation department is interested in evaluating the efficiency of these programs.

Outcomes of the project implied by the goals are an increase in educational aspirations and a reduction in arrests. Educational aspirations are measured in terms of the change in the number of students who intend to pursue a university education in the year prior to implementation of the ETR program, as compared to the year during which the program has been implemented. Changes in numbers of arrests are also of interest. Results of the evaluation may be used to restructure programs or to reallocate resources.

		Arrests			Educational Aspirations	
	Total Cost*	% decrease in arrests	CE Ratio		% increase in intent	CE Ratio
Program						
After School	80	28	0.35		20	0.25
Recess	40	3	0.13		3	0.13
Weekend	60	26	0.43		21	0.35

Table 9.3 Hypothetical Cost-Effectiveness Analysis

* In thousands

Hypothetical results are presented in Table 9.3. The table reports cost-efficiency in terms of both arrests and educational aspirations. For the hypothetical arrests data, the ratios are the percentage decrease totals divided by the total cost of the program. For educational aspirations, the CE ratios are the percentage increase totals divided by the program cost.

In terms of arrests, the weekend programs appear to be the most cost-effective. Each thousand dollars invested in the weekend program corresponds to an increase of .43 toward the total reduction in arrests. In contrast, the much more expensive after-school program was slightly less cost-effective. Each thousand dollars spent on the after-school program corresponded to a contribution of .35 to the percentage decrease in arrests. The recess program was relatively inexpensive, but did not seem to be cost-effective, relative to the other programs (CE= .08).

Table 9.3 also provides cost-effectiveness (CE) ratios associated with education aspirations. In our hypothetical example, the CE ratios reveal that the weekend program was again the most cost-effective. Each thousand dollars spent on the weekend program produced a contribution of .35 toward the percentage increase in intent to pursue university studies following high school graduation. Results of this evaluation suggest that the department might consider replacing the after-school and recess programs with the less expensive and more cost-effective weekend programs.

Summary

The intent of this chapter has been to introduce you to evaluation and how it might be applied toward understanding therapeutic recreation programs in terms of ethics, efficacy, and efficiency. Using this information, let us return to the scenario presented at the beginning of the chapter. In that scenario, you were in the role of a wealthy philanthropist who was being asked to provide financial support for a program that provides adventure recreation programs for at-risk youth. This chapter implies that, as you investigate your interest in supporting this program, you might be interested in such questions as the following:

Questions related to knowledge about the program
- Does knowledge about the program exist? What evidence exists that a reasonable person would trust as being indicative of the effects of the program on participants?
- To what extent is the manager's testimonial influenced by his or her passion for the program as opposed to knowledge about the program?

Questions related to ethics of the program
- Are the outcomes that the program is producing good, right, and desirable?
- Are the activities and experiences within the program good, right, and desirable?

Questions about efficacy of the program
- What kinds of evaluation studies have been conducted to determine the efficacy of the program in effecting changes? Is the program an effective agent?
- What evidence exists that would suggest that the program is successfully providing outcomes that participants and their families consider to be important?

Questions about the efficiency of the program
- How efficient is the program? What evidence exists to suggest that the philanthropist would create more desirable change by investing in this program rather than some alternative program with similar goals and objectives?

Finally, another word of caution is advised. This chapter involved only introductory comments and basic illustrations of a variety of very complex topics, ranging from the nature of knowledge to experimental design and cost-benefit analyses. Further, a number of highly beneficial techniques well-deserving of introduction in a chapter of this type are not mentioned here. A prime example is Goal Attainment Scaling (Kiresuk, Smith & Cardillo, 1994; Touchstone, 1984), a creative technique for synthesizing evaluation results and establishing a common basis for comparison of program outcomes across diverse programs and services. Other examples of topics and techniques that would be highly useful tools in any evaluator's tool box include benefits-based management (e.g., Allen 1996; Allen, Stevens & Harwell, 1996), use of focus groups (e.g., Krueger, 1994), possible applications of quantitative models such as multiattribute utility technology (Edwards & Newman, 1982), case study methods (e.g., Stake, 1995; Yin, 1994), and systems analysis (e.g., Bonnicksen, 1987). Readers are encouraged to use this chapter as a point of departure in developing skills in select techniques that can help them defend the services that they provide and make informed decisions about the programs and services that they provide.

Recommended Readings

Henderson, K. A. and Bialeschki, M. D. (1995). *Evaluating leisure services: Making enlightened decisions*. State College, PA: Venture Publishing, Inc.

Kraus, R. and Allen, L. (1998). *Research and evaluation in recreation, parks, and leisure studies* (2nd ed.). Needham Heights, MA: Allyn & Bacon.

Lankford, M. (1999). *Research methods in park, recreation, and leisure services*. Champaign, IL: Sagamore.

Loomis, J. B. and Walsh, R. G. (1997). *Recreation economic decisions: Comparing benefits and costs* (2nd ed.). State College, PA: Venture Publishing, Inc.

Magafas, A. and Pawelko, K. (1997). Therapeutic recreation evaluation: Problems and possibilities. In D. M. Compton (Ed.), *Issues in therapeutic recreation: Toward the new millennium* (2nd ed.), (pp. 383–401). Champaign, IL: Sagamore.

Malkin, M. and Howe, C. (Eds.). (1993). *Research in therapeutic recreation: Concepts and methods*. State College, PA: Venture Publishing, Inc.

Riddick, C. and Russell, R. (1999). *Evaluative research in recreation, park, and sport settings: Searching for useful information*. Champaign, IL: Sagamore.

Section

Technical Aspects of Therapeutic Recreation Programming

Therapeutic recreation programs enable clients to develop skills and knowledge necessary for experiencing leisure and engaging in freely chosen activities. For example, programs may allow clients to gain the social abilities that lead to friendships or the knowledge necessary for negotiating barriers to participation. Programs may also provide participants with the opportunity to enjoy their favorite music with others. In Sections One and Two we discussed the foundations and theories that provide the conceptual framework for the development of therapeutic recreation programs. Section Three presents skills, methods, and techniques that professionals use when developing therapeutic recreation programs. In addition, we describe how professional foundations and theories inform the development of comprehensive and individual program plans.

Chapter 10 describes the development of comprehensive and specific program plans. The comprehensive program plan articulates the overall mission of a therapeutic recreation department and the general goals outlined for people who engage in services. The conceptual foundation, philosophy, and practice model on which the comprehensive program is based gives direction and substance to the plan. For example, a conceptual foundation built on leisure and selection of the Leisure Ability Model (Stumbo & Peterson, 1998) may result in a mission statement and goals aimed at the development of participants' independent leisure behavior. The comprehensive program plan then guides the creation of specific program plans. Such plans provide an outline for each program, including the purpose, goals, and content.

In Chapter 11 we discuss individualized care plans. Individual care plans result from client assessment. Goals and objectives are then developed to address the client's needs. Specific programs are selected to build on a client's strengths and interests and allow for the achievement of care goals and objectives.

Many of the applied concepts in Chapter 11 draw on the theories presented in Sections One and Two. For example, the assessment paradigms and principles in Chapter 5 are referred to as we discuss the applied aspects of selecting and using a therapeutic recreation assessment tool. The counseling theories presented in Chapter 6 may guide the therapeutic recreation specialist's interactions with a client. For example, if behavioral modification techniques were used with a client such information would be included in the individualized care plan. Lastly, discharge planning and life care planning are discussed, drawing on many of the principles of recreation inclusion presented in Chapter 8.

The aspects of therapeutic recreation programming presented in Section Three are the culmination of this textbook. Students are challenged to consider how their values, beliefs, and philosophies influence their conceptualization of program delivery. We encourage students to reevaluate regularly how they use theories and philosophies to guide the development and implementation of therapeutic recreation programs.

Chapter

Therapeutic Recreation Program Planning: Comprehensive and Specific Program Plans

In this chapter we examine the components and processes involved in design-ing comprehensive and specific program plans. A comprehensive plan details the mission and scope of an agency's overall therapeutic recreation program. It further leads to the development of specific therapeutic recreation programs for the clientele served by the agency.

Comprehensive Plan

The comprehensive plan consists of a mission statement, goals, and specific programs. Articulating the mission statement is the first step in developing the plan. The mission statement guides the development of departmental goals and specific programs and communicates the focus of the agency to participants, funding agencies, administrators, and professionals from other disciplines (O'Morrow & Carter, 1997).

Assessment

Developing a mission statement requires an assessment of the domains that influence the delivery of therapeutic recreation services, including external forces (external to the department and therapeutic recreation profession);

professional standards and procedures; agency or internal forces; and partici-pants/clientele (see Table 10.1).

External Forces

Accreditation verifies that an agency meets minimum standards set by an accrediting body. For example, the Joint Commission on Accreditation of Healthcare Organizations (JCAHO) and the Commission on Accreditation of Rehabilitation Facilities (CARF) accredit many hospitals. JCAHO and CARF outline standards of care regarding the type of hospital units or programs that must provide therapeutic recreation services. Facilities that receive Medicare funding (i.e., federal funding of health care for adults 65 and over) must adhere to the Health Care Financing Administration's (HCFA) guidelines and standards.

Knowledge of federal, state, and local legislation is also needed to develop a comprehensive program that reflects legal mandates (Smith, Austin & Kennedy, 1996). For example, the Americans with Disabilities Act (ADA) has influenced public recreation opportunities for people with disabilities. Title II of the ADA mandates that public services, such as public recreation, may not refuse a person the opportunity to participate due to a disability. Therefore, a

---

Table 10.1 Domains Influencing Mission Statement

External Forces:
  Accrediting Bodies (JCAHO, CARF)
  Legislation (ADA)

Professional Standards and Procedures:
  Philosophy, Conceptual Foundation
  Practice Models
  Standards of Practice
  Code of Ethics

Agency Forces:
  Agency Mission
  Staff Resources
  Disciplines/Professionals Other Than Therapeutic Recreation

Participants/Clientele:
  Demographic Characteristics
  Functional Abilities and Needs
  Leisure Abilities and Needs
  Community Characteristics and Opportunities
  Vocational Needs and Interests

public recreation agency would be required to provide community integration opportunities for constituents with disabilities. Another example is the impact that the 1987 Omnibus Budget Reconciliation Act had on the assessment and treatment of nursing home residents.

Professional Standards and Procedures

NTRS's *Standards of Practice* (1991), ATRA's *Standards for Practice* (1991), NTRS's *Code of Ethics* (1990), and ATRA's *Code of Ethics* (1998) provide guidance when designing a comprehensive program plan (see Appendices A, B, C, and D). Standards of practice set a template for acceptable delivery of services, such as assessment, documentation, and interventions. The ATRA and NTRS Codes of Ethics express moral standards expected of therapeutic recreation specialists. All of these guidelines may shape the services provided by a therapeutic recreation department.

Agency Forces

Numerous forces internal to the agency will impact the comprehensive mission statement. Knowing the agency's overall mission is important if the therapeutic recreation department is within a large agency, such as a hospital or municipal recreation agency. The mission of the therapeutic recreation department should complement that of the overall organization. In addition, the therapeutic recreation specialist must know the staff and volunteer resources that are available to the therapeutic recreation department.

Knowledge of the other disciplines employed by the agency is also important. For example, a therapeutic recreation specialist employed in a physical rehabilitation hospital typically works on an interdisciplinary team consisting of physicians, nurses, physical therapists, occupational therapists, speech therapists, and dieticians. The interdisciplinary team helps to establish the scope of services and supports the goals and efforts of each other. The therapeutic recreation specialist may involve participants in community outings following accomplishments in transferring from wheelchair to toilet (e.g., physical therapy). Alternatively, when a client participating in therapeutic recreation renews his interest in swimming, physical therapy may target strength training that promotes the client's skills in swimming. A therapeutic recreation specialist may also co-lead community outings with a physical therapist. In such cases, the therapeutic recreation specialist may focus on clients' socialization skills, while the physical therapist addresses mobility.

Participants/Clientele

The participants or clientele served constitute the major force shaping the department's mission statement. The therapeutic recreation specialist must know the range of characteristics, needs, and abilities of the clientele. Basic demographic data, such as age, gender, race/ethnicity, religion, socioeconomic status, and educational attainment, allow for an initial description of clientele. Information gathered on the disabilities, diagnoses, functional abilities, health status, and leisure abilities and interests of the clientele will also be important to the therapeutic recreation specialist. Information may deal with any or all of the following:

- Demographic information (e.g., age, gender, race/ethnicity, religion, educational attainment, socioeconomic status),
- Specific disabilities and diagnoses,
- Cognitive functioning (e.g., intelligence, memory, ability to follow instructions),
- Emotional functioning (e.g., express emotions appropriately, recognize emotions),
- Physical functioning (e.g., strength, range of motion, ability to transfer from wheelchair to van or bed),
- Social functioning (e.g., initiate conversation, respond to inquiries, make eye contact),
- Independence in activities of daily living (e.g., toileting, dressing, eating),
- Health status,
- Diagnoses,
- Knowledge of and ability in leisure activities,
- Knowledge of leisure resources,
- Attitudes and beliefs about leisure, recreation, and play, and
- General quality of life.

Information on the communities from which participants are referred and subsequently return is also pertinent. Such information directly affects a client's leisure behavior prior to entry into a therapeutic recreation program, as well as the leisure opportunities available upon discharge. Clients may enter service delivery from their homes (e.g., hospitalization for depression) or from another institution (e.g., from a medical hospital to a free standing physical rehabilitation unit). A basic understanding of how long clients have been away from their home environments will provide insight into their leisure challenges. For example, an individual who gardens may have little opportunity to do so while receiving inpatient services on a physical rehabilitation unit. Facilities that provide services to individuals who are unable to pursue familiar and enjoyable recreation activities should develop a comprehensive program plan that mandates the provision of freely chosen recreation pursuits (e.g., recreation participation component of the Leisure Ability Model).

Therapeutic recreation specialists must also understand the settings and communities to which participants return after discharge. In institutional settings participants may be discharged to their home, while others may be discharged to a new community. Clients who participate in a community based therapeutic recreation program will return home immediately following partici- pation in a specific program. Knowledge of discharge placement allows a therapeutic recreation specialist to consider leisure education needs. For example, if most clients were discharged to new communities it would be necessary to provide educational programs on the development and mainte- nance of leisure pursuits in the new community. In a community therapeutic recreation program, knowledge of community recreation opportunities facili- tates the integration of clients in general recreation programs.

Planning

Mission Statement

Following the collection and examination of the information on the domains that affect service delivery, the therapeutic recreation staff writes a mission statement. The *mission statement* communicates "the basic purpose of an organization, that is, what it is trying to accomplish" (Kotler & Andreasen, 1996, p. 66). The mission statement conveys the values of a department as well as the focus of services.

Mission statements vary in length, from a few sentences to several pages. Shorter examples from three departments are included here.

#1: MISSION STATEMENT of the Therapeutic Recreation Department, Psychiatric Hospital

> Our mission is to promote healthy social and emotional functioning and independence in daily leisure among all patients. We are commit- ted to providing therapy and education services that promote health and independence during hospitalization and following discharge to the community.

#2: MISSION STATEMENT of the Therapeutic Recreation Department, Community and Residential Services for Adults with Developmental Disabilities

Our mission is to promote healthy social, emotional, physical functioning, and independence in leisure pursuits among the clients of the Community and Residential Services Program. We are committed to providing quality programs, including functional intervention, leisure education, and recreation services, for clients residing in residential group homes and community-based dwellings.

#3: MISSION STATEMENT of the Special Recreation Division, Public Parks and Recreation Agency

Our mission is to promote residents' highest level of integration in community recreation programs. We are committed to the provision of quality leisure education and recreation services that facilitate participants' engagement with family and friends and their integration into community programs.

Each mission statement reflects the practice model underlying therapeutic recreation services. For example, the department in #1 exemplifies a mission statement that draws on the Van Andel (1998) Therapeutic Recreation Service Delivery Model and reflects the specific components of treatment/rehabilitation and education. The departments in #2 and #3 draw from the Peterson and Stumbo (2000) Leisure Ability Model. The therapeutic recreation department in #2 provides treatment, leisure education, and recreation participation. The therapeutic recreation department in #3 provides leisure education and recreation participation services.

Agencies vary in how they develop a mission statement. Some agencies write a mission statement that expresses their philosophy of care, which may entail several pages. Other agencies may include value statements as part of their mission. For the purpose of developing a comprehensive program plan, a mission statement describing the valued outcomes and focus of services is the minimum needed by a department. We encourage readers to consult other resources to examine the different approaches for developing mission statements (see Kotler & Andreasen, 1996; O'Morrow & Carter, 1997).

Goals

Comprehensive program goals support the department's mission statement. The goals target the client needs to be addressed in the therapeutic recreation programs. Goals are typically one sentence in length and are not directly measurable. Below are goals developed by the three departments.

#1: MISSION STATEMENT of the Therapeutic Recreation Department, Psychiatric Hospital

Our mission is to promote healthy social and emotional functioning and independence in daily leisure among all patients. We are committed to providing therapy and education services that promote health and independence during hospitalization and following discharge into the community.

Goals: Programs are designed to allow participants:
1. To develop social interaction skills.
2. To develop means of acknowledging and appropriately expressing emotions.
3. To develop ability to make appropriate decisions regarding daily care, time use, and recreation.
4. To develop a broad range of leisure activity skills.
5. To gain knowledge of leisure resources in the home, neighborhood, and community.

#2: MISSION STATEMENT of the Therapeutic Recreation Department, Community and Residential Services for Adults with Developmental Disabilities

Our mission is to promote healthy social, emotional, physical functioning, and independence in leisure pursuits among the clients of the Community and Residential Services Program. We are committed to providing quality programs, including functional intervention, leisure education, and recreation services, for clients residing in residential group homes and community-based dwellings.

Goals: Programs are designed to allow participants:
1. To develop social interaction skills.
2. To develop awareness and appropriate expression of emotions.

3. To enhance independence through improved physical strength and mobility.
4. To develop a range of leisure activity skills.
5. To develop knowledge of residential and community based leisure resources.
6. To engage in social and recreational activities both independently and with family and friends.

#3: MISSION STATEMENT of the Special Recreation Division, Public Parks and Recreation Agency

Our mission is to promote residents' highest level of integration in community recreation programs. We are committed to the provision of quality leisure education and recreation services that facilitate participants' engagement with family and friends and their integration into community programs.

Goals: Programs are designed to allow participants:
1. To examine leisure related values, beliefs, and attitudes.
2. To develop a broad repertoire of leisure activity skills.
3. To gain knowledge of the community based leisure resources.
4. To engage in recreation activities during evening and weekend hours that reinforce healthy leisure pursuits.

Case Example

The Wilderness Group (WG) recently hired a new program director who decided to develop a comprehensive program plan. The Wilderness Group is a nonprofit organization which contracts with state agencies to provide treatment for young offenders. The average adjudicated youth serves either nine months in a traditional juvenile correctional institution or one month in WG and eight months at home on parole. The young people have volunteered readily to participate in the program and selection has been based on a subjective evaluation by the WG program director. Past program participants included males and females ranging in age from 15 to 17 years. Their personal histories varied and their violations range from status offenses to multiple felonies.

A WG program usually consists of ten participants and two instructors, lasts 30 days, and involves an extended lake/flat-river canoe trip, rock climbing, rappelling, trust exercises, and ropes course activities. A run followed by a dip-in-the river and group incentives are daily features. Reality Therapy is used to guide instructor/participant interactions. The program is not coeducational and costs about $3,000 per participant. A new WG program begins approximately every two weeks with the number of programs split evenly between males and females. (Wilhite & Keller, 1992, pp. 181-182)

The director and staff developed the comprehensive program plan by identifying the information needed to write a mission statement (see Table 10.1, p. 276). The *external forces* effecting WG are the legal system and the subsequent sentencing participants receive. Further information on the legal system and the state and local laws affecting the sentencing of adolescents was needed.

Little information on *professional standards and procedures* was available. Staff discussed the conceptual foundations, practice model, standards of practice, and code of ethics guiding service delivery at WG. They agreed that its conceptualization of therapeutic recreation was based on the link of leisure to health and well-being. Given the diversity of skills and abilities addressed in the WG programs, Van Andel's Therapeutic Recreation Service Delivery Model guided the delivery of services. Professional standards of practice and codes of ethics were also considered.

The new program director had detailed information on *agency forces,* including number and expertise of the staff. Due to liability of the high-risk program and need for confidentiality, no volunteers are involved in the WG programs. The *clientele* are adjudicated youth between 15 and 17 years of age. The WG does have documentation as to the functional abilities of the partici-pants, including social skills, ability to acknowledge and express emotions, physical abilities, and leisure participation patterns prior to entry into the legal system. Participants come from all over the state to participate in WG. Further information was sought about the communities from which participants entered the program, as well as the communities in which participants serve their parole.

Following an in-depth discussion of the forces influencing service delivery, the WG staff developed the following mission statement and goals:

MISSION STATEMENT: Our mission is to promote healthy social and emotional functioning, knowledge of appropriate leisure pursuits and lifelong leisure abilities among all participants. We are committed to providing quality treatment and educational services that foster these outcomes.

Goals: Wildness Group programs are designed to allow participants:
1. To develop appropriate social skills for recreation, school, and work environments.
2. To develop an awareness and appropriate expression of emotions.
3. To gain knowledge of healthy leisure pursuits.
4. To gain leisure related decision-making skills.
5. To develop a broad range of leisure activity skills.

Departmental Goals and Programs

A number of specific programs are designed to support the department goals in the comprehensive program plan. An agency's comprehensive program plan will include the mission statement and goals, as well as a list of the specific programs that support each goal. The comprehensive program plan for a psychiatric hospital may be as follows:

#1: MISSION STATEMENT of the Therapeutic Recreation Department, Psychiatric Hospital
Our mission is to promote healthy social and emotional functioning and independence in daily leisure among all patients. We are committed to providing therapy and education services that promote health and independence during hospitalization and following discharge to the community.

Goals:	**Specific Programs:**
1.To develop social interaction skills.	• Socializing with Friends and Family • Family Communication Skills • Afternoon or Evening Social
2. To develop means of acknowledging and appropriately expressing emotions.	• Self Esteem: A Personal Journey • Expressive Arts: Journaling • Expressive Arts: Dance and Movement • Expressive Arts:Painting and Drawing • Relaxation
3. To develop ability to make appropriate decisions regarding daily care, time use, and recreation.	• Daily Tasks: Ready, Set, Go! (co-lead with Nursing and OT) • Leisure Education: Time Use • Leisure Values and Choices

4. To develop a broad range of leisure activity skills

• Leisure Activity Skill Classes: Swimming, Exercise, Volleyball, Softball, Board Games, Crafts

5. To gain knowledge of leisure resources in the home, neighborhood, and community.

• Leisure Education: Home Activities
• Leisure Education: Family Leisure
• Leisure Education: That's My Neighborhood
• Leisure Education: Resources Galore!
• Community Outings

Specific Program Plans

Specific program plans are written documents for each program offered by a department. Each plan includes a statement regarding the particular departmental goals that are supported by the program. Additionally, specific program plans include a written statement of purpose, goals, objectives, content, process, and general information. The *statement of purpose* is written to articulate the general purpose of the program. *Goals* describe the general outcomes for participants. Goals are further broken down into *objectives*, which identify specific knowledge or behaviors clients need to demonstrate to achieve their goals. Typically, two to four objectives are written for each goal. Readers should note that the objectives developed for specific programs identify knowledge and behaviors that are potentially measurable. However, specific program objectives have not been assigned the criteria that make them directly measurable. While clients assigned to a specific program will share similar goals and objectives, the measurable content of their objectives will vary depending on their individual needs and levels of development. Accordingly, expectations regarding performance will vary from client to client. Objectives receive the performance criteria that make them measurable during the development of individual care plans, which will be discussed in Chapter 11.

When designing the program, the learning activities are selected which allow participants to demonstrate the knowledge and behavior outlined in the objectives. The *content* of a program plan consists of the activities to be implemented in the session. The *process* outlines the actions and procedures used by the leader during the session. Finally, the program plan includes *general information* pertaining to the range of participants appropriate for the program, program length, location, equipment, and staff competencies needed for implementation.

In the following section we discuss activity analysis, a tool used to match the content of a program to the intended goals and objectives. The elements of a specific program plan and the steps followed to develop a plan will also be presented. Lastly, we provide an example of a specific program plan.

Activity Analysis

Activity analysis involves examining an activity along social, physical, cognitive, and affective domains to determine the knowledge, skills, and materials required to participate in an activity; and the effectiveness of the activity for contributing to participants' acquisition of knowledge and skill or change in attitudes and affect, as outlined in the objectives. According to Peterson and Stumbo (2000), activity analysis provides:

- A better comprehension of the expected outcomes of participants,
- A greater understanding of the complexity of activity components, which can then be compared to the functional level of an individual or group to determine the appropriateness of the activity,
- A basis for comparing and contrasting the relative contributions of several activity options to the desired participant outcomes,
- Information about whether the activity will contribute to the desired behavioral outcomes when specific behavioral goals or objectives are being used,
- Directions for the modification or adaptation of an activity for individuals with limitations,
- Useful information for selecting an intervention, instructional, or leadership technique, and
- A rationale or explanation for the therapeutic benefits of activity involvement. (p. 144)

An activity is analyzed using a series of questions pertaining to physical, cognitive, affective, and social domains (see Table 10.2, p. 288). The physical domain considers means of movement (e.g., walking, running, jumping), use of body parts (e.g., arms, legs), endurance, strength, and speed. The cognitive domain considers the demands an activity would place on memory, concentration, and intellectual skills, such as reading and writing. The affective domain assesses the experience and expression of feelings, such as joy, anger, fear, guilt, and success. Finally, the social domain considers the demands for cooperation, competition, social interaction, and leadership.

An example of therapeutic recreation specialists using activity analysis speaks to its importance in developing specific program plans. For instance, the therapeutic recreation staff in a nursing home are considering activities that would support the department goal "to develop social interaction skills." One therapeutic recreation specialist suggests gardening. Other staff are enthusiastic about this suggestion since many residents talk about gardening. When gardening is analyzed, however, they realized that the skills involved in gardening place demands on cognitive abilities (e.g., to follow and remember instructions) and physical abilities (e.g., bending, lifting, grasping). A basic gardening group would not promote social interaction. The staff then considered either modifying the activity to include a discussion on gardening that would demand the use of social interaction skills or selecting another activity to promote the departmental goal of developing social interaction skills.

Once activity analysis has been conducted, it is possible to decide what modifications are required. Peterson and Gunn (1984) recommended several factors when modifying activities:

1.   Keep the activity and action as close to the original or traditional activity as possible.
2.   Modify only the aspects of the activity that need adapting.
3.   Individualize the modification (p. 205).

An example of a modification would be a therapeutic recreation staff in a rehabilitation hospital that is considering a gardening group to support the departmental goal "to maintain participation in lifelong leisure pursuits." Many patients have expressed the desire to spend time in the sun weeding and planting seedlings. Activity analysis of gardening, however, indicates that participants must be able to squat down and bend. Since a majority of patients use wheelchairs, staff members recognize the need to modify the activity. Creating raised garden beds that allow participants to weed and plant from a sitting position are considered an appropriate modification. Such a modification maintains the basic nature of the activity.

General feasibility of the proposed activity must also be considered, including equipment, resources, and staff competence. The therapeutic recreation specialist should consider the number of staff needed to implement the program, as well as their qualifications. For example, therapeutic recreation specialists who implement an aquatic therapy program would need special training and certification. The adequacy of facilities and equipment and sufficiency of time are also evaluated.

Activity analysis can be straightforward, as it was in the preceding example. It can also be extensive and complex, as in the case of a severely disabled person who is leaving an institution for the first time at age eighteen. Moreover, activity analysis should not be an exercise in finding and modifying

Table 10.2 Activity Analysis*

Activity Analysis is the examination of the social, physical, cognitive, and affective domains of an activity to assess the knowledge, skills, and materials required to participate in an activity and the effectiveness of the activity for contributing to clients' goals and objectives.

Domains	Examples
Physical	• What body parts are used when participating in the activity? • Does the activity require flexibility? • What types of movements are required when participating in the activity? (e.g., reaching, pushing, bending) • Does the activity require independence in mobility? • Does the activity require physical strength? (e.g., upper body strength, lower body strength?) • Does the activity require coordination? • Does the activity require speed?
Cognitive	• Does the activity require ability to follow directions? • Does the activity require an understanding of numbers? • Does the activity require short-term memory skills? Long-term memory skills? • Does the activity require concentration? • Does the activity require sensory abilities? • Does the activity require abstract thinking skills? Concrete thinking skills?
Affective	• Does the activity allow for expression of feelings? (e.g., happiness, sadness, frustration) • Does the activity demand control of feelings? (e.g., anger, frustration)
Social	• Does the activity require one-on-one interaction? Small group interaction? Large group interaction? • Does the activity require communication? • Does the activity require competition? Cooperation? • Does the activity require leadership on the part of all participants?
Feasibility	• Availability of appropriate equipment? • Availability of appropriate location? • Availability of staff expertise and time?

* Adapted from Carter, Browne, LeConey, and Nagle (1991) and Peterson and Stumbo (2000).

activities solely for their value as treatment interventions. One of the ultimate goals of therapeutic recreation is for individuals to *choose* leisure activities that contribute to their health and well-being. As such, their autonomy and personal interests should be respected and promoted as much as possible. In the long run, therapeutic recreation specialists will find it most productive to help clients find activities that suit their personal interests because they are then more likely to pursue intrinsically motivated activities after discharge. Therefore, clients should have a prominent role in the process of activity analysis.

The next section presents a case example. The case demonstrates the steps a therapeutic recreation specialist follows when developing a specific program plan.

Case Example

The therapeutic recreation staff employed in a psychiatric hospital are developing a number of specific program plans. The staff follow a series of steps as they develop the specific program plans (see Table 10.3, p. 303). First, the department's comprehensive program plan is reviewed. For example, the mission statement for the Therapeutic Recreation Department in this hospital is as follows:

> #1: MISSION STATEMENT *of the Therapeutic Recreation Department, Psychiatric Hospital*
>
> > Our mission is to promote healthy social and emotional functioning and independence in daily leisure among all patients. We are committed to providing therapy and education services that promote health and independence during hospitalization and following discharge to the community.

A departmental goal is then selected for program development. The intent is to create specific programs that support the following departmental goal:

> To gain knowledge of leisure resources in the home, neighborhood, and community.

Several leisure education programs are needed to support the department goal listed above. The therapeutic recreation specialist begins by deciding whether to target resources in the home, neighborhood, or community. The purpose of a program addressing community leisure resources may be to *facilitate participants' awareness of leisure resources available in their communities*. The overall goal of such a program would be for participants to *demonstrate knowledge of leisure resources in the neighborhood.* The goal is then further developed into two objectives.

Program Statement of Purpose: To facilitate participants' awareness of the leisure resources available in their communities.

Goal: Demonstrate knowledge of leisure resources in the neighborhood.
Objective 1: Describe leisure resources previously accessed in the neighborhood.
Objective 2: Identify new leisure resources in the neighborhood.

The next step in the process involves brainstorming activities that would result in participants demonstrating the targeted knowledge or skill. For the second objective in the program outlined above, the therapeutic recreation specialist may consider a scavenger hunt using a telephone book, creating maps of neighborhood resources, or visiting community recreation facilities.

For the specific program developed in this section, the therapeutic recreation specialist may decide to have participants draw a map of their neighborhoods and indicate leisure resources they have used. The participants may be given a copy of a Community Resource Guidebook and instructions on how to use it to add newly identified resources to their neighborhood maps. The decision to use these activities is based on both the findings of the activity analysis and feasibility of implementation.

After the activities are identified, the therapeutic recreation specialist begins to outline the content of the program. The content for the proposed leisure education program is as follows:

Program Statement of Purpose: To facilitate participants' awareness of the leisure resources available in their communities.

Goal: Demonstrate knowledge of leisure resources in the neighborhood.
Objective 1: Describe leisure resources previously accessed in the neighborhood.
    Content:
    • Discuss types of recreation and leisure pursuits typically found in neighborhoods and communities.
    • Draw a map of his or her neighborhood indicating recreation and leisure pursuits.
    • Discuss previously accessed recreation and leisure pursuits.

Table 10.3 Steps in Development of a Specific Program Plan

1. Review comprehensive program plan.

2. Select one department goal for program development.

3. Develop the purpose and general outcome (i.e., goals) of the program.

4. Develop objectives for each goal.

5. Consider a variety of activities that will allow for participants to achieve objectives.

6. Select activities based on feasibility (e.g., equipment, staff, time, facilities).

7. Develop an outline of program content (i.e., activities used).

8. Develop an outline of the process used to implement program content (i.e., leadership and counseling methods and techniques).

9. Develop a description of abilities needed in order to participate, length of session, location, equipment and staff competencies needed for implementation.

Objective 2: Identify new leisure resources in the neighborhood.
Content:
- Introduce the Community Resources Guidebook and neighborhood newspapers.
- Revise neighborhood maps based on information discovered in the guidebook and newspapers.
- Discuss newly discovered resources.
- Identify one goal for use of neighborhood recreation and leisure opportunities after discharge.

Next the therapeutic recreation specialist considers the actions he or she must take when facilitating the group. Actions may include providing participants with equipment, asking participants to discuss their experiences, or providing reinforcement for participation. The process is as follows:

Goal: Demonstrate knowledge of leisure resources in the neighborhood.
Objective 1: Describe leisure resources previously accessed in the neighborhood.

Content:	**Process:**
• Discuss neighborhoods, types of recreation and leisure pursuits typically found in neighborhoods and communities.	• Ask group to identify recreation and leisure pursuits in their neighborhoods.
• Draw a map of his or her neighborhood indicating recreation and leisure pursuits.	• Provide participants with paper and markers.
• Discuss previously accessed recreation and leisure pursuits.	• Ask each participant about neighborhood recreation pursuits they have used. • Provide positive reinforcement for each participant's contribution to the discussion.

Objective 2: Demonstrate ability to identify new leisure resources in the neighborhood.

Content:	**Process:**
• Introduce the Community Resources Guidebook and neighborhood newspapers.	• Distribute Guidebooks and newspapers; provide assistance as needed.
• Revise their neighborhood maps based on information discovered in the Guidebooks and newspapers.	• Provide assistance as needed.
• Discuss newly discovered resources.	• Ask participants to share information on newly discovered resources.
• Identify one goal for use of neighborhood recreation and leisure opportunities after discharge.	• Provide positive reinforcement for each participant's engagement in the activity.

The final step in the development of the specific program plan is providing a title for the program, as well as information pertinent to implementation. Implementation information may include the abilities needed by participants, location, equipment, session length, and staffing needs. The finalized plan is as follows:

TITLE: That's My Neighborhood!

Statement of Purpose: To facilitate participants' awareness of the leisure resources available in their communities.

Participants: Must be able to listen to instructions, to concentrate on independent tasks for up to five minutes, read, respond to questions.

Location: Room free of distractions with tables and chairs situated to allow participants to see and hear one another.

Equipment/Supplies: Paper, markers, pencils, Community Resource Guidebook, neighborhood newspapers.

Length of Session: Approximately 45 minutes.

Staffing Needs: One therapeutic recreation specialist and one nursing staff member for each eight participants.

Goal: Demonstrate knowledge of leisure resources in the neighborhood.

Objective 1: Describe leisure resources previously accessed in the neighborhood.

Content:	*Process:*
• Discuss types of recreation and leisure pursuits typically found in neighborhoods and communities.	• Ask group to identify recreation and leisure pursuits in their neighborhoods.
• Draw a map of his or her neighborhood indicating recreation and leisure pursuits.	• Provide participants with paper and markers.
• Discuss previously accessed recreation and leisure pursuits.	• Ask each participant about neighborhood recreation pursuits they have used. • Provide positive reinforcement for each participant's contribution to the discussion.

Objective 2: Identify new leisure resources in neighborhood.

Content:	*Process:*
• Introduce the Community Resources Guidebook and neighborhood newspapers.	• Distribute Guidebooks and newspapers.
• Revise their neighborhood maps based on information discovered in the Guidebooks and newspapers.	• Provide assistance as needed

- Discuss newly discovered resources.

- Ask participants to share information on newly discovered resources.

- Identify one goal involving the use of neighborhood recreation and leisure opportunities after discharge.

- Provide positive reinforcement for each participant's engagement in the discussion.

Matching Participants to Specific Programs

On an ongoing basis the therapeutic recreation specialist who implements "That's My Neighborhood" will identify clients in need of leisure education. A match between the program's goals and objectives and the client's assessed needs determines whether or not a client is included in the program. Clients lacking knowledge about their community leisure resources are ideal candidates for "That's My Neighborhood." For example:

> *Sara* is a 29-year-old female. For the past two years she has been depressed and has left her home only to go to the grocery store. One of her treatment goals is to increase the time spent outside her home engaged in familiar activities.

> *Mark* is a 23-year-old male. During his teen years he was an active basketball player, reader, and video game wizard. Several years ago, due to a number of family pressures, he started drinking and stopped participating in many activities. One of his treatment goals is to increase awareness of leisure opportunities available in his neighborhood.

The therapeutic recreation specialist and the client decide on the specific behaviors (knowledge or skill) to be demonstrated during participation in the program. As part of the client's individualized care plan, measurable behavioral objectives are written to specify the exact behaviors to be demonstrated. (The development of measurable objectives for individual care plans will be discussed in Chapter 11.)

Types of Specific Programs

In this section several specific programs that have been used extensively by therapeutic recreation specialists are presented. Programs presented include: (1) social skills training, (2) reminiscence, (3) sensory stimulation, (4) adventure programming, (5) aquatic therapy, and (6) horticulture therapy. The brief descriptions includes citations that provide further detail as to the content and outcomes of the program.

Social Skills Training

Social skills are an essential prerequisite to an appropriate leisure lifestyle (Peterson & Gunn, 1984; Sneegas, 1989; Stumbo, 1995). Socially competent people demonstrate verbal and nonverbal communication skills. In addition, they have the ability and knowledge to respond appropriately in a variety of situations. For example, an individual participating in a relaxation group may enter the room and speak quietly with other participants. In contrast, when the same individual joins a group of friends who are tailgating before the football game, his verbal interactions may be boisterous and loud.

The content of *social skills training* addresses overt social behaviors and cognitive processes. Overt social behaviors include nonverbal and verbal communication. Cognitive processes include "problem-solving skills, role-playing skills, and information processing" (Sneegas, 1989, p. 33). Examples of therapeutic recreation programs addressing social skills are found in Stumbo's leisure education manuals (Stumbo, 1992).

Reminiscence

Many therapeutic recreation specialists implement reminiscence groups with older adults. *Reminiscence* is the "recall [of] previous life experiences and facilitate the group's affirmation of these experiences" (Bowlby, 1993, p. 210). The benefits of reminiscence occur from the acknowledgment of personal accomplishments and meaningful relationships and experiences (Butler & Lewis, 1986; Hawkins, May, & Rogers, 1996). Therapeutic recreation special- ists have reported using reminiscence to enable recall of home life and travel experiences (Weiss, 1989; Weiss & Thurn, 1987).

Sensory Stimulation

Sensory stimulation programs enable participants "to experience the pleasures of life through the senses" (Bowlby, 1993, p. 93). Participants typically have limited cognitive and verbal abilities. Sensory objects are used to evoke an active response. For example, the smell of a freshly baked chocolate chip cookie may evoke the response of eating the cookie, as well as reminiscing about baking.

Sensory stimulation may occur at the beginning of a group program. For example, sensory cues such as holiday music and colorful decorations may serve as the introduction to a holiday program. Sensory stimulation programs may also stand alone and consist of a series of sensory objects used to stimulate participants' active responses. Familiar objects (plants, bean bags, sponges), natural materials (smooth stones, pine, mint), and materials associated with a functional response (throwing a colorful, smooth beachball) may be used (Bowlby, 1993).

Adventure Programming

Adventure programming typically consists of outdoor experiences that are both physically and psychologically challenging (Dattilo & Murphy, 1987b). Adventure program activities range from cooperative games to ropes courses to outdoor pursuits, such as rock climbing and whitewater rafting. The specific activities are designed so that participants must work together to accomplish the assigned task. For example, a group of eight participants may be assigned the task of every group member going over an eight-foot wall within ten minutes.

A key element of adventure programming is the final discussion and processing of the participants' experiences (Luckner & Nadler, 1995). The processing of experiences addresses the roles and reactions of the participants as they worked together. In addition, participants discuss how these experiences relate to their daily lives. For example, following the eight-foot wall activity, participants may identify one or two group members who took on leadership roles or were the group cheerleader. Further discussion may reflect on the positive and negative aspects of being a leader or cheerleader in real life interactions with family, friends, or colleagues.

Aquatic Therapy

In the past decade, therapeutic recreation specialists have become increasingly knowledgeable of using aquatic therapy as an intervention. Broach and Dattilo (1996) defined *aquatic therapy* as "water exercise and swimming as modes of prescribed activity . . . to achieve goals of improved physiological, psychological, psychosocial, and/or life activity function under the supervision of individuals qualified and competent in its techniques and utilization" (p. 214). Water provides buoyancy that allows movement that may not be possible on land for individuals with physical impairments. Using water exercises and movement may decrease pain and increase strength, endurance, and mood (Broach & Dattilo, 1996; Beaudouin & Keller, 1994). Descriptions of aquatic therapy content and outcomes have been reported by a number of therapeutic recreation specialists (Broach, Groff, & Dattilo, 1997; Broach, Groff, Dattilo, Yaffe & Gast, 1997/98).

Horticulture Therapy

Many facilities sponsor horticulture programs. Such programs range from indoor gardening, to planting and caring for the perennials and annuals that surround the facility, to planting and caring for gardens at a local park. Some facilities actually have a horticultural therapist on staff, while other facilities may provide horticulture or gardening programs under the umbrella of therapeutic recreation. "*Horticultural therapy* is a process through which plants, gardening activities, and the innate closeness we all feel towards nature are used as vehicles in professionally conducted programs of therapy and rehabilitation" (Davis, 1998, p. 3).

Protocols

The concept of *protocols* has become popular in the design and implementation of therapeutic recreation programs. A protocol is a standardized set of steps implemented to achieve an outcome. For example, imagine that improved self-esteem is one of the desired outcomes for a depressed adolescent. Research has confirmed that adventure activities are effective for improving the self-esteem of depressed adolescents. Logically the therapeutic recreation specialist would use the protocol of adventure activities as an intervention to achieve the outcome of improved self-esteem. As therapeutic recreation practice evolves, research productivity increases, and the body of knowledge grows, protocols will be designed for specific needs and problems (Ferguson, 1997). Standardized protocols are especially appealing because they are conducive to efficient care.

Several similarities exist between standardized protocols and specific program plans. For example, both protocols and program plans indicate the type of client appropriate for participation and contain detailed information on the intervention (specific activities). Sound protocols, however, are based on efficacy research in relation to clients' symptoms and diagnoses. In contrast, specific program plans are developed to support the departmental mission and goals. Until further research in therapeutic recreation is completed, many therapeutic recreation departments will deliver services based on specific program plans. Appendix F provides an example of a therapeutic recreation protocol that was developed based on the efficacy research of strength training with older adults (Mobily & Mobily, 1997; Mobily, Mobily, Lane & Semijaner, 1998).

While standardized protocols have their merits, they are not without controversy. First, while individuals may share a diagnosis, they are typically different with regard to their beliefs, values, backgrounds, interests, and experiences. Protocols are thus ill-advised if they are regarded as "one intervention fits all." Second, one of the principles of recreation and leisure is that individuals are unique in their needs and interests. Therapeutic recreation specialists, therefore, should attempt to promote choice and self-expression, which may be restricted by standardization. There may indeed be times when standardized protocols are appropriate, but professionals must be cautious not to implement protocols without first considering clients' quality of life goals. Moreover, standardized protocols are not consistent with a multicultural approach to therapeutic recreation programming. Assuming that the same intervention will work with individuals from different cultures is simplistic and potentially unethical.

Summary

This chapter provided an introduction to comprehensive program planning. We reviewed the domains (external and internal forces, professional standards, participant characteristics) that influence a therapeutic recreation department's mission statement. We also discussed the departmental goals that are developed to support the mission statement. The steps in designing specific activity plans supporting departmental goals were reviewed. Several specific programs used extensively by therapeutic recreation specialists were introduced. Lastly, we discussed the components of protocols.

We encourage readers to consider means of evaluating departmental programs. Following the development of a comprehensive program plan, as well as specific program plans, a department typically evaluates how well specific programs support departmental goals. In Chapter 9 we discussed means of evaluating the ethics, efficacy, and efficiency of therapeutic recreation programs. Many departments, for example, use satisfaction surveys or importance-performance measures to evaluate programs. Evaluation of the comprehensive program plan is an important aspect of managing a therapeutic recreation department (see Chapter 9; O'Morrow & Carter, 1997).

Recommended Readings

Dattilo, J. and Murphy, W. D. (1991). *Leisure education program planning: A systematic approach*. State College, PA: Venture Publishing, Inc.

Grote, K., Hasl, M., Krider, R., and Mortensen, D. (1995). *Behavioral health protocols for recreational therapy*. Ravensdale, WA: Idyll Arbor.

O'Morrow, G. and Carter, M. J. (1997). *Effective management in therapeutic recreation*. State College, PA: Venture Publishing, Inc.

Peterson, C. and Stumbo, N. J. (2000). *Therapeutic recreation program design: Principles and procedures* (3rd ed.). Boston, MA: Allyn and Bacon.

Chapter

Individualized Care Plans

Chapter 10 discussed comprehensive and specific programs. Clients are assigned to specific programs depending on their needs. Because clients in a particular setting are typically similar to one another in terms of diagnosis and other key characteristics, they are usually grouped in the same specific programs. As such, they often will share goals and objectives. Nevertheless, each client is a unique individual. Therefore, care plans should be *individualized* for each client. Care plans should include an assessment of an individual client's strengths and problems, specific programs and interventions used to build on personal strengths and address problem areas, and evaluation methods.

This chapter discusses individual care plans. We begin by building on the theoretical foundations of assessment provided in Chapter 5. Following a review of assessment, the components of individual care plans are examined. Finally, documentation methods used to report client behavior and progress are presented.

Client Assessment

Assessment is a process for collecting information on select areas of a client's functioning, providing the therapeutic recreation specialist with data on the client's problems and strengths. The data are then used to develop a care plan or evaluate the effectiveness of an intervention.

Selecting an assessment involves more than pulling a couple of handy instruments from the shelf or throwing open a book and finding something that looks appropriate. In this section we will discuss the selection of assessment tools, review assessment principles, and survey types of assessment tools.

Selection of Assessment Tools

Assessments should be selected based on professionals' best judgment of what methods and instruments are appropriate for their clientele and agencies. The ultimate concern is selecting a tool that will best serve the needs of the individuals who receive services. The therapeutic recreation specialist should ask: What constructs will be measured by the assessment tool? What method will be appropriate for measuring the selected constructs?

The behaviors, knowledge, and attitudes of the client that require attention guide selection of an assessment tool. The department's comprehensive program plan, specifically the mission statement (see Chapter 10), articulates the functional domains or leisure behaviors targeted by the therapeutic recreation interventions. The department's mission statement guides the development of specific programs to address relevant behaviors. Therefore, the assessment tool should measure the same functional domains or leisure behaviors addressed in the department's specific programs.

Observational, survey, and interview methods are typically used in therapeutic recreation assessment. When using observational methods the therapeutic recreation specialist will watch and rate a client's behavior. For example, a specialist may observe a client's social skills and rate his or her ability to initiate conversation and maintain eye contact. Survey methods involve a client completing a questionnaire. An example of a questionnaire is a leisure interest survey that asks for information on past and present leisure interests. Lastly, many therapeutic recreation specialists use an interview as part of the assessment. An interview typically consists of predetermined questions about the client's daily functioning and leisure behavior. We have provided several examples of therapeutic recreation departments' mission statements. Relevant behaviors and the construct to be measured by the assessment tool are identified in each example. Potential methods for assessing the construct are also provided.

> *MISSION STATEMENT: Therapeutic Recreation Department, Psychiatric Hospital*
>
> Our mission is to promote healthy *social and emotional functioning* and independence in *daily leisure* among all patients. We are committed to providing therapy and education services that promote health and independence during hospitalization and following discharge to the community.

CONSTRUCTS: social skills, appropriate expression of emotion, leisure behavior

POTENTIAL METHODS OF ASSESSMENT:
Social Skills: Comprehensive Evaluation in Recreational Therapy (Observational; see burlingame & Blaschko, 1997)

Social and Emotional Skills: Functional Assessment of Characteristics for Therapeutic Recreation, Revised (FACTR-R) (Observational; see burlingame & Blaschko, 1997)

Leisure Behavior: Leisure Competence Measure (Observational; see Kloseck, Crilly, Ellis & Lammers, 1996)

Leisure Behavior: Leisure Diagnostic Battery – Short Form (Questionnaire; see Ellis & Witt, 1986)

MISSION STATEMENT: Special Recreation Division, Public Parks & Recreation Agency

Our mission is to promote residents' highest level of *integration in community recreation programs*. We are committed to the provision of quality leisure education and recreation services that facilitate participants' engagement with family and friends and their integration into community programs.

CONSTRUCTS: leisure skills, leisure attitudes

POTENTIAL METHODS OF ASSESSMENT:
Leisure Attitudes: Leisure Diagnostic Battery Parts One and Two (Questionnaire; see Ellis & Witt, 1986)

Leisure Skills: Agency Specific Interview

Assessment Principles

Several key assessment principles, including validity, reliability, and usability, should be taken into account in the selection of assessment tools. Readers should consult Chapter 5 for a more extensive discussion of assessment principles.

- *Validity*: Does the instrument assess the desired construct (e.g., boredom, self-esteem, leisure)? A ruler is the correct assessment for height, but not intelligence. An activity checklist can tell you what activities an individual is interested in, but it cannot validly assess freedom, boredom, or motivation.
- *Reliability*: Does the assessment yield consistent measures? A ruler is usually a carefully calibrated assessment instrument. However, if the person using it cannot read the numbers, it is going to be a source of large error, making it unreliable. Similarly, if the words on an instrument surpass an individual's vocabulary, the assessment is likely to be unreliable.
- *Practical Considerations*: Are there adequate resources for conducting the assessment (e.g., time, materials, sufficient staff, proper training)? For example, selecting an assessment that takes so much staff time to administer that it leaves little opportunity to use its results to develop quality programs for clients would be absurd. Similarly, the most powerful assessment cannot overcome a staff that is not trained to administer the instrument.

Assessment Tools

Assessments can provide a wide range of information about an individual. Besides data regarding a person's social, physical, cognitive, and emotional needs, assessment can reveal important information about a person's interests, aptitudes, and needs regarding such areas as work, leisure, and education. Assessment data should also be gathered on the individual's environment, including accessibility and social supports. In this section we will discuss general assessments and assessments specifically developed for therapeutic recreation practice.

General Assessments

A plethora of general assessment tools exists. Typically, therapeutic recreation specialists do not administer general assessments, unless they are designed for interdisciplinary use. Nonetheless, therapeutic recreation specialists should be sufficiently familiar with general assessments to understand the implications of their results for therapeutic recreation practice. For example, a therapeutic recreation specialist should be able to apply results from a personality test to plan an intervention or to use the score of an intelligence test to adapt an activity. Similarly, the therapeutic recreation specialist should be able to use the results of a fitness test for selecting and adjusting adaptive equipment.

Physical assessments include physical examinations and fitness tests. Assessment of physical functioning is important in therapeutic recreation, especially if the client intends to participate in physical activities. An example of a physical assessment for older persons is the Functional Fitness Assessment for Adults over 50 Years (Osness, Adrian, Clark, Hoeger, Raab, and Wiswell, 1990). *Psychological assessments* cover a gamut of variables, such as affect, motivation, self-concept, personality, intelligence, and cognitive functioning. One of the most widely used tests is the Minnesota Multiphasic Personality Inventory (MMPI), which was designed to be an inventory of psychiatric disturbance, but has also been used as a measure of personality (Maloney & Ward, 1976). *Social assessment* is an especially paramount area in therapeutic recreation because of the importance of social skills to leisure experience and community integration (Sneegas, 1989; Stumbo, 1994/95). Stumbo (1994/95) has done a thorough job of addressing the assessment of social skills for therapeutic recreation. Besides discussing views of social competence and models for the implementation of social skills assessment and training, she examined particular social behaviors that might be deficient (e.g., social aggressiveness) and listed 20 tools for assessing social skills and behaviors.

The *Resident Assessment Instrument* is an example of a general assessment that affects therapeutic recreation specialists working in long-term care. In response to the 1987 Omnibus Budget Reconciliation Act's mandate for uniformed assessment in long-term care facilities, the Health Care Finance Administration developed a comprehensive assessment tool (Morris, Hawes, Fries, Phillips, Mor, Katz, Murphy, Drugovich & Friedlob, 1990). The Resident Assessment Instrument consists of two parts: (1) the Minimum Data Set (MDS) and (2) the Resident Assessments Protocol (RAP). The MDS assesses a resident's functioning in the following domains: cognitive patterns, communi-cation/hearing patterns, vision patterns, physical functioning, continence, psychosocial well-being, mood and behavior patterns, activity pursuit patterns, disease diagnoses, health conditions, oral/nutritional status, oral/dental status, skin condition, and medication use. Data from the MDS trigger problem areas that are then addressed using the RAP. The care team develops an individual-ized plan of care in accordance with the treatment guidelines in the RAP. A care team member, typically a nurse, gathers data from team members about the resident's functioning in each domain of the MDS. Although the therapeutic recreation specialist provides input on many of the domains, he or she is typically responsible for the data on activity pursuit patterns (see Table 11.1, p. 307). The MDS data may then trigger RAP, which guides the development of the individual care plan. For example, MDS data trigger the activities RAP if the resident is awake most of the day, spends a majority of his or her time in activities, and tires during most days (see Table 11.2, page 308). Given this scenario, the therapeutic recreation specialist may consider whether participation in activities should be decreased or whether the resident should take a rest or nap between activities.

Therapeutic recreation specialists also need to have a working familiarity with quality of life assessments, another form of general assessment. *Quality of life* pertains to a life that the individual perceives as good, satisfying, and meaningful. A major part of quality of life planning is getting to know the client as a unique person. Galambos (1995) has done a splendid job discussing quality of life planning. In particular, she recommended developing personal profiles for each individual. The role of assessment in the construction of personal profiles includes:

- *Life story.* Rather than the client's medical history, this is the account of the individual as a person who has had a life beyond the patient role. This information puts a human face on persons who too often are treated as disabilities or diagnoses. Life stories can be developed in a variety of ways, including writing, conversation, and photography. Whatever strategy is used, the point is to get to know the person's likes, dislikes, values, interests, accomplishments, disappointments, hopes, and fears.

- *Quality of life.* Since quality of life is the goal of planning, attention must be given to the individuals' perceptions of their present quality of life and their hopes for the future. In assessing quality of life, Galambos (1995) recommended "including the ideas and opinions of the person, your own direct observations, and input from others who play important roles in their life" (p. 47).

- *Portfolios.* A portfolio includes artifacts of achievements, interests, memories, dreams, and inspirations. Portfolios may include schoolwork, favorite songs, poems, athletic awards, or pictures—anything that gives *authentic* testimony to the person's hopes, interests, abilities, and achievements.

Once a personal profile has been constructed, therapeutic recreation specialists will be in a position to develop individualized care plans around quality of life goals. Therapeutic recreation assessment further contributes to that process.

	Table 11.1 Minimum Data Set: Activity Pursuit Patterns	
1	TIME AWAKE	Resident awake all or most of the time in the: a. morning b. afternoon c. evening d. none of the above
2	AVERAGE TIME INVOLVED IN ACTIVITIES	0. most - more than 2/3 time 1. some - 1/3 to 2/3 time 2. little - less than 1/3 time 3. none
3	PREFERRED ACTIVITY SETTINGS	a. own room b. day/activity room c. inside NH/off unit d. outside facility e. none of the above
4	GENERAL ACTIVITY PREFERENCES	a. cards, other games b. crafts or art c. exercise or sports d. music e. reading, writing f. spiritual or religious activities g. trips or shopping h. walking/wheeling outside i. watching TV j. gardening or plants k. talking or conversing l. helping others m. none of the above
5	PREFER MORE OR DIFFERENT ACTIVITIES	Resident expresses or indicates preferences for other activities or choices. 0. No 1. Yes
6	ISOLATION ORDERS	Resident is under medical orders for isolation which prohibits participation in group activities. 0. No 1. Yes
7	SENSORY STIMULATION	Resident has a condition which prevents participation in usual activities and would benefit from a sensory stimulation program. 0. No 1. Yes

	Table 11.2 Examples of Minimum Data Set Data Triggering Resident Assessment Protocols	
MDS Data checked *plus*	**MDS Data checked *equals***	**Triggering of RAP**
1 TIME AWAKE checked for morning, afternoon, or evening	**AND** both of the following: 2 AVERAGE TIME IN ACTIVITIES = 0 *(most >2/3)* PHYSICAL FUNCTIONING 10f tires noticeably during most days	Review Activity Care Plan *Things to consider: Should activities be restricted or decreased? Should activities be less physically strenuous? Should residents rest or take a nap between activities?*
6 ISOLATION ORDERS	**AND** both of the following: 1 TIME AWAKE checked for morning, afternoon, or evening 2 AVERAGE TIME IN ACTIVITIES = 2 or 3 (little or no involvement in activities)	Review Activity Care Plan *Things to consider: What are the preferences of the residents? How may the residents' preferences be adapted for in-room and solitary participation?*
PHYSICAL FUNCTIONING/ BODY CONTROL PROBLEMS bedfast	**AND** both of the following: AVERAGE TIME IN ACTIVITIES = 2 or 3 (little or no involvement) Any TWO of the following: PSYCHOSOCIAL WELL-BEING = indicators of unsettled relationships PSYCHOSOCIAL WELL-BEING = sadness over lost roles or status MOOD AND BEHAVIOR = verbal expressions of sad mood ACTIVITY PURSUIT PATTERNS= 4 (no general activity preferences)	Review Activity Care Plan *Things to consider: What types of activities may decrease distress? How may activities be adapted for in-room participation?*

Therapeutic Recreation Assessment

Therapeutic recreation assessment has experienced slow and uneven progress (Howe, 1984, 1989; Stumbo, 1991, 1994/95, 1997; Sneegas, 1989; and Witt, Connolly & Compton, 1980). Many issues remain according to Peterson and Stumbo (2000, pp. 237-238), who list 35 serious problems associated with therapeutic recreation assessment, including lack of availability, cost, inadequate conceptualization, lack of training on the part of therapeutic recreation specialists, and lack of motivation/opportunities for training. As such, therapeutic recreation assessment continues to be "problematic" (Peterson & Stumbo, 2000, p. 237), requiring improvement in the current state of affairs. Therapeutic recreation specialists, therefore, must take great care in the selection and administration of assessment instruments because the results impact the lives of people receiving care.

Below is information on two therapeutic recreation assessments whose validity and reliability have been rigorously developed: the Leisure Diagnostic Battery and the Leisure Competence Measure. For each assessment tool we will briefly discuss the construct measured and then present a case exemplifying the use of the tool in therapeutic recreation practice. Finally, we discuss environmental assessment as an important, but underutilized, component of therapeutic recreation assessment.

Leisure Diagnostic Battery. The Leisure Diagnostic Battery (LDB) (Ellis & Witt, 1986) consists of two parts. Part One includes five scales that measure a client's perceived freedom in leisure (Perceived Leisure Competence Scale, Perceived Leisure Control Scale, Depth of Involvement in Leisure Scale, Leisure Needs Scale, and Playfulness Scale). Each scale has a series of questions in which clients indicate the extent to which each statement "sounds like" them. For example, the long form of the Perceived Freedom in Leisure Scale includes the following statements:

1. My recreation activities help me to feel important.
2. I usually decide with whom I do recreation activities.
3. I am able to be creative during my recreation activities.

The five scales collectively measure an individual's level of perceived freedom in leisure, ranging from dependence (helplessness) to independence (freedom). Higher scores indicate more independence and greater leisure functioning. Conversely, lower scores indicate deficits in leisure functioning. Part Two consists of three scales: The Barriers to Leisure Involvement Scale, the Knowledge of Leisure Opportunities Scale, and the Leisure Preferences Scale. Each scale provides useful information relative to barriers, knowledge, and preferences for assisting individuals to enhance their leisure functioning.

Blake (1991) published a case history that demonstrates the use of the LDB in practice. The client, Fred, was 24 years of age and had suffered a spinal cord injury at age 19. He was admitted to a freestanding rehabilitation hospital following reparative surgery on decubitus ulcers (bed sores). Fred's scores on the LDB at admission and discharge are presented in Table 11.3, p. 311.

Average scores for Part One are based on a five-point scale with five representing the highest level of the construct and one representing the lowest level.
Fred's overall perceived freedom in leisure score was 3.36. Compared to other
patients who had participated in the therapeutic recreation program at the
rehabilitation hospital, Fred's score fell in the 38th percentile (i.e., 62% of the
clients scored higher in perceived freedom in leisure). Fred's score indicated
that he experienced a greater degree of dependence and helplessness in leisure
than his peers. His scores on Part Two were used to design a care plan building
on his preferences and addressing perceived barriers. Fred preferred sports and
nature activities in group settings. Difficulty with decision making and perceived ability were his greatest barriers in leisure.

Blake, along with input from Fred, created a care plan that included leisure
education sessions and community reentry. Fred decided to explore participation opportunities in alpine snow skiing, water skiing, wheelchair basketball,
and billiards. Given that Fred was hospitalized during the winter, alpine skiing
was selected for actual participation. He attended a ski school two hours per
week for six weeks. Following his first session at the ski school he displayed
increased positive affect and motivation to gain physical strength that would
enhance his ability in alpine skiing. Upon discharge Fred completed Part One
of the LDB. His score increased and rose to the 88th percentile, indicating his
increase in perceived freedom in leisure.

Leisure Competence Measure. The Leisure Competence Measure (LCM)
was designed to assess leisure functioning (Kloseck, Crilly, Ellis & Lammers,
1996). Modeled after the Functional Independence Measure (FIM), an assessment tool that measures the functional abilities of individuals with physical
disabilities, the LCM:

> identifies specific skills, knowledge and behaviour which
> individuals must possess in order to function independently and
> successfully in their leisure. Deficiencies in competencies
> identified through the LCM may then be worked on to improve
> or develop behaviours necessary for more independent living and
> to ensure that individuals enjoy their leisure optimally. (Kloseck,
> Crilly, Ellis, & Lammers, 1996, p. 16)

The LCM assesses seven domains, including leisure awareness, attitude,
skills, social appropriateness, group interaction skills, social contact, and
community-based participation (Table 11.4, p. 312). Each domain is scored on
a seven-point scale according to the same levels used with the FIM:

Table 11.3 Case Example:
Fred's Admission and Discharge Scores on the Leisure Diagnostic Battery*

LDB Part One:	*Admission*		*Discharge*	
	Score	Average	Score	Average
Total Perceived Freedom	319	3.36	386	4.06
Competence	60	3.00	80	4.00
Control	59	3.47	66	3.88
Needs Satisfaction	67	3.35	83	4.15
Depth of Involvement	65	3.61	78	4.33
Playfulness	68	3.40	79	3.95

LDB Part Two:

Barriers Scale	Score	Average
Communication	9.99	3.33
Social	12.00	4.00
Decision Making	6.99	2.33
Opportunities	9.99	3.33
Motivation	8.01	2.67
Ability	6.00	2.00
Money	12.00	4.00
Time	9.99	3.33
Activities Preference Scale		
Nature and Outdoor	75%	
Music and Drama	42%	
Arts and Crafts	17%	
Sports	75%	
Mental and Linquistic	42%	
Activities Style Scale		
Active/Passive	50%	
Group/Individual	100%	
Risk/Non-risk	80%	

* Ellis and Witt, 1986.

- Seven = complete independence,
- Six = modified independence,
- Five = modified dependence,
- Four = modified dependence with minimal assistance,
- Three = modified dependence with moderate assistance,
- Two = modified dependence with maximal assistance, and
- One = total dependence with total assistance.

The LCM allows for initial levels of leisure functioning to be determined. Rankings of five or below indicate dependent functioning, while rankings of six and seven indicate independent leisure functioning. Goals can then be set and interventions selected to achieve outcomes for enhancing leisure functioning.

Table 11.4. Leisure Competence Measure*		
LCM	**Description**	**Behaviors Exhibited by Client**
Leisure Awareness	Client's knowledge and understanding of leisure	• personal beliefs • knowledge of leisure opportunities • awareness of strengths and weaknesses • realistic expectations
Leisure Attitude	Behaviors exhibited and/ or feelings expressed by the client which suggest attitude toward leisure involvement	• initiative • self-directedness • willingness to develop • new skills and hobbies
Leisure Skills	Skills possessed by the client which affect leisure involvement	• ability to make choices • activity skills necessary to participate in chosen activities • ability to identify, locate, and access leisure resources
Social Appropriateness	Specific social behaviors exhibited by the client which affect ability to function in leisure activities	• manners • dress • hygiene • tolerance of others
Group Interaction Skills	Client's ability to participate in various types of group situations	• sharing • cooperation task is the focus • minimal interaction with others • 1:1 interaction • withdrawal; isolation
Social Contact	Type and duration of social contact client has with others	• type, duration, and frequency of social contact • custodial vs. social contact
Community Participation	Client's overall leisure participation pattern	• type, duration, and frequency of leisure involvement

* Adapted from Klosek, Crilly, Ellis, and Lammers, 1996.

Lane, Montgomery, and Schmid (1995) used the LCM to assess the leisure competence of Andrew, a 16-year-old admitted to a residential treatment center for adolescent males. Andrew had a history of physical abuse and had attempted suicide prior to admission. His LCM scores, as shown in Table 11.5, indicate dependent functioning. Interpretation of the LCM findings indicated that Andrew was unable to follow through with community reintegration without reassurance, became easily agitated with others, and did not seek social contact with others. Therefore, the therapeutic recreation specialist designed a care plan to result in Andrew being able: "1. to identify positive attributes about self, 2. to identify coping mechanisms which are socially acceptable, and 3. to learn basic problem-solving skills" (Lane, Montgomery & Schmid, 1995, p. 296). Although this case exemplifies the use of the LCM, readers are cautioned

---

Table 11.5 Leisure Competence Measure: Assessment Results

Domain	Score*
Leisure Awareness	4
Leisure Attitude	5
Leisure Skills	4
#Social Behavior (Social Appropriateness)	4
#Interpersonal Skills (Group Interaction Skills)	4
Social Contact	5
Community Participation	3

* 1= total dependence with total assistance
2= modified dependence with maximal assistance
3= modified dependence with moderate assistance
4= modified dependence with minimal assistance
5= modified dependence
6= modified independence
7= complete independence

\# Domains listed reflect an early version of the LCM. Current names of domains are in parentheses.

to question the validity of the assessment data since the LCM was developed for use with adults with physical disabilities.

Environmental Assessment. Howe-Murphy and Charboneau (1987) proposed an ecological approach to therapeutic recreation assessment. Environmental assessment typically examines physical, social, economic, and political aspects. It involves assessing the individual, the environment, and the interaction between the two. For example, assessment results may report that a client has few leisure skills. The leisure skills to be addressed in the care plan must be of interest to the client *and* be supported in his or her home, neighborhood, or community. The client may learn how to play pickup basketball, but without basketball courts in her neighborhood she would have limited opportunity to participate. In contrast, if the environmental assessment finds that the client's family and friends enjoy bicycling and there are extensive bicycle trails in her neighborhood, the therapeutic recreation specialist may work with the client on learning how to bicycle (skill) and about bicycle safety (knowledge).

An example of an environmental assessment is presented in Table 11.6, pp. 315 and 316. This assessment was developed for use with older adults with dementia who reside in the community with a family caregiver (Voelkl, St. Pierre & Buettner, 1999). Therapeutic recreation students who worked in the home with the older adult and caregiver complete the assessment in an effort to design the home environment to promote the older adult's independent engagement in leisure. The student, caregiver, and client select a room for assessment and identify the independent activities that the older adult would like to participate in when in the selected room. Both the physical environment and environmental resources are assessed.

The assessment process generates information on a client's problems and strengths, as well as aspects of his or her environment. Assessment data allows the therapeutic recreation specialist to develop a care plan that responds to the specific needs of a client. In the next section we will discuss the components of an individualized care plan.

Care Plans

Care plans provide an individualized "road map" that describes a client's problems and strengths, targeted changes in behavior, and interventions that will be used to assist a client in making changes in his or her behavior. The specific format of an individualized care plan may differ from facility to facility; however, there are several basic components found in most care plans:

- *Demographic data* may include the client's age, gender, place of residency, educational attainment, occupation, family unit.

Table 11.6 Examples of an Environmental Assessment*

This questionnaire has been designed to assist the volunteer in working with the older adult and caregiver to optimize the design of the room where the older adult spends most of his or her time. Please keep in mind that the focus is on the room where the older adult will spend time engaged in recreation activities, both independently and shared. The design of such an area or room will be different from a room designed for quiet or rest time.

1. Selected room: _____

2. Individual and shared pleasant activities identified on Pleasant Events Scale:

Individual (older adult)	Shared (caregiver and older adult)
_____	_____
_____	_____
_____	_____

3. Does the layout of the room and arrangement of the furniture allow for engagement in preferred activities?

Layout: _____

_____

Furniture: _____

_____

_____

4. Complete the following questions:

	YES	NO
a. Does the room permit accurate perceptions with clocks and calendars set consistently?	_____	_____
b. Is the lighting adequate for engagement in preferred activities?	_____	_____
c. Is there distracting stimulation (noise, movement, clutter)?	_____	_____
d. Are recreation resources available for independent recreation by the older adult?	_____	_____
e. Does the older adult have easy access to the selected location?	_____	_____

Table 11.6 Examples of an Environmental Assessment* (continued)

	YES	NO
f. From the selected location, can the older adult easily access the bathroom?	_____	_____
eating area?	_____	_____
bedroom?	_____	_____
g. A majority of the independent and shared recreation preferences listed in item #2 are available in this room.	_____	_____
h. Are there opportunities for the older adult to choose and select which recreation resource he or she would like to manipulate?	_____	_____

Additional Comments/Suggestions for modification: _____

_____

5. Needed or Planned Modifications/Changes

Suggested modifications/changes in layout of room: _____

_____

Suggested modifications/changes/additions to recreation resources available in the room:

_____

_____

---

* Voelkl, St. Pierre, and Buettner (1999).

- *Assessment results* include a summary and interpretation of the client's needs and the problems to be addressed in the care plan. Additionally, the client's strengths, including recreation interests and abilities, are identified.
- *Goals and measurable objectives* are developed based on the problems and strengths identified in the assessment, responding to specific needs of a client. Readers will recall the distinction made in Chapter 10 between objectives prepared for specific programs and those prepared for individualized care plans. Specific program objectives refer to knowledge or behaviors that clients are expected to demonstrate in order to

achieve their goals; however, it is in the individualized care plan that objectives receive the performance criteria that make them measurable.

- *Specific activities and interventions* that will allow a client to achieve his or her goals and objectives.
- *Means of evaluating* the client's participation in activities and achievement of behavioral objectives is stated. Typically, frequency of documentation on the client's performance is stated.

In this section we will discuss the creation of the care plan, including development of the individual's goals and objectives, selection of activities and interventions that support attainment of the goals and behavioral objectives, and the evaluation of a client's behavior as he or she participates in the selected interventions.

Developing Goals and Behavioral Objectives

Individual care goals are expressed in general terms, indicating an area for improvement. For example, a client's need may relate to alleviating depression. The care goal "to relieve depression," however, does not specify what behaviors need to occur to indicate that the depression has been sufficiently alleviated. Similarly, the goal "to become involved in community leisure opportunities" is also nonspecific. Does it mean involvement in *all* community opportunities? Does the individual need to know how to identify and access community leisure opportunities? Further, what kind of involvement is appropriate for the individual in light of his or her condition and level of development? A 45-year-old woman with a spinal-cord injury will differ from a 12-year-old boy with a developmental disability. Finally, consider the goal "to improve self-esteem." Here the problem pertains to the matter of theoretical constructs. How do you know when you have accomplished something that does not physically exist? Specific *behaviors* must be identified that *represent* the construct of self-esteem. These behaviors or *measurable objectives* are accepted as signs that the care goal has been achieved.

Goals may be associated with functional and quality of life domains. Functional goals or outcomes pertain to the capacity to execute the basic social, physical, emotional, and cognitive competencies needed to sustain life, such as feeding, dressing, and solving problems. They relate to the specific skills, such as memory (cognitive), motivation (emotional), endurance (physical), and cooperation (social), that enable people to meet their basic needs and to function in their various capacities as students, parents, partners, workers, and players. Quality of life domains relate to activities and experiences that provide meaning, purpose, and satisfaction in the lives of people. Friendship, challenge, learning, achievement, autonomy, community, spirituality, self-determination, and creative expression are examples of quality of life goals. Functional domains and goals are important to quality of life. People need to possess physical, social, psychological, and cognitive abilities for the sake of work, play, family, friendships, spirituality, and the like. Strength, intelligence, and motivation, would lose much of their relevance if people did not have meaningful activities in their lives. Motivation, a psychological function, is intensified by the presence of purposeful and meaningful activities. People are more highly *motivated* to use their energies, abilities, and talents, as well as improve their health, *for the sake of* quality of life goals. Because it is in the wholeness and quality of life that healthy functioning achieves importance, therapeutic recreation specialists have a valued role to play in holistic healthcare. Perhaps more than any other healthcare professional, they are uniquely prepared to serve clients' quality of life needs. Following are examples of typical therapeutic goals:

Functional Goals

Cognitive
- Improve time management skills,
- Increase attention span,
- Improve memory,
- Enhance leisure awareness,
- Increase knowledge of community leisure resources, and
- Increase leisure-related skills.

Psychological
- Increase anger control,
- Improve self-esteem,
- Decrease depression,
- Increase motivation for leisure, and
- Increase leisure-related skills.

Physical
- Increase physical fitness,
- Increase flexibility, and
- Increase leisure-related skills.

Social
- Increase social skills,
- increase cooperation, and
- Increase leisure-related skills.

Quality of Life/Functional Goals

- Establish friendships/improve social skills,
- Explore spirituality/improve reading skills (e.g., through sacred and secular literature),
- Sexual relations/learn to use sexual aids for a person with a spinal cord injury,
- Creative expression/improve fine motor skills,
- Increased autonomy/improve decision-making skills,
- Self-determination/provide opportunities to make decisions and use abilities, and
- Broaden leisure interests and abilities/increase leisure awareness, skills, and resources.

Because goals are typically expressed in general terms, measurable objectives are written for each goal. A measurable objective has three elements. First, it describes a measurable *behavior*. Second, it includes a *performance criterion* that indicates whether the behavior has been satisfactorily achieved. Third, it states any pertinent *conditions* or *circumstances* under which the behavior is to occur. Consider the behavioral objective: "When in the company of a family member, the client will suggest at least one social leisure activity he and the family member can do together on the weekend." *In the company of a family member* and *on the weekend* are conditions.

Imagine a client's goal is to increase self-esteem. Assessment data would provide information regarding the client's developmental needs and level of psychosocial functioning for the purpose of designing appropriate behavioral objectives. The next step is to decide what behaviors the client needs to demonstrate as evidence that he or she has achieved the desired outcome of self-esteem. Accordingly, the therapeutic recreation specialist determines that the client will need to demonstrate his or her ability to:

(1) *understand* the meaning and importance of self-esteem, (2) *recognize* feelings of self-esteem, (3) *identify* sources of self-esteem, and (4) *participate* in self-chosen activities that produce feelings of self-esteem.

The therapeutic recreation specialist must next decide the performance criteria that indicate whether the behavior has been satisfactorily achieved. Criteria may be described in various ways, as long as they can be objectively assessed. For example, "initiates social interaction three times in the course of the activity," or "demonstrates proper tennis serve," or "identifies five leisure resources within a three mile radius of the client's home." Performance criteria are determined by assessment results, which provide a baseline and a target. For example, an assessment of community leisure resources would reveal what the client actually knows about leisure resources, which becomes the baseline. Progress would be evaluated by comparing the client's baseline knowledge of community leisure resources against what he needs to learn in order to have sufficient understanding of community leisure resources to meet his needs. The number and variety of resources that the client would need to learn would depend on what he already knows about community leisure resources (baseline) and what he needs to know (target).

Consider another example that pertains to social skills. Social skills assessment shows that a client is capable of initiating conversations, but cannot sustain them sufficiently to achieve social interaction. Skills related to initiating conversations, therefore, do not need to be addressed. Instead, target goals would include behaviors such as using eye contact to encourage interaction, using questions as a means to sustain conversation, and becoming familiar with topics useful for facilitating social interaction.

With respect to the goal of self-esteem, the following behavioral objectives were developed for a client of normal intelligence diagnosed with clinical depression who was placed in an outdoor challenge program:

1. By the third activity session, when prompted, explain the importance of self-esteem as judged appropriate by the therapeutic recreation specialist. (In this instance, the client would have received instruction regarding the importance of self-esteem. The professional would judge whether he or she has successfully expressed the importance of self-esteem.)
2. By the fourth session, share with the therapeutic recreation specialist at least two times when feelings of self-esteem have been experienced during the activity. (Taking a step beyond understanding the importance of self-esteem, the client is now expected to recognize feelings of self-esteem, incorporating both intellectual and emotional dimensions of self-esteem.)
3. After the fifth activity session, identify at least three areas in life that have provided feelings of self-esteem. (This behavioral objective is yet another progression in enhancing self-esteem by helping the client

       consciously identify areas in his or her life that are reliable sources for feelings of self-esteem.)

4.   Choose a recreation activity that contributes to feelings of self-esteem and report the experience to the therapeutic recreation specialist within 24 hours after the activity. (The final behavioral objective involves personally chosen experiences of self-esteem.)

Achieving the four behavioral objectives would indicate that the client had attained the goal of increased self-esteem.

    The next example of a therapeutic recreation care goal and accompanying behavioral objectives involves both quality of life and functional domains. Imagine that the client in this case was an avid skier prior to an automobile accident that resulted in amputation of both legs above the knees. Because of complications, her rehabilitation has been long, resulting in deterioration of her overall fitness. The activity of skiing has been a lifelong source of enjoyment, adventure, competition, and social participation for the client. In short, the client can live without her legs, but she cannot, in her words, "live without skiing." Therefore, the client is absolutely determined to ski again. She understands that maximal physical fitness is essential to an expedient and successful return to the slopes. The quality of life goal can be stated simply as "skiing again," which will entail learning how to use a mono-ski. At this juncture, however, the client needs to regain her physical fitness, realizing that besides the usual rigors of skiing, recovery from her accident will be hastened by increased fitness.

    The functional goal, therefore, is to improve physical fitness. Once again, the therapeutic recreation specialist must decide what is appropriate for the client in light of her condition. The client is in her mid-twenties, intelligent, and well-informed on matters of physical fitness. As such, a fitness appraisal is initially performed to establish baseline data for setting and evaluating objectives. The following behavioral objectives were developed:

Quality of Life Goal: Skiing
Functional Goal: To improve physical fitness
Program: Ongoing physical fitness class
Behavioral Objectives:

1.   Write three fitness goals and corresponding objectives in consultation with the therapeutic recreation specialist. (For this behavioral objective, the client decides what areas of fitness, such as strength, endurance, flexibility, she needs to work on and what performance levels she needs to attain.)

2. Attend 60-minute fitness sessions three times weekly over the duration of rehabilitation.
3. Prior to discharge, complete a fitness assessment, meeting 100% of goals.

In sum, to achieve her goal of improved physical fitness, which was chosen *for the sake of* skiing, an activity essential to her quality of life, the client needed to demonstrate three behaviors: (1) write her fitness objectives, (2) attend fitness sessions, and (3) complete a fitness assessment. If she satisfactorily achieves all three objectives, her functional goal will have been reached. Her quality of life goal should be included in her discharge plan and evaluated on the basis of her successful return to the slopes. This case again shows how quality of life and functional goals operate synergistically. Because she was intrinsically motivated to ski, her commitment to improved functioning was enhanced.

An infinite number of behavioral objectives could conceivably be written for a goal. Clearly that is not practical. Ideally, a minimum number of behavioral objectives should be written that conveys successful achievement of the goal. In some cases, a few objectives will suffice. In others, more will be required. For example, the practice of chaining requires linking a series of behaviors to achieve a particular task or goal. Depending on the complexity of the task and the condition of the client, numerous objectives may be required. The number of behavioral objectives should be sufficient to enable the individual to reach his or her goal.

Activity Analysis

As discussed in Chapter 10, activity analysis involves examining an activity along social, physical, cognitive, and affective domains to determine: (1) the knowledge, skills, and materials required to participate in an activity and (2) the effectiveness of the activity for contributing to individual care goals, including functional improvements, education, and quality of life. In addition to its value for developing specific programs, activity analysis also guides the modification or adaptation of activities for an individual client. The following example demonstrates the use of activity analysis in individual care plans.

Take the previous case of the young woman who is a double amputee. Her goal is to improve her physical fitness in order to ski again. Accordingly, the therapeutic recreation specialist needs to analyze various fitness activities to determine what is required for the purpose of participation and how well these activities will contribute to the client's fitness objectives. The therapeutic recreation specialist begins by analyzing the cognitive requirements of fitness activities (e.g., memory, concentration, verbalization). Assume that the client in this case has the required cognitive abilities to participate in the activity. Next, the therapeutic recreation specialist would examine social requirements, such as assertiveness, cooperation, competition, interaction patterns, and cultural factors as they relate to age, gender, ethnicity, etc. Again, analysis indicated that the client possessed the necessary social skills and knowledge. The therapeutic recreation specialist would also wish to assess emotional requirements for participation. How much confidence is needed? What is the client's threshold for frustration? Is she sufficiently motivated? Will the satisfaction of success be sufficient to sustain her motivation? Here, too, the client was deemed ready.

Next, physical requirements would be examined. What must the client be able to do to participate physically in a fitness program? Much of the information may already have been collected as part of an inventory of the client's comprehensive functioning. Nonetheless, the therapeutic recreation specialist will need to determine the client's baseline fitness relative to strength, balance, endurance, flexibility, speed, etc. The fitness program can then be planned so the client can progress toward her goals. Furthermore, specific fitness activities can be selected and adapted that are best suited for her quality of life goal of skiing. For example, learning to use a mono-ski requires exceptional balance, as opposed to wheelchair basketball, which emphasizes speed and strength. Therefore, specific fitness activities that focus on balance and flexibility, as well as strength, would be recommended for the client.

Finally, it makes no sense to assist people to recover functionally if they are unable to recapture those activities and experiences that give them a full, meaningful, and satisfying life. Therefore, activity analysis should be extended to an assessment of opportunities, constraints, and supports. For example, what will be required in terms of transportation, finances, and special equipment for the client to continue her fitness program and to put it to the ultimate test of skiing? Can individuals in the community with similar interests be found so the client has normal companionship and does not need to depend on professionals for participation?

The next section provides several examples of care plans. These examples show how many of the tools and techniques discussed earlier in this chapter (e.g., developing functional and quality of life goals, writing behavioral objectives, activity analysis) are used when creating an individualized care plan.

Examples of Care Plans

Case Study #1

Jan is a 62-year-old woman with an inoperable brain tumor. She is receiving hospice care until she dies. What kind of care plan does a therapeutic recreation specialist write for someone who has less than a month to live? What assessments should be done? What goals should be written? Besides being made as comfortable as possible, the idea of functional outcomes appears ludicrous. Jan is not going to improve; she is going to die. Her goals should be oriented to the quality of life. Rather than functionally oriented, her goals are *existentially* based, concerned with what she finds personally meaningful and important in her existence. At the least, this would entail such values as life accomplishments, family, friends, and spiritual commitments. In short, the remaining weeks should provide Jan opportunities to celebrate her life with others, to reflect and rejoice personally on her life, and to prepare for death in ways that are spiritually appropriate for her.

Although an assessment instrument is selected based on the department's mission statement, we recognize the difficulty of identifying an assessment instrument suitable for persons who are dying. On a critical note, O'Keefe (1996) wrote:

> What our clients really want us to know . . . is their stories. By knowing their stories we come to know their hearts and spirits, the source of their motivation and actions, their philosophies of life. Yet our assessments give little room for story . . . (p. 4)

In this situation, then, we recommend interviewing Jan as a way to understand her needs during these final weeks. Of course, the therapeutic recreation specialist should also talk with Jan's friends and family as a means of assessing the situation.

Suppose that the assessment revealed the following information. Jan was a music teacher who loves the classics. She is also a devoted gardener. Besides raising three children, she enjoys hikes with her husband and dog. Jan is not formally religious, belonging to no church. Yet she believes in a personal God and finds peace, comfort, and meaning in a variety of sacred and secular literature.

The therapeutic recreation specialist meets with Jan to formulate goals for the final weeks of her life. The idea of "goals" amuses the good-natured woman, but she understands the intention, commenting wryly that she will check with St. Peter upon reaching the "pearly gates" to see if she achieved her goals. Quality of life goals were developed for Jan. These goals do not involve behavioral change, therefore objectives were not written. Successful achievement of the goals occurs when Jan is able to participate in the identified activities.

HOSPICE PROGRAM RECREATION CARE PLAN

Client: Jan
Gender: Female
Age: 62
Diagnosis: Cancer, Brain Tumor
Admission to Hospice Program: 2-15-00
Assessment Results: Jan reports enjoying music, gardening, and spending time with family and friends. She expresses a need to review meaningful experiences in her life, reflect on her spiritual journey through reading, listening to music, and sharing with others.

Quality of Life Goals:
1. Enjoy favorite music.
2. Experience gardening.
3. To revisit her life experiences.
4. To spend time with family and friends.
5. To reflect on the next stage of her spiritual journey through reading, reflection, and discussion.

Plan:
1. CTRS will provide CD and tape player. Family will be asked to bring in Jan's favorite tapes and CDs.
2. CTRS will invite Jan to engage in gardening in the unit lounge or patio area (weather permitting).
3. CTRS will inform Jan and her family and friends as to the areas available for socialization and/or spiritual contemplation (lounge, private family lounges, chapel, patio).
4. CTRS will inform Jan as to the unit resources for spiritual inquiry (library, tapes, books, discussion groups).

Evaluation: Progress notes written two times per week to report on Jan's time use and experiences.

Date: 2-17-00   TRS: B. Barker

The aim of activity analysis in this case would be to identify participation requirements and to make necessary modifications. Different interventions could be used, though we see the humanistic or client-centered approach as being most suitable in this instance.

Case Study #2

Wally is a 35-year-old male. Three months ago he had a rock-climbing accident that paralyzed him below the waist. He is married, has two children (ages eight and ten) and works as a computer analyst. Based on the departmental mission statement, the therapeutic recreation specialist asked Wally to complete a variety of assessment tools. His physical needs include improvement of strength and range of motion. Psychometric assessment further revealed reactive depression. Subsequent interviews indicated Wally was profoundly discouraged regarding his prospects of returning to his leisure interests. He is anxious about his ability to continue activities that his wife and he enjoy sharing, including skiing and backpacking. Finally, he is afraid that his disability will severely restrict his involvement with his children's activities, which constituted a significant portion of his leisure. Wally's quality of life domains were also assessed in an interview. His life revolves around his family. He enjoys his work as a computer analyst and is relieved that he will be able to continue his job. Nonetheless, his job has mainly been a means to provide his family and him a comfortable living to support the activities they share.

Based on assessment results, the following goals and behavioral objectives were developed. Initially, quality of life goals were identified: Return to outdoor interests he shares with his wife (including skiing and hiking) and remain active in his children's lives.

Wally's care goals and behavioral objectives were subsequently developed in the context of these quality of life goals. His first quality of life goal, returning to outdoor interests, will require improvement of physical abilities and learning adapted outdoor activity skills. His second quality of life goal, remaining active in his children's lives, will mainly necessitate accessibility. Wally's care plan is as follows:

THERAPEUTIC RECREATION CARE PLAN

Client: Wally
Gender: Male
Age: 35
Diagnosis: spinal cord injury
Date of Admission: 4-30-00

Assessment Results: Findings indicate a sense of hopelessness and anxiety over returning to previous leisure pursuits. Client expresses concern about maintaining preferred leisure (skiing, hiking) and social activities with his wife and children.

Quality of Life Goal: Return to outdoor activities
Care Goal: Improve physical fitness

Objectives:
1. Increase upper body strength by 10% after 6 weeks of strength training, 3 times per week.
2. Increase range of motion by 15% after 6 weeks of flexibility training, 3 times per week.
3. Increase endurance by 20% after 6 weeks of cardiovascular training, 3 times per week.

Quality of Life Goal: Return to outdoor activities
Care Goal: Learn adapted skiing techniques.

Objectives:
1. Complete a six-week adapted skiing program, satisfactorily passing all course requirements, including: clothing, safety, equipment care and use, chair lift use and safety, tethered mono-ski with partner, and independent monoski.

Quality of Life Goal: Return to outdoor activities
Care Goal: Locate and use hiking trails.

Objectives:
1. Identify all accessible hiking trails within a two-hour driving distance of home.
2. Review safety procedures and precautions for hiking with his wife prior to each trip.
3. Evaluate trail accessibility by keeping a log and sharing the results with the appropriate authority in charge of maintaining the trail.

Quality of Life Goal: Remain active in children's lives.
Care Goal: Participate in children's leisure activities.

Objectives:
1. Identify, with his family, barriers to participation in his children's leisure activities.
2. Problem solve with his family ways to eliminate barriers to involvement in his children's leisure activities.
3. Become involved in his children's leisure activities by successfully attending all activities of his choice.

Plan:
1. Participate in the Physical Fitness Program three times per week for six weeks.
2. Participate in six-week Community-Based Adapted Skiing Program.
3. Participate in Leisure Education Program, focus on hiking.
4. Participate in Family Leisure Counseling, focus on children's leisure activities.

Evaluation: Weekly charting as to progress made on goals and objectives.

Date: 5-3-00   TRS: B. Barker

The likelihood is that Wally will not require a specific counseling intervention. Instead, the therapeutic recreation specialist will be mainly functioning as a teacher and a resource.

Case Study #3

The final example involves Winston, a 45-year-old man who was hospitalized for severe depression. Winston recently lost his job and is separated from his wife of 15 years. They have no children. Winston was once active in the outdoors, but does nothing now, choosing instead to sit at home watching television. Assessment revealed that low self-esteem exacerbates Winston's clinical depression.

The therapeutic recreation specialist decides the course of action for Winston: go fishing. The therapeutic recreation specialist had conducted an analysis of various activities and had found that fishing was especially effective with depressed men. It created a suitable environment for sharing personal thoughts and feelings while reflecting on the cosmic qualities of fishing. The activity is structured such that Winston and the therapeutic recreation specialist can talk informally about self-esteem. Accordingly, the following plan was outlined:

THERAPEUTIC RECREATION CARE PLAN

Client: Winston
Gender: Male
Age: 45
Diagnosis: Major Depression
Date of Admission: 6-20-00

Assessment Results: Reports no participation in activities outside the home. In-home activity is watching TV. Previous activity participation included hiking, fishing, woodworking. General assessment conducted by psychologist indicates low self-esteem.
Quality of Life Goal: Return to favorite outdoor interests, particularly fishing.
Care Goal: Enhance self-esteem.
Program: Outdoor Interests Group

Objectives:
1. By the second fishing trip, explain the meaning and importance of self-esteem when prompted by the therapeutic recreation specialist.
2. By the second fishing trip, share with the therapeutic recreation specialist at least two times in the past year when he has experienced feelings of self-esteem.
3. By the third fishing trip, identify at least three areas in his life that have provided feelings of self-esteem.
4. Choose an outdoor activity that contributes to self-esteem and report his experience to the therapeutic recreation specialist within 24 hours.

Plan:
1. Participate in the Outdoor Interests Group outings to local fishing pond three times per week.
2. Participate in an independently selected outdoor activity one time per week.
3. CTRS will ask client to describe the benefits of independent outdoor activity.
4. CTRS will use client-centered approach to develop therapeutic relationship with client and cognitive approaches in response to negative self-statements.

Evaluation: Weekly charting as to the progress made on goals and objectives.

Date: 6-22-00   TRS: T. Miller

Winston is an intelligent person who would respond well to cognitive approaches. At the same time, Winston suffers from emotional conflict. Consequently, a client-centered approach that allows him to explore and express his feelings, especially as they relate to self-esteem, would be recommended.

Although agencies may differ as to the format of an individualized care plan, most care plans are similar in their content. Recently, however, care plans have become more complex in response to the changing health care environment. Increasing numbers of individuals with multiple disabilities are being transitioned from hospital or residential settings into the community. Therapeutic recreation specialists are responding to these changes through their involvement in developing transitional and life care plans.

Transitional and Life Care Planning

Managed care has reduced the length of hospital stays. Consequently, many individuals, while well enough to leave the hospital, require ongoing care in the community. Furthermore, the U.S. Supreme Court, in a June 1999 decision, said that states must provide community-based care for persons with mental disabilities. Federal officials are interpreting this ruling to extend to people with all types of disabilities (Pear, 2000). Advances in medical technology and health practices have made it possible to preserve and extend the lives of persons who have suffered severe injuries or debilitating illnesses. This results in a growing population of persons who will require community-based assistance to manage their disabilities. As such, transitional and life care planning are critical aspects of rehabilitation.

Transitional planning involves assisting clients to find the services they need to make a successful return to their lives in the community. For example, a person who has been treated for an eating disorder might be encouraged to join an eating disorder support group in the community. Further, her goals would include locating leisure activities in the community that suit her needs and interests. Generally, transition planning entails the following elements:

- Summary of the client's progress, shared with all pertinent parties (e.g., client, family, social worker, therapeutic recreation professional),
- Functional abilities assessment, indicating the client's level of functioning, what areas require further attention, and the supports that will be needed in new environments, such as work and leisure. (e.g., a client's social skills may still necessitate attention, calling for further coaching in the community; or a client may have been discharged before she had an

opportunity to learn the transportation system or gain activity skills needed for participation in community leisure programs),

- Recommendations of programs and services that will enable the client to make a successful transition into the community (e.g., home attendant, transportation, community-based leisure education), and
- Follow-up plan for tracking the client's progress as he or she transitions into the community. The follow-up plan should involve the client and all relevant parties, such as family and caregivers.

Life care planning, according to Zasler (1996), "is an organized method of identifying and addressing the long-term comprehensive needs of an individual and their family with a disability due to a catastrophic injury or a chronic disabling condition" (p. 79). In addition to a report describing the history and current status of the condition, social situation, functional abilities, and lifestyle concerns, the life care plan includes:

- Projected evaluations (e.g., physical therapy, occupational therapy, speech therapy, therapeutic recreation, vocational, diet, transportation — evaluations required to sustain the highest level of functioning and quality of life),
- Therapeutic modalities (e.g., occupational therapy, physical therapy, therapeutic recreation, psychological counseling, vocational counseling),
- Drug and supply needs,
- Orthotics and prosthetics,
- Wheelchair equipment and supplies,
- Special home furnishings and structural modifications (e.g., adaptive eating utensils, environmental control systems, ramps),
- Level of long-term home or facility care,
- Routine medical care (e.g., medical tests, dental examinations),
- Other medical care (e.g., surgical interventions),
- Transportation requirements,
- Leisure and recreation needs, including special equipment, and
- Educational needs. (Zasler, 1996)

The effectiveness of transitional and life care planning, and the success of rehabilitation in general, should be measured by the degree of successful community integration and social inclusion. (Readers are encouraged to review the chapter on recreation inclusion.)

Individualized care plans, transitional plans, and life care plans all include evaluation methods. Written documentation and verbal reporting are typically used to evaluate a client's progress. Several documentation methods are presented in the next section.

Documentation

A primary communication tool, documentation is the written record regarding the client's health status, needs, care, and response to care. Its main aspects include information on assessments, care plan, interventions, outcomes, and communication among disciplines (Eggland & Heinemann, 1994). Eggland and Heinemann (1994) identify six purposes of documentation:

- Communication: Documentation is the main communication tool among healthcare professionals. Effective communication keeps everyone informed about the client's needs, care, and progress.
- Legal protection: Documentation provides a description of the client's care, including significant incidents and how they occurred. Documentation can serve as a legal defense in the event of litigation, which demands accurate, complete, and objective records.
- Reimbursement: Documentation provides a database for reimbursement by Medicare, Medicaid, and private insurers.
- Education: Documentation serves as an educational tool by helping students to recognize symptoms, treatments, and the effects of care for various diagnoses.
- Quality assurance: Audits are conducted on documentation to compare information in the client's chart with standards of care.
- Research: Documentation can be a source for identifying research needs and data.

Documentation Methods

Narrative Progress Notes

Documentation has traditionally been done using narrative progress notes, also referred to as source-oriented records. Narrative progress notes are written entries made in the client's record. Each discipline involved in the client's care contributes narrative progress notes. Besides the fundamentals of good charting, there is no prescribed format for writing narrative notes. The following is an example of a narrative progress note.

Date: 12-3-99   Time: 4:30 p.m.
Patient said she didn't understand directions for craft activity.
Wandered around the craft room for less than a minute. Returned

to her seat when directed by the nursing assistant. Did not participate in activity. Smiled and nodded when comments were directed at her. Made no other responses. Said "Thank you" when the activity ended and left the room on her own, saying she was "going to a wedding."

(signed) M. Smith, CTRS

Narrative progress notes can be useful when a concise description is required. On the other hand, narrative progress notes can be time-consuming to read because different disciplines make entries. The information may also be irrelevant, inappropriate, or repetitive (Eggland & Heinemann, 1994).

Problem-Oriented Record

The Problem-Oriented Record (POR) standardized documentation around specific client problems or goals. According to Lindberg, Hunter, and Kruszewski (1983), the objectives of POR are:

- To individualize care by focusing on the client's needs,
- To encourage health professionals to look for relationships among problems,
- To promote communication among healthcare members involved in direct care of the client, and
- To organize the healthcare record so that all information from all health disciplines is recorded in the same way. (p. 243)

Organized around clients' problems, POR contain four components: database, problem list, initial plan, and progress note. The *database* is the collected information on the client, such as medical history and assessments. A *problem* or *needs list* is then generated based on analysis of the database. Problems are numbered chronologically. Once a problem list has been derived from the database, an *initial plan* is written for each need or problem. An initial plan will vary among agencies, but it generally includes the problem or need, goals and behavioral objectives, and interventions. *Progress notes* provide a written record of the client's status according to a SOAP format, whereby:

- S—Subjective data (what the client said)
- O—Objective (behaviors and other factual data that were observed)
- A—Assessment (conclusions reached based on subjective and objective data)
- P—Plan (course of action)

While SOAP is the standard format for progress notes using POR, variations are employed. One variation is SOAPIER, whereby:

- I—Intervention (indicates a particular action taken by a discipline)
- E—Evaluation (indicates client response to intervention)
- R—Revision (indicates changes prompted by evaluation)

The following are examples of SOAP progress notes:

Date: 10/19/99   Time: 10:00 a.m.   Problem No.: 3   Problem: Isolation

Progress Note:

S: I don't get out much. I don't have a car and the bus makes me nervous.
O: Client taps foot repeatedly. Doesn't make eye contact. Speaks softly.
A: Client is apprehensive about using public transportation
P: 1.   Assess transportation skills.
   2.   If indicated, expand leisure education to include transportation training
   3.   Evaluate in two weeks

(signed) M. Smith, CTRS

The next example has two parts. The first illustrates an improperly written SOAP progress notes. The second shows the same note, correctly written.

Date: 9/23/99   Time: 3:00 p.m.   Problem No.: 2   Problem: Socialization

Progress Note:

S: The client yelled in a threatening tone, "I don't have to be here, you know. The whole bunch of you can go to hell."
(The *subjective* component only includes what the client said, not the professional's interpretation of its tone.)
O: Came to group inappropriately dressed. Client spat at the therapeutic recreation specialist and raised his fist like he was going to attack.
(The *objective* component is based on observable facts and behaviors. "Inappropriate" is an inference, not objective evidence. Similarly, the therapeutic recreation specialist has assumed that the client is going to attack. Objectively, he only raised his arm and made a fist.)

A: Client is argumentative, hostile, and shows signs of a personality disorder. (There is probably enough evidence to suggest that the client is hostile and argumentative. Leaping to the conclusion that this constitutes a "personality disorder" is unwarranted, leaving the client with an unjustified label.)

A proper SOAP progress note would read:

S: I don't have to be here, you know. The whole bunch of you can go to hell.
O: Came to group activity unshaven and dressed in pajamas with no top. Client spat at and raised a clenched fist when approached by the therapeutic recreation specialist.
A: Client is argumentative and hostile.
P: Remove client from group until further notice. Do 1:1, 2 x day, a.m. & p.m.

(signed) M. Smith, CTRS 9/23/99 3:00 p.m.

Because we have stressed quality of life goals in this text, we wish to illustrate a SOAP progress note oriented to quality of life.

Date: Time: Need No.1   Need: Enhance spirituality

Progress Note:

S: Gardening is so peaceful. It reminds me of the cycle of life. I think I'll write in my journal about it tonight. Oh dear, I don't have it here. Can I get something to write in?
O: Client smiles while cultivating soil. Interacts with other clients.
A: Client finds gardening spiritually meaningful. Enjoys sharing activity with others.
P: 1. Continue as planned
    2. Provide client with journal

(Signed) M. Smith, CTRS 6-10-98 4:30 p.m.

Charting by Exception

Charting by Exception (CBE) is a method of documentation in which a narrative progress note is only entered in the client's chart if there has been a deviation or variance from the expected course of care. Accordingly, CBE is referred to as variance documentation in some settings.

Consider the following situation using CBE. The care plan calls for the client who is recovering from severe facial burns to attend a meeting in the community on leisure resources. Because the client's nonattendance was an exception or variance from the care plan, it is recorded in the chart. As such, the therapeutic recreation specialist might report the following:

> Failed to attend community leisure resources meeting. Explained that he got nervous and became nauseous thinking about appearing in public alone. Indicated he would prefer to have company at his first meeting. Next meeting is postdischarge. Suggest that wife accompany him to first meeting. Incorporate into discharge plan.
>
> (Signed) M. Smith, CTRS   6/10/98 9:00 a.m.

Guidelines to Good Documentation

A well-documented entry should be:
- Factual,
- Accurate,
- Concise,
- Legible,
- Dated (include time),
- Signed (first initial, last name, and 's title—M. Winston, CTRS), and
- Properly corrected where errors have occurred. (Dittos and erasures are not permitted. A single line should be drawn through an incorrect entry; the word "error" should be written beside an incorrect entry; the entry should be rewritten correctly; and the person making and correcting the error should identify him or herself.)

Additional guidelines:
- Blank or partially blank lines are not permitted. A single line is drawn through unused space. Blank spaces can raise doubt about the addition of entries made later.
- Only approved abbreviations and symbols should be used.
- Each page of the record should be identified with the patient's name.
- Entries should clearly and specifically show how a health practitioner fulfilled responsibility to the patient. (Wolff, Weitzel, & Fuerst, 1979)
- Entries should be timely and logical ordered. (Eggland & Heinemann, 1994)

Reporting

Reporting is a verbal means of communicating about clients. Reporting involves an exchange of information for the purposes of problem-solving and continuity of care (Eggland & Heinemann, 1994). Therapeutic recreation specialists deliver verbal reports in meetings with an interdisciplinary team or family members. In both situations the therapeutic recreation specialist is expected to report on some facet of the client's behavior (assessment results, care plan, progress, etc.).

Reporting comprises two chief phases: preparation and delivery. In the *preparation phase*, the therapeutic recreation specialist should determine what information is pertinent to report, such as assessment results, interventions, or changes in conditions. He or she should have specific goals for the report, careful not to digress into irrelevant material. In short, the therapeutic recreation specialist should know what he or she wants to say and why he or she wants to say it.

Regarding the *delivery phase*, the therapeutic recreation specialist needs to consider how the report is made. Eggland and Heinemann (1994) recommend the following in delivering verbal reports:

- Avoid technical phrases and acronyms,
- Talk at participant's level,
- Avoid prejudicial comments,
- Allow time for questions,
- Be receptive to questions and feedback, and
- Encourage participation.

Critical Pathways

A growing trend in managed care is the use of *critical pathways*. According to Grote, Hasl, Krider, and Mortensen (1995), a critical pathway is a master plan of care that "describes a prescribed and expected course of hospitalization for patients with similar problems" (p. 3). A critical pathway includes the diagnosis, anticipated length of stay, and expected outcomes. It also includes a daily list of tasks, such as assessments, medications, tests, interventions, and discharge planning, as well as each discipline's contribution. Table 11.7 (p. 338) provides a list of ancillary terms. An abbreviated example of a critical pathway is presented in Table 11.8 (pp. 340–341). The therapeutic recreation specialist individualizes the patient's treatment by listing the specific groups for participation on days two and three. Such flexibility is critical because while patients may have the same diagnosis, they are individuals with unique interests and abilities.

To develop a critical pathway, a team of healthcare providers identifies the responsibilities of each discipline and the timing of interventions conducted by each discipline. Disciplines may be asked to identify practice standards, such as

---

Table 11.7 Abbreviations and Symbols Commonly Used in Healthcare Settings

$\overline{a}$	before	OOB	out of bed
abd	abdomen	$\overline{p}$	post (after)
ad lib	as desired	P	pulse
ADL	activities of daily living	PE	physical exam
AMA	against medical advice	PT	physical therapy
BRP	bathroom privileges	pt	patient
C	Celsius	rt	right
$\overline{c}$	with	Rx	treatment
c/o	complains of	stat	at once
CPR	cardiopulmonary resuscitation	Sx	symptoms
CVA	cerebrovascular accident	T	temperature
dc	discontinue	x	times
Dx	diagnosis	>	greater than
EKG (ECG)	electrocardiogram	<	less than
F	Fahrenheit	↑	increase
GI	gastrointestinal	↓	decrease
h/o	history of	=	equal
hs	hours of sleep	≠	unequal
lt	left		
neg	negative		

standardized programs or interventions that are effective with clients with a specific diagnosis. When creating critical pathways, providers may also conduct literature reviews on the efficacy of treatment interventions.

Managed care, critical pathways, and protocols are all aimed at streamlining patient care. The design of protocols and critical pathways is based on research documenting the efficacy of interventions. Therefore, therapeutic recreation specialists will find increasing pressure to substantiate the effectiveness of their programs and uniform the delivery of interventions. We anticipate that the challenge will be in maintaining the individualized nature of care that taps into the quality of life goals that are central to human motivation and self-determination.

Table 11.8 Abbreviated Example of a Critical Pathway: Psychiatric-Geriatric Clinical Pathway*			
PROBLEM/FOCUS OF CARE	**DAY 1**	**DAY 2**	**DAY 3**
DIAGNOSIS/PROCEDURE • Medical history • Allergies • Patient Involvement			
DIAGNOSIS TESTS	ECG, CXR, CBC, Chem. Profile, Urine Tox, etc.	ECG, CXR done Blood work done, results in chart	ECG, CXR results in chart
MEDICATIONS • Neuroleptic meds orders • Need for additional titration assessed by Day 3 • Need for mood stabilizer assessed by Day 3	• Neuroleptic meds ordered • Response monitored • Vital signs qd	• Vital signs qd	• Medication titration provided by MD • Vital signs qd
PLANS	Interdisciplinary plans of care		
RECREATION THERAPY	Initial functional evaluation	• Participation in structured and unstructured recreation/social activities • Participation in the following groups: _____ _____	• Participation in functional task group/individual therapy • Demonstrates higher level of independent functioning • Participation in following groups: _____
PSYCH • Demonstrates a decrease in symptoms as evidenced by score on Beck Depression Inventory • Attends and participates in groups • Verbalizes feelings during 1:1 session • Returns to normal sleep patterns Pt signature: _____	• MMS • Beck Depression Inventory • Sleeping patterns assessed	• MMS • Sleeping 3-4 hours/night minimum	• MMS • Sleeping 3-4 hours/night minimum

Table 11.8 Abbreviated Example of a Critical Pathway: Psychiatric-Geriatric Clinical Pathway* (continued)			
PROBLEM/FOCUS OF CARE	**DAY 1**	**DAY 2**	**DAY3**
PATIENT EDUCATION • Attends to own ADL • Verbalizes understanding of medication/side effects Pt signature: _____	Educational needs assessment • Medication • Coping skills • Substance abuse • Self-care	• Attending group based on needs assessment	• Attending groups based on needs assessment
LENGTH OF STAY	Expected LOS:8 days		
CLINICAL PATHWAY REVIEWED • 11PM-7AM • 7AM-3PM • 3PM-11PM	RN SIGNATURES	RN SIGNATURES	RN SIGNATURES

* Modified from Dykes (1998).

Summary

The material in this chapter pertains to the typical work responsibilities of therapeutic recreation specialists who provide client care on a daily basis. The steps of the individualized therapeutic recreation process were examined, including client assessment, the development of care plans, and methods for documenting client progress. Section Three (Chapters 10 and 11) emphasized the applied aspects of therapeutic recreation. As the conclusion of this text draws near, we wish to reiterate the vital importance among conceptual foundations (Section One), theories of practice (Section Two), and practice (Section Three) in the work and development of professionals.

Recommended Readings

burlingame, j. and Blaschko, T. M. (1997). *Assessment tools for recreational therapy* (2nd Edition). Ravensdale, Washington: Idyll Arbor, Inc.

Ellis, G. D. and Witt, P. (1986). The Leisure Diagnostic Battery: Past, present, and future. *Therapeutic Recreation Journal, 20* (4), 31-47.

Galambos, D. (1995). *Planning to have a life: Individualized planning for quality of life*. Oakville, ON: Sheridan College.

Kloseck, M., Crilly, R., Ellis, G. D., and Lammers, E. (1996). Leisure Competence Measure: Development and reliability testing of a scale to measure functional outcomes in therapeutic recreation. *Therapeutic Recreation Journal, 30* (1), 13-26.

Epilogue

People say that what we're all seeking is a meaning for life...
I think that what we're really seeking is an experience of being
alive so that our life experiences on the purely physical plane
will have resonance within our innermost being and reality, so
that we can actually feel the rapture of being alive.

Joseph Campbell

For our readers, the conclusion of this book marks a point of departure on a new and important journey. Travelers on that journey are colleagues in a very noble and exciting profession, a profession that is committed not only to life, but also to what it means to be fully alive. In Joseph Campbell's words, these travelers are devoted to helping people with major life challenges to feel the rapture of being alive. A significant measure of the success of these professionals is the extent to which they are able to find creative ways of facilitating a full and healthy life based on sound theory and effective practices. We have endeavored to introduce some of that knowledge in this book. Being a therapeutic recreation professional, however, demands more than the creative application of theoretical principles. Knowledge is both relative and dynamic. Just as we begin to believe that we have mastered a facet of knowledge, it suddenly becomes elusive. Capturing knowledge is akin to catching the wind. As you clutch your fingers around what you believe to be its essence, you find that it quickly vanishes. As such, therapeutic recreation professionals are challenged not only to apply knowledge, but also to use their experience to construct and reconstruct knowledge that helps them in their quest to promote the rapture of living among the people they serve. They must build upon that which proves worthy of being built upon, reject that which becomes obsolete, unreliable, unsound, or unjust, and pave paths that lead toward the advancement of the human condition.

As authors, we recognize the challenge of building on the theoretical foundations of leisure when delivering therapeutic recreation services. Success depends on the willingness of the professional to engage in continuous inquiry and question skeptically even the knowledge that he or she holds most dear.

Such a challenge was the impetus for writing this textbook. Further we recognize that therapeutic recreation specialists are faced with the tension that often exists between fostering meaningful leisure in the lives of their clients while simultaneously documenting functional outcomes for the agencies that employ them. The tension is played out in the differences between:

- An individualized care plan designed to facilitate quality of life through meaningful leisure experiences for a client and standardized guidelines followed in critical pathways,
- Specific program plans aimed at outcomes pertaining to meaningful leisure experiences and protocols aimed solely at client symptoms or diagnoses, and
- Services and goals cited in our models of practice.

As a profession we seek to create meaningful experiences in clients' lives. Such meaning does not always translate readily into the outcomes sought by health and human service agencies. So, readers are challenged to bring together the focus on meaningful leisure experiences and functional outcomes. Furthermore, readers are challenged to explain the linkages between leisure, quality of life, and health-related outcomes to colleagues, administrators, families, and clients, to name a few. In learning how to respond to such a challenge, each therapeutic recreation professional will create a philosophy that guides his or her words and actions.

As readers take leave of this textbook, we encourage them to confront directly the challenges facing them as they enter the professional arena. Much of the challenge lies in connecting the theories presented in Sections One and Two to the professional practices discussed in Section Three. We have only touched the surface of these challenges through discussion and examples. Full integration of theory and practice emerges as professionals conduct their day-to-day practices. For example, the thoughtful practitioner striving to integrate theory and practice is faced with:

- Considering how leisure theory and models of practice shape service delivery as outlined in a comprehensive program,
- Recognizing and responding to the diversity among the clients served,
- Reflecting on and using ethical principles,
- Considering how a departmental mission guides the selection of assessment tools and the development of specific programs,
- Considering how counseling and learning theories guide the design and implementation of specific programs, evaluating the ethics, efficacy, and efficiency of specific programs,

- Creating means of integrating clients into their communities, and
- Considering means to revise programs and create mechanisms to move clients toward the most meaningful leisure experiences possible.

As educators, we will continue to grapple with the complexity of theory and practice. To do so, we draw on our experiences as practitioners and those of our colleagues who currently promote enraptured living for the people we serve. As the future of the profession, we invite you to join us and other professionals on this ongoing journey.

APPENDIX A

American Therapeutic Recreation Association
Code of Ethics

The American Therapeutic Recreation Association's Code of Ethics is intended to be used as a guide for promoting and maintaining the highest standards of ethical behavior. The code applies to all Therapeutic Recreation personnel. The term Therapeutic Recreation personnel includes Certified Therapeutic Recreation Specialists (CTRS), Certified Therapeutic Recreation Assistants (CTRA) and Therapeutic Recreation students. Acceptance of membership in the American Therapeutic Recreation Association commits a member to adherence to these principles.

PRINCIPLE 1: Beneficence/Non-Maleficence

Therapeutic Recreation personnel shall treat persons in an ethical manner not only by respecting their decisions and protecting them from harm but also by actively making efforts to secure their well-being. Personnel strive to maximize possible benefits, and minimize possible harms. This serves as the guiding principle for the profession. The term "persons" includes not only persons served but colleagues, agencies and the profession.

PRINCIPLE 2: Autonomy

Therapeutic Recreation personnel have a duty to preserve and protect the right of each individual to make his/her own choices. Each individual is to be given the opportunity to determine his/her own course of action in accordance with a plan freely chosen.

PRINCIPLE 3: Justice

Therapeutic Recreation personnel are responsible for ensuring that individuals are served fairly and that there is equity in the distribution of services. Individuals receive service without regard to race, color, creed, gender, sexual orientation, age, disability/disease, social and financial status.

PRINCIPLE 4: Fidelity

Therapeutic Recreation personnel have an obligation to be truthful, faithful and meet commitments made to persons receiving services, colleagues, agencies and the profession.

PRINCIPLE 5: Veracity/Informed Consent

Therapeutic Recreation personnel are responsible for providing each individual receiving service with information regarding the service and the professional's training and credentials; benefits, outcomes, length of treatment, expected activities, risks, limitations. Each individual receiving service has the right to know what is likely to take place during and as a result of professional intervention. Informed consent is obtained when information is provided by the professional.

PRINCIPLE 6: Confidentiality And Privacy

Therapeutic Recreation personnel are responsible for safeguarding information about individuals served. Individuals served have the right to control information about themselves. When a situation arises that requires disclosure of confidential information about an individual to protect the individual's welfare or the interest of others, the Therapeutic Recreation professional has the responsibility/obligation to inform the individual served of the circumstances in which confidentiality was broken.

PRINCIPLE 7: Competence

Therapeutic Recreation personnel have the responsibility to continually seek to expand one's knowledge base related to Therapeutic Recreation practice. The professional is responsible for keeping a record of participation in training activities. The professional has the responsibility for contributing to changes in the profession through activities such as research, dissemination of information through publications and professional presentations, and through active involvement in professional organizations.

PRINCIPLE 8: Compliance With Laws & Regulations

Therapeutic Recreation personnel are responsible for complying with local, state and federal laws and ATRA policies governing the profession of Therapeutic Recreation.

March 1990/Revised 1998

APPENDIX B

American Therapeutic Recreation Association
Standards of Practice

Developed by the American Therapeutic Recreation Association, the Standards reflect levels of service provision for therapeutic recreation professionals to implement in a variety of settings. The Standards will assist the therapeutic recreation professional in assuring the systematic provision of quality therapeutic recreation services.

Standard 1: The therapeutic recreation specialist conducts an individualized assessment to collect systematic, comprehensive and accurate data necessary to determine a course of action and subsequent individualized treatment plan.

Standard 2: The therapeutic recreation specialist plans and develops the individualized treatment plan that identifies goals, objectives and treatment intervention strategies.

Standard 3: The therapeutic recreation specialist implements the individualized treatment plan using appropriate intervention strategies to restore, remediate or rehabilitate in order to improve functioning and independence as well as reduce or eliminate the effects of illness or disability. Implementation of the treatment plan by the therapeutic recreation specialist is consistent with the overall patient/client treatment program.

Standard 4: The therapeutic recreation specialist systematically evaluates and compares the client's response to the individualized treatment plan. The treatment plan is revised based upon changes in the interventions, diagnoses and patient/client responses.

Standard 5: The therapeutic recreation specialist develops a discharge plan in collaboration with the patient/client, family, and other treatment team members in order to continue treatment, as appropriate.

Standard 6: Recreation opportunities are available to patients/clients to promote or improve their general health and well-being.

Standard 7: The therapeutic recreation specialist adheres to the ATRA Code of Ethics.

Standard 8: The therapeutic recreation department is governed by a written plan of operation that is based upon ATRA Standards of the Practice of Therapeutic Recreation and standards of other accrediting/regulatory agencies, as appropriate.

Standard 9: The therapeutic recreation department has established provisions for assuring that therapeutic recreation staff maintain appropriate credentials and have opportunities for professional development.

Standard 10: Within the therapeutic recreation department, there exists an objective and systematic quality improvement program for the purposes of monitoring and evaluating the quality and appropriateness of care, and to identify and resolve problems in order to improve therapeutic recreation services.

Standard 11: Therapeutic recreation services are provided in an effective and efficient manner that reflects the reasonable and appropriate use of resources.

Standard 12: The therapeutic recreation department engages in routine, systematic program evaluation and research for the purpose of determining appropriateness and efficacy.

ATRA Standards of Practice Task Force
American Therapeutic Recreation Association, 1991

APPENDIX C

National Therapeutic Recreation Society
Code of Ethics

Preamble

Leisure, recreation, and play are inherent aspects of the human experience, and are essential to health and well-being. All people, therefore, have an inalienable right to leisure and the opportunities it affords for play and recreation. Some human beings have disabilities, illnesses, or social conditions which may limit their participation in the normative structure of society. These persons have the same need for and right to leisure, recreation, and play.

Accordingly, the purpose of therapeutic recreation is to facilitate leisure, recreation, and play for persons with physical, mental, emotional or social limitations in order to promote their health and well-being. This goal is accomplished through professional services delivered in clinical and community settings. Services are intended to develop skills and knowledge, to foster values and attitudes, and to maximize independence by decreasing barriers and by increasing ability and opportunity.

The National Therapeutic Recreation Society exists to promote the development of therapeutic recreation in order to ensure quality services and to protect and promote the rights of persons receiving services. The National Therapeutic Recreation Society and its members are morally obligated to contribute to the health and well-being of the people they serve. In order to meet this important social responsibility, the National Therapeutic Recreation Society and its members endorse and practice the following ethical principles.

I. The Obligation of Professional Virtue

Professionals possess and practice the virtues of integrity, honesty, fairness, competence, diligence, and self-awareness.

A. Integrity: Professionals act in ways that protect, preserve and promote the soundness and completeness of their commitment to service. Professionals do not forsake nor arbitrarily compromise their principles. They strive for unity, firmness, and consistency of character. Professionals exhibit personal and professional qualities conducive to the highest ideals of human service.

B. Honesty: Professionals are truthful. They do not misrepresent themselves, their knowledge, their abilities, or their profession. Their communications are sufficiently complete, accurate, and clear in order for individuals to understand the intent and implications of services.

C. Fairness: Professionals are just. They do not place individuals at unwarranted advantage or disadvantage. They distribute resources and services according to principles of equity.

D. Competence: Professionals function to the best of their knowledge and skill. They only render services and employ techniques of which they are qualified by training and experience. They recognize their limitations, and seek to reduce them by expanding their expertise. Professionals continuously enhance their knowledge and skills through education and by remaining informed of professional and social trends, issues and developments.

E. Diligence: Professionals are earnest and conscientious. Their time, energy, and professional resources are efficiently used to meet the needs of the persons they serve.

F. Awareness: Professionals are aware of how their personal needs, desires, values, and interests may influence their professional actions. They are especially cognizant of where their personal needs may interfere with the needs of the persons they serve.

II. The Obligation of the Professional to the Individual

A. Well-Being: Professionals' foremost concern is the well-being of the people they serve. They do everything reasonable in their power and within the scope of professional practice to benefit them. Above all, professionals cause no harm.

B. Loyalty: Professionals' first loyalty is to the well-being of the individuals they serve. In instances of multiple loyalties, professionals make the nature and the priority of their loyalties explicit to everyone concerned, especially where they may be in question or in conflict.

C. Respect: Professionals respect the people they serve. They show regard for their intrinsic worth and for their potential to grow and change. The following areas of respect merit special attention:

1. Freedom, Autonomy, and Self-Determination: Professionals respect the ability of people to make, execute, and take responsibility for their own choices. Individuals are given adequate opportunity for self-determination in the least restrictive environment possible. Individuals have the right of informed consent. They may refuse participation in any program except where their welfare is clearly and immediately threatened and where they are unable to make rational decisions on their own due to temporary or permanent incapacity. Professionals promote independence and avoid fostering dependence. In particular, sexual relations and other manipulative behaviors intended to control individuals for the personal needs of the professional are expressly unethical.

2. Privacy: Professionals respect the privacy of individuals. Communications are kept confidential except with the explicit consent of the individual or where the welfare of the individual or others is clearly imperiled. Individuals are informed of the nature and the scope of confidentiality.

D. Professional Practices: Professionals provide quality services based on the highest professional standards. Professionals abide by standards set by the profession, deviating only when justified by the needs of the individual. Care is used in administering tests and other measurement instruments. They are used only for their express purposes. Instruments should conform to accepted psychometric standards. The nature of all practices, including tests and measurements, are explained to individuals. Individuals are also debriefed on the results and the implications of professional practices. All professional practices are conducted with the safety and well-being of the individual in mind.

III. The Obligation of the Professional to Other Individuals and to Society

A. General Welfare: Professionals make certain that their actions do not harm others. They also seek to promote the general welfare of society by advocating the importance of leisure, recreation and play.

B. Fairness: Professionals are fair to other individuals and to the general public. They seek to balance the needs of the individuals they serve with the needs of other persons according to principles of equity.

IV. The Obligation of the Professional to Colleagues

A. Respect: Professionals show respect for colleagues and their respective professions. They take no action that undermines the integrity of their colleagues.

B. Cooperation and Support: Professionals cooperate with and support their colleagues for the benefit of the persons they serve. Professionals demand the highest professional and moral conduct of each other. They approach and offer help to colleagues who require assistance with an ethical problem. Professionals take appropriate action toward colleagues who behave unethically.

V. The Obligation of the Professional to the Profession

A. Knowledge: Professionals work to increase and improve the profession's body of knowledge by supporting and/or by conducting research. Research is practiced according to accepted canons and ethics of scientific inquiry. Where subjects are involved, their welfare is paramount. Prior permission is gained from subjects to participate in research. They are informed of the general nature of the research and any specific risks that may be involved. Subjects are debriefed at the conclusion of the research, and are provided with results of the study on request.

B. Respect: Professionals treat the profession with critical respect. They strive to protect, preserve, and promote the integrity of the profession and its commitment to public service.

C. Reform: Professionals are committed to regular and continuous evaluation of the profession. Changes are implemented that improve the profession's ability to serve society.

VI. The Obligation of the Profession to Society

A. Service: The profession exists to serve society. All of its activities and resources are devoted to the principle of service.

B. Equality: The profession is committed to equality of opportunity. No person shall be refused service because of race, gender, religion, social status, ethnic background, sexual orientation, or inability to pay. The profession neither conducts nor condones discriminatory practices. It actively seeks to correct inequities that unjustly discriminate.
C. Advocacy: The profession advocates for the people it is entrusted to serve. It protects and promotes their health and well-being and their inalienable right to leisure, recreation, and play in clinical and community settings.

National Therapeutic Recreation Society
Revised 1990

APPENDIX D

National Therapeutic Recreation Society
Standards of Practice for Therapeutic Recreation Services

Introduction

The National Therapeutic Recreation Society (NTRS) Board of Directors approved the revised Standards of Practice for Therapeutic Recreation Services in September, 1994. What follows are the basic Standards of Practice, without the criteria for each standard.

Standard 1 - Scope of Service

A. Treatment services are available which are goal-oriented and directed toward rehabilitation, amelioration and/or modification of specific physical, emotional, cognitive, and/or social functional behaviors. Therapeutic recreation intervention targeting these functional behaviors is warranted when the behaviors impede or otherwise inhibit participation in reasonable and customary leisure participation. (Note: This may not apply to all therapeutic recreation settings for all clients.)

B. Leisure education services are available which are goal-oriented and directed toward the development of knowledge, attitudes, values, behaviors, skills and resources related to socialization and leisure involvement. (Note: This may not apply for all clients.)

C. Recreation services are available that provide a variety of activities designed to meet client needs, competencies, aptitudes, capabilities and interest. These services are directed toward optimizing client leisure involvement and are designed to promote health and well-being, and improve the quality of life.

Standard II - Mission and Purpose, Goals, and Objectives

Mission, purpose, goals and specific objectives are formulated and stated for each type of therapeutic recreation service based upon the philosophy and goals of the agency. These are then translated into operational procedures and serve as a blueprint for program evaluation.

Standard III - Individual Treatment/Program Plan

The therapeutic recreation specialist develops an individualized treatment/ program plan for each client referred to the agency for therapeutic recreation services.

Standard IV - Documentation

The therapeutic recreation specialist records specific information based on client assessment, involvement and progress. Information pertaining to the client is recorded on a regular basis as determined by the agency policy and procedures, and accrediting body standards.

Standard V - Plan of Operation

Therapeutic recreation services are considered a viable aspect of treatment, rehabilitation, normalization and development. Appropriate and fair scheduling of services, facilities, personnel and resources is vital to client progress and the operation of therapeutic recreation services. (See the NTRS Guidelines for the Administration of Therapeutic Recreation Services for additional reference information.)

Standard VI - Personnel Qualifications

Therapeutic recreation services are conducted by therapeutic recreation specialists whose training and experiences have prepared them to be effective at the functions they perform. Therapeutic recreation specialists have opportunities for involvement in professional development and lifelong learning.

Standard VII - Ethical Responsibilities

Professionals are committed to advancing the use of therapeutic recreation services in order to ensure quality, protection, and to promote the rights of persons receiving services.

Standard VIII - Evaluation and Research

Therapeutic recreation specialists implement client and service-related evaluation and research functions to maintain and improve the quality, effectiveness, and integrity of therapeutic recreation services.

APPENDIX E

National Recreation and Park Association
Position Statement on Inclusion

Diversity is a cornerstone of our society and culture and thus should be celebrated. Including people with disabilities in the fabric of society strengthens the community and its individual members. The value of inclusive leisure experiences in enhancing the quality of life for all people, with and without disabilities, cannot be overstated. As we broaden our understanding and acceptance of differences among people through shared leisure experiences, we empower future generations to build a better place for all to live and thrive.

Inclusive leisure experiences encourage and enhance opportunities for people of varying abilities to participate and interact in life's activities together with dignity. It also provides an environment that promotes and fosters physical, social, and psychological inclusion of people with diverse experiences and skill levels. Inclusion enhances individuals' potential for full and active participation in leisure activities and experiences.

Additionally, the benefits of this participation may include:

- providing positive recreational experiences which contribute to the physical, mental, social, emotional, and spiritual growth and development of every individual,
- fostering peer and intergenerational relationships that allow one to share affection, support, companionship, and assistance, and
- developing community support and encouraging attitudinal changes to reflect dignity, self-respect, and involvement within the community.

Purpose

The purpose of the National Recreation and Park Association (NRPA) Position Statement on Inclusion is to encourage all providers of park, recreation, and leisure services to provide opportunities in settings where people of all abilities can recreate and interact together.

This document articulates a commitment to the leisure process and the desired outcomes. Accordingly, the NRPA Position Statement on Inclusion encompasses these broad concepts and beliefs:

Right to Leisure

- The pursuit of leisure is a condition necessary for human dignity and well-being.
- Leisure is a part of a healthy lifestyle and a productive life.
- Every individual is entitled to the opportunity to express unique interests and pursue, develop, and improve talents and abilities.
- People are entitled to opportunities and services in the most inclusive setting.
- The right to choose from the full array of recreation opportunities offered in diverse settings and environments and requiring different levels of competency should be provided.

Quality of Life

- People grow and develop throughout the life span.
- Through leisure an individual gains an enhanced sense of competence and self-direction.
- A healthy leisure lifestyle can prevent illness and promote wellness.
- The social connection with one's peers plays a major role in his/her life satisfaction.
- The opportunity to choose is an important component in one's quality of life; individual choices will be respected.

Support, Assistance and Accommodations

- Inclusion is most effective when support, assistance, and accommodations are provided.
- Support, assistance and accommodations can and should be responsive to people's needs and preferences.
- Support, assistance, and accommodations should create a safe and fun environment, remove real and artificial barriers to participation, and maximize not only the independence but also the interdependence of the individual. People want to be self-sufficient.
- Support, assistance, and accommodations may often vary and are typically individualized. Types of support, assistance and accommodations include, but are not limited to: qualified staff, adaptive equipment, alternative formats for printed or audio materials, trained volunteers, or flexibility in policies and program rules.

Barrier Removal

- Environments should be designed to encourage social interaction, "risk-taking," fun, choices and acceptance that allow for personal accomplishment in a cooperative context.
- Physical barriers should be eliminated to facilitate full participation by individuals with disabilities.
- Attitudinal barriers in all existing and future recreation services should be removed or minimized through education and training of personnel (staff, volunteers, students, and/or community at-large).

The National Recreation and Park Association is dedicated to the four inclusion concepts of:

- *Right to Leisure* (for all individuals),
- *Quality of Life* (enhancements through leisure experiences),
- Support, Assistance, and Accommodations, and
- Barrier Removal.

in all park, recreation, and leisure services. Properly fostered, inclusion will happen naturally. Over time, inclusion will occur with little effort and with the priceless reward of an enlightened community. Encouraged in the right way, inclusion is the right thing to plan for, implement, and celebrate.

Adopted by the NRPA Board of Trustees as an NRPA Policy
October 24, 1999

APPENDIX F

Research Based Protocol: Progressive Resistance Training

PURPOSE
The purpose of this research-based protocol is to improve and maintain the functional fitness of older adults through Progressive Resistance Training (PRT). The purpose of PRT is to improve the participant's prospects for independent living, reduce risk of falls, enhance commitment to regular exercise, and increase overall quality of life.

DEFINITIONS
Progressive resistance training is the use of weights and other forms of resistance (e.g., Therabands™) to provide resistance in a series of exercises with intent of increasing muscle strength. As the subject becomes stronger, the amount of resistance (weight) must be progressively increased in order to continue to elicit strength gains. At some point the participant and practitioner may find that the strength gains are satisfactory and decide to use PRT for maintenance or muscle strength instead of improvement.
Low muscle strength is defined as strength insufficient to meet the ordinary demands of daily life enabling one to live independently and safely in the community.

INDIVIDUALS AT RISK FOR LOW LEVELS OF MUSCLE STRENGTH
Through research reviews, several risk factors have been identified that increase a participant's chances of developing low levels of muscle strength. Older adults at risk for low muscle strength or who presently have low muscle strength should be placed on an appropriate PRT intervention. Risk factors for low muscle strength in older adults include the presence of one or more of the following:

- Postural instability or balance difficulties (Fiatrone, et al., 1994; Kauffmann, 1994; Lord & Clark, 1996).
- Frailty (Speechley & Tinetti, 1991).
- Chronic muscle weakness, especially in the lower extremities (Buchner & Larson, 1987; Rosado, et al., 1989; Tinetti, Speechley & Ginter, 1988).
- History of minor falls (Hayes, et al., 1996; Tideiksaar, 1994; Nevitt, 1990).
- Difficulty with activities of daily living (Cutler, 1994; Dunkle, Kart & Lockery, 1994).

- Difficulty with self-care (Sonn, Frandin & Grimby, 1995; Potter, Evans & Duncan, 1995).
- Sedentary lifestyle (Fiatrone, 1992; Haskell, 1985; Rantanen, Era, Kauppinen & Heikkinen, 1994).

ASSESSMENT FOR PROGRESSIVE RESISTANCE TRAINING

Assessment for progressive resistance training consists of two separate measures:
1. Assessment of physical activity readiness
2. Assessment of functional fitness

Assessment of physical activity readiness

Prior to beginning this or any program of regular physical activity, the older adult should be screened using any of a number of good health screening devices. We experienced good results with the revised Physical Activity Readiness Questionnaire (rPAR-Q) developed by Shephard and his colleagues (1991), but other good screening instruments are available. Whatever health screening device is used, anyone reporting a contraindication for exercise should obtain a physician's approval to participate in the program.

Research reported by Cardinal (1997) suggests that the rPAR-Q is a conservative screening devise. Cardinal screened 181 older adults (60-89 years of age) using the rPAR-Q and found that more than one-half answered "yes" to one of the seven items. The blood pressure item was most frequently answered in the affirmative by Cardinal's subjects. Cardinal concluded that the rPAR-Q is a useful means for identifying older adults who may participate safely in low to moderate intensity exercise programs.

Cardinal's work suggests that practitioners screening older adults for low to moderate intensity exercise programs (such as the one described here) should anticipate that about one-half or more of the potential participants will answer "yes" to one or more of the rPAR-Q items. Accordingly, a phone call by the participant to his/her physician to obtain permission to participate in PRT may be a usual experience.

In anticipation of this phone call, the practitioner should develop a short descriptive summary of what the participant will experience during the PRT protocol described here. The summary can then be mailed to the physician for review prior to approval, or read to the physician over the phone. Our experience in three years of conducting the PRT program has been that no physician has denied an interested individual who is asymptomatic with respect to cardiopulmonary disease.

Assessment of functional fitness

The most comprehensive assessment inventory is the 1996 Functional Fitness Assessment for Adults Over 60 Years (2nd ed.) developed by the Council on Aging and Adult Development of the American Alliance of Health, Physical Education, Recreation and Dance (AAHPERD). The battery includes five tests of functional fitness described in detail below.

The tests of fitness are designed to be administered under conditions of minimal risk to the participant. "The test will not need physician approval. It bears no more risk than life itself" (Osness et al. 1996, p. vii). Measurement of each of the five functional fitness criteria is as follows:

- *Flexibility.* The participant assumes a seated position on the floor and stretches and reaches as far as comfortably possible along a measured line in front of him/her. The flexibility score is the length the participant can reach in inches.
- *Agility and dynamic balance.* The participant assumes a seated position in a chair. On a signal from the tester, the participant rises and turns, walking at a 45-degree angle toward a cone (or other marker) placed in a corner approximately five feet away. On circling the cone and returning to the chair, the participant rises and negotiates a cone (or other marker) placed in the opposite corner at a 45-degree angle the same distance away as the first cone. One trial consists of four trips around the cones (two left and two right). The best trial is recorded as the score.
- *Coordination.* Using the preferred hand, the participant moves small cans from one station to the next and back two times. The best time on two trials equals the coordination score.
- *Strength and muscle endurance.* In a seated position (chair should not have arms), and using the dominant hand, the participant grasps a weight (8 lbs. for men, 4 lbs. for women). Next, the participant flexes the forearm, bringing the weight upwards toward the shoulder until the forearm touches the bicep. The strength and muscle endurance score is the number of repetitions completed in 30 seconds. The participant is limited to one trial.
- *Endurance.* The participant walks an 880 yard measured course at a comfortable pace. The endurance score is the length of time required to complete the 880 yard course. The participant is limited to one trial.

DESCRIPTION OF INTERVENTION

The following PRT intervention program describes activities that should begin on a two-month, three workouts per week basis.

The following activities should be performed as part of the PRT program. During each 40 minute session, participants should complete the following activities:

- Warm-up: 5 minutes of light exercises designed to prepare the participant for muscle conditioning and to improve overall flexibility.
- Muscular conditioning: 30 minutes of exercises designed to improve muscular strength and endurance. Most of the exercises use light weight (hand-held dumbbells with typical resistance of 4 to 15 pounds for most exercises) and are progressive in nature (i.e., participant advances to higher demand levels at their own pace, according to personal ability to tolerate the exercises and accommodate the increases in demand). Generally, these exercises are performed for three sets of 8 to 10 repetitions each, progressing to three sets of 15 repetitions each.
- Cool-down: 5 minutes of light exercises (using some of the same flexibility exercises employed in the warm-up phase). The purpose of the cool-down is to return respiration levels back to normal levels and to stretch the muscles worked in the exercise session.

This program is consistent with recommendations from the American Alliance for Health, Physical Education, Recreation and Dance (n.d.) and weight training authorities (e.g., Westcott, 1987).

Any number of exercises can be introduced. Generally, most older adults in normal health are able to complete eight different exercises at a rate of three sets per exercise in about 30-40 minutes without discomfort. Introduce at least one flexibility stretching/exercise within the context of the workout. Also, try to introduce exercises that will work all parts of the body, and include:

1. Upper extremities and shoulder girdle
2. Trunk and abdomen
3. Lower extremities and pelvic girdle

[NOTE: The protocol contains description of arm curls, shoulder shrug, leg lunge, toe raises, rowing, abdominal crunches, tricep extension, side bends, quadriceps extension, hamstring curls.]

EVALUATION OF PARTICIPANT OUTCOMES AND PROCESS FACTORS

In order to evaluate the use of this protocol among participants at risk for low muscle strength, both outcome and process factors should be evaluated.

OUTCOME FACTORS

Use of the Functional Fitness Assessment (Osness et al. 1996), described under Assessment of Functional Fitness at one month intervals following the start of the PRT program. Compare baseline assessment with progress following each month in the program. Also, the participant's functional fitness performance may be compared to norms. An improvement in this functional fitness should be observed following two months.

- For the individual implementing the PRT program, this information will provide information about how effective the program is.
- For the participant, this information can be rewarding and, hopefully, encouraging enough to motivate continued participation in a program of regular exercise.

The PRT Management Monitor is an outcome measure based upon participant interviews that elicits specific information regarding the PRT program and increases in functional fitness. Please use the Monitor on at least a monthly basis.

Other participant outcomes may be included as dictated by the specific aims of the program and for each individual participant. Examples of other outcomes that can be assessed include:

1. Record number of and severity of reported falls before, during, and after the PRT program
2. Record functional ability through standardized tests (e.g., tests of hand function, functional reach, sit-to-stand, timed up-and-go)
3. Record reported ability to carry on independent living and self-care activities
4. Record any increases in the participant's reported level of quality of life

PROCESS FACTORS

A sample of the nurses and/or physicians who are using this protocol need to be given the Process Evaluation Monitor approximately one month following his/her use of the protocol. The purpose of this monitor is to determine his/her understanding of the protocol and to assess the support for carrying out the protocol.

Mobily & Mobily, 1997

References

Achenbach, T. M. (1985). *Assessment and taxonomy of child and adolescent psychopathology*. Newbury Park, CA: Sage Publications.

Adler, M. (1970). Freedom as natural, acquired, and circumstantial. In R. Dewey and J. Gould (Eds.), *Freedom: Its history, nature, and varieties* (pp. 68-75). Toronto, ON: MacMillan.

Agich, G. (1993). *Autonomy and long-term care*. New York, NY: Oxford University Press.

Allen, L. R. (1996). A primer: Benefits-based management of recreation services. *Parks and Recreation 31*(3), 64-76.

Allen, L. R., Stevens, B., and Harwell, R. (1996). Benefits-based management in activity planning model for youth in at-risk environments. *Journal of Park and Recreation Administration 14* (3), 10-19.

Allison, M. and Smith, S. (1990). Leisure and the quality of work: Issues facing racial and ethnic minority elderly. *Therapeutic Recreation Journal, 23*(3), 50-63.

American Psychiatric Association. (1994). *Diagnostic and statistical manual of mental disorders* (4th ed.). Washington, DC: Author.

American Therapeutic Recreation Association. (n.d.). *What is the American Therapeutic Recreation Association?* Washington, DC: Author.

American Therapeutic Recreation Association. (1988). Definition statement. *American Therapeutic Recreation Newsletter, 4*(3).

American Therapeutic Recreation Association. (1998). *Code of ethics*. Hattiesburg, MS: Author.

American Therapeutic Recreation Association. (1993). *Recreational therapy: An integral aspect of comprehensive healthcare*. Hattiesburg, MS: Author.

American Therapeutic Recreation Association. (1996). Definition/Vision Statement. In *American Therapeutic Recreation Association* [Online]. Available: http://www.atra-tr.org/defvis.html

American Therapeutic Recreation Association (1998). *Code of ethics* (rev.). Hattiesburg, MS: Author.

American Therapeutic Recreation Association Reimbursement Committee. (1994). Reimbursement for partial hospitalization. *American Therapeutic Recreation Association Newsletter, 9*(7), 3.

American Therapeutic Recreation Association. (1999). *Educational/Career Information, Therapeutic Recreation*. (Approved, 1987). [Online]. Available: http://www/atra/org/educat.html

American Therapeutic Recreation Association and National Therapeutic Recreation Society. (1993) *Therapeutic recreation: Responding to the challenges of health care reform*. Hattiesburg, MS: Authors.

Annas, G. and Densberger, J. (1986). Competence to refuse medical treatment: Autonomy vs. paternalism. In E. Friedman (Ed.), *Making choices: Ethical issues for health care professionals* (pp. 149-168). Chicago, IL: American Hospital Publishing.

Armstrong, M. and Lauzen, S. (1994). *Community integration program* (2nd ed.). Ravensdale, WA: Idyll Arbor.

Atteberry-Rogers, M. (1993). *Leisure and family fun*. State College, PA: Venture Publishing, Inc.

Austin, D. R. (1991a). Introduction and overview. In D. R. Austin and M. E. Crawford (Eds.). *Therapeutic Recreation: An Introduction* (pp. 1-18). Englewood Cliffs, NJ: Prentice Hall, Inc.

Austin, D. R. (1991b). *Therapeutic recreation processes and techniques*. Champaign, IL: Sagamore.

Austin, D. R. (1997). *Therapeutic recreation: Processes and techniques*. (3rd ed.). Champaign, IL: Sagamore.

Austin, D. R. (1998). The health protection/health promotion model. *Therapeutic Recreation Journal, 32,* 109-117.

Axelson, J. (1993). *Counseling and development in a multicultural society* (2nd ed). Pacific Grove, CA: Brooks/Cole.

Babbi, E. R. (1998). *The practice of social research* (8th ed.). Belmont, CA: Wadsworth.

Baltes, P. B. and Baltes, M. M. (1990). Selective optimization with compensation. In P. B. Baltes and M. M. Baltes (Eds.), *Successful aging: Perspectives from the behavioral sciences* (pp. 1-34). New York, NY: Cambridge University Press.

Banks, J. A. (1994). *Multiethnic education: Theory and practice*. Boston, MA: Allyn and Bacon.

Barbarash, L. (1997). *Multicultural games*. Brooklyn, NY: Human Kinetics.

Barker, K. (Ed.) (1985). *The NIV study bible*. Grand Rapids, MI: Zondervan.

Bartling v. Glendale Adventist Medical Center. (1985). 209 Cal. 220.

Beauchamp, T. and Childress, J. (1994). *Principles of biomedical ethics* (4th ed.). New York, NY: Oxford University Press.

Beaudouin, M. and Keller, J. (1994). Aquatic solutions: A continuum of services for individuals with physical disabilities in the community. *Therapeutic Recreation Journal, 28,* 193-202.

Beck, A. T. (1976). *Cognitive therapy and the emotional disorders*. New York: Penguin Group.

Beck, A. T. (1985). *Anxiety disorders and phobias: A cognitive perspective.* New York, NY: Basic Books.

Bedini, L. (1998). Attitudes toward disability. In F. Brasile, T. Skalko, and j. burlingame (Eds.), *Perspectives in recreational therapy: Issues of a dynamic profession* (pp. 287-309). Ravensdale, WA: Idyll Arbor.

Bedini, L, Bullock, C., and Driscoll, L. (1993). The effects of leisure education on factors contributing to the successful transition of students with mental retardation from school to adult life. *Therapeutic Recreation Journal, 27*(2), 70-82.

Bellah, R., Madsen, R., Sullivan, W., and Tipton, S. (1985). *Habits of the heart.* Berkeley, CA: University of California Press.

Benn, S. and Peters, R. (1959). *Social principles and the democratic state.* London, UK: Allen & Unwin.

Bennett, C. (1995). *Comprehensive multicultural education: Theory and practice (3rd ed.).* Boston, MA: Allyn and Bacon.

Blake, J. G. (1991). Therapeutic recreation assessment and intervention with a patient with quadriplegia. *Therapeutic Recreation Journal, 25*(4), 71-75.

Blankfield, A. (1987). The concept of dependence. *The International Journal of the Addictions, 22,* 1069-1086.

Bloom, B. S., Englehart, M. D., Furst, E. J., Hill, W. H., and Krathwohl, D. R. (1956). *Taxonomy of educational objectives: The classification of educational goals. Handbook 1: cognitive domain.* New York, NY: McKay.

Boardman, A. E., Greenberg, D. H., Vining, A. R., and Weimer, D. L. (1996). *Cost-benefit analysis: Concepts and practice.* Upper Saddle River, NJ: Prentice Hall.

Bonnicksen, T. M. (1987). *EZ-Impact: The judgement-based systems modeling and decision analysis program.* College Station, TX: Biosocial Decision Systems.

Bourgeois, M. S. (1993). Effects of memory aids on dyadic conversations of individuals with dementia. *Journal of Applied Behavior Analysis, 26*(1), 77-87.

Bourne, L. E. and Ekstrand, B. R. (1973). *Psychology: Its principles and meanings.* Hinsdale, IL: The Dryden Press.

Bowlby, C. (1993). *Therapeutic activities with persons disabled by Alzheimer's disease and related disorders.* Gaithersburg, MD: Aspen Publishers, Inc.

Boyer, E. L. (1987). *College: The undergraduate experience in America.* New York, NY: Harper & Row.

Brannon, S. A., Chinn, K. B., and Verhoven, P. J. (1981). *What is leisure education? A primer for persons working with handicapped children and youth*. Washington, DC: Hawkins and Associates, Inc.

Brightbill, C. (1960). *The challenge of leisure*. Englewood Cliffs, NJ: Prentice Hall.

Brightbill, C. K. and Mobley, T. A. (1977). *Educating for leisure-centered living* (2nd ed.). New York: John Wiley & Sons.

Broach, E. and Dattilo, J. (1996). Aquatic therapy: A viable therapeutic recreation intervention. *Therapeutic Recreation Journal, 30*(3), 213-229.

Broach, E., Groff, D., and Dattilo, J. (1997). Effects of an aquatic therapy swimming program on adults with spinal cord injuries. *Therapeutic Recreation Journal, 31*(3), 160-173.

Broach, E., Groff, D., Dattilo, J., Yaffe, R., and Gast, D. (1997/98). Effects of aquatic therapy on adults with multiple sclerosis. *Annual in Therapeutic Recreation, 7*, 1-20.

Bullock, C. (1993). Ways of knowing: The naturalistic and positivistic perspectives on research. In M. J. Malkin and C. Z. Howe (Eds.), *Research in therapeutic recreation: Concepts and methods* (pp. 25-42). State College, PA: Venture Publishing, Inc.

Bullock, C. and Howe, C. (1991). A model therapeutic recreation program for reintegration of persons with disabilities into the community. *Therapeutic Recreation Journal, 25*(1), 6-17.

burlingame, j. and Blaschko, T. (1990). *Assessment tools for recreational therapy*. Ravensdale, WA: Idyll Arbor.

burlingame, j. and Blaschko, T. (1997). *Assessment tools for recreational therapy* (2nd ed.). Ravensdale, WA: Idyll Arbor.

burlingame, j. and Skalko, T. (1997). *Glossary for therapists*. Ravensdale, WA: Idyll Arbor.

Burn, D. (1992). Ethical implications in cross-cultural counseling and training. *Journal of Counseling and Development, 70*, 578-583.

Butler, R. N. and Lewis, M. I. (1986). *Aging and mental health: Positive psychosocial and biomedical approaches*. Columbus, OH: Charles E. Merrill Publishing Company.

Caldwell, L. L. (1998). In response to Dattilo, Kleiber and Williams' "Self-determination and enjoyment enhancement: A psychologically-based service delivery model for therapeutic recreation." *Therapeutic Recreation Journal, 32*(4), 283-289.

Cantania, A. C. (1998). *Learning* (4th ed.). Upper Saddle River, NJ: Prentice Hall.

Callahan, D. (1973). The WHO definition of health. In P. Steinfels (Ed.), *The Hastings Center Studies: The Concept of Health, 1*(3), 77-87.

Callahan, D. (1977). Health and society: Some ethical imperatives. In J. Knowles (Ed.), *Doing better and feeling worse*, (pp. 23-33). New York, NY: W. W. Norton.

Callahan, D. (1990). *What kind of life? The limits of medical progress*. New York, NY: Simon & Schuster.

Carruthers, C., Sneegas, J. J., and Ashton-Shaeffer, C. (1986). *Therapeutic recreation: Guidelines for activity services in long-term care*. Champaign-Urbana, IL: University of Illinois.

Carter, M. J., Browne, B., LeConey, S. P., and Nagle, C. J. (1991). *Designing therapeutic recreation programs in the community*. Reston, VA: American Alliance for Health, Physical Education, Recreation and Dance.

Carter, M. J., Van Andel, G., and Robb, G. (1995). *Therapeutic recreation: A practical approach* (2nd ed.). Prospect Heights, IL: Waveland Press.

Chambless, D. L. and Goldstein, A. J. (1989). Behavioral psychotherapy. In R. Corsini (Ed.), *Current psychotherapies* (2nd ed.) (pp. 230-272). Itasca, IL: F. E. Peacock Publishers, Inc.

Cogan, M. L. (1953. Toward a definition of a profession. *Harvard Educational Review*, *23*, 33-50.

Collopy, B. (1996). Bioethics and therapeutic recreation: Expanding the dialogue. In C. Sylvester (Ed.), *Philosophy of therapeutic recreation: Ideas and issues: Vol. 2* (pp. 10-19). Arlington, VA: National Recreation and Park Association.

Combs, A. W. (1989). *A theory of therapy: Guidelines for counseling practice*. Newbury Park, CA: Sage Publications.

Compton, D. (1989). On shaping a future for therapeutic recreation. In D. Compton, (Ed.), *Issues in therapeutic recreation: A profession in transition* (pp. 485-500). Champaign, IL: Sagamore.

Connolly, P. (n.d.). *A message from the president*. Sand Springs, OK: American Therapeutic Recreation Association.

Connolly, P. and Keogh-Hoss, M. A. (1991). The development and use of intervention protocols in therapeutic recreation: Documenting field-based practices. In B. Riley (Ed.), *Quality management applications for therapeutic recreation* (pp. 117-136). State College, PA: Venture Publishing, Inc.

Corbin, H. D. and Tait, W. J. (1973). *Education for leisure*. Englewood Cliffs, NJ: Prentice Hall.

Corey, G. (1996). *Theory and practice of counseling and psychotherapy*. Pacific Grove, CA: Brooks/Cole Publishing Co.

Corey, G., Corey, M., and Callanan, P. (1993). *Issues and ethics in the helping professions*. Pacific Grove, CA: Brooks/Cole Publishing Co.

Coyle, C. P. (1998). Integrating service delivery and outcomes: A practice model for the future? *Therapeutic Recreation Journal, 32*(3), 194-201.

Coyle, C., Kinney, W., and Shank, J. (1991). A summary of benefits common to therapeutic recreation. In C. Coyle, W. Kinney, B. Riley, and J. Shank (Eds.), *Benefits of therapeutic recreation: A consensus view*. Philadelphia, PA: Temple University.

Coyne, J. (1976). The place of informed consent in ethical dilemmas. *Journal of Consulting and Clinical Psychology, 44*, 1015-1017.

Crawford, D. W., Jackson, E. L., and Godbey, G. (1987). A hierarchical model of leisure constraints. *Leisure Sciences, 13*, 309-320.

The Creation of Man. (2000, June 28). [Online] Available: http://www.peaknet.net/~aardvark/birth.html

Crider, A. B., Goethals, G. R. , Kavanaugh, R. D., and Solomon, P. R. (1983). *Psychology*. Glenview, IL: Scott, Foresman & Company.

Cronbach. L. J. (1990). *Essentials of psychological testing*. (5th ed.). New York, NY: Harper & Row.

Csikszentmihalyi, M. (1975). *Beyond boredom and anxiety*. San Francisco, CA: Jossey-Bass.

Csikszentmihayli, M. (1988). The flow experience and its significance for human psychology. In M. Csikszentmihayli and I. S. Csikszentmihalyi (Eds.), *Optimal experience: Psychological studies of flow in consciousness* (pp. 15-35). New York, NY: Cambridge University Press.

Csikszentmihalyi, M. (1990). *Flow: The psychology of optimal experience*. New York, NY: Harper & Row Publishers.

Dattilo, J. (1994). *Inclusive leisure services: Responding to the rights of people with disabilities*. State College, PA: Venture Publishing, Inc.

Dattilo, J. (1999). *Leisure education program planning: A systematic approach*. State College, PA: Venture Publishing, Inc.

Dattilo, J. and Barnett, L. (1985). Therapeutic recreation for individuals with severe handicaps: An analysis of the relationship between choice and pleasure. *Therapeutic Recreation Journal, 19*(3), 79-91.

Dattilo, J. and Kleiber, D. (1993). Psychological perspectives for therapeutic recreation research: The psychology of enjoyment. In M. J. Malkin and C. Z. Howe (Eds.), *Research in therapeutic recreation: Concepts and methods* (pp. 57-76). State College, PA: Venture Publishing, Inc.

Dattilo, J., Kleiber, D., and Williams, R. (1998). Self-determination and Enjoyment Enhancement: A psychologically-based service delivery model for therapeutic recreation. *Therapeutic Recreation Journal, 32*(4), 258-271.

Dattilo, J. and Murphy, W. D. (1987a). *Behavior modification in therapeutic recreation*. State College, PA: Venture Publishing, Inc.

Dattilo, J. and Murphy, W. D. (1987b). The challenge of adventure recreation for individuals with disabilities. *Therapeutic Recreation Journal, 21*(3), 14-21.

Dattilo, J. and Murphy, W. D. (1991). *Leisure education program planning: a systematic approach*. State College, PA: Venture Publishing, Inc.

Dattilo, J. and Smith, R. (1990). Communicating positive attitudes toward people with disabilities through sensitive terminology. *Therapeutic Recreation Journal, 24*(1), 8-17.

Davis, S. (1998). Development of the profession of horticultural therapy. In S. P. Simson and M. C. Straus (Eds.), *Horticulture as therapy: Principles and practice* (pp. 3-20). New York, NY: The Food Products Press.

Deaux, K. and Wrightsman, L. S. (1988). *Social psychology* (5th ed). Belmont, CA: Wadsworth.

de Grazia, S. (1964). *Of time, work, and leisure*. Garden City, NY: Anchor Books.

Dieser, R. B. (1999). Letter to the guest editors of the practice models series. *Therapeutic Recreation Journal, 33*(3), 193-194.

Dieser, R. B. and Peregoy, J. (1999). A multicultural critique of three therapeutic recreation service models. *Annual in Therapeutic Recreation, 8*, 56-69.

Denzin, N. K. and Lincoln, Y. S. (1994). *Handbook of qualitative research*. Thousand Oaks, CA: Sage Publications.

DeVellis, R. F. (1991). *Scale development: Theory and applications*. Newbury Park, CA: Sage Publications.

Dobson, K. S. (1988). *Handbook of cognitive-behavioral therapies*. New York, NY: The Guilford Press.

Driver, B., Brown, P., and Peterson, G. (Eds.). (1991). *Benefits of leisure*. State College, PA: Venture Publishing, Inc.

Dryden, W. and DiGiuseppe, R. (1990). *A primer on rational-emotive therapy*. Champaign, IL: Research Press.

Dubos, R. (1980). *Man adapting*. New Haven, CT: Yale University Press.

Dunn, N. J. and Wilhite, B. (1997). The effects of a leisure education program on leisure participation and psychological well-being of two older women who are home-centered. *Therapeutic Recreation Journal, 31*, 53-71.

Dykes, P. C. (1998). *Psychiatric clinical pathways: An interdisciplinary approach*. Gaithersburg, MD: Aspen Publishers, Inc.

Earle, W. J. (1992). *Introduction to philosophy*. New York, NY: McGraw-Hill.

Edwards, W. and Newman, J. R. (1982). *Multiattribute evaluation.* Newbury Park, CA: Sage Publications.

Egan, G. (1994). *The skilled helper: A problem-management approach to helping.* Pacific Grove, CA: Brooks/Cole Publishing Company.

Eggland, E. and Heinemann, D. (1994). *Nursing documentation: Charting, recording, and reporting.* Philadelphia, PA: J. B. Lippincott.

Ellis, A. (1962). *Reason and emotion in psychotherapy.* New York, NY: L. Stuart.

Ellis, A. (1973). *Humanistic psychotherapy: The rational-emotive approach.* New York, NY: Julian Press.

Ellis, A. (1985). *Clinical application of rational-emotive therapy.* New York, NY: Plenum Press.

Ellis, G. and Niles, S. (1989). Development, reliability, and preliminary validation of a brief leisure rating scale. In National Therapeutic Recreation Society (Ed.), *The best of Therapeutic Recreation Journal: Assessment* (pp. 153-164). Alexandria, VA: National Recreation and Park Association.

Ellis, G. D. & Witt, P. A. (1984). The measurement of perceived freedom in leisure. *Journal of Leisure Research, 16,* 110-123.

Ellis, G. and Witt, P. (1986). The leisure diagnostic battery: Past, present, and future. *Therapeutic Recreation Journal, 20*(4), 31-47.

Etzioni, A. (Ed.). (1969). *The semi-professions and their organization.* New York, NY: The Free Press.

Farnham-Diggory, S. (1994). Paradigms of knowledge and instruction. *Review of Educational Research, 64,* 463-467.

Ferguson, D. D. (1997). Protocols in therapeutic recreation: Dancing on the bubble. In D. Compton (Ed.), *Issues in therapeutic recreation: Toward the new millennium* (pp. 403-418), Champaign, IL: Sagamore.

Finnis, J. (1980). *Natural law and natural rights.* London, UK: Oxford University Press.

Floyd, K. and Negley, S. (1989). *I Believe In Me: Project I.B.I.M.* Salt Lake City, UT: Authors.

Frankl, V. (1959). *Man's search for meaning: An introduction to logotherapy.* New York, NY: Simon & Schuster.

Frankl, V. (1992). *Man's search for meaning: An introduction to logotherapy* (4th ed.). Boston, MA: Beacon Press.

Franklin, L. and Rios, D. (1999, September). *Mental illness: Cultural implications within the therapeutic process.* Paper presented at the American Therapeutic Recreation Association Conference, Portland, OR.

Freund, P. (1982). *The civilized body: Social domination, control, and health.* Philadelphia, PA: Temple University Press.

Freysinger, V. J. (1999). A critique of the "Optimizing Lifelong Health Through Therapeutic Recreation" (OLH-TR) Model. *Therapeutic Recreation Journal, 33*(2), 109-115.

Gagne, R. M. (1970). *The conditions of learning*. New York, NY: Holt, Rinehart & Winston.

Galambos, D. (1995). *Planning to have a life: Individualized planning for quality of life*. Oakville, ON: Sheridan College.

Gallwey, W. T. (1971). *The inner game of tennis*. New York, NY: Random House.

Gay, G. (2000). *Culturally responsive teaching: Theory, research, and practice*. New York, NY: Teachers College.

Gerber, L. (1994/95). Keynote address for the first annual ATRA research institute. *Annual in Therapeutic Recreation, 5*, 1-4.

Gloria, A. M. and Peregoy, J. J. (1996). Counseling Latino alcohol and other substances users/abusers: Clinical considerations for counselors. *Journal of Substance Abuse Treatment, 13(2)*, 1-8.

Goode, W. (1960). Encroachment, charlatanism, and the emerging professions: Psychology, sociology, and medicine. *American Sociological Review, 25*, 902-914.

Green, F. P. and DeCoux, V. (1994). A procedure for evaluating the effectiveness of a community recreation integration program. *Therapeutic Recreation Journal, 28*(1), 41-47.

Greenwood, E. (1966). Attributes of a profession. In H. M. Vollmer and D. L. Mills (Eds.), *Professionalization* (pp. 10-19). Englewood Cliffs, NJ: Prentice Hall.

Griffin, J. (1986). *Well-being: Its meaning, measurement, and moral importance*. New York, NY: Oxford University Press.

Grote, K., Hasl, M., Krider, R., and Mortensen, D. (1995). *Behavioral health protocols for recreational therapy*. Ravensdale, WA: Idyll Arbor.

Guess, R. (1981). *The idea of a critical theory: Habermas and the Frankfurt School*. Cambridge, UK: Cambridge University Press.

Gunn, S. L. and Peterson, C. A. (1978). *Therapeutic recreation program design: Principles and procedures*. Englewood Cliffs, NJ: Prentice Hall.

Hambleton, R. K., Swaminathan, H., and Rogers, H. J. (1991). *Fundamentals of item response theory*. Newbury Park, CA: Sage Publications.

Hamilton, E. and Anderson, S. (1991). Effects of leisure activities on attitudes toward people with disabilities. *Therapeutic Recreation Journal, 17*(3), 363-372.

Haslett, D. (1994). *Capitalism with morality*. Oxford, UK: Clarendon Press.

Haun, P. (1966). *Recreation: A medical viewpoint*. New York, NY: Teachers College Press.

Havitz, M. E., Twynam, G. D. and DeLorenzo, J. M. (1991). Important-performance analysis as a staff evaluation tool. *Journal of Park and Recreation Administration, 9*(1), 43-54.

Hawkins, B., May, M. E., and Brattain Rogers, N. (1996). *Therapeutic activity intervention with the elderly: Foundations and practices*. State College, PA: Venture Publishing, Inc.

Hearn, F. (1976/77). Toward a critical theory of play. *Telos, 30*(Winter), 145-160.

Hemingway, J. (1987). Building a philosophical defense of therapeutic recreation: The case of distributive justice. In C. Sylvester, J. Hemingway, R. Howe-Murphy, K. Mobily, and P. Shank (Eds.), *Philosophy of therapeutic recreation: Ideas and issues* (pp. 1-16). Alexandria, VA: National Recreation and Park Association.

Henderson, K. A. (1995). *Evaluating leisure services: Making enlightened decisions*. State College, PA: Venture Publishing, Inc.

Herman, J. L. (Ed.) (1987). *Program evaluation kit*. (2nd Ed.). Thousand Oaks, CA: Sage Publications.

Hickman, C. M. (1992). *Effects of behavioral group leisure counseling programs on leisure independence, depression, and depression related variables of adult women*. Unpublished doctoral dissertation, University of Utah, Salt Lake City, UT.

Hill, W. F. (1997). *Learning: A survey of psychological interpretations* (6th ed.). New York, NY: Longman.

Honer, S. M., Hunt, T. C., and Okholm, D. L. (1992). *Invitation to philosophy: Issues and options* (6th ed.). Belmont, CA: Wadsworth.

Howe, C. (1984). Leisure assessment and counseling. In E. T. Dowd (Ed.), *Leisure counseling: Concepts and applications* (pp. 214-233). Springfield, IL: C. C. Thomas.

Howe, C. (1989). Assessment instruments in therapeutic recreation: To what extent do they work? In D. Compton (Ed.), *Issues in therapeutic recreation: A profession in transition* (pp. 205-221). Champaign, IL: Sagamore.

Howe-Murphy, R. and Charboneau, B. G. (1987). *Therapeutic recreation intervention: An ecological perspective*. Englewood Cliffs, NJ: Prentice Hall.

Hughes, E. C. (1963). Professions. *Daedalus, 92*, 655-668.

Humphrey, F. (1970). Therapeutic recreation and the 1970s: Challenge or progress? *Therapeutic Recreation Annual, 7*, 9.

Hunt, J. (1990). *Ethical issues in experiential education*. Boulder, CO: The Association for Experiential Education.

Hutchison, P. and Lord, J. (1979). *Recreation integration: Issues and alternatives in leisure services and community involvement*. Ottawa, ON: Leisurability Publications.

Hutchison, P. and McGill, J. (1998). *Leisure, integration, and community*. Toronto, ON: Leisurability Publications.

Ibrahim, F. and Arredondo, P. (1986). Ethical standards for cross-cultural counseling: Counselor preparation, practice, assessment, and research. *Journal of Counseling and Development, 64*, 349-352.

The Institute for Career and Leisure Development. (1993). *Leisure learning system II: Leisure and the group home*. Washington, DC: Author.

Iso-Ahola, S. (1988). Research on therapeutic recreation. *Therapeutic Recreation Journal, 22*(1), 7-13.

Iso-Ahola, S. E. and Crowley, E. D. (1991). Adolescent substance abuse and leisure boredom, *Journal of Leisure Research, 23*, 260-271.

Iso-Ahola, S. E. and Weissinger, E. (1990). Perceptions of boredom in leisure: Conceptualization, reliability, and validity of the Leisure Boredom Scale. *Journal of Leisure Research, 22*, 1-17.

James, A. (1998). The conceptual development of recreational therapy. In F. Brasile, T. Skalko, and j. burlingame (Eds.), *Perspectives in recreational therapy: Issues of a dynamic profession* (pp. 7-38). Ravensdale, WA: Idyll Arbor.

Jones, R. L. (Ed.). (1996) *Handbook of test and measurements for Black populations* (Vols. 1-2). Hampton, VA: Cobb & Henry.

Jourard, S. (1964). *The transparent self*. New York, NY: D. Van Nostrand.

Kass, L. (1975). Regarding the end of medicine and the pursuit of health. *The Public Interest, 40*(Summer), 11-42.

Kazdin, A. E. (1994). *Behavior modification in applied settings*. Pacific Grove, CA: Brooks/Cole Publishing Company.

Kelly, J. (1982). *Leisure*. Englewood Cliffs, NJ: Prentice Hall.

Kimble, G.A. (1961). *Hilgard & Marquis' conditioning and learning* (2nd ed.). New York, NY: Appleton-Century-Crofts.

King, A. (1990). Enhancing peer interaction and learning in the classroom through reciprocal questioning. *American Educational Research Journal, 27*, 664-687.

Kiresuk, T. J., Smith, A., and Cardillo, J. E. (Eds.). (1994). *Goal attainment scaling: Applications, theory, and measurement*. Hillsdale, NJ: Lawrence Erlbaum Associates.

Kitchener, K. (1996). There is more to ethics than principles. *The Counseling Psychologist, 24*, 92-97.

Kloseck, M. and Crilly, R. G. (1997). *Leisure Competence Measure: Adult version professional manual and user's guide*. London, ON: Leisure Competence Measure Data System.

Kloseck, M., Crilly, R., Ellis, G. D., and Lammers, E. (1996). Leisure Competence Measure: Development and reliability testing of a scale to measure functional outcomes in therapeutic recreation. *Therapeutic Recreation Journal, 30*(1), 13-26.

Knight, L. and Johnson, D. (1991). Therapeutic recreation protocols: Client problem centered approach. In B. Riley (Ed.), *Quality management: Applications for therapeutic recreation* (pp. 137-147). State College, PA: Venture Publishing, Inc.

Kotler, P. and Andreasen, A. R. (1996). *Strategic marketing for non-profit organizations*. Upper Saddle River, NJ: Prentice Hall.

Kraus, R. and Allen. L. (1998). *Research and evaluation in recreation, parks, and leisure studies*. (2nd ed.). Boston, MA: Allyn & Bacon.

Kraus, R. and Shank, J. (1992). *Therapeutic recreation: Principles and practices* (4th ed.). Dubuque, IA: Wm. C. Brown.

Krueger, R. A. (1994). *Focus groups: A practical guide for applied research* (2nd ed.). Thousand Oaks, CA: Sage Publications.

Kuhn, T. (1970). *The structure of scientific revolutions*. Chicago, IL: University of Chicago Press.

Lahey, M. (1987a, September). Foundational questions in therapeutic recreation. Paper presented at the Leisure Research Symposium, New Orleans, LA.

Lahey, M. (1987b). The ethics of intervention in therapeutic recreation. In C. Sylvester, J. Hemingway, R. Howe-Murphy, K. Mobily and P. Shank (Eds.), *Philosophy of therapeutic recreation: Ideas and issues: Vol 1* (pp. 17-26). Arlington, VA: National Recreation and Park Association.

Lahey, M. (1991). Serving the new poor: Therapeutic recreation values in hard times. *Therapeutic Recreation Journal, 25*(2), 9-18.

Lahey, M. (1996). The commercial model and the future of therapeutic recreation. In C. Sylvester (Ed.), *Philosophy of therapeutic recreation: Ideas and issues: Vol 2* (pp. 20-29). Arlington, VA: National Recreation and Park Association.

Lane, S., Montgomery, D., and Schmid, W. (1995). Understanding differences to maximize treatment interventions: A case history. *Therapeutic Recreation Journal, 29*(4), 294-299.

Langer, E. and Rodin, J. (1976). The effects of choice and enhanced personal responsibility for the aged: A field experiment in an institutional setting. *Journal of Personality and Social Psychology, 34,* 191-198.

Lee, Y. (1998). A critique of the Health Protection/Health Promotion Model. *Therapeutic Recreation Journal, 32*(2), 118-123.

Leitner, M. J., Leitner, S. F. and Associates. (1996). *Leisure enhancement.* (2nd ed.). New York, NY: Haworth Press.

Lewinsohn, P. M. and Graf, J. (1973). Pleasant activities and depression. *Journal of Consulting and Clinical Psychology, 41*, 261-268.

Lewinsohn, P. M. and Libert, J. (1972). Pleasant events, activity schedules, and depression. *Journal of Abnormal Psychology, 79*, 291-295.

Lieb, I. (1976). The image of men in medicine. *Journal of Medicine and Philosophy, 1*, 162-176.

Lincoln, Y. S. and Guba, E. G. (1985), *Naturalistic inquiry.* Newbury Park, CA: Sage Publications.

Lindberg, J., Hunter, M., and Kruszewski, A. (1983). *Introduction to person-centered nursing.* New York, NY: J. B. Lippincott.

Loomis, J. B. and Walsh, R. G. (1997). *Recreation economic decisions: Comparing benefits and costs.* State College, PA: Venture Publishing, Inc.

Luckner, J. L. and Nadler, R. S. (1995). Processing adventure experiences: It's the story that counts. *Therapeutic Recreation Journal, 29*(3), 175-183.

MacLean, J. R., Peterson, J. A., and Martin, W. D. (1985). *Recreation and leisure: The changing scene* (4th ed.). New York, NY: John Wiley & Sons.

MacPhillamy, D. J. and Lewinsohn, P. M. (1982). The pleasant events schedule: Studies on reliability, validity, and scale correlation. *Journal of Consulting and Clinical Psychology, 50*, 363-380.

Mahon, M. (1994). The use of self-control techniques to facilitate self-determination skills during leisure in adolescents and young adults with mild and moderate mental retardation. *Therapeutic Recreation Journal, 28*(2), 58-72.

Mahon, M. M. and Bullock, C. C. (1992). Teaching adolescents with mild mental retardation to make decisions in leisure through the use of self-control techniques. *Therapeutic Recreation Journal, 26*, 9-26

Mahon, M. J., Bullock, C. C., Luken, K., and Martens, C. (1996). Leisure education for persons with severe and persistent mental illness: Is it a socially valid process? *Therapeutic Recreation Journal, 30*, 197-212.

Malkin, M. J. and Howe, C. Z. (1993). *Research in therapeutic recreation: Concepts and methods.* State College, PA: Venture Publishing, Inc.

Maloney, M. and Ward, M. (1976). *Psychological assessment: A conceptual approach.* New York, NY: Oxford.

Mannell, R. and Kleiber, D. (1997). *A social psychology of leisure*. State College, PA: Venture Publishing, Inc.

Mannell, R. C., Zuzanek, J., and Larson, R. (1988). Leisure states and "flow" experiences: Testing perceived freedom and intrinsic motivation hypotheses. *Journal of Leisure Research, 20,* 289-304.

Manning, S. (1997). The social worker as a moral citizen: Ethics in action. *Social Work, 42,* 223-230.

Martilla, J. A. and James, J. C. (1977). Importance-performance analysis. *Journal of Marketing 41*(1), 77-79.

May, R. and Yalom, I. (1995). Existential psychotherapy. In R. J. Corsini and D. Wedding (Eds.), *Current psychotherapies* (pp. 262-292). Itasca, IL: F. E. Peacock Publishers, Inc.

McAvoy, L., Schatz, E., Schleien, S., and Lais, G. (1989). Integrated wilderness adventure: Effects on personal and lifestyle traits of persons with and without disabilities. *Therapeutic Recreation Journal, 23*(3), 50-64.

McGinn, F., Flowers, C., and Rubin, S. (1994). In quest of an explicit multicultural emphasis in ethical standards for rehabilitation counselors. *Rehabilitation Education, 7,* 261-268.

Meara, N., Schmidt, L., and Day, J. (1996). Principles and virtues: A foundation for ethical decisions, policies, and character. *The Counseling Psychologist, 24,* 4-77.

Merrill, M. D. (1983). Component display theory. In C. M. Reigeluth (Ed.), *Instructional-design theories and models: An overview of their current status*. Hillsdale, NJ: Lawrence Erlbaum Associates.

Messick, S. (1989). Validity. In Linn, R. F. (Ed.), *Educational measurement* (3rd ed.). New York, NY: Macmillan.

Meyer, L. (1980, May). *Philosophical alternatives and the professionalization of therapeutic recreation*. Paper submitted as part of the Philosophical Statement Task Force to the National Therapeutic Recreation Society. Alexandria, VA: National Recreation and Park Association.

Mitra, A. and Lankford, S. (1999). *Research methods in park, recreation, and leisure services*. Champaign, IL: Sagamore.

Miller, D. (1976). *Social justice*. Oxford: Clarendon Press.

Miller, N. (1967). Recreation and the therapeutic environment. *Therapeutic Recreation Journal, 1*(2),

Miller, N. and Robinson, D. (1963). *The leisure age*. Belmont, CA: Wadsworth.

Mobily, K. E. (1999). New horizons in models of practice in therapeutic recreation. *Therapeutic Recreation Journal, 33*(3), 174-192.

Mobily, K. E., Mobily, P. R., Lane, B. K., and Semerjian, T. (1998). Using progressive resistance training as an intervention with older adults. *Therapeutic Recreation Journal, 32* (1), 42-53.

Mobily, K. E., Weissinger, E., and Hunnicutt, B. K. (1987). The means/ends controversy: A framework for understanding the value potential of TR. *Therapeutic Recreation Journal, 21*(3), 7-13.

Mordacci, R. and Sobel, R. (1998). Health: A comprehensive concept. *Hastings Center Report, 28*(1), 34-37.

Morris, C. and Ellis, G. (1993). The attributional basis of perceived freedom in leisure. *Therapeutic Recreation Journal, 27,* 172-185.

Morris, J. N., Hawes, C., Fries, B. E., Phillips, C. D., Mor, V., Katz, S., Murphy, K., Drugovich, M. L., and Friedlob, A. S. (1990). Designing the National Resident Assessment Instrument for nursing homes. *Gerontologist, 30*(3), 293-307.

Mundy, J. and Odum, L. (1979). *Leisure education: Theory and practice.* New York, NY: John Wiley & Sons.

Murray, S. (1998). A practitioner critique of the Self-Determination and Enjoyment Enhancement Model. *Therapeutic Recreation Journal, 32,* 272-282.

National Therapeutic Recreation Society. (1982). *Philosophical position statement of the National Therapeutic Recreation Society.* Arlington, VA: Author.

National Therapeutic Recreation Society. (1990). *National Therapeutic Recreation Society Code of Ethics.* Arlington, VA: Author.

National Therapeutic Recreation Society. (2000). *Definition statement.* (Rev.). Ashburn, VA: Author.

National Therapeutic Recreation Society. (1996). *National Therapeutic Recreation Society Philosophical Position Statement* (Rev. ed.). Ashburn, VA: Author.

National Therapeutic Recreation Society. (1997). *National Therapeutic Recreation Society Position Statement on Inclusion.* Ashburn, VA: Author.

National Therapeutic Recreation Society. (1999). *NTRS Report, 24*(3).

Nemeroff, C. J. and Karoly, P. (1991). Operant methods. In F. H. Kanfer and A. P. Goldstein (Eds.), *Helping people change: A textbook of methods* (pp. 122-160). New York, NY: Pergamon Press.

Neulinger, J. (1981). *To leisure: An introduction.* Boston, MA: Allyn and Bacon.

Ninth Southern Regional Institute (1969). *Therapeutic recreation position paper.* Developed at the Ninth Southern Regional Institute on Therapeutic Recreation, University of North Carolina.

Nowicki, S. and Strickland, B. R. (1973). A locus of control scale for children. *Journal of Consulting and Clinical Psychology, 40,* 148-154.

O'Keefe, C. (1996). The importance of philosophy: An introductory address to students, educators, and practitioners. In C. Sylvester (Ed.), *Philosophy of therapeutic recreation: Ideas and Issues Vol. II* (pp. 1-9). Arlington, VA: National Recreation and Park Association.

Okun, B. F. (1997). *Effective helping: Interviewing and counseling techniques.* Pacific Grove, CA: Brooks/Cole Publishing Company.

Oles, G. (1992). "Borrowing" activities from another culture: A Native American's perspective. *The Journal of Experiential Education, 15*(3), 20-22.

O'Morrow, G. and Carter, M. J. (1997). *Effective management in therapeutic recreation service.* State College, PA: Venture Publishing, Inc.

Osness. W., Adrian, M., Clark, B., Hoeger, W., Raab, D., and Wiswell, R. (1990). Functional assessment for adults over 60 years. Reston, VA: American Alliance for Health, Physical Education, Recreation and Dance.

Pacific Northwest Regional Council, National Recreation and Park Association. (1994). *Benefits of Parks and Recreation* [Film]. (Available from National Recreation and Park Association, 22377 Belmont Ridge Road, Ashburn, Virginia 20148)

Pear, R. (2000, February 13). U.S. seeks more care for disabled outside institutions. *The New York Times,* p. 24.

Pedersen, P. (1994). *A handbook for developing multicultural awareness* (2nd ed.). Alexandria, VA: American Counseling Association.

Pedersen, P. (1997). The cultural context of the American Counseling Association Code of Ethics. *Journal of Counseling & Development, 76,* 23-28.

Peregoy J., and Dieser, R. (1997). Multicultural awareness in therapeutic recreation: Hamlet living. *Therapeutic Recreation Journal, 31,* 174-188.

Peregoy, J., Schliebner, C., and Dieser, R. (1997). Diversity issues in therapeutic recreation. In D. Compton (Ed.), *Issues in therapeutic recreation: Toward the new millennium* (2nd ed.) (pp. 275-298). Champaign, IL: Sagamore.

Peterson, C. A. (1989). The dilemma of philosophy. In D. Compton (Ed.), *Issues in therapeutic recreation: A profession in transition* (pp. 21-33). Champaign, IL: Sagamore.

Peterson, C. A. and Gunn, S. L. (1984). *Therapeutic recreation program design: Principles and procedures* (2nd ed.). Englewood Cliffs, NJ: Prentice Hall.

Peterson, C. A. & Stumbo, N. J. (2000). *Therapeutic recreation program design: Principles and procedures* (3rd ed.). Boston, MA: Allyn & Bacon.

Pojman. L. (1999). *Ethics: Discovering right and wrong* (3rd ed.). Belmont, CA: Wadsworth.

Privacy Protection Study Committee. (1977). *Personal privacy in an information society*. Washington, DC: U.S. Government Printing Office.

Rabin, A. I. (Ed.). (1981). *Assessment with projective techniques*. New York, NY: Springer.

Rancourt, A. (1989). Older adults with developmental disabilities/mental retardation: Implications for professional services. *Therapeutic Recreation Journal, 23*(1), 47-57.

Redlich, F. (1976) Editorial reflections on the concepts of health and disease. *Journal of Medicine and Philosophy, 1*, 269-280.

Remley, T. (1990). Counseling records: Legal and ethical issues. In B. Herlihy and L. Golden (Eds.), *Professionals in distress: Issues, syndromes and solutions in psychology* (pp. 162-169). Alexandria, VA: American Association for Counseling and Development.

Rescher, N. (1972). *Welfare: The social issues in philosophical perspective*. Pittsburgh, PA: University of Pittsburgh.

Reynolds, R. P. and O'Morrow, G. S. (1985). *Problems, issues and concepts in therapeutic recreation*. Englewood Cliffs, NJ: Prentice Hall.

Richter, K. and Kaschalk, S. (1996). The future of therapeutic recreation: An existential outcome. In C. Sylvester (Ed.), *Philosophy of therapeutic recreation: Ideas and issues: Vol. 2* (pp. 86-91). Arlington, VA: National Recreation and Park Association.

Ridley C., Li, L., and Hill, C. (1998). Multicultural assessment: Reexamination, reconceptualization, and practical application. *Counseling Psychologist, 26,* 827-910.

Rifkin, J. (1995). *The end of work: The decline of the global labor force and the dawn of the post-market era*. New York, NY: G. P. Putnam's Sons.

Rogers, C. R. (1961). *On becoming a person*. Boston, MA: Houghton Mifflin Company.

Roper Center. (1990, May/June). *The public perspective: A Roper center review of public opinion polling. 1.*

Ross, J. E. (1998). A critique of the Health Protection/Health Promotion Model. *Therapeutic Recreation Journal, 32*(2), 124-129.

Rossi, P. H. and Freeman, H. E. (1993). *Evaluation: A systematic approach*. Newbury Park, CA: Sage Publications.

Rusalem, H. (1973). An alternative to the therapeutic model in therapeutic recreation. *Therapeutic Recreation Journal, 7*(1), 8-15.

Russoniello, C. (1992). President's Message. *American Therapeutic Recreation Newsletter, 8*(2).

Russoniello, C. (1994). Recreational therapy: A medicine model. In D. Compton and S. Iso-Ahola (Eds.), *Leisure and mental health* (pp. 247-258). Park City, UT: Family Development Resources.

Sandstrom, R., Hoppe, K., and Smutko, N. (1996). Comprehensive medical rehabilitation in the 1990s: The community integration rehabilitation model. *The Health Care Supervisor, 15*(2), 44-54.

Sanford, R. C. (1985). An inquiry into the evolution of the client-centered approach to psychotherapy. In J. K. Zeig (Ed.), *The evolution of psychotherapy* (pp. 179-189). New York, NY: Brunner/Mazel, Publishers.

Schleien, S. and Green, F. (1992). Three approaches for integrating persons with disabilities into community recreation. *Journal of Park and Recreation Administration, 10*(2), 51-66.

Schelein, S. and Ray, M. T. (1988). *Community recreation and persons with disabilities: Strategies for integration.* Baltimore, MD: Paul H. Brookes.

Schleien, S., Ray, M., and Green, F. (1997). *Community recreation and people with disabilities: Strategies for inclusion* (2nd ed.). Baltimore, MD: Paul H. Brookes.

Schleien, S., Ray, M., Soderman-Olson, M., and McMahon, K. (1987). Integrating children with moderate to severe cognitive deficits into a community museum program. *Education and Training in Mental Retardation, 22*(2), 112-120.

Searle, M. S. and Mahon, M. J. (1993). The effects of a leisure education program on selected social-psychological variables: A three month follow-up investigation. *Therapeutic Recreation Journal, 27*(1), 9-21.

Shah, S. (1970). Privileged communication, confidentiality, and privacy: Privacy. *Professional Psychology, 1*, 243-252.

Shank, J. (1985). Bioethical principles and the practice of therapeutic recreation in clinical settings. *Therapeutic Recreation Journal, 19*(4), 31-40.

Shank, J. and Kinney, T. (1987). On the neglect of clinical practice. In C. Sylvester, J. L. Hemingway, R. Howe-Murphy, K. Mobily, and P. A. Shank (Eds.), *Philosophy of therapeutic recreation: Ideas and issues* (pp. 65-75). Alexandria, VA: National Recreation and Park Association.

Shank, P. (1996). Doing ethics: Toward the resolution of ethical dilemmas. In C. Sylvester (Ed.), *Philosophy of therapeutic recreation: Ideas and issues: Vol. 2* (pp. 30-56). Arlington, VA: National Recreation and Park Association.

Sherwin, S. (1992). *No longer patient: Feminist ethics and health care*. Philadelphia, PA: Temple University Press.

Siegal, M. (1979). Privacy, ethics, and confidentiality. *Professional Psychology, 10*, 249-258.

Skinner, B. F. (1950). Are theories of learning necessary? *Psychological Review, 57*, 193-216.

Smith, R., Austin, D., and Kennedy, D. (1996). *Inclusive and special recreation: Opportunities for persons with disabilities*. Madison, WI: Brown & Benchmark.

Smith, S. L. J. (1985). On the biological basis of pleasure: Some implications for leisure policy In T. L. Goodale and P. A. Witt (Eds.), *Recreation and leisure: Issues in an era of change* (Rev. ed.) (pp. 56-68). State College, PA: Venture Publishing, Inc.

Sneegas, J. (1989). Social skills: An integral component of leisure participation and therapeutic recreation services. *Therapeutic Recreation Journal, 23*(2), 30-40.

Solomon, A. (1992, June). Clinical diagnosis among diverse populations: A multicultural perspective. *Families in Society: The Journal of Contemporary Human Services*, 371-377.

Spiegler, M. D. (1983). *Contemporary behavioral therapy*. Palo Alto, CA: Mayfield Publishing Company.

Stake, R. E. (1995). *The art of case study research*. Thousand Oaks, CA: Sage Publications.

Stumbo, N. (1991). Selected assessment resources: A review of instruments and references. *Annual in Therapeutic Recreation, 2*(2), 8-24.

Stumbo, N. J. (1992). *Leisure education II: More activities and resources*. State College, PA: Venture Publishing, Inc.

Stumbo, N. J. (1995). Social skills instruction through commercially available resources. *Therapeutic Recreation Journal, 29*(1), 30-55.

Stumbo, N. J. (1994/95). Assessment of social skills for therapeutic recreation intervention. *Annual in Therapeutic Recreation, 5*, 68-82.

Stumbo, N. J. and Peterson, C. A. (1998). The Leisure Ability Model. *Therapeutic Recreation Journal, 32*(2), 82-96.

Sue, D. W. and Sue, D. (1990). *Counseling the culturally different: Theory and practice* (2nd ed.). New York, NY: John Wiley & Sons.

Sue, D. W., Carter, R., Casas, J., Fouad, N., Ivey, A., Jensen, M. LaFromboise, T., Manese, J., Ponterotto, J., and Vazquez-Nutall, E. (1998). *Multicultural counseling competencies*. Thousand Oaks, CA: Sage Publications.

Suen, H. K. (1990). *Principles of test theories*. Hillsdale, NJ: Lawrence Erlbaum and Associates.

Sylvester, C. (1985). Freedom, leisure, and therapeutic recreation: A philosophical view. *Therapeutic Recreation Journal, 19*(1), 6-13.

Sylvester, C. (1986). Wonder, doubt, and thoughtfulness in therapeutic recreation: An invitation to philosophize. *Therapeutic Recreation Journal, 20* (3), 6-10.

Sylvester, C. (1989a). Impressions of the intellectual past and future of therapeutic recreation: Implications for professionalization. In D. M. Compton (Ed.), *Issues in therapeutic recreation: A profession in transition* (pp. 1-20). Champaign, IL: Sagamore.

Sylvester, C. (1989b). Quality assurance and quality of life: Accounting for the good and healthy life. *Therapeutic Recreation Journal, (2),* 7-22.

Sylvester, C. (1992). Therapeutic recreation and the right to leisure. *Therapeutic Recreation Journal, 26*(2), 9-20.

Sylvester, C. (1994/95). Critical theory, therapeutic recreation, and health care reform: An instructive example of critical thinking. *Annual in Therapeutic Recreation, 5,* 94-109.

Sylvester, C. (1995). Critical theory and therapeutic recreation: Breaking new ground. *Abstracts from the 1995 Symposium on Leisure Research*. Alexandria, VA: National Recreation and Park Association, 33.

Sylvester, C. (1996). Instrumental rationality and therapeutic recreation: Revisiting the issue of means and ends. In C. Sylvester (Ed.), *Philosophy of therapeutic recreation: Ideas and issues: Vol 2* (pp. 92-105). Arlington, VA: National Recreation and Park Association.

Sylvester, C. (1998). Careers, callings, and the professionalization of therapeutic recreation. *Journal of Leisurability, 25*(2), 3-13.

Sylvester, C. and Patrick, G. (1991). Guest editors' comments. *Therapeutic Recreation Journal, 25*(2), 7-8.

Tate, D. and Dieser, R. (1997). The linear model for individualized treatment: Still an effective guide for therapeutic recreation service delivery. *Therapeutic Recreation Journal 31*(4), 259-265.

Temkin, O. (1973). Health and disease. In P. Weiner (Ed.), *Dictionary of the history of ideas Vol. II* (pp. 395-407), New York, NY: Charles Scribner's Sons.

Thomasa, D. (1984). The goals of medicine in society. In D. Brock and A. Harward (Eds.), *The culture of biomedicine: Studies in science and culture* (pp. 34-54). Newark, DE: University of Delaware Press.

Thompson, A. and Ozanne, P. (1982). *Ethical concerns in psychotherapy and their legal ramifications*. Eugene, OR: Authors.

Ting-Toomey, S. (1999). *Communicating across cultures*. New York, NY: The Guilford Press.

Tjeltveit, A. (1999). *Ethics and values in psychotherapy*. New York, NY: Routledge.

Touchstone, W. A. (1984). A personalized approach to goal planning and evaluation in clinical settings. *Therapeutic Recreation Journal 18*(2), 25-31.

U.S. Bureau of the Census. (1998). *Population profile of the United States: 1997* (Population Reports Series P23-194). Washington, DC: U.S. Government Printing Office.

Van Andel, G. (1998). TR Service Delivery and TR Outcome Models. *Therapeutic Recreation Journal, 32*(3), 180-193.

Van der Linden, W. J. and Hambleton, R. K. (1997). *Handbook of modern item response theory*. New York, NY: Springer.

Voelkl, J. E., Carruthers, C., and Hawkins, B. (1997). Special Issue on Therapeutic Recreation Practice Models: Guest Editors' Introductory Comments. *Therapeutic Recreation Journal, 31*(4), 210-212.

Voelkl, J. E., St. Pierre, J., and Buettner, L. (1999). *The at-home recreation program manual*. Iowa City, IA: Authors.

Vollmer, H. and Mills, D. (1966). *Professionalization*. Englewood Cliffs, NJ: Prentice Hall.

Wassman, K. B. and Iso-Ahola, S. E. (1985). The relationship between participation and depression in psychiatric patients. *Therapeutic Recreation Journal, 19*, 63-70.

Watson, J. (1930). *Behaviorism*. Chicago, IL: University of Chicago Press.

Weinrach, S. (1995). Rational emotive behavior therapy: A tough-minded therapy for a tender-minded profession. *Journal of Counseling and Development, 73*, 296-300.

Weiss, C. R. (1989). TR and reminiscing: The pursuit of elusive memory and the art of remembering. *Therapeutic Recreation Journal, 23*(3), 7-18.

Weiss, C. R. and Thurn, J. M. (1987). A mapping project to facilitate reminiscence in a long-term care facility. *Therapeutic Recreation Journal, 21*(2), 46-53.

Weissinger, E., Ellis, G., Compton, D., Rosegard, E., and Haggard, L. (1996, May 11). *Direct and indirect effects of leisure boredom on quality of life within the PRECEDE/PROCEED Model*. Ottawa, ON: Canadian Congress on Leisure Research, University of Ottawa.

West, R. (1993). American Recreational Therapy Association? *American Therapeutic Recreation Association Newsletter, 9*(3), 5-8.

Widmer, M. A. (1993). *Measuring ethical behavior in leisure from an Aristotelian foundation*. Unpublished doctoral dissertation, University of Utah, Salt Lake City, UT.

Widmer, M. and Ellis, G. (1998). The Aristotelian Good Life Model: Integration of values into therapeutic recreation service delivery. *Therapeutic Recreation Journal, 32,* 290-302.

Wilhite, B. and Keller, M. J. (1992). *Therapeutic recreation: Cases and exercises.* State College, PA: Venture Publishing, Inc.

Wilhite, B., Keller, M. J., and Caldwell, L. (1999). Optimizing lifelong health and well-being: A health enhancing model of therapeutic recreation. *Therapeutic Recreation Journal, 33*(2), 98-108.

Williams, R. and Dattilo, J. (1997). Effects of leisure education on choice making, social interaction, and positive affect of young adults with mental retardation. *Therapeutic Recreation Journal, 31,* 244-258.

Wilson, J. (2000, June 28). WOVOKA [Online]. Available: http://www.peaknet.net/~aardvark/WOVOKA.HTML

Wise, J. B. (1999). *Effects of a curriculum to generalize self-efficacy from weight training exercises to activities of daily living in adults with spinal cord injuries or spina bifida.* Unpublished doctoral dissertation, University of Utah, Salt Lake City, UT.

Witt, P. (1988). Leisure programs and services for special populations. In L. Barnett. (Ed.), *Research about leisure: Past, present, and future* (pp. 127-139). Champaign, IL: Sagamore.

Witt, P. (1990). Overview and conclusions based on recent studies utilizing the Leisure Diagnostic Battery. In Bryan Smale (Ed.). *Leisure challenges: Bringing people, resources, and policy into play.* (pp. 70-75). Waterloo, ON: Ontario Research Council on Leisure.

Witt, P., Connolly, P., and Compton, D. (1980). Assessment: A plea for sophistication. *Therapeutic Recreation Journal, 14*(1), 5-8.

Witt, P. A. and Ellis, G. D. (1989). *The Leisure Diagnostic Battery: Users Manual and Sample Forms.* State College, PA: Venture Publishing, Inc.

Witman, J. P. and Shank, J. W. (1987). Professionalization in therapeutic recreation: State leaders's perceptions of progress, priorities, and strategies. *Therapeutic Recreation Journal, 21*(4), 32-42.

Wolfensberger, W. (1972). *The principle of normalization in human services.* Toronto, ON: National Institute of Mental Retardation.

Wolfensberger, W. (1983). Social role valorization: A proposed new term for the principle of normalization. *Mental Retardation, 21,* 234-239.

Wolfensberger, W. (1985). An overview of social role valorization and some reflections on elderly mentally retarded persons. In M.P. Janicki and H. M. Wisniewski (Eds.), *Aging and developmental disabilities: Issues and approaches* (pp. 61-76). Baltimore, MD: Brookes.

Wolff, L., Weitzel, M., and Fuerst, E. (1979). *Fundamentals of nursing* (6th ed.). Philadelphia, PA: J. B. Lippincott.

Woolfolk. A. E. (1998). *Educational psychology* (7th ed.). Boston, MA: Allyn and Bacon.

World Health Organization. (1997). [Online] *Female genital mutilation: A joint WHO/UNICEF/ UNFPA statement*. [Online]. Available: http://www.who.int/dsa/cat98/mat8.htm#Female Genital Mutilation

Wrenn, C. (1962). The culturally encapsulated counselor. *Harvard Educational Review*, *32*, 444-449.

Yaffe, R. M. (1998). The Leisure Ability Model: A response from a service perspective. *Therapeutic Recreation Journal, 32*(2), 103-108.

Yalom, I. (1980). *Existential psychotherapy*. New York, NY: Basic Books.

Yin, R. K. (1994). *Case study research: design and methods*. Thousand Oaks, CA: Sage Publications.

Zasler, C. (1996). Primer for the rehabilitation professional on the life care planning process. *Neurorehabilitation, 7*(2), 79-93.

Zeyen, D., Odum, L. L , Lancaster, R. A., Fernandez, A., Tinker, S., and Verhoven, P. J. (1977). *Kangaroo kit: Leisure education curriculum for kindergarten-grade 12*. Arlington, VA: National Recreation and Park Association.

Zinn, H. (1980). *A people's history of the United States*. New York, NY: Harper-Collins.

Zoerink, D. A. and Lauener, K. (1991). Effects of a leisure education program on adults with traumatic brain injury. *Therapeutic Recreation Journal, 25*, 19-28.

Zola, I. (1977). Healthism and disabling medicalization. In I. Illich et al. (Eds.), *Disabling professions* (pp. 41-67), London, UK: Marion Boyars Publishers Ltd.

Index

A

B

C

E

F

S

# Other Books From Venture Publishing, Inc.

The A•B•Cs of Behavior Change: Skills for Working With Behavior Problems in
Nursing Homes
    by Margaret D. Cohn, Michael A. Smyer, and Ann L. Horgas

Activity Experiences and Programming Within Long-Term Care
    by Ted Tedrick and Elaine R. Green

The Activity Gourmet
    by Peggy Powers

Advanced Concepts for Geriatric Nursing Assistants
    by Carolyn A. McDonald

Adventure Programming
    edited by John C. Miles and Simon Priest

Aerobics of the Mind: Keeping the Mind Active in Aging—A New Perspective on
Programming for Older Adults
    by Marge Engelman

Assessment: The Cornerstone of Activity Programs
    by Ruth Perschbacher

Behavior Modification in Therapeutic Recreation: An Introductory Manual
    by John Datillo and William D. Murphy

Benefits of Leisure
    edited by B. L. Driver, Perry J. Brown, and George L. Peterson

Benefits of Recreation Research Update
    by Judy M. Sefton and W. Kerry Mummery

Beyond Bingo: Innovative Programs for the New Senior
    by Sal Arrigo, Jr., Ann Lewis, and Hank Mattimore

Beyond Bingo 2: More Innovative Programs for the New Senior
    by Sal Arrigo, Jr.

Both Gains and Gaps: Feminist Perspectives on Women's Leisure
    by Karla Henderson, M. Deborah Bialeschki, Susan M. Shaw, and Valeria J.
    Freysinger

Dimensions of Choice: A Qualitative Approach to Recreation, Parks, and Leisure Research
    by Karla A. Henderson

Diversity and the Recreation Profession: Organizational Perspectives
    edited by Maria T. Allison and Ingrid E. Schneider

Effective Management in Therapeutic Recreation Service
    by Gerald S. O'Morrow and Marcia Jean Carter

Evaluating Leisure Services: Making Enlightened Decisions
    by Karla A. Henderson with M. Deborah Bialeschki

Everything From A to Y: The Zest Is up to You! Older Adult Activities for Every Day of the Year
    by Nancy R. Cheshire and Martha L. Kenney

The Evolution of Leisure: Historical and Philosophical Perspectives (Second Printing)
    by Thomas Goodale and Geoffrey Godbey

Experience Marketing: Strategies for the New Millennium
    by Ellen L. O'Sullivan and Kathy J. Spangler

Facilitation Techniques in Therapeutic Recreation
    by John Dattilo

File o' Fun: A Recreation Planner for Games & Activities—Third Edition
    by Jane Harris Ericson and Diane Ruth Albright

The Game and Play Leader's Handbook: Facilitating Fun and Positive Interaction
    by Bill Michaelis and John M. O'Connell

The Game Finder—A Leader's Guide to Great Activities
    by Annette C. Moore

Getting People Involved in Life and Activities: Effective Motivating Techniques
    by Jeanne Adams

Glossary of Recreation Therapy and Occupational Therapy
    by David R. Austin

Great Special Events and Activities
    by Annie Morton, Angie Prosser, and Sue Spangler

Group Games & Activity Leadership
    by Kenneth J. Bulik

Hands on! Children's Activities for Fairs, Festivals, and Special Events
    by Karen L. Ramey

Inclusive Leisure Services: Responding to the Rights of People With Disabilities
    by John Dattilo

Internships in Recreation and Leisure Services: A Practical Guide for Students—Second Edition
    by Edward E. Seagle, Jr., Ralph W. Smith, and Lola M. Dalton

Interpretation of Cultural and Natural Resources
    by Douglas M. Knudson, Ted T. Cable, and Larry Beck

Intervention Activities for At-Risk Youth
    by Norma J. Stumbo

Introduction to Leisure Services—7th Edition
    by H. Douglas Sessoms and Karla A. Henderson

Introduction to Writing Goals and Objectives: A Manual for Recreation Therapy
Students and Entry-Level Professionals
    by Suzanne Melcher

Leadership and Administration of Outdoor Pursuits, Second Edition
    by Phyllis Ford and James Blanchard

Leadership in Leisure Services: Making a Difference, Second Edition
    by Debra J. Jordan

Leisure and Leisure Services in the 21st Century
    by Geoffrey Godbey

The Leisure Diagnostic Battery: Users Manual and Sample Forms
    by Peter A. Witt and Gary Ellis

Leisure Education: A Manual of Activities and Resources
    by Norma J. Stumbo and Steven R. Thompson

Leisure Education II: More Activities and Resources
    by Norma J. Stumbo

Leisure Education III: More Goal-Oriented Activities
    by Norma J. Stumbo

Leisure Education IV: Activities for Individuals With Substance Addictions
    by Norma J. Stumbo

Leisure Education Program Planning: A Systematic Approach—Second Edition
    by John Dattilo

Leisure Education Specific Programs
    by John Dattilo

Leisure in Your Life: An Exploration—Fifth Edition
    by Geoffrey Godbey

Leisure Services in Canada: An Introduction—Second Edition
    by Mark S. Searle and Russell E. Brayley

Leisure Studies: Prospects for the Twenty-First Century
    edited by Edgar L. Jackson and Thomas L. Burton

The Lifestory Re-Play Circle: A Manual of Activities and Techniques
    by Rosilyn Wilder

Marketing for Parks, Recreation, and Leisure
    by Ellen L. O'Sullivan

Models of Change in Municipal Parks and Recreation: A Book of Innovative Case
Studies
    edited by Mark E. Havitz

More Than a Game: A New Focus on Senior Activity Services
by Brenda Corbett

Nature and the Human Spirit: Toward an Expanded Land Management Ethic
edited by B. L. Driver, Daniel Dustin, Tony Baltic, Gary Elsner, and George
Peterson

Outdoor Recreation Management: Theory and Application, Third Edition
by Alan Jubenville and Ben Twight

Planning Parks for People, Second Edition
by John Hultsman, Richard L. Cottrell, and Wendy Z. Hultsman

The Process of Recreation Programming Theory and Technique, Third Edition
by Patricia Farrell and Herberta M. Lundegren

Programming for Parks, Recreation, and Leisure Services: A Servant Leadership
Approach
by Donald G. DeGraaf, Debra J. Jordan, and Kathy H. DeGraaf

Protocols for Recreation Therapy Programs
edited by Jill Kelland, along with the Recreation Therapy Staff at Alberta Hospital
Edmonton

Quality Management: Applications for Therapeutic Recreation
edited by Bob Riley

A Recovery Workbook: The Road Back From Substance Abuse
by April K. Neal and Michael J. Taleff

Recreation and Leisure: Issues in an Era of Change, Third Edition
edited by Thomas Goodale and Peter A. Witt

Recreation Economic Decisions: Comparing Benefits and Costs (Second Edition)
by John B. Loomis and Richard G. Walsh

Recreation for Older Adults: Individual and Group Activities
by Judith A. Elliott and Jerold E. Elliott

Recreation Programming and Activities for Older Adults
by Jerold E. Elliott and Judith A. Sorg-Elliott

Recreation Programs That Work for At-Risk Youth: The Challenge of Shaping the
Future
by Peter A. Witt and John L. Crompton

Reference Manual for Writing Rehabilitation Therapy Treatment Plans
by Penny Hogberg and Mary Johnson

Research in Therapeutic Recreation: Concepts and Methods
edited by Marjorie J. Malkin and Christine Z. Howe

Simple Expressions: Creative and Therapeutic Arts for the Elderly in Long-Term Care
Facilities
by Vicki Parsons

A Social History of Leisure Since 1600
 by Gary Cross

A Social Psychology of Leisure
 by Roger C. Mannell and Douglas A. Kleiber

Steps to Successful Programming: A Student Handbook to Accompany Programming for Parks, Recreation, and Leisure Services
 by Donald G. DeGraaf, Debra J. Jordan, and Kathy H. DeGraaf

Therapeutic Activity Intervention With the Elderly: Foundations & Practices
 by Barbara A. Hawkins, Marti E. May, and Nancy Brattain Rogers

Therapeutic Recreation: Cases and Exercises—Second Edition
 by Barbara C. Wilhite and M. Jean Keller

Therapeutic Recreation in the Nursing Home
 by Linda Buettner and Shelley L. Martin

Therapeutic Recreation Protocol for Treatment of Substance Addictions
 by Rozanne W. Faulkner

Tourism and Society: A Guide to Problems and Issues
 by Robert W. Wyllie

A Training Manual for Americans With Disabilities Act Compliance in Parks and Recreation Settings
 By Carol Stensrud